W9-ADB-247

Occupational Outlook Handbook™

Second Edition   The Editors @ JIST

Based on information from the U.S. Department of Labor

JIST®
Works
America's Career Publisher®

EZ Occupational Outlook Handbook, Second Edition

© 2011 by JIST Publishing

Published by JIST Works, an imprint of JIST Publishing
7321 Shadeland Station, Suite 200
Indianapolis, IN 46256-3923
Phone: 800-648-JIST   Fax: 877-454-7839
E-mail: info@jist.com   Web site: www.jist.com

> **To Educators, Counselors, and Other Professionals:** The *EZ Occupational Outlook Handbook* can be used with JIST's videos, workbooks, and career assessments for workshops, for courses, and in other settings. Call 800-648-JIST or visit www.jist.com for more information.
>
> Quantity discounts are available for JIST products. Please call 800-648-JIST or visit www.jist.com for a free catalog and more information.
>
> Visit www.jist.com for information on JIST, free job search information, tables of contents, sample pages, and ordering information for our many products.

Acquisitions Editor: Susan Pines
Development Editor: Stephanie Koutek
Writing and Database Work: Laurence Shatkin
Cover Photo: IStock
Cover Designer and Interior Layout: Toi Davis
Interior Designer: Marie Kristine Parial-Leonardo
Proofreaders: Chuck Hutchinson, Jeanne Clark

Printed in the United States of America

16 15 14 13 12 11   9 8 7 6 5 4 3 2 1

Library of Congress Cataloging-in-Publication Data is on file with the Library of Congress.

ISBN 978-1-59357-831-2

One of These Pages Contains the Career of Your Dreams

This book is designed to help you explore careers. It includes descriptions for more than 250 major jobs, plus 14 green jobs, which together employ about 90 percent of the U.S. workforce.

The job descriptions answer questions such as these:

* What do people in this job do all day?

* Where do they work and during what hours and days?

* What training or education will I need to do the job?

* How much does the job pay?

* Will the job be in demand in the future?

* What jobs are related to this one?

* Where can I find out more about this job?

Although it contains an immense amount of information, this book is actually very easy to use (it says so in the title, after all). Simply thumb through the Table of Contents to find one or more job titles that interest you and turn to the page indicated. Alternatively, you can use the appendixes to find jobs listed by personality type or by the education and training required.

The Introduction provides additional information that can help you use this book in your career exploration. We hope it helps you to discover jobs and careers that match your interests, goals, needs, and dreams.

Acknowledgments and Limitations on Use of the Data

This book features data obtained from the U.S. Department of Labor as used in various works it publishes, including the *Occupational Outlook Handbook* and the O*NET. The data collection process is an enormous one. We are thankful for the department's tireless efforts and immense contributions to the career development field. In using the information, however, we want to warn you of its limitations by adapting the language used by the department in the original works:

The occupational information contained in this book reflects jobs as they have been found to occur, but they may not coincide in every respect with the content of jobs as performed in particular establishments or at certain localities. Users of this information demanding specific job requirements should supplement this data with local information detailing jobs in their community.

In using this book, note that the U.S. Employment Service, the U.S. Department of Labor, and JIST Publishing have no responsibility for establishing wage levels for workers in the United States or settling jurisdictional matters in relation to different occupations. In the preparation of vocational definitions, no data was collected concerning these and related matters. Therefore, the occupational information in this book cannot be regarded as determining standards for any aspect of the employer-employee relationship. Data contained in this publication should not be considered a judicial or legislative standard for wages, hours, or other contractual or bargaining elements.

The use of any information, no matter how carefully collected, researched, screened, or presented, has its limitations. The information provided in the *OOH* and O*NET database–and this book–has been carefully collected and thoughtfully presented. Even so, errors and inaccuracies can be introduced and, for this reason, we can accept no responsibility for any errors in fact nor in any decisions made or actions taken as a result of the information provided. As in all things, we humbly suggest that you follow your own judgment regarding important decisions.

Table of Contents

Service Occupations 159

Introduction

What This Book Can Do for You

Once upon a time, the U.S. Department of Labor created a book with descriptions of the vast majority of jobs in the market. The book was called the *Occupational Outlook Handbook (OOH)*, and it became the most widely used source of career information around. It has helped millions of people explore their career options and make educated decisions. The book is still the most popular source of career information, and it is updated every two years.

It is also more than 700 pages long and weighs as much as a watermelon. Undoubtedly the *OOH* is so popular because of the wealth of information it offers, but it can also be intimidating for some readers. Those people who are in the early stages of career exploration may not even know where to get started with such a thick book.

If only it were possible to squeeze the most pertinent information out of the *OOH* and put it in a format that was simpler to use, easier to read, and more accessible for the everyday job seeker. A book that contained all of the relevant content but none of the excess, trimmed down for people like you and me.

A book like this one.

Like the book it was based on, this EZ version presents information on the more than 250 major jobs that the *OOH* describes in full, and you are very likely to work in one or more of them during your life. Also like the *OOH*, the *EZ OOH* groups similar jobs together, making it simple to explore related jobs you might not know about. Unlike the *OOH*, the job descriptions in this book are only one page long. Yet they still contain all the necessary information about earnings, working conditions, and job opportunities, as well as information the *OOH* doesn't include, such as personality types best suited to the career and interesting facts related to each job.

This edition of the *EZ OOH* also includes an exclusive "Green Occupations" section: 14 job descriptions based on information included in the 2010–2011 JIST edition of the *OOH*. This information, here in an EZ format, is not available on the Department of Labor's *OOH* Web site.

This introduction will give you information to help you understand and use the book. In looking over these job descriptions, we suggest that you consider every one that interests you. Remember that you are exploring job *possibilities*. The information presented will help you discover what jobs match your personality and what additional training or education you will need to do that job. If a job requires more training or education than you currently have, consider it anyway. After all, there are many ways to finance an education.

Once upon a time there was a golden-haired girl who stumbled upon a house in the woods. She apparently didn't have very good manners because she started eating, sitting on, and sleeping in everything in sight. She was also a little picky. She couldn't have her porridge too hot or her bed too small. She wanted something that was a good fit for her. Nothing too big or overwhelming, but certainly something rich enough to meet her needs. In short, she was looking for something just right.

We think she would have liked this book.

We hope you do, too.

Getting the Most from an *EZ OOH* Job Description

The table of contents lists all the jobs in this book, arranged into groups of similar jobs. Look through the list and choose one or more of the job groups that sound most interesting to you. Make a list of the jobs that interest you, and then read the descriptions for those jobs.

Each job description in this book (except those in the special section on Green Occupations) uses the same format. They include the following sections:

At a Glance: This section provides a short description of the job, including the most common work activities and responsibilities. Essentially, it gives you a sense of what people in this job *do* for a living.

Career in Focus: Most of the occupations from the *OOH* cover a wide range of jobs within a particular field. This section focuses on a more specific job within that career category, a highly related job, or an opportunity for advancement. The description can give you a better idea of what people with specific job titles do.

Where and When: This section describes the working conditions of the job, including the work environment, the number of hours, possible job hazards, and other information that can help you decide whether the job is a good fit for you.

Did You Know? Because career exploration should be exciting and interesting, this section offers facts, anecdotes, or other unique information designed to give you a better perspective on the job.

For More Information: This section offers associations, agencies, and other organizations you can contact for more information. Internet addresses have been listed whenever possible. For even more information, see Appendix C, "Additional Sources of Career Information."

Data Bank: The Data Bank contains the facts and figures you need to make an informed decision, from earnings to job openings. The following section describes how to get the most of this information. (This section is not included for the Green Occupations because labor statistics for them are not yet available.)

Entry Ramp: This topic, shown only for the Green Occupations, explains how workers typically prepare to enter the career. Most of the green jobs are still emerging and do not have well-established entry requirements, so this section usually covers several optional pathways. In a few cases or in some locations, licensing may be required or helpful, but there was not room here to note such cases.

Using the Data Bank

Each job description is accompanied by a Data Bank that includes the most pertinent information every job seeker is looking for. This can help you compare one job with another to find the one with the right earnings and the most potential that best matches your interests. Unless otherwise stated, all of the data found in this section is based on information from the *Occupational Outlook Handbook* and the Department of Labor.

Education & Training: This section tells you the education and training levels most employers expect for someone just starting out in the job. Almost all jobs now require a high school diploma, so we do not include "high school graduate" as an option. Instead, we list the *additional* training or education the average high school graduate needs to get the job.

Here are brief explanations of the categories we've used for the levels of training and education:

* **Work experience:** Work experience in a related job.
* **Short-term on-the-job training:** On-the-job training that can be as short as a week or last up to six months.
* **Moderate-term on-the-job training:** On-the-job training that can last from six months to a year.
* **Long-term on-the-job training:** On-the-job training that lasts up to two or more years. This training can take the form of apprenticeships, especially in the construction trades and production, installation, maintenance, and repair occupations.
* **Vocational/technical training:** Formal vocational or technical training received in a school, apprenticeship, or cooperative education program or in the military. This training can last from a few months to two or more years and may combine classroom training with on-the-job experience.
* **Associate degree:** A two-year college degree, usually from a trade school, technical school, or community college.
* **Bachelor's degree:** A four-year college degree.
* **Master's degree:** A bachelor's degree plus one or two years of additional education.
* **Doctoral degree:** A master's degree plus two or more years of additional education.
* **Professional degree:** Typically, a bachelor's degree plus two or more years of specialized education (for example, education to be an attorney, physician, or veterinarian).
* **Plus Related Work Experience:** Some jobs require work experience in a related job *as well as* formal education.

Some descriptions in this section present a range of possible requirements (for example, vocational/technical training to bachelor's degree). This means that certain positions within that career or certain industries within that field may require more training than others. Keep in mind that this represents the *minimal* requirements to get the job and that many employers would prefer individuals with even more education and training. (That's particularly true in careers where technology is advancing rapidly.) In addition, some occupations may require certification or licensing for entry, advancement, or private practice. Certification and licensing usually require completing coursework or passing examinations.

To research jobs by the education and training level, start your exploration with Appendix B, "Job Titles by Education and Training Requirements."

Average Earnings: These figures are based on the earnings of the middle 50 percent of workers in that field. In all cases, earnings are presented as annual income, even if the job usually pays by the hour. This allows you to easily compare one job's potential earnings with another's. Cases where the average earnings only apply to particular jobs are noted.

Keep in mind that the range of earnings given here excludes both the bottom and top 25 percent of earners. That is, half of the people in these jobs make *less* or *more* than the figures listed here—perhaps substantially more or less. We can all think of actors and top executives who make more than $100,000 a year. Likewise, some waiters and waitresses earn more than $50,000 a year, although the average earnings for these jobs are much lower.

It is generally true, however, that those jobs requiring higher levels of training and education pay more. Earnings also vary widely for similar jobs with different employers or in different parts of the country. Finally, young workers usually earn less than the average because they have less work experience than older workers in the same job.

Earnings Growth Potential: Most people who start a new career get a low rate of pay at first, but they expect to get higher wages later as they acquire experience. In some careers, earnings have the potential for a great increase. In other careers, the potential for increasing earnings is small, and to get better pay you generally need to move on to a different occupation. The Earnings Growth Potential statement answers the question, "*How much* higher can the earnings get for the average workers?"

To calculate this potential, we took two figures that the Bureau of Labor Statistics provides for every job: the highest earnings of the bottom 10 percent of wage earners and the earnings at the median (half earn more, half earn less). We took the *difference* between these two figures and calculated it as a *percentage* of the median. Because a percentage figure would be hard to interpret, we represent it as an easy-to-understand verbal tag that expresses the Earnings Growth Potential: "very low" when the percentage is less than 25 percent, "low" for 25 to 35 percent, "medium" for 36 to 40 percent, "high" for 41 to 50 percent, and "very high" for any figure higher than 50 percent.

Total Jobs Held: This provides an estimate of the total number of people currently employed in this job. This is useful when considering potential job openings. The more people in a given career, generally the more openings that will be available from turnover and retirement.

Job Outlook: This tells you whether the job is likely to employ more or fewer people in the future. The possible categories are as follows:

* **Declining:** Employment is expected to decrease.
* **Little change:** Employment is expected to remain about the same or increase as much as 6 percent.
* **Average increase:** Employment is expected to increase between 7 percent and 13 percent.
* **Above-average increase:** Employment is expected to increase between 14 percent and 19 percent.
* **Rapid increase:** Employment is expected to increase by 20 percent or more.

Annual Job Openings: This figure represents both the number of new jobs that will be created and the number of already established positions that will come open each year. It's important to note that even jobs expecting a decline in job growth may still have thousands of openings each year because of turnover and retirement.

Related Jobs: This section lists similar jobs you can consider, all of which are referenced elsewhere in this book.

Personality Types: This section describes the personality types that best match the work and environment required of each job. Personality types are derived from the work of vocational psychologist John L. Holland. The information here is based on O*NET jobs that are linked to each *OOH* job title. The O*NET, or Occupational Information Network, is a database of job information developed and continuously updated by the U.S. Department of Labor. Most jobs fit a primary personality type plus one or more secondary types, separated by hyphens.

We recommend you look over the following types and find the two or three that you think best describe your personality and interests. As you research the job descriptions, pay attention to the personality types listed in the Data Bank. While a personality type that differs from your own shouldn't keep you from considering a job, one that matches your personality and interests might be an even more appealing career choice. In short, if you are an artistic person and the job says it is a good fit for artistic people, you may be on to something.

Descriptions of the Six Personality Types

✳ **Realistic:** These occupations frequently involve practical, hands-on problems and solutions. Workers often deal with plants; animals; and real-world materials such as wood, tools, and machinery. Many of the occupations require working outside and do not involve a lot of paperwork or working closely with other people.

✳ **Investigative:** These occupations frequently involve working with ideas and require lots of critical thinking and analysis. These occupations can involve searching for facts and solving complex problems.

✳ **Artistic:** These occupations frequently involve working with forms, designs, and patterns. They often require self-expression, and the work can be done without following a clear set of rules.

✳ **Social:** These occupations frequently involve working with, communicating with, and teaching people. They almost always involve helping or providing service to others.

✳ **Enterprising:** These occupations frequently involve starting up and carrying out projects. They often require leading people, taking risks, and making important decisions. They often deal with business.

✳ **Conventional:** These occupations frequently involve following set procedures and routines. They often entail working with data and details more than with ideas. Usually there is a clear line of authority to follow.

To research jobs by personality type, start your exploration with Appendix A, "Job Titles by Personality Type," found near the back of the book.

Dare to Compare

Make photocopies of the worksheet on the following page and use it to compare the jobs that interest you most. Simply fill in the information about each job, giving each characteristic (earnings, working conditions, education requirements, and so on) a rating from 1 (undesirable) to 5 (most desirable). Adding the ratings and comparing the totals for each can give you some idea of which jobs you'd like to pursue further.

Career Comparison Worksheet

Job Characteristic Ratings Scale

←——1——2——3——4——5——→

Undesirable   **Desirable**   **Most Desirable**

	Job 1	Job 2	Job 3
Job Title			
Job Description Does the "At a Glance" description appeal to you?			
Working Conditions Does the "Where and When" of the job appeal to you?			
Education Required Jobs that match your current or future educational level are more desirable.			
Average Earnings Generally, the higher the earnings, the more desirable the job.			
Job Outlook Generally, the better the outlook, the more desirable the job.			
Personality Type Jobs that match your perceived personality type may offer more satisfaction.			
Totals			

Green Occupations

Biofuels Production Workers

At a Glance

Biofuels production workers operate, maintain, and manage facilities that produce fuels from plant and animal sources. Grains and recycled greases are already being processed into ethanol and biodiesel to power cars and trucks. Biofuels production technicians load the feedstock, monitor the chemical processing, separate the useful fuel from byproducts, test the quality of the fuel, and keep the production area clean. The equipment is complex, consisting of a mixture of mechanical, electrical, and electronic components, and it requires routine inspection and maintenance, plus repairs as needed.

Entry Ramp

Biofuels production technicians may learn their trade through postsecondary classes, a formal training program such as an apprenticeship, or informal on-the-job training. Many managers in this industry learn their skills through several years of experience in a related occupation. Some college graduates may be hired directly into lower-level management positions.

Did You Know?

At present, most biofuels are not as green as they should be; the process of growing the crops and refining the fuel consumes more energy than it produces. Researchers are experimenting with new processes, such as making diesel fuel from oil-rich microalgae. Microalgae are much more efficient processors of sunlight than soybeans because they have a simple cell structure and don't waste energy on forming stems. They can be grown in tanks, tubes, and ponds instead of in crop rows planted in topsoil. They can grow in salt water, even when temperatures fall below zero.

Career in Focus: *Biofuels Production Manager*

Biofuels production managers supervise operations of the plant, including production, shipping, maintenance, and quality assurance. Safety is always a concern because of the high temperatures of some equipment and the caustic or flammable properties of some of the liquids, so these managers formulate safety policies and train the employees in how to comply. Similarly, they are responsible for keeping the plant in line with environmental standards and regulations. By reviewing logs, datasheets, and reports, they ensure that production is on track and identify emerging problems with equipment or processes.

Where and When

The facilities where biofuels are produced include areas that are noisy, hot, dusty, and foul-smelling. Technicians are trained to safeguard against fire and chemical burns from the fluids involved in production. They must sometimes move heavy machinery and stoop, crawl, or climb to access equipment. Production managers divide their workday between a clean and comfortable office environment and the production areas of the facility. Biofuels production plants often operate around the clock, so workers may be required to work on rotating shifts.

For More Information

* Renewable Fuels Association, One Massachusetts Ave. NW, Suite 820, Washington, DC 20001. Internet: www.ethanolrfa.org

* National Biodiesel Board, P.O. Box 104898, Jefferson City, MO 65110-4898. Internet: www.biodiesel.org

* "Careers in Renewable Energy," by the National Renewable Energy Laboratory for the U.S. Department of Energy, 2001. Internet: www.nrel.gov/docs/fy01osti/28369.pdf

Biomass Energy Production Workers

At a Glance

Biomass plant technicians control and monitor activities at a facility that produces power from plant-derived materials such as wood, agricultural residues, and waste paper. Many installations burn biomass to generate power, sometimes diverting the waste heat to other purposes. When heated in a low-oxygen environment, biomass gives off a synthetic gas ("syngas") that can be used like natural gas. All of these processes generate carbon dioxide gas, but the plants that produce biomass consume this gas as they grow, so biomass is considered a "green" fuel. Technicians may preprocess biomass, chopping it up and pelletizing it. They operate valves, pumps, engines, or generators to control and adjust production of power. They also perform maintenance as needed.

Career in Focus: *Biomass Production Manager*

Biomass production managers direct work activities at the plant, including supervision of the operations and maintenance staff. They monitor the production processes, making sure that the plant complies with regulatory requirements. They compile and record operational data on forms or in logbooks. They also plan and schedule plant activities.

Where and When

Biomass plants contain equipment that is noisy or hot and may produce high-pressure steam and high-voltage electricity. The work environment may be dusty. To access equipment, technicians may need to stoop, crawl, or be exposed to heights or confined spaces. The work tends to be steady year-round, although there is usually more preprocessing activity during seasons when feedstocks (for example, agricultural wastes) become available.

Education and Training

Biomass energy production technicians may learn their trade through postsecondary classes, a formal training program such as an apprenticeship, or informal on-the-job training. Most managers in this industry learn their skills through several years of experience in a related occupation.

For More Information

* American Bioenergy Association, 1001 G St. NW, Suite 900 E, Washington, DC 20001. Internet: www.biomass.org
* Biomass Energy Research Association, 901 D St. SW, Suite 100, Washington, DC 20024. Internet: http://beraonline.org

Entry Ramp

Biofuels production technicians may learn their trade through postsecondary classes, a formal training program such as an apprenticeship, or informal on-the-job training. Many managers in this industry learn their skills through several years of experience in a related occupation. Some college graduates may be hired directly into lower-level management positions.

Did You Know?

In one experimental technique for preprocessing biomass, the materials are roasted like coffee beans. This method, called torrefaction, drives off moisture from the raw biomass, increasing its energy density, making it more economical to ship over a distance, and improving its stability during storage. As the biomass is roasted, it gives off gas that can be burned to provide some or all of the heat that the process requires. The torrefied biomass is brittle and can be ground up to be mixed with coal powder.

Brownfield Redevelopment Specialists and Site Managers

At a Glance

Brownfield redevelopment specialists and site managers participate in planning and directing cleanup and redevelopment of contaminated properties. Many parcels of land have excellent locations, perhaps near a city, but are neglected or underused because they have been abandoned by companies that have shut down or moved on. Environmental contamination, known or feared, often discourages developers from acquiring these sites, which are known as brownfields. Brownfield redevelopment specialists assess the amount and kind of environmental damage at the site. They facilitate negotiations between the buyer and the seller to determine such issues as who is responsible for the cleanup. Then they plan and supervise the cleanup project.

Entry Ramp

Many brownfield redevelopment specialists and site managers get into the field by getting a bachelor's degree in engineering. Another route to this job is a master's degree in public administration or in urban, community, and regional planning, especially if combined with an undergraduate major or minor in environmental studies. Some workers get a bachelor's or master's degree in landscape architecture and then specialize in designing the landscape components of redevelopment projects.

Did You Know?

The U.S. General Accounting Office estimates that there are somewhere between 450,000 and 1 million brownfield sites in the United States. They are not confined to states with big cities; Iowa is estimated to have 4,000 sites.

Career in Focus:
Brownfield Site Manager

Site managers oversee a rehabilitated property and deal with any lingering concerns, perhaps doing periodic testing and reporting. Sometimes they must deal with continuing operation and maintenance of remedial systems, such as groundwater treatment systems, asphalt caps, and fences.

Where and When

Brownfield redevelopment specialists and site managers spend most of their time in offices consulting with clients, developing reports and plans, and working with engineers and contractors. However, they often visit brownfield sites to conduct inspections and review the progress of projects. Although most redevelopers work approximately 40 hours per week, they sometimes have to work nights and weekends to meet deadlines or to attend community meetings.

For More Information

* National Brownfield Association, 8765 W. Higgins Rd., Suite 280, Chicago, IL 60631. Internet: www.brownfieldassociation.org

* Environmental Protection Agency, Brownfields and Land Revitalization. Internet: www.epa.gov/brownfields

Energy Auditors

At a Glance

Energy auditors help businesses and homeowners learn where their energy dollars are going and how they can use energy more efficiently. They inspect building envelopes, mechanical systems, electrical systems, or industrial processes to determine the energy consumption of each component. They analyze records, such as energy bills, to detect annual or monthly patterns of energy use. Then they identify energy-saving measures and prepare an audit report containing the results of the energy analysis and recommendations for energy cost savings.

Career in Focus: *Residential Energy Auditor*

Residential energy auditors advise homeowners about energy efficiency or answer questions about the costs of running household appliances and how to select energy-efficient appliances. They may prepare job-specification sheets for home energy improvements such as attic insulation, window retrofits, and heating system upgrades.

Where and When

Energy auditors spend much of their time in comfortable offices, where they analyze data and prepare reports, specifications, and budgets. However, they must also visit homes, commercial buildings, and industrial facilities to perform tests and inspections, take measurements, and meet with clients. At these locations, they may need to do some work in cramped or damp spaces. Some industrial sites are noisy or foul-smelling. Safety procedures and equipment (such as a hard hat) may be required. Energy auditors must sometimes work evening or weekend shifts to be able to meet with homeowners.

For More Information

✳ The Residential Energy Services Network (RESNET) has information about certifications and the training programs that can prepare for them. P.O. Box 4561, Oceanside, CA 92052-4561. Phone: (760) 806-3448. Internet: www.resnet.us

✳ A state-by-state listing of programs that certify home energy auditors is maintained at the Energy Circle blog. Internet: http://energycircle.com/blog/learn-about-home-energy/energy-auditing/home-energy-audits-iii-audit-certification

✳ Association of Energy Engineers, 4025 Pleasantdale Rd., Suite 420, Atlanta, GA 30340. Internet: www.aeecenter.org

Entry Ramp

Energy auditors have several entry routes that represent several levels of skill, from on-the-job training to a bachelor's degree. HVAC (heating, ventilating, and air-conditioning) is an especially relevant trade, and some workers enter the energy-conservation field from a background as an HVAC mechanic. Another relevant construction trade in which to get training is insulation worker, either through informal on-the-job training, which typically takes six months, or through a formal apprenticeship, which takes four or five years. Energy auditors who work in industrial settings often have a bachelor's degree in engineering; so do some who work in household settings. Some industry organizations offer certification programs that teach energy-auditing skills.

Did You Know?

You may think that utility companies want to sell more and more power so they can earn more money. However, they lose money when they have to build generating facilities that are needed only on the coldest days of winter and the hottest days of summer. That's why the utilities encourage energy conservation. Some employ energy auditors and offer homeowners and businesses free or low-cost energy audits.

Environmental Restoration Planners

At a Glance

Environmental restoration planners use scientific methods to design and monitor projects that reintroduce natural balances to an ecosystem, restoring its health, integrity, and sustainability. They often begin by gathering data at the site of the degraded ecosystem—for example, taking measurements of tree rings, soil strata, or stream deposits. This evidence indicates what the site was like before it was damaged, as well as its current state. Next, they propose interventions to roll back at least some of the damaging forces, collaborating with energy engineers, biologists, geologists, or other professionals, plus appropriate technicians. Their plans include schedules and budgets, plus explanations of how the project will comply with any standards, laws, or regulations that apply.

Entry Ramp

Strong technical knowledge is essential for environmental restoration planners. Some begin their careers as engineers, after completing a bachelor's degree in an engineering field related to the environment. Others begin as scientists, such as environmental scientists, hydrologists, or wildlife scientists. Most scientists engaged in basic research have a Ph.D. degree; some who work in applied research and other activities may have a bachelor's or master's degree. Experience or coursework in business is a helpful addition to technical credentials.

Did You Know?

These workers sometimes need to make plans that will soften the environmental impact of energy-related projects, such as power transmission lines, natural gas pipelines, and fuel refineries. The public is particularly sensitive to the impact of projects that are intended to harvest sustainable energy, such as geothermal plants, wind farms, or solar farms.

Career in Focus: *Restoration Technician*

Restoration technicians help planners by gathering data about a site—for example, the number of plant species. They also participate in the restoration work. For example, they may cut and burn out invasive plant species and then gather and plant seeds of native species. They need to be able to identify a wide range of plants and animals, as well as soils.

Where and When

Environmental restoration planners spend most of their time in an office, where they analyze data, create plans, and communicate with project staff. They may spend some time in a lab or in the field at sites to do testing and gather data. Site visits sometimes involve strenuous physical activity and require outdoor work in all kinds of weather. These workers sometimes attend public hearings about environmental issues. Most planners work 40 hours a week and may work longer on occasion to meet project deadlines.

For More Information

* U.S. Army Corps of Engineers, 441 G St. NW, Washington, DC 20314-1000. Internet: www.usace.army.mil
* Society for Ecological Restoration International, 285 W. 18th St., Suite 1, Tucson, AZ 85701. Internet: www.ser.org

Fuel Cell Technicians

At a Glance

Fuel cell technicians design, modify, repair, and construct fuel cell components and systems. Fuel cells produce electricity by a process that's more efficient than burning fuels. Several types of fuel can be used to power fuel cells, including hydrogen, diesel fuel, and various kinds of alcohol. The technology is still evolving, so many fuel cell technicians currently are working in research and development, helping engineers measure the potential of new designs by building prototypes and testing their performance. As usage of fuel cells expands to vehicles, some technicians may work as specialized vehicle mechanics.

Career in Focus: *Fuel Cell Field Service Technician*

Field service technicians maintain and repair installations in residential or industrial settings. They interpret engineering specifications, use test equipment, and analyze test data and performance records.

Where and When

Fuel cell technicians work in laboratories, offices, or industrial plants. Some may be exposed to hazards from equipment, but they are trained in safety procedures. Field technicians spend part of their workday traveling to sites where equipment needs to be tested or serviced.

For More Information

* Fuel Cells 2000: Internet: www.fuelcells.org
* U.S. Army Corps of Engineers, Engineer Research and Development Center, Construction Engineering Research Laboratory, Fuel Cell. Internet: http://dodfuelcell.cecer.army.mil/index.php
* US Fuel Cell Council, 1100 H St. NW, Suite 800, Washington, DC 20005. Internet: www.usfcc.com

Entry Ramp

An associate degree in engineering technology is a good route for entering the occupation. At present, only a handful of programs are designed specifically for training in fuel cell technology, but many of the necessary skills can be learned in programs for electrical or electronics engineering technology. Such programs are offered at technical institutes and community colleges. The military is exploring uses of fuel cell technology and probably will eventually develop training programs for technicians.

Did You Know?

Fuel cells may be used to make solar and wind power more affordable. These sources produce electric power at times that are not entirely predictable and may not coincide with the times when power is needed; therefore, we need ways to store the energy. One attractive option is to use surplus electric power to break down water into hydrogen and oxygen, store these gases, and then use fuel cells to generate electricity from them when demand exceeds supply.

Geothermal Energy Production Workers

At a Glance

Geothermal energy production workers operate, maintain, and manage facilities that generate energy from heat within the earth. Water may be forced into red-hot rock formations to heat up or may occur naturally there. Either way, the water turns to steam when it emerges from the earth, and this can drive a turbine to generate power. Geothermal production managers assess sites for their suitability, obtain permits for drilling, and oversee construction of geothermal power plants. During operation, they keep logs of maintenance tasks, power production, and other operations. Like managers in any industrial facility, they plan and budget, supervise workers, devise safety policies, and communicate with facility owners. Geothermal technicians operate and service equipment.

Entry Ramp

Geothermal energy production technicians may learn their trade through postsecondary classes, a formal training program such as an apprenticeship, or informal on-the-job training. Most managers in this industry learn their skills through several years of experience in a related occupation. Some college graduates may be hired directly into lower-level management positions.

Did You Know?

Hot water extracted for geothermal power generation sometimes contains large amounts of dissolved minerals or gases. Much of the maintenance work at the power plant may be directed at dealing with corrosion caused by these substances. The chemicals are often extracted from the water or steam, partly to avoid release of pollution and partly to obtain commercially valuable substances. In one installation at an arid setting in East Africa, condensed steam provides drinking water for the community.

Career in Focus: *Geothermal Heat Pump Technician*

Some geothermal technicians work on installations that tap into heat found just below the earth's surface. A heat pump, working like an air conditioner in reverse, extracts heat from water that is drawn from a well or that circulates in a buried loop. Technicians construct the water-circulation system, install the heat pump, and hook it up to the air ducts and hot water plumbing of a building.

Where and When

Many parts of geothermal power plants are noisy, hot, and sometimes foul-smelling. Technicians sometimes need to stoop, crawl, or be exposed to heights or confined spaces. Parts of the facility house water and steam under high pressure and high-voltage electric wiring. Managers work in an office, but they also supervise workers and inspect production areas. Power plants operate around the clock, so workers may work rotating shifts. Geothermal technicians who install and maintain systems for heat pumps do much of their work outdoors. The equipment is noisy and potentially hazardous. Routing pipes into a building may require working in a confined space.

For More Information

* The International Ground Source Heat Pump Association (IGSHPA), 374 Cordell South, Stillwater, OK 74078. Internet: www.igshpa.okstate.edu

* Geothermal Energy Association, 209 Pennsylvania Ave. SE, Washington, DC 20003. Internet: www.geo-energy.org

* "Fact Sheet: Jobs from Renewable Energy and Energy Efficiency" by the Environmental and Energy Study Institute, 2008. Internet: www.eesi.org/110708_Jobs_factsheet

Hydroelectric Energy Production Workers

At a Glance

Hydroelectric energy production workers operate, maintain, and manage facilities that generate energy from the force of moving water. Hydroelectric plant technicians monitor the operation and performance of equipment and make adjustments and repairs as necessary. A hydropower plant is a very complex collection of electrical, mechanical, and electronic equipment. Technicians change oil, hydraulic fluid, or other lubricants. They cut, bend, or shape metal parts and weld or bolt them together. The machines may be huge, but they sometimes have tolerances smaller than the width of a human hair.

Career in Focus:
Hydroelectric Production Manager

Hydroelectric production managers supervise operations at the power plant. They provide technical direction in the construction and commissioning of hydroelectric equipment and the supporting electrical or mechanical systems and supervise the plant technicians. They keep operations within prescribed operating limits, such as loads, voltages, and temperatures.

Where and When

Some parts of hydroelectric power plants are very noisy environments. The water roars through pipes and turbines, and the generators whine. In outdoor parts of the facility, workers are exposed to extremes of weather. Accessing the water channels and power-generating equipment may sometimes require climbing, stooping, or crawling. Those in managerial positions do much of their work in a clean and comfortable office environment, but they must visit production areas of the hydroelectric installation to supervise workers and conduct inspections. Power plants operate around the clock, so workers may be required to work on rotating shifts.

For More Information

✳ National Hydropower Association, 25 Massachusetts Ave. NW, Suite 450, Washington, DC 20001. Internet: www.hydro.org

✳ "Fact Sheet: Jobs from Renewable Energy and Energy Efficiency" by the Environmental and Energy Study Institute, 2008. Internet: http://www.eesi.org/110708_Jobs_factsheet

✳ The Web site of the U.S. Department of Energy's Office of Energy Efficiency and Renewable Energy has links to job listings and providers of education and training. Internet: http://www1.eere.energy.gov/education

Entry Ramp

Hydroelectric plant technicians do not need a college degree, but the more postsecondary learning they have, the higher the level of the job they can hold. Managers typically learn their skills through several years of experience in a related occupation. Some college graduates may be hired directly into lower-level management positions.

Did You Know?

Hydropower is sometimes used to store energy: Water can be pumped uphill from a lower reservoir to a higher one and then later released to flow downhill through a turbine. Although this cycle consumes more energy than it produces, it can be useful to even out temporary mismatches between power that is available and power that is needed by customers. Because wind and sunshine vary in availability, the more those power sources are used, the more pumped-storage hydropower and similar technologies (perhaps using compressed air) may be needed.

Industrial Ecologists

At a Glance

Industrial ecologists study or investigate industrial production and natural ecosystems to achieve high production, sustainable resources, and environmental safety or protection. They look at the inputs and outputs of industrial activity and what processes connect them. They try to find ways to recycle outputs as inputs so that the entire system can be a closed loop—sustainable and not wasteful. Industrial ecologists use scientific methods in their work; they make hypotheses, gather data, and analyze the data to confirm or reject the hypotheses. They review the work of other researchers and publish their own methods and findings.

Career in Focus: *Environmental Economist*

Environmental economists study how the natural environment interacts with the global economy. To understand these complex and dynamic interactions, they use mathematical models. They focus on issues such as the environmental impact of economic forces, the carrying capacity of an ecosystem that is being exploited, or the benefits and costs of environmental regulations.

Where and When

Industrial ecologists divide their time between outdoor work in the field and indoor work in an office or laboratory. They may also do some fieldwork indoors at industrial or commercial sites. The outdoor work may be physically taxing and expose workers to all kinds of weather. Academic researchers may face stress when looking for funding. Occasionally, those who write technical reports for business clients and regulators may be under pressure to meet deadlines and thus have to work long hours.

For More Information

* "Industrial Ecology," video by University of Leiden and Delft University of Technology, Netherlands. Internet: www.youtube.com/watch?v=bk5vwFbGEP4

* "The Best of Both Worlds: A Beginner's Guide to Industrial Ecology," *MIT Undergraduate Research Journal*, Volume 15, Spring 2007, pp. 19–22. Internet: http://web.mit.edu/murj/www/v15/v15-Features/v15-f6.pdf

* The Center for Industrial Ecology, Yale University, 380 Edwards St., New Haven, CT 06511. Internet: cie.research.yale.edu

Methane/Landfill Gas Production Workers

At a Glance

Methane/landfill gas production workers operate, maintain, and manage facilities that collect gas from landfills and process it as a substitute for natural gas. The gas is produced by microorganisms that feed on the garbage. Methane/landfill gas generation system technicians operate the equipment that taps into landfills, extracts the gas, filters it, purifies it, compresses it, and distributes it. They diagnose or troubleshoot problems with the mechanical and electronic systems. They read, interpret, and adjust monitoring apparatus and maintain a log of wellhead pressure readings and other data. Technicians routinely conduct walking inspections of the landfill's surface, measuring the vegetative covering, installing additional covering where it is required, and detecting leaks.

Career in Focus: *Methane/ Landfill Gas Collection System Operator*

Collection system operators oversee the construction, maintenance, and repair of equipment and play a supervisory role in ensuring compliance with environmental regulations. Operators supervise technicians, prepare and manage budgets for the system, and develop and enforce procedures for normal operation, startup, and shutdown.

Where and When

Safety is an important concern for workers in the production of an explosive gas. Some processing equipment may be hot or noisy or generate high-voltage electric current. Liquids in the equipment may contain hazardous substances, and the untreated gas is notorious for its foul odor. Technicians must learn the facility's safety policies and not cut corners. Those in managerial positions work in an office environment. However, the job requires them to supervise workers and conduct inspections in the outdoor areas of the facility. Technicians are sometimes on call around the clock to deal with emergencies.

Entry Ramp

Methane/landfill gas generation system technicians may be hired with only a high school diploma, but usually some postsecondary classes are helpful or expected. System operators either learn their skills through several years of experience as technicians or enter directly with a college degree.

Did You Know?

Operators sometimes are assigned to work at abandoned landfills, which present special problems. The old landfill may be leaky because it was constructed without a clay lining at its base or without a system of pipes and pumps for collecting liquids. There may be no records of the depth or composition of the waste or the geology that underlies it. Housing may be located nearby, with the risk that migrating gas can enter basements. These situations require a lot of testing to determine possible environmental hazards and the appropriate corrective measures.

For More Information

* Solid Waste Association of North America, 1100 Wayne Ave., Suite 700, Silver Spring, MD 20910. Internet: www.swana.org

* The overheads for a training course in landfill gas management, developed by Earth Tech, Inc., for the Illinois Environmental Protection Agency, are available at www.epa.gov/reg5rcra/wptdiv/solidwaste/slides/PART1LF_Gas_Mgmt_Sections.pdf

* U.S. Department of Energy's Office of Energy Efficiency and Renewable Energy. Internet: http://www1.eere.energy.gov/education

Solar Energy Production Workers

At a Glance

Solar energy production workers operate, maintain, and manage facilities that collect heat or generate electric energy from sunlight. Solar photovoltaic (PV) installers set up systems that generate electricity directly from sunlight and perform whatever maintenance is needed. They mount PV panels on rooftops or frames and connect the panels to wiring, perhaps linking to the local utility's power grid. Solar thermal installers and technicians work on systems that absorb and use heat from the sun, either for hot water, for climate control in a building, or for a boiler that generates power. They install and maintain pipes, insulation, tanks, heat exchangers, and perhaps mirrors.

Entry Ramp

Solar energy technicians may learn their trade through postsecondary classes, formal training programs such as an apprenticeship, or informal on-the-job training. (At present, the Department of Labor's Office of Apprenticeship does not have registered apprenticeship programs in this field, but they may be developed as the industry expands.) The majority of managers in this industry learn their skills through several years of experience in a related occupation, such as solar energy installer or construction manager. Some college graduates may be hired directly into lower-level management positions.

Did You Know?

A report from the Renewable and Appropriate Energy Laboratory in Berkeley found that renewable energy creates more jobs per megawatt of power installed, per unit of energy produced, and per dollar of investment than the sector of the energy industry based on fossil fuel. The Renewable Energy Policy Project estimated that almost two-thirds of solar PV-related jobs are for assembling modules, connecting systems, and contracting, so even if most solar PV units are manufactured abroad, an expansion of solar PV usage will create a large number of American jobs.

Career in Focus: *Solar Energy Installation Manager*

Installation managers prepare project proposals, including budgets and schedules. As a project gets under way, they ensure that installers and subcontractors comply with the plans and with standards of quality and safety. At completion, they schedule building inspections and help the technicians with startup and testing of the system.

Where and When

Installation projects often involve working on rooftops—difficult work for people who are afraid of heights. Even ground-based installation work requires exposure to the weather. Connecting a panel array to a building's electric or hot-water system may involve working in basements or confined crawl spaces. Technicians are trained in safety procedures to follow when dealing with electricity or hot fluids. Those in managerial positions do much of their work in a clean and comfortable office environment, but they also supervise workers and conduct inspections at installation sites. All kinds of workers need to travel to installation sites.

For More Information

* "Finding Your Dream Job in Solar" by Andy Black, *Solar Today*, September/October, 2005. Internet: www.ongrid.net/papers/SolarTodayDreamJob2005.pdf

* For information about certification of solar PV and thermal installers, contact the North American Board of Certified Energy Practitioners (NABCEP), 634 Plank Rd., Suite 102, Clifton Park, NY 12065. The Web site itemizes the competencies that are needed for certification. Internet: www.nabcep.org

Water Resource Specialists

At a Glance

Water resource specialists find ways to ensure ample supplies of clean freshwater. Most of them are employed by county governments or by municipal water-supply agencies. They work to protect or rehabilitate watersheds, especially from pollution. Pollutants often are carried far from their source, so finding the source may require considerable research. Water resource specialists monitor the health of a water resource by overseeing or conducting regular testing and sampling. They also measure the quantities of accumulated water and water flow rates in resources, in storage and distribution systems, and from wastewater outlets.

Career in Focus: *Water Resource Engineer*

Water resource engineers design projects that distribute water or collect and treat wastewater. Using data from field studies, they construct mathematical models to determine how best to operate a network of rivers and reservoirs in a manner than will improve water quality and reduce flooding. They consult with the managers who oversee the construction of water detention facilities, storm drains, flood control facilities, or other hydraulic structures.

Where and When

Water resource specialists divide their time between comfortable offices and field work. In the field, they may visit treatment plants for water and wastewater, which may be noisy or bad-smelling. Field trips expose the workers to bad weather conditions, insects, and driving on dirt roads, plus some physical exertion. The work week is usually 40 hours, but field work may require up to a 14-hour shift, and workers may need to appear at public meetings held in the evening.

For More Information

* U.S. Bureau of Reclamation, Water Resources Planning and Operations Support, P.O. Box 25007, Denver Federal Center, Mail Stop 86-68210, Denver, CO 80225. Internet: www.usbr.gov/pmts/water_use

* American Water Works Association, 6666 W. Quincy Ave., Denver, CO 80235. Internet: www.awwa.org

* "Careers in Water Resources" brochure, Universities Council on Water Resources, 4543 Faner Hall, Southern Illinois University at Carbondale, Carbondale, IL 62901-4526. Internet: www.ucowr.siu.edu/Careers/CareersInWater.html

Entry Ramp

Employers usually require the combination of a bachelor's degree and a few years of relevant work experience. The degree might be in engineering, geology, hydrology, or a related field, as long as it includes substantial coursework in hydrology, earth science, chemistry, engineering, and water resources. Appropriate experience beyond the degree might include working as an engineer, hydrologist, or geologist. Experience or a master's degree in public administration is also helpful. Water resource specialists need to be skilled with computer modeling, data analysis and integration, digital mapping, remote sensing, and Geographic Information Systems (GIS). Global Positioning Systems (GPS) are growing in importance.

Did You Know?

In some places, the groundwater was deposited thousands or even millions of years ago—"fossil" water that gets little or no replenishment from the surface. Like fossil fuel, this water is a nonrenewable resource that can be used only once and then is exhausted. Water resource specialists try to minimize use of such water by encouraging recycling and highly efficient use.

Weatherization Installers and Technicians

At a Glance

Weatherization installers and technicians perform a variety of activities to weatherize homes and make them more energy efficient. These workers schedule visits to homes or buildings, which they inspect to identify needed weatherization measures, including repair work, modification, or replacement. Based on what they see and the energy regulations and codes that apply, they recommend weatherization techniques to the owners of the home or building and prepare specifications and cost estimates for the work they plan to do. They often apply heat-trapping materials such as loose, blanket, board, and foam insulation.

Entry Ramp

Short-term on-the-job training is usually enough for jobs that require laying insulation blankets, wielding a caulking gun, or installing door sweeps. Somewhat longer-term on-the-job training is needed before workers can conduct routine energy-leak tests and install conservation components with demanding tolerances, such as heat-efficient doors and windows. The Department of Energy estimates that it takes six to eight weeks to train a work crew in home weatherization. Those who install HVAC units usually need formal training, such as a two-year program in HVAC technology at a technical or community college, or perhaps training in an apprenticeship or the military.

Did You Know?

Weatherization workers sometimes do more than save money for householders; sometimes they save lives, because many heat-leaking old buildings also have other problems. A weatherization program conducted by a utilities company in Louisville in 1997 found that 23 percent of the households served had gas leaks, 26 percent had inadequate draft for heaters, and 16 percent had elevated levels of deadly carbon monoxide gas. Weatherization workers who do HVAC work are trained to detect these hazards and remedy them.

Career in Focus: *Weatherization Shell Technician*

Shell technicians focus on the shell of the building rather than on the interior. They may install storm windows, storm doors, weatherstripping, glazing, caulking, or door sweeps to reduce energy losses. Some also improve the efficiency of heating and hot water systems by wrapping air ducts and water lines with insulating materials or by wrapping water heaters with fiberglass blankets.

Where and When

Weatherization technicians who specialize in insulating heating, ventilating, and air-conditioning (HVAC) systems or plumbing spend much of their time in basements or in attics and crawl spaces. When applying insulation, they wear protective clothing, including filter masks. Some work on windows and walls is outdoors and at heights. All technicians must travel to work sites at homes and businesses. Most work at least a 40-hour week. They sometimes work evening or weekend shifts to meet with homeowners.

For More Information

* The Department of Energy developed a set of "Core Competencies for the Weatherization Assistance Program," listing skills and knowledge that weatherization technicians and crew chiefs need for success in the state programs to weatherize low-income neighborhoods. This may be useful for evaluating the topics covered in any training program you consider. Internet: www.waptac.org/si.asp?id=1259

* The Web site of the U.S. Department of Energy's Office of Energy Efficiency and Renewable Energy has links to job listings and providers of education and training. Internet: http://www1.eere.energy.gov/education. Information about the Weatherization Training Conference is available at http://www1.eere.energy.gov/weatherization/conference

Wind Energy Production Workers

At a Glance

Wind energy production workers operate, maintain, and manage facilities that generate energy from wind power. Wind energy project managers oversee the development and evaluation of potential wind energy business opportunities, including environmental studies, proposals, permitting, and sometimes construction. As the project progresses, they supervise the work of subcontractors and keep tabs on expenditures to ensure that costs stay within budget limits. Wind energy operations managers supervise operations of existing wind farms, including personnel, maintenance, financial activities, and planning.

Career in Focus: *Wind Turbine Service Technician*

Because wind turbines have many moving parts and are exposed to strong forces of nature, the equipment requires frequent service. Wind turbine service technicians are trained to detect and fix malfunctions in electrical, mechanical, and hydraulic systems. Some help assemble components during the construction of a wind farm.

Where and When

To access the power-generating equipment and service tower structures, technicians are exposed to heights. The nacelle (which houses the generating equipment) sways and rotates in the wind and can induce motion sickness; inside, the technician is exposed to heat and cold and may need to work in confined spaces. The work sometimes involves high-voltage electric wiring. Work hours may be longer during seasons of peak wind activity, when equipment needs more attention. Project managers spend part of their time in offices, but they also must spend time at construction sites where they are exposed to many of the same discomforts and hazards as the technicians.

Entry Ramp

Wind turbine service technicians may learn their trade through postsecondary classes, a formal training program, or informal on-the-job training. (At present, the Department of Labor's Office of Apprenticeship does not have registered apprenticeship programs in this field, but they are likely to be developed as the industry expands.) The majority of managers in this industry learn their skills through several years of experience in a related occupation, such as wind turbine service technician, millwright, or construction manager. Some college graduates may be hired directly into lower-level management positions.

Did You Know?

When a community college in New Mexico started an associate degree program for wind energy technicians in 2008, an official of General Electric promised to hire all graduates of the program for the next three years.

For More Information

* American Wind Energy Association, 1501 M St. NW, Suite 1000, Washington, DC 20005. Internet: www.awea.org

* "Fact Sheet: Jobs from Renewable Energy and Energy Efficiency," by the Environmental and Energy Study Institute, 2008. Internet: www.eesi.org/110708_Jobs_factsheet

* U.S. Department of Energy's Office of Energy Efficiency and Renewable Energy. Internet: http://www1.eere.energy.gov/education and www.windpoweringamerica.gov/schools_training.asp

Management and Business and Financial Operations Occupations

Administrative Services Managers

At a Glance

Administrative services managers work for large and small businesses and government agencies. They manage the services that keep businesses running smoothly: mailroom, food, travel, data processing, security, parking, printing, purchasing, and payroll. They can work as office managers, contract administrators, or unclaimed property officers. In large companies, they may manage other workers. In small companies, they may be responsible for any or all of these services themselves.

Data Bank

Education and Training: Bachelor's or higher degree plus related work experience

Average Earnings: $54,000–$101,000

Earnings Growth Potential: High

Total Jobs Held: 259,000

Job Outlook: Average increase

Annual Job Openings: 8,700

Related Jobs: Cost estimators; office and administrative support worker supervisors and managers; property, real estate, and community association managers; purchasing managers, buyers, and purchasing agents; top executives

Personality Types: Enterprising-Conventional

Did You Know?

Facility managers looking for advice can find it in *American School & Hospital Facility*, a magazine designed for managers of institutional buildings. It includes articles on everything from the best floor cleaner to the latest grounds security surveillance systems. In fact, whatever your ideal career is, there is probably a magazine for it.

Career in Focus: *Facility Manager*

Facility managers plan, design, and manage workplace facilities. They are responsible for budgeting, buying and selling real estate, and making renovations. They may assist with the architectural design of the buildings. Often they are responsible for keeping the facility safe and well maintained. Such jobs require a combination of engineering skill and business experience.

Where and When

Administrative service managers generally work in comfortable office settings. Most work a standard 40-hour week, though some overtime may be expected to meet deadlines. Depending on the type of job, frequent travel could be required.

For More Information

* International Facility Management Association, 1 E. Greenway Plaza, Suite 1100, Houston, TX 77046-0194. Internet: www.ifma.org
* Association of Professional Office Managers, P.O. Box 1926, Rockville, MD 20849. Internet: www.apomonline.org

Advertising, Marketing, Promotions, Public Relations, and Sales Managers

At a Glance

Advertising, marketing, promotions, public relations, and sales managers can be found in almost every industry and are responsible for helping businesses sell their products and services. They coordinate market research, marketing strategy, sales, advertising, promotion, pricing, product development, and public relations activities. Advertising managers dictate what kind of advertising campaign will best sell the product, including the kinds of media used (radio, television, magazines, and so on). Marketing managers estimate how much of a product will sell and to which markets. Promotions managers direct programs that combine advertising with discounts, rebates, and contests to increase sales. Public relations managers help companies create a positive image in the community through interviews, press releases, and special events. Sales managers assign sales territories, set goals, and help train and motivate the sales force. Most of these managers are responsible for coordinating a team of workers to meet goals under strict deadlines.

Career in Focus: *Creative Director*

The creative director is an advertising manager who is specifically responsible for the written and visual parts of an ad campaign. This career combines business sense and experience with an imaginative and artistic personality.

Where and When

Advertising, marketing, promotions, public relations, and sales managers work in comfortable office settings. Long hours, including evenings and weekends, are common. In fact, about two-thirds of these managers usually work more than 40 hours per week. Substantial travel may be involved. The high stress of meeting deadlines can make this a challenging but rewarding career.

For More Information

* American Association of Advertising Agencies, 405 Lexington Ave., 18th Floor, New York, NY 10174-1801. Internet: www.aaaa.org
* Public Relations Society of America, 33 Maiden Ln., 11th Floor, New York, NY 10038-5150. Internet: www.prsa.org

---

Data Bank

Education and Training: Bachelor's or higher degree plus related work experience

Average Earnings: $68,000–$141,000

Earnings Growth Potential: High

Total Jobs Held: 624,000

Job Outlook: Average increase

Annual Job Openings: 21,700

Related Jobs: Actors, producers, and directors; advertising sales agents; artists and related workers; authors, writers, and editors; demonstrators and product promoters; market and survey researchers; models; public relations specialists; sales representatives, wholesale and manufacturing

Personality Types: Enterprising-Conventional-Artistic

Did You Know?

As the top-selling soft drink in the world, Coca-Cola spends a hefty sum to keep its brand on the minds of consumers. Its annual advertising and marketing budget hovers around $2.5 billion. With that kind of investment, any new slogan better be catchy.

Computer and Information Systems Managers

At a Glance

Computer and information systems managers plan and direct the installation and use of computer systems. They hire computer programmers and support specialists and plan what new technology is needed to keep their company successful. They also decide what workers and equipment are needed to do certain jobs. Often they are involved in the upkeep, maintenance, and security of computer networks as well. Such responsibilities require them to constantly stay aware of the latest advances in technology.

Data Bank

Education and Training: Bachelor's or higher degree plus related work experience

Average Earnings: $89,000–$144,000

Earnings Growth Potential: Medium

Total Jobs Held: 293,000

Job Outlook: Above-average increase

Annual Job Openings: 9,700

Related Jobs: Advertising, marketing, promotions, public relations, and sales managers; computer network, systems, and database administrators; computer scientists; computer software engineers and computer programmers; computer support specialists; computer systems analysts; engineering and natural sciences managers; financial managers; top executives

Personality Types: Enterprising-Conventional-Investigative

Did You Know?

According to the Symantec company, more than 1.1 million known computer viruses were in circulation in 2008. Computer and information systems managers have their work cut out for them in protecting their businesses' networks and data, whether they are protecting against a worm or filtering out spam.

Career in Focus: *Network Manager*

Otherwise known as LAN/WAN (local area network/wide area network) managers, these individuals are responsible for designing and maintaining the network that connects all workers within an organization. When an employee on the second floor can't log in or a computer virus suddenly spreads throughout the network, you can be sure this manager is on the case.

Where and When

Computer and information systems managers work in comfortable office settings. They sometimes need to work evenings and weekends to solve unexpected problems, because companies often need their computer systems in order to keep their businesses running. Extensive computer use can lead to eyestrain and back, hand, and wrist problems.

For More Information

* Association for Computing Machinery (ACM), 2 Penn Plaza, Suite 701, New York, NY 10121-0701. Internet: http://computingcareers.acm.org

* Institute of Electrical and Electronics Engineers Computer Society, Headquarters Office, 2001 L St. NW, Suite 700, Washington, DC 20036-4910. Internet: www.computer.org

* National Workforce Center for Emerging Technologies, 3000 Landerholm Circle SE, Bellevue, WA 98007. Internet: www.nwcet.org

Construction Managers

At a Glance

Construction managers plan and direct construction projects, including roads, bridges, plants, schools, hospitals, and other buildings. On small projects they are responsible for all the people, materials, and equipment at a job site. They direct the building process from the concept stage through the final construction. They hire and schedule workers, make sure materials are delivered on time, and oversee the safety of the work site. They are also responsible for staying within budget. Anyone interested in being a construction manager needs a background in building science, business, and management, as well as experience in the construction industry.

Career in Focus: *Specialty Trade Contractor*

Most construction managers are concerned with all aspects of construction. But some aspects of a building are important enough to require a construction manager who specializes in that line of work, often known as a specialty trade contractor. Examples of specialties include plumbing, heating and air conditioning, and electrical work. After all, you don't want just anyone overseeing the plumbing work in your new house.

Where and When

Construction managers often work out of a central office where they coordinate activity. However, they spend a great deal of time on site as well, which could mean extensive travel. In addition, they are usually on call 24 hours a day to deal with delays, bad weather, and emergencies. Though safety precautions are always taken, work around a construction site can still be hazardous.

For More Information

* American Institute of Constructors, P.O. Box 26334, Alexandria, VA 22314. Internet: www.aicnet.org

* Construction Management Association of America, 7926 Jones Branch Dr., Suite 800, McLean, VA 22102. Internet: www.cmaanet.org

* American Council for Construction Education, 1717 North Loop 1604 E, Suite 320, San Antonio, TX 78232. Internet: www.acce-hq.org

* National Center for Construction Education and Research, 3600 NW 43rd St., Bldg. G, Gainesville, FL 32606. Internet: www.nccer.org

Data Bank

Education and Training: Bachelor's degree

Average Earnings: $63,000–$111,000

Earnings Growth Potential: Medium

Total Jobs Held: 551,000

Job Outlook: Above-average increase

Annual Job Openings: 13,800

Related Jobs: Architects, except landscape and naval; cost estimators; engineering and natural sciences managers; engineers; landscape architects

Personality Types: Enterprising-Realistic-Conventional

Did You Know?

There is an increased demand for certification of construction managers. Volunteer certification programs such as those offered by the American Institute of Constructors (AIC) and the Construction Management Association of America (CMAA) provide proof to potential employers and clients of a manager's knowledge and experience.

Education Administrators

At a Glance

Education administrators manage the day-to-day activities in schools, preschools, daycare centers, and colleges and universities. They also direct the educational programs of businesses, correctional institutions, museums, and community service organizations. Education administrators set standards and goals and establish the policies and procedures to carry them out. They develop academic programs, monitor students' progress, and train and motivate teachers. They also may prepare budgets and handle relations with parents, students, employers, and the community. They might be school principals, college presidents or deans, or school-district superintendents. Many education administrators begin their careers as teachers.

Did You Know?

Do you have what it takes to be Principal of the Year? Every year MetLife and the National Association of Secondary School Principals award this prestigious honor to one middle school and one high school principal out of those nominated by the 50 states. First-place winners get a $5,000 grant and an honorary banquet in Washington, DC. Four finalists receive $1,500 each. The award may not be as glamorous as Miss America, but the competition is still intense (though there is no swimsuit competition as far as we know).

Career in Focus: *College Registrar*

College registrars keep track of college students' records. They register students, record grades, prepare student transcripts, plan commencement, and oversee the preparation of college course offerings. Most students (and many parents) know them primarily for one other responsibility: collecting tuition and fees. Contrary to what many students would say, they really are nice people.

Where and When

Unlike most teachers, the majority of educational administrators work 11 or 12 months out of the year, often more than 40 hours per week. While the job is mostly indoors in comfortable settings, the stress level can be high. These administrators must deal with the concerns of students, parents, teachers, and government agencies all at once.

For More Information

* American Association of Collegiate Registrars and Admissions Officers, One Dupont Circle NW, Suite 520, Washington, DC 20036-1171. Internet: www.aacrao.org

* The National Association of Elementary School Principals, 1615 Duke St., Alexandria, VA 22314-3483. Internet: www.naesp.org

* The National Association of Secondary School Principals, 1904 Association Dr., Reston, VA 20191-1537. Internet: www.nassp.org

* The Educational Leadership Constituent Council, 1904 Association Dr., Reston, VA 20191. Internet: www.npbea.org/ncate.php

Engineering and Natural Sciences Managers

At a Glance

Engineering and natural sciences managers plan and direct research, development, and production in large and small companies and labs. They hire and supervise engineers, chemists, and biologists. They manage and review the work in a business or lab and help determine salaries. They also decide what workers and equipment are needed to do certain jobs. Many coordinate the design, installation, and operation of equipment in industrial plants. These positions require a good mix of administrative and managerial skills with a scientific or engineering education and background. In fact, most of these managers begin their careers as engineers or scientists.

Career in Focus: *Science Manager*

Most science managers specialize in a particular branch of science, such as biology, chemistry, or geology. They coordinate the research of others and oversee testing, quality control, and production. Most have their Ph.D. in their chosen scientific field and conduct their own research as well.

Where and When

Engineering and natural sciences managers work in offices or laboratories and are sometimes exposed to potentially harmful substances. Most of these managers work at least 40 hours per week. They are often under pressure to meet deadlines and stay within budget.

For More Information

* ABET, Inc., 111 Market Place, Suite 1050, Baltimore, MD 21202. Internet: www.abet.org

Data Bank

Education and Training: Bachelor's or higher degree plus related work experience

Average Earnings: $92,000–$146,000

Earnings Growth Potential: Medium

Total Jobs Held: 229,000

Job Outlook: Average increase

Annual Job Openings: 6,900

Related Jobs: Agricultural and food scientists; atmospheric scientists; biological scientists; chemists and materials scientists; engineers; environmental scientists and specialists; geoscientists and hydrologists; mathematicians; medical scientists; physicists and astronomers; top executives

Personality Types: Enterprising-Investigative

Did You Know?

For a long time, almost no management jobs in engineering (or any jobs in engineering, for that matter) were held by women. But in the last two decades, more and more women have moved up the ranks to become engineering managers. In fact, today's engineering companies are actively recruiting women at all levels. In 2006, about 7 percent of all engineering managers were women. That's still only a small number, but it can be expected to increase as more women enter engineering.

Farmers, Ranchers, and Agricultural Managers

At a Glance

American farmers, ranchers, and agricultural managers direct the activities of one of the world's largest agricultural producers. Farmers and ranchers own and operate family-owned or leased farms. They are responsible for preparing, planting, fertilizing, cultivating, and harvesting crops. After the harvest, they make sure that the crops are properly packaged, stored, or marketed. Livestock, dairy, and poultry farmers must feed and care for their animals. Horticultural specialty farmers oversee the production of ornamental plants; flowers, bulbs, and shrubbery; and fruits and vegetables grown in greenhouses. Agricultural managers manage the day-to-day activities of one or more farms, ranches, and nurseries. They all focus on the business aspects of running a farm.

Data Bank

Education and Training: Long-term on-the-job training to bachelor's or higher degree plus related work experience

Average Earnings: $41,000–$74,000

Earnings Growth Potential: High

Total Jobs Held: 1,234,000

Job Outlook: Declining

Annual Job Openings: 12,500

Related Jobs: Agricultural and food scientists; agricultural inspectors; agricultural workers, other; engineers; farm and home management advisors; purchasing managers, buyers, and purchasing agents

Personality Types: Enterprising-Realistic-Conventional

Did You Know?

Like most other businesses, farming has become more complex due to changes in technology. The result is that many farmers and agricultural managers now use computers and scanners to keep track of inventory and manage their businesses. Being a successful farmer means keeping track of economic trends as well as having good business sense, making it an even more demanding job than before.

Career in Focus: *Aquaculture Farmer*

Aquaculture farmers raise fish and shellfish for food or recreational fishing. They must stock, feed, and protect the aquatic life raised in ponds or floating net pens. It's easier to trust the Gorton's fisherman when you know he raises his own fish in a floating pen.

Where and When

The work of farmers, ranchers, and agricultural managers is demanding. The hours are long and the work can be quite physical. Work usually increases or decreases with the season. In addition, this line of work can be dangerous. Farm machinery can cause serious injury, and exposure to chemicals is a concern.

For More Information

* National FFA Organization, Attention: Career Information Requests, P.O. Box 68690, Indianapolis, IN 46268-0960. Internet: www.ffa.org

* American Society of Farm Managers and Rural Appraisers, 950 Cherry St., Suite 508, Denver, CO 80246-2664. Internet: www.asfmra.org

* Family and Small Farm Program, U.S. Department of Agriculture, National Institute of Food and Agriculture, 1400 Independence Ave. SW, Stop 2201, Washington, DC 20250-2201. Internet: www.csrees.usda.gov/smallfarms.cfm

* The Beginning Farm Center, 10861 Douglas Ave., Suite B, Urbandale, IA 50322-2042. Internet: www.farmtransition.org/netwpart.html

Financial Managers

At a Glance

Financial managers work for all kinds of businesses and agencies. They analyze data in order to offer advice on how to maximize profits. They prepare financial reports and make sure the business pays its taxes and has enough money to operate. They watch over the cash flow, manage the company's stocks, and communicate with investors. They also decide whether the business needs to borrow money, lend money, or invest in stocks and bonds. Controllers direct the preparation of reports that summarize the organization's financial position. Treasurers and finance officers direct the organization's financial goals, objectives, and budgets. Other managers oversee the firm's credit and collections and monitor the flow of cash.

Career in Focus: *Risk and Insurance Manager*

Risk and insurance managers oversee programs to minimize risks and losses that might arise from financial transactions and business operations. They also manage the organization's insurance budget. They are watchdogs, making sure a company doesn't stretch its financial resources too far.

Where and When

While they do get to work in comfortable office settings and often have access to the latest technology, financial managers are also prone to working long hours. They often work more than 50 hours per week. The job can be stressful and may require some travel as well.

For More Information

* Financial Management Association International, College of Business Administration, University of South Florida, 4202 E. Fowler Ave., BSN 3331, Tampa, FL 33620. Internet: www.fma.org

* Association for Financial Professionals, 4520 East-West Hwy., Suite 750, Bethesda, MD 20814. Internet: www.afponline.org

* CFA Institute, 560 Ray Hunt Dr., Charlottesville, VA 22903. Internet: www.cfainstitute.org

* American Bankers Association, 1120 Connecticut Ave. NW, Washington, DC 20036. Internet: www.aba.com

* Institute of Management Accountants, 10 Paragon Dr., Montvale, NJ 07645. Internet: www.imanet.org

Data Bank

Education and Training: Bachelor's or higher degree plus related work experience

Average Earnings: $74,000–$138,000

Earnings Growth Potential: High

Total Jobs Held: 539,000

Job Outlook: Average increase

Annual Job Openings: 13,800

Related Jobs: Accountants and auditors; budget analysts; financial analysts; insurance sales agents; insurance underwriters; loan officers; personal financial advisors; real estate brokers and sales agents; securities, commodities, and financial services sales agents

Personality Types: Enterprising-Conventional

Did You Know?

While a bachelor's degree is a minimum requirement for landing a job as a financial manager, many companies are seeking individuals with even more education: preferably a master's degree in business administration, economics, finance, or risk management. The number of students graduating with MBAs continues to rise, suggesting keen competition for careers like these.

Food Service Managers

At a Glance

Food service managers are responsible for the daily operations of restaurants and other establishments that serve food and drinks. They coordinate the activities of the kitchen, dining room, and banquet operations and ensure that customers are satisfied with their dining experience. Food service managers select and price the food on a restaurant's menu. They hire and train workers and manage staffing, payroll, and bookkeeping. They also oversee food preparation, order supplies and ingredients, and make sure the restaurant is clean and well maintained. Managers must be able to communicate with a diverse clientele and staff and motivate employees to work as a team.

Data Bank

Education and Training: Work experience in a related occupation

Average Earnings: $37,000–$61,000

Earnings Growth Potential: Medium

Total Jobs Held: 339,000

Job Outlook: Little change

Annual Job Openings: 8,400

Related Jobs: First-line supervisors or managers of food preparation and serving workers; gaming services occupations; lodging managers; sales worker supervisors

Personality Types: Enterprising-Conventional-Realistic

Did You Know?

Have you ever heard of Hamburger University? Students come from around the world to attend McDonald's manager-training school in Oak Brook, Illinois. There they learn about maintaining product quality, hiring and supervising workers, advertising and publicity, equipment repair, and other aspects of restaurant management. The training lasts two weeks, and graduates are qualified to manage a McDonald's restaurant. They do not, as far as we know, get fries with that.

Career in Focus: *Special Food Services Manager*

Though the name might suggest that they serve exotic fare like poached ostrich eggs or alligator steaks, special food services managers are actually contractors who supply food services at institutional, governmental, commercial, or industrial locations. In other words, they may supply the food for a school cafeteria, a hotel buffet, or the entire menu at a nursing home.

Where and When

These managers are among the first to arrive and the last to leave. They often work 12 to 15 hours per day and 50 or more hours per week. Those who work in schools, factories, and hospitals may have more regular hours. Managers must be calm under pressure, as they are the ones called upon to resolve problems. Dealing with angry customers or uncooperative employees can be stressful. Managers may also experience muscle aches, cuts, or burns.

For More Information

* National Restaurant Association Educational Foundation, 175 W. Jackson Blvd., Suite 1500, Chicago, IL 60604-2702. Internet: www.nraef.org

* National Restaurant Association, 1200 17th St. NW, Washington, DC 20036-3097. Internet: www.restaurant.org

* The International Council on Hotel, Restaurant, and Institutional Education, 2810 N. Parham Rd., Suite 230, Richmond, VA 23294. Internet: www.chrie.org

Funeral Directors

At a Glance

Although Americans express a wide range of beliefs, funeral practices usually share some common elements: preparing the remains, performing a ceremony that honors the deceased and addresses the spiritual needs of the family, and carrying out the final burial or cremation of the body. Funeral directors, also called morticians or undertakers, arrange and direct these tasks for grieving families. They also help the family plan the funeral, prepare the obituary notice, and handle the paperwork. Funeral directors often run the business as well: They prepare bills, keep financial records, and hire and manage a staff.

Career in Focus:
Embalmer

Most funeral directors are also licensed embalmers. Embalming is a sanitary, cosmetic, and preservative process that prepares the body for burial or cremation. Embalmers wash the body and replace the blood with embalming fluid to preserve the tissues. They may also reshape and reconstruct disfigured or maimed bodies, using materials such as clay, cotton, plaster of paris, and wax. This job may not be for everybody.

Where and When

Funeral directors can work long, irregular hours, in part because they are often on call. There are very few worries about health concerns in working with human remains as long as strict regulations are followed.

For More Information

* The National Funeral Directors Association, 13625 Bishop's Dr., Brookfield, WI 53005. Internet: www.nfda.org

* The American Board of Funeral Service Education, 3414 Ashland Ave., Suite G, St. Joseph, MO 64506. Internet: www.abfse.org

Data Bank

Education and Training: Associate degree

Average Earnings: $40,000–$72,000

Earnings Growth Potential: High

Total Jobs Held: 30,000

Job Outlook: Average increase

Annual Job Openings: 1,000

Related Jobs: Physicians and surgeons; psychologists; social workers

Personality Types: Enterprising-Social-Conventional

Did You Know?

It may be possible to bury the dead in your backyard, provided it's big enough. State laws vary widely on whether bodies must be buried in cemeteries or can be laid to rest on a private residence. Regulations are established for how far the burial must be from a dwelling (or water source) to how far down in the ground the remains should be. We do not recommend opening up a cemetery in your backyard, however, no matter how big it is.

Human Resources, Training, and Labor Relations Managers and Specialists

At a Glance

Human resources, training, and labor relations managers and specialists find the best employees they can and match them with jobs in their company. They interview job candidates and train new workers. They may hold job fairs to find applicants. They are often responsible for handling employee benefits and creating and maintaining a fair pay system. They help to resolve conflicts among workers or between workers and management. They also provide some employee training and are concerned with maintaining worker satisfaction. They often provide for mental and physical health services, on-the-job safety programs, and child care. Increasingly, they take part in the company's strategic planning, discussing how personnel resources can best be used.

Data Bank

Education and Training: Bachelor's degree to bachelor's or higher degree plus related work experience

Average Earnings: $44,000–$77,000

Earnings Growth Potential: High

Total Jobs Held: 905,000

Job Outlook: Rapid increase

Annual Job Openings: 42,700

Related Jobs: Counselors; education administrators; lawyers; psychologists; public relations specialists; social and human service assistants; social workers

Personality Types: Enterprising-Social-Conventional

Did You Know?

Human resources managers are responsible for taking care of the economy's most important natural resource. No—not oil. People. By 2018, the number of salaried workers in the U.S. labor force is expected to reach 166 million. And that population is expected to grow even more diverse, meaning that human resources managers and specialists must be especially sensitive to cultural differences in order to be successful.

Career in Focus: *Recruiter*

Recruiters maintain contacts within the community and may travel considerably, often to college campuses, to search for promising job applicants. Recruiters screen, interview, and occasionally test applicants. They also may check references and extend job offers. These workers must keep informed about equal employment opportunity (EEO) and affirmative action guidelines and laws.

Where and When

Most human resources managers work a standard 35- to 40-hour week in comfortable office settings. Although many work in the office, some travel extensively.

For More Information

* Society for Human Resource Management, 1800 Duke St., Alexandria, VA 22314. Internet: www.shrm.org

* American Society for Training and Development, 1640 King St., Box 1443, Alexandria, VA 22313-2043. Internet: www.astd.org

* International Foundation of Employee Benefit Plans, 18700 W. Bluemound Rd., Brookfield, WI 53045. Internet: www.ifebp.org

* WorldatWork, 14040 N. Northsight Blvd., Scottsdale, AZ 85260. Internet: www.worldatwork.org

Industrial Production Managers

At a Glance

Industrial production managers plan the activities needed to produce millions of goods every year in the United States. They direct scheduling, staffing, equipment, quality control, and inventory in factories. Their main job is to get goods produced the right way, on time, and within budget. They decide what equipment and workers to use and in what order. They also monitor the production run to make sure it stays on schedule and to fix any problems that arise. They are often responsible for thinking up ways to improve the production process as well. For that reason, they must keep up with changes in technology and new innovations by competitors.

Career in Focus: *Quality Control Manager*

Quality control managers are primarily responsible for ensuring that a product meets certain standards. They sample products before they are shipped and make recommendations for how they might be improved. They are also responsible for troubleshooting problems in the production process. One can only assume that Hanes Inspector #12 has already made it up to management level.

Where and When

Most industrial production managers spend equal time in the production area and their offices. While in the production area, they must follow the established health and safety practices and wear protective clothing and equipment. Most work more than 40 hours per week to meet production deadlines. Some facilities work around the clock, requiring the need for late-shift managers or managers on call.

For More Information

❉ APICS, the Association for Operations Management, 8430 W. Bryn Mawr Ave., Suite 1000, Chicago, IL 60631. Internet: www.apics.org

❉ American Society for Quality, 600 N. Plankinton Ave., Milwaukee, WI 53203. Internet: www.asq.org

Data Bank

Education and Training: Work experience in a related occupation

Average Earnings: $66,000–$112,000

Earnings Growth Potential: Medium

Total Jobs Held: 156,000

Job Outlook: Declining

Annual Job Openings: 5,500

Related Jobs: Advertising, marketing, promotions, public relations, and sales managers; construction managers; engineers; management analysts; operations research analysts; top executives

Personality Types: Enterprising-Conventional

Did You Know?

In 1913 Henry Ford introduced moving assembly belts into his auto plants, starting a small industrial revolution. By 1918, half of all cars on the road were Ford Model Ts. Ford is famous for the changes he made to automobiles, production methods, and economic theory. He is also famous for having written about the Model T, "Any customer can have a car painted any color that he wants so long as it is black." At that time, only black paint dried quickly enough to suit a fast-moving assembly line.

Lodging Managers

At a Glance

Vacationers and business travelers expect good food, a friendly staff, and a comfortable room. Lodging managers are responsible for providing these things. These managers hire, train, and supervise the people who work in hotels, motels, and inns. They set room rates, handle billing, order food and supplies, and oversee the day-to-day operations. Managers who work for hotel chains may staff a new hotel, refurbish an older one, or reorganize one that is not operating well. Some of these managers specialize in one aspect of the lodging business, whether it's helping to coordinate special events, managing housekeeping, or overseeing the food operations. All lodging managers are primarily responsible for keeping their guests happy and comfortable.

Data Bank

Education and Training: Work experience in a related occupation

Average Earnings: $35,000–$64,000

Earnings Growth Potential: Medium

Total Jobs Held: 60,000

Job Outlook: Little change

Annual Job Openings: 1,600

Related Jobs: Food service managers; gaming services occupations; property, real estate, and community association managers; sales worker supervisors

Personality Types: Enterprising-Conventional-Social

Did You Know?

Imagine spending $10,000 for one night in a hotel room. In fact, many of the most luxurious suites in the world's five-star hotels go for that rate or more. The Bridge Suite at the Atlantis resort in the Bahamas runs $25,000 a night. Of course, such prices often get you a 5,000-square-foot room complete with private cinema and maybe even a chauffeured Rolls-Royce for personal use. But at that rate, you might just be better off buying a house everywhere you go.

Career in Focus: *Front Office Manager*

Front office managers coordinate reservations and room assignments. They also train and direct the hotel's front desk staff. They ensure that guests are treated courteously, complaints and problems are resolved, and requests for special services are carried out. They are also the ones who address all those questions you have about mysterious telephone and cable charges on your bill.

Where and When

Most hotels are open around the clock, meaning lodging managers commonly work nights and weekends and spend much of their time on call. Coordinating a wide range of activities and managing a staff can be stressful. Conventions and large groups of tourists can require managers to work extra hours. Dealing with angry guests can be difficult at times, especially since kicking them out is seldom an option.

For More Information

* American Hotel and Lodging Association, 1201 New York Ave. NW, Suite 600, Washington, DC 20005. Internet: www.ahla.com

* Educational Institute of the American Hotel and Lodging Association, 800 N. Magnolia Ave., Suite 300, Orlando, FL 32803. Internet: www.ei-ahla.org

* International Council on Hotel, Restaurant, and Institutional Education, 2810 N. Parham Rd., Suite 230, Richmond, VA 23294. Internet: www.chrie.org

* Accreditation Commission for Programs in Hospitality Administration, P.O. Box 400, Oxford, MD 21654. Internet: www.acpha-cahm.org

Medical and Health Services Managers

At a Glance

Medical and health services managers—also called health-care administrators or health-care executives—organize and supervise the delivery of health care. They determine staffing and equipment needs. They also direct the public relations, marketing, and finances of hospitals, nursing homes, clinics, and doctor's offices. They may be in charge of an entire organization or only one department within it. Medical and health services managers must be constantly aware of changes in technology and medicine. Because of the rising cost of health care, these managers are also often responsible for improving efficiency to reduce cost without sacrificing quality.

Career in Focus: *Health Information Manager*

Health information managers are responsible for maintaining and protecting patient records. Federal regulations require that all health-care providers maintain electronic patient records and that these records be secure. Health information managers ensure that databases are complete, accurate, and available only to authorized personnel.

Where and When

While the pay is often good, most medical and health services managers work long hours. Most health-care facilities operate around the clock, and administrators and managers may be called at all hours to deal with problems. Some travel can also be required to conferences or other facilities. These managers often work out of comfortable private offices or share space with other managers and staff.

For More Information

* Association of University Programs in Health Administration, 2000 N. 14th St., Suite 780, Arlington, VA 22201. Internet: www.aupha.org

* Commission on Accreditation of Healthcare Management Education, 2111 Wilson Blvd., Suite 700, Arlington, VA 22201. Internet: www.cahme.org

* American College of Healthcare Executives, 1 N. Franklin St., Suite 1700, Chicago, IL 60606. Internet: www.healthmanagementcareers.org

* American College of Healthcare Administrators, 1321 Duke St., Suite 400, Alexandria, VA 22314. Internet: www.achca.org

Data Bank

Education and Training: Bachelor's or higher degree plus related work experience

Average Earnings: $64,000–$106,000

Earnings Growth Potential: Medium

Total Jobs Held: 283,000

Job Outlook: Above-average increase

Annual Job Openings: 9,900

Related Jobs: Insurance underwriters; social and community service managers

Personality Types: Enterprising-Social-Conventional

Did You Know?

The number of patients using some form of home health care has been rising. More than a million patients rely on qualified professionals to help treat them in their homes. Medical and health service managers are responsible for coordinating their care as well. With the cost of hospital stays rising, home health care can be a good option financially and is sometimes better for the comfort of the patient.

Property, Real Estate, and Community Association Managers

At a Glance

Property and real estate managers maintain and increase the value of real estate. They oversee apartment buildings, rental houses, businesses, and shopping malls. They sell empty space to renters, prepare leases, collect rent, and handle the book-keeping. They also make sure the property is maintained and handle complaints from renters. Managers may purchase supplies and equipment for the property. They make arrangements for repairs that cannot be handled by regular maintenance staff. They make sure that their properties comply with all government regulations and building codes. Some property and real estate managers act as a property owner's economic adviser as well.

Data Bank

Education and Training: Bachelor's degree

Average Earnings: $34,000–$71,000

Earnings Growth Potential: Very high

Total Jobs Held: 304,000

Job Outlook: Average increase

Annual Job Openings: 7,800

Related Jobs: Administrative services managers; education administrators; food service managers; lodging managers; medical and health services managers; real estate brokers and sales agents; urban and regional planners

Personality Types: Enterprising-Conventional

Did You Know?

Property managers don't just manage apartments and houses. Did you ever wonder who is in charge of all that open space at the shopping mall? Mall property managers provide security, replace light bulbs, hire cleaning crews, and make sure the flowers are watered. They collect rent from the stores and restaurants (the mall's tenants) and make sure the mall is clean, comfortable, and open for business.

Career in Focus: *Community Association Manager*

Community association managers work for condominium or neighborhood owners' associations. They collect dues, prepare budgets, negotiate with contractors, and help resolve complaints. They interact with homeowners and other residents on a daily basis. They are hired by the volunteer board of directors of the association. They oversee the maintenance of property and facilities that the homeowners own and use jointly, such as playgrounds and swimming pools.

Where and When

Although they work out of offices, these managers spend most of their time away from their desks, investigating problems, showing apartments, or managing staff. Some of these managers are required to live in the apartments or neighborhoods where they work. Night and weekend work is common, though many receive time off during the week to make up for having to work weekends.

For More Information

* Institute of Real Estate Management, 430 N. Michigan Ave., Chicago, IL 60611. Internet: www.irem.org

* Building Owners and Managers Institute, 1 Park Place, Suite 475, Annapolis, MD 21401. Internet: www.bomi.org

* Community Associations Institute, 225 Reinekers Ln., Suite 300, Alexandria, VA 22314. Internet: www.caionline.org

* National Board of Certification for Community Association Managers, 225 Reinekers Ln., Suite 310, Alexandria, VA 22314. Internet: www.nbccam.org

Purchasing Managers, Buyers, and Purchasing Agents

At a Glance

These workers look for the highest quality merchandise at the lowest possible price for their employers or for resale. They find the best products, negotiate the price, and make sure the right amount is received at the right time. They study sales records and inventory levels, identify suppliers, and study changes in the marketplace. Wholesale and retail buyers purchase goods for resale, such as clothing or electronics. Purchasing agents buy goods and services for use by their own company or organization, such as raw materials for manufacturing or office supplies. Many managers assist in planning sales promotions.

Career in Focus:
Merchandise Manager

Merchandise managers buy finished goods for resale. They are employed by wholesale and retail establishments, where they commonly are known as *buyers*. Wholesale buyers purchase goods directly from manufacturers or from other wholesale firms for resale to retail firms, commercial establishments, and other organizations.

Where and When

Most purchasing managers, buyers, and purchasing agents work in comfortable offices, though they commonly work long hours, evenings, or weekends—especially before holiday and back-to-school seasons. Many of them travel several days out of the month, sometimes internationally.

For More Information

* American Purchasing Society, P.O. Box 256, Aurora, IL 60506.
* APICS, The Association for Operations Management, 8430 W. Bryn Mawr Ave., Suite 1000, Chicago, IL 60631. Internet: www.apics.org
* Institute for Supply Management, P.O. Box 22160, Tempe, AZ 85285-2160. Internet: www.ism.ws
* National Institute of Governmental Purchasing, Inc., 151 Spring St., Suite 300, Herndon, VA 20170-5223. Internet: www.nigp.org

Data Bank

Education and Training: Long-term on-the-job training to bachelor's or higher degree plus related work experience

Average Earnings: $45,000–$77,000

Earnings Growth Potential: Medium

Total Jobs Held: 527,000

Job Outlook: Average increase

Annual Job Openings: 18,000

Related Jobs: Advertising, marketing, promotions, public relations, and sales managers; food service managers; insurance sales agents; lodging managers; procurement clerks; sales engineers; sales representatives, wholesale and manufacturing

Personality Types: Enterprising-Conventional

Did You Know?

Purchasing specialists often work closely with other employees in their own organization, an arrangement sometimes called "team buying." For example, before submitting an order, they may discuss the design of products with company engineers, talk about the quality of purchased goods with production supervisors, or mention shipment problems to managers in the receiving department. This may also keep them from having to take all the blame when something doesn't go as well as they hoped.

Top Executives

At a Glance

Although they carry a wide range of titles—CEO, COO, board chair, president, superintendent, or commissioner—all top executives are responsible for guiding their business or corporation, government organization, or nonprofit institution to reach its goals. Top executives make policies and direct operations. They meet with other executives, boards of directors, government heads, and consultants to discuss policy and direction. They are responsible for the organization's ultimate success or failure, so they are always under pressure. They provide the company's vision and share it with its employees and the public.

Data Bank

Education and Training: Bachelor's or higher degree plus related work experience

Average Earnings: $70,000–$118,000

Earnings Growth Potential: Very high

Total Jobs Held: 2,134,000

Job Outlook: Declining

Annual Job Openings: 61,500

Related Jobs: Administrative services managers; advertising, marketing, promotions, public relations, and sales managers; computer and information systems managers; education administrators; financial managers; food service managers; industrial production managers; lodging managers; medical and health services managers

Personality Types: Enterprising-Conventional-Social

Did You Know?

In addition to being responsible for the success of a company, top executives are increasingly held accountable for the ethics of their business practices. Since the Enron bankruptcy and the Wall Street wheeling and dealing that almost caused a depression, the American public has become skeptical of top executives and their dealings. Still, while the occasional CEO appears before a grand jury or a Congressional hearing, plenty more share their success with others, such as Bill Gates, whose charitable foundation gives billions of dollars to people and programs in need.

Career in Focus: *Chief Financial Officer*

Chief financial officers (CFOs) direct the organization's financial goals, objectives, and budgets. They oversee investments and cash flow, raise capital, deal with mergers and acquisitions, and manage a business's expansion. In short, they control the company's purse strings.

Where and When

Top executives usually get the biggest offices with the cushiest chairs, but it comes at the price of long hours, including evenings and weekends. Many executives spend a good deal of time traveling, often outside the country. In addition, top executives are always under pressure to succeed and to look after the welfare of their employees.

For More Information

* American Management Association, 1601 Broadway, 6th Floor, New York, NY 10019. Internet: www.amanet.org

* National Management Association, 2210 Arbor Blvd., Dayton, OH 45439. Internet: www.nma1.org

* Financial Executives International, 200 Campus Dr., Florham Park, NJ 07932. Internet: www.financialexecutives.org

* Financial Management Association International, College of Business Administration, University of South Florida, 4202 E. Fowler Ave., BSN 3331, Tampa, FL 33620. Internet: www.fma.org

* Institute for Certified Professional Managers, James Madison University, MSC 5504, Harrisonburg, VA 22807. Internet: www.icpm.biz

Accountants and Auditors

At a Glance

Accountants and auditors prepare and check financial reports and taxes. Public accountants perform a broad range of accounting, auditing, tax, and consulting activities for corporations, governments, nonprofit organizations, or individuals. Management accountants record and analyze financial information. They are responsible for budgeting, performance evaluation, and cost and asset management. Internal auditors verify the accuracy of internal records and check for mismanagement, waste, or fraud. Government accountants maintain and examine the records of government agencies. They also audit the records of private businesses. Increasingly, accountants act as personal financial advisors, helping clients develop personal budgets, manage investments, and plan for retirement.

Career in Focus: *Forensic Accountant*

Forensic accountants investigate white-collar crimes such as securities fraud and embezzlement, bankruptcies and contract disputes, and money laundering. They combine their knowledge of accounting and finance with law and investigative techniques to determine whether an activity is illegal. Forensic accountants appear as expert witnesses during trials. Think of it as *CSI* with a lot more math.

Where and When

Most accountants and auditors work in office settings. Some are self-employed and can work from home. Those whose primary responsibility involves auditing other companies' finances have to travel extensively. While most work the standard 40-hour week, overtime is common during tax season.

For More Information

* AACSB International—Association to Advance Collegiate Schools of Business, 777 S. Harbour Island Blvd., Suite 750, Tampa FL 33602. Internet: www.aacsb.edu/accreditation/AccreditedMembers.asp

* American Institute of Certified Public Accountants, 1211 Avenue of the Americas, New York, NY 10036. Internet: www.aicpa.org

* AICPA Examinations Team, Parkway Corporate Center, 1230 Parkway Ave., Suite 311, Ewing, NJ 08628-3018. Internet: www.cpa-exam.org

* National Association of State Boards of Accountancy, 150 Fourth Ave. N, Suite 700, Nashville, TN 37219-2417. Internet: www.nasba.org

* Institute of Management Accountants, 10 Paragon Dr., Montvale, NJ 07645-1718. Internet: www.imanet.org

Data Bank

Education and Training: Bachelor's degree

Average Earnings: $47,000–$79,000

Earnings Growth Potential: Medium

Total Jobs Held: 1,291,000

Job Outlook: Rapid increase

Annual Job Openings: 49,800

Related Jobs: Bookkeeping, accounting, and auditing clerks; budget analysts; computer network, systems, and database administrators; computer software engineers and computer programmers; cost estimators; financial analysts; loan officers; management analysts; personal financial advisors; tax examiners, collectors, and revenue agents

Personality Types: Conventional-Enterprising-Investigative

Did You Know?

In the 1920s, Al Capone boasted that he owned the city of Chicago. He raked in millions of dollars in gambling, prostitution, and bootleg alcohol (during the age of Prohibition), and the police seemed helpless to stop him. That is, until government accountants stepped in and looked at his financial records. Capone was finally convicted and imprisoned, not for the murders he ordered, but for the taxes he didn't pay.

Appraisers and Assessors of Real Estate

At a Glance

Real estate appraisers and assessors estimate the value of all kinds of property, from farmland to shopping centers. Their evaluations are used to help decide property taxes, mortgages, sale prices, or whether property is a good investment for a client. Assessors determine the value of all properties in an area for tax purposes, and they primarily work for the government.

Data Bank

Education and Training: Associate degree

Average Earnings: $35,000–$67,000

Earnings Growth Potential: High

Total Jobs Held: 92,000

Job Outlook: Little change

Annual Job Openings: 2,100

Related Jobs: Claims adjusters, appraisers, examiners, and investigators; construction and building inspectors; real estate brokers and sales agents

Personality Types: Conventional-Enterprising

Did You Know?

Property taxes are the primary source of income for local governments, and much of our everyday life—such as our public school systems—depends on them. Assessors are responsible for researching and helping set the property tax for each city and county. Based on figures from the Tax Foundation, the states with the highest local property taxes per capita are New Jersey, Connecticut, New York, New Hampshire, Rhode Island, and Wyoming.

Appraisers evaluate properties one at a time for a variety of purposes. After visiting the property, the appraiser or assessor will determine the fair value by considering things such as lease records, location, previous appraisals, and income potential. They then put all of their research and observations together in a detailed report.

Career in Focus: *Residential Appraiser*

Residential appraisers focus on appraising homes or other residences. Sellers use appraisers to know what their home is worth. Buyers use appraisals to decide if the price is right and if the property will keep or increase its value. In addition, banks and other lending institutions use appraisers when deciding whether to give home loans.

Where and When

While they spend much of their time researching and writing reports, appraisers and assessors are able to spend more and more time on site due to advances in mobile technology. Four out of ten appraisers are self-employed and can often work out of their homes.

For More Information

* The Appraisal Foundation, 1155 15th St. NW, Suite 1111, Washington, DC 20005. Internet: www.appraisalfoundation.org

* Appraisal Subcommittee (ASC), 1401 H St. NW, Suite 760, Washington, DC 20005. Internet: www.asc.gov

* American Society of Appraisers, 555 Herndon Pkwy., Suite 125, Herndon, VA 20170. Internet: www.appraisers.org

* Appraisal Institute, 550 W. Van Buren St., Suite 1000, Chicago, IL 60607. Internet: www.appraisalinstitute.org

* International Association of Assessing Officers, 314 W. 10th St., Kansas City, MO 64105. Internet: www.iaao.org

Budget Analysts

At a Glance

Budget analysts help businesses decide how much money they need in order to run and how best to spend it. They check reports and accounts during the year to make sure the business is staying within its budget and spending its money wisely. Budget analysts work in private industry, nonprofit organizations, and the public sector. They are always on the lookout for new ways to improve efficiency and make the most of the company's resources. Budget analysts create a plan for the coming year and beyond and then help the chief operating officer, agency head, or other top managers analyze the proposal. Computer software has greatly increased the amount of information that budget analysts are able to analyze.

Career in Focus: *Cost Accountant*

A cross between a budget analyst and an accountant, cost accountants record, research, and analyze the costs (in terms of time and resources) associated with running the company. Like budget analysts, they are interested in finding ways to use their company's resources more efficiently.

Where and When

Most budget analysts work at least 40 hours per week in comfortable office settings. They often work independently, though they usually work under deadlines, especially during mid-year and end-of-year reviews.

For More Information

* Advancing of Government Accountability, 2208 Mount Vernon Ave., Alexandria, VA 22301. Internet: www.agacgfm.org
* National Association of State Budget Officers, Hall of the States Building, Suite 642, 444 N. Capitol St. NW, Washington, DC 20001. Internet: www.nasbo.org

Data Bank

Education and Training: Bachelor's degree

Average Earnings: $53,000–$83,000

Earnings Growth Potential: Medium

Total Jobs Held: 67,000

Job Outlook: Above-average increase

Annual Job Openings: 2,200

Related Jobs: Accountants and auditors; cost estimators; financial analysts; financial managers; insurance underwriters; loan officers; management analysts; tax examiners, collectors, and revenue agents

Personality Types: Conventional-Enterprising-Investigative

Did You Know?

Balancing the budget is not an easy task, especially if you are the federal government. With its yearly budget of about 3.5 trillion dollars (not to mention the 13 trillion dollars of debt and the money that's owed to Social Security), one can only imagine the headaches of budget analysts trying to find ways to stretch the U.S. tax dollar and make it pay for everything voters and lawmakers want it to.

Claims Adjusters, Appraisers, Examiners, and Investigators

At a Glance

Individuals and businesses purchase insurance policies to protect against loss. In the event of a loss (such as a house fire), policyholders submit claims, seeking compensation. Insurance claims adjusters and claims investigators check to make sure that the claims filed are covered by their company's policies. Then they decide how much should be paid (called the settlement) and authorize the payment. If the claim is not covered, they deny payment. They are often asked to testify in legal disputes. Appraisers travel to see damaged property and assess how much the damage is worth.

Data Bank

Education and Training: Long-term on-the-job training to vocational/technical training

Average Earnings: $43,000–$72,000

Earnings Growth Potential: Medium

Total Jobs Held: 306,000

Job Outlook: Average increase

Annual Job Openings: 9,900

Related Jobs: Accountants and auditors; appraisers and assessors of real estate; automotive body and related repairers; automotive service technicians and mechanics; bill and account collectors; billing and posting clerks and machine operators; bookkeeping, accounting, and auditing clerks; construction and building inspectors; cost estimators; credit authorizers, checkers, and clerks; fire inspectors and investigators; medical records and health information technicians; private detectives and investigators; tax examiners, collectors, and revenue agents

Personality Types: Conventional-Enterprising

Did You Know?

Insurance companies insure the rest of us, but who insures insurance companies? Believe it or not, such companies exist. They are called reinsurance companies, and they are responsible for helping other insurance companies cover the cost of claims when catastrophes and natural disasters strike, such as Hurricane Katrina, which caused an estimated $125 billion of damage, of which $66 billion was insured.

Career in Focus: *Insurance Investigator*

Insurance investigators handle claims in which the company suspects criminal activity, such as arson, staged accidents, or unnecessary medical treatments. Investigators can access certain personal information, such as Social Security numbers, aliases, driver's license numbers, addresses, phone numbers, criminal records, and past claims histories, to establish whether a person has ever attempted insurance fraud. Investigators often consult with legal counsel and can be expert witnesses in court cases.

Where and When

Most claims adjusters, appraisers, examiners, and investigators work a standard 40-hour week in comfortable office environments. Many claims adjusters must also work outside of the office inspecting damaged automobiles and buildings. Sometimes they need to adjust their schedules to meet with clients on evenings and weekends. They may have some extended travel with long investigations, for instance, visiting the scene of a natural disaster to assess the total damage.

For More Information

* Insurance Information Institute, 110 William St., New York, NY 10038. Internet: www.iii.org
* American Institute for Chartered Property Casualty Underwriters and the Insurance Institute of America, 720 Providence Rd., Suite 100, Malvern, PA 19355-3433. Internet: www.aicpcu.org
* International Claim Association, 1155 15th St. NW, Suite 500, Washington, DC 20005. Internet: www.claim.org

Cost Estimators

At a Glance

When a company is thinking about developing a new product, the owner needs to know how much it will cost to produce. Cost estimators research and evaluate all of the resources that will be necessary, including materials, new machinery, additional labor, taxes, and insurance. They then find the least expensive way to make the best product. They decide what supplies to use, estimate labor costs, and report back to the owner. Computers play an integral role in this line of work because estimating often involves complex mathematical calculations.

Career in Focus: *Construction Cost Estimator*

More than half of all cost estimators work in construction. These estimators gather information on the proposed building site and the availability of electricity, water, and other services. They then research, analyze, and compile a cost summary for the entire project, including the costs of labor, equipment, materials, and subcontracts. Construction cost estimators also may be hired to track actual costs as the project develops.

Where and When

Cost estimators split their time between doing research in the comfort of their offices and visiting the site or factory floor. Although they normally work 40-hour weeks, overtime is common. In some industries, frequent travel is also required.

For More Information

* AACE International, 209 Prairie Ave., Suite 100, Morgantown, WV 26501. Internet: www.aacei.org

* American Society of Professional Estimators (ASPE), 2525 Perimeter Place Dr., Suite 103, Nashville, TN 37214. Internet: www.aspenational.org

* Society of Cost Estimating and Analysis, 527 Maple Ave. E, Suite 301, Vienna, VA 22180. Internet: www.sceaonline.org

Data Bank

Education and Training: Bachelor's degree

Average Earnings: $43,000–$75,000

Earnings Growth Potential: High

Total Jobs Held: 218,000

Job Outlook: Rapid increase

Annual Job Openings: 10,400

Related Jobs: Accountants and auditors; budget analysts; claims adjusters, appraisers, examiners, and investigators; construction managers; economists; financial analysts; financial managers; industrial production managers; insurance underwriters; loan officers; market and survey researchers; operations research analysts; personal financial advisors

Personality Types: Conventional-Enterprising

Did You Know?

A company called a cost estimator to estimate the value of a load of scrap copper in the Mojave Desert. The manager warned the estimator that he might have trouble with the job. When the estimator arrived on site, he understood why. The company had been having such problems with thieves, it had dug a huge pit and put the copper inside. Then, for added security, it had thrown rattlesnakes on top of the copper. The estimator just peered into the pit and made his best guess.

Financial Analysts

At a Glance

Financial analysts help businesses and individuals with their investment decisions. They gather and analyze financial information in order to make recommendations to their clients. Some financial analysts research the economic performance of other companies and industries for institutions with money to invest. Others help banks and other firms sell stocks, bonds, and other investments. All of these workers must be able to use spreadsheet and statistical software to analyze financial data, spot trends, and develop forecasts.

Data Bank

Education and Training: Bachelor's degree

Average Earnings: $56,000–$99,000

Earnings Growth Potential: Medium

Total Jobs Held: 251,000

Job Outlook: Rapid increase

Annual Job Openings: 9,500

Related Jobs: Accountants and auditors; actuaries; budget analysts; financial managers; insurance sales agents; insurance underwriters; personal financial advisors; securities, commodities, and financial services sales agents

Personality Types: Conventional-Investigative-Enterprising

Did You Know?

What's the difference between a bull and a bear? When you are being chased by one, probably not much (except bulls can't climb trees). In the stock market, however, a bull market indicates a prolonged period of time where prices rise faster than they have in the past (generally indicating economic growth). A bear market, on the other hand, indicates a period of time where prices fall faster. Most investors obviously prefer the bull, but there are ways to profit from a bear market.

Career in Focus: *Ratings Analyst*

Ratings analysts evaluate the ability of companies or governments to repay their debts on bonds. On the basis of their evaluation, a management team can assign a rating to a company's or government's bonds. Based on these ratings, investors can make more sound decisions about where to invest their money.

Where and When

Though they have the benefit of working in comfortable office settings, financial analysts may work long hours. They may work long hours, travel frequently to visit companies or potential investors, and face the pressure of deadlines. Much of their research must be done after office hours because their days are filled with telephone calls and meetings.

For More Information

* Financial Industry Regulatory Authority (FINRA), 1735 K St. NW, Washington, DC 20006. Internet: www.finra.org

* Securities Industry and Financial Markets Association, 120 Broadway, 35th Floor, New York, NY 10271. Internet: www.sifma.org

* American Academy of Financial Management, 200 L&A Rd., Suite B, Metairie, LA 70001. Internet: www.aafm.us

* CFA Institute, 560 Ray C. Hunt Dr., Charlottesville, VA 22903. Internet: www.cfainstitute.org

Insurance Underwriters

At a Glance

How much should an insurance company charge for insurance? That depends on how likely a customer is to have an accident. Using national statistics, underwriters first decide whether a person applying for insurance is a good risk. They then help write the policies and decide how much to charge. If they set the rates too low, the company will lose money. If they set the rates too high, the company will lose business to competitors. Most underwriters specialize in one of three major categories of insurance: life, health, and property and casualty. Life and health insurance underwriters may further specialize in group or individual policies.

Career in Focus: *Property and Casualty Underwriter*

Property and casualty underwriters usually specialize in either commercial or personal insurance for a particular type of risk, such as fire, homeowners', automobile, or liability insurance. In cases where casualty companies provide package insurance, the underwriter must be familiar with *all* the different lines of insurance.

Where and When

These jobs tend to be desk jobs in comfortable office settings. Most underwriters typically work a standard 40-hour week, and travel is usually kept to a minimum.

For More Information

* Insurance Information Institute, 110 William St., New York, NY 10038. Internet: www.iii.org
* American Institute for Chartered Property and Casualty Underwriters and Insurance Institute of America, 720 Providence Rd., Suite 100, Malvern, PA 19355. Internet: www.aicpcu.org
* CPCU Society, 720 Providence Rd., Malvern, PA 19355. Internet: www.cpcusociety.org
* The American College, 270 S. Bryn Mawr Ave., Bryn Mawr, PA 19010. Internet: www.theamericancollege.edu

Data Bank

Education and Training: Bachelor's degree

Average Earnings: $44,000–$78,000

Earnings Growth Potential: Medium

Total Jobs Held: 103,000

Job Outlook: Declining

Annual Job Openings: 3,000

Related Jobs: Accountants and auditors; actuaries; budget analysts; claims adjusters, appraisers, examiners, and investigators; cost estimators; credit analysts; financial managers; insurance sales agents; loan officers

Personality Types: Conventional-Enterprising-Investigative

Did You Know?

Underwriters often calculate risk based on national averages. Underwriters look at accident statistics from all over the country to decide which drivers are most likely to be involved in an accident. They use this information to create a profile of a high-risk driver. For example, anyone under the age of 21 or over the age of 70 tends to be considered "high-risk" for automobile insurance. Driving a red Ferrari isn't going to help keep your rates down either. Though if you can afford a Ferrari, you probably don't care.

Loan Officers

At a Glance

Individuals often need loans to afford a house, a car, or a college education. Businesses need loans to start companies, buy inventory, or invest in equipment. Loan officers help these individuals and businesses apply for those loans. They help potential clients fill out the applications, answering any questions. Then they collect and analyze information on a potential client's work, assets and debts, and credit rating. Loan officers usually specialize in commercial, consumer, or mortgage loans. Commercial loans help companies start up or expand; consumer loans help individuals buy cars, make renovations, or pay for other personal expenses; and mortgage loans are made to purchase real estate. Loan officers often act as salespeople as well, trying to give potential clients the best deal and rate with as little risk to the bank as possible.

Did You Know?

More and more students are planning to go to college, yet tuition continues to rise. That means more school loans taken by both parents and students alike. The average student earning a four-year degree graduates with almost $20,000 in debt. This is good news for loan officers who see college graduates as a sound investment—after all, they are bound to get a job and start paying it back eventually. Aren't they?

Career in Focus: *Loan Collection Officer*

Loan collection officers contact borrowers with overdue loan accounts to help them find a method of repayment and keep them from defaulting on the loan. If they cannot agree on a repayment plan, the loan collection officer begins the "collateral liquidation" process: The lender seizes the collateral used to secure the loan—a home or car, for example—and sells it to repay the loan.

Where and When

Most loan officers work a standard 40-hour week in comfortable office settings. Travel can be frequent, especially for commercial loan officers. Many loan officers intentionally carry heavy caseloads, which can cause them to work extra hours. Business picks up when interest rates drop, making loans more attractive to consumers but increasing the stress on loan officers.

For More Information

* Mortgage Bankers Association, 1331 L St. NW, Washington, DC 20005. Internet: www.mortgagebankers.org

Management Analysts

At a Glance

Companies hire management analysts to solve problems. They analyze a company's policy and performance and suggest ways to improve that organization's structure, efficiency, or profits. The work varies from project to project. Some analysts and consultants specialize in a specific industry, such as health care or telecommunications. Others specialize by type of business function, such as human resources, marketing, or information systems. Once they have analyzed the problem and decided on a course of action, consultants report their findings and recommendations to the client. For some projects, management analysts help implement the suggestions they have made.

Career in Focus:
Technology and Electronic Commerce Consultant

Recently, advances in information technology and electronic commerce have provided new opportunities for management analysts. Companies often hire consultants to help them enter and/or remain competitive in the new electronic marketplace. These analysts must mix their knowledge of computers and technology with their business sense to find the right solutions for their clients.

Where and When

Most management analysts split their time between their home office and the site of the client they are helping, so frequent travel is common. Overtime is also common, and the stress of meeting clients' demands on tight schedules can make this a challenging job. Many management analysts are self-employed, however, and can set their own schedule and workload.

For More Information

* Association of Management Consulting Firms, 370 Lexington Ave., Suite 2209, New York, NY 10017. Internet: www.amcf.org
* Institute of Management Consultants USA, Inc., 2025 M St. NW, Suite 800, Washington, DC 20036. Internet: www.imcusa.org

Data Bank

Education and Training: Bachelor's or higher degree plus related work experience

Average Earnings: $56,000–$101,000

Earnings Growth Potential: High

Total Jobs Held: 747,000

Job Outlook: Rapid increase

Annual Job Openings: 30,600

Related Jobs: Accountants and auditors; administrative services managers; advertising, marketing, promotions, public relations, and sales managers; budget analysts; computer scientists; computer systems analysts; cost estimators; economists; financial analysts; financial managers; human resources, training, and labor relations managers and specialists; industrial production managers; market and survey researchers; operations research analysts; personal financial advisors; top executives

Personality Types: Investigative-Enterprising-Conventional

Did You Know?

Almost everybody can use a little outside support from time to time, including the federal government. To prepare for a possible avian flu epidemic in the spring of 2006, the U.S. Department of Health and Human Services (HHS) awarded Tunnell Consulting a multi-million dollar contract to assist it in preparing for a potential pandemic. Government departments with problems like these are just one possible client for management analysts.

Meeting and Convention Planners

At a Glance

Meeting and convention planners make sure that such gatherings come off without a hitch. They arrange speakers and locations, acquire the necessary provisions and equipment, and deal with any problems that may arise. They work for nonprofit organizations, professional associations, hotels, corporations, and the government. Planners often must negotiate contracts with facilities and suppliers. They are also responsible for measuring how well the meeting's purpose was achieved by collecting and analyzing survey data. An important part of being a planner is establishing and maintaining relationships. Meeting and convention planners interact with a variety of people and must be good communicators.

Data Bank

Education and Training: Bachelor's degree

Average Earnings: $35,000–$58,000

Earnings Growth Potential: Medium

Total Jobs Held: 57,000

Job Outlook: Above-average increase

Annual Job Openings: 2,100

Related Jobs: Food service managers; lodging managers; public relations specialists; travel agents

Personality Types: Enterprising-Conventional-Social

Did You Know?

There are conventions for just about everything from tattoos to biotechnology to frozen foods, and planning some of these can be a monumental task. For example, more than one million people attend the annual Chicago Auto Show, where new cars are showcased for the coming year. Such conventions are not only important for the attendees, but also for the area hotels and restaurants, who are more than happy to provide those people with a place to sleep and eat.

Career in Focus: *Convention Service Manager*

Convention service managers work in hotels, convention centers, and similar establishments and act as the contact person between the meeting facility and event planners. They present food service options to outside planners, coordinate special requests, suggest hotel services based on the planners' budgets, and offer any other assistance.

Where and When

This job is fast-paced and requires a great deal of energy and sharp organization skills. Planners travel regularly, and working hours can be long and irregular, especially right before and during the meeting or convention. Some physical activity in the form of moderate lifting may be required. The job offers a high level of independence.

For More Information

* Convention Industry Council, 700 N. Fairfax St., Suite 510, Alexandria, VA 22314. Internet: www.conventionindustry.org

* Society of Government Meeting Professionals, 908 King St., Lower Level, Alexandria, VA 22314. Internet: www.sgmp.org

* Professional Convention Management Association, 2301 S. Lake Shore Dr., Suite 1001, Chicago, IL 60616-1419. Internet: www.pcma.org

* Meeting Professionals International, 3030 Lyndon B. Johnson Fwy., Suite 1700, Dallas, TX 75234-2759. Internet: www.mpiweb.org

Personal Financial Advisors

At a Glance

Personal financial advisors assess the financial needs of individuals and assist them with investments, tax laws, and insurance decisions. Advisors help their clients identify and plan for short-term and long-term goals. Advisors help clients plan for retirement, education expenses, and general investment choices. Many also provide tax advice or sell insurance. Although most planners offer advice on a wide range of topics, some specialize in areas such as retirement and estate planning or risk management.

Career in Focus: *Private Banker*

Private bankers (also known as wealth managers) are personal financial advisors who work for people who have a lot of money to invest. Private bankers manage portfolios for these individuals, using the resources of a bank, including teams of financial analysts, accountants, lawyers, and other professionals. Private bankers generally spend most of their time working with a small number of clients.

Where and When

Personal financial advisors usually work in offices or their own homes. They usually work standard business hours, but they also schedule meetings with clients in the evenings or on weekends. Many also teach evening classes or hold seminars to bring in more clients. Some personal financial advisors spend a fair amount of their time traveling to attend conferences or training sessions or to visit clients.

For More Information

* Financial Industry Regulatory Authority (FINRA), 1735 K St. NW, Washington, DC 20006. Internet: www.finra.org

* Securities Industry and Financial Markets Association, 120 Broadway, 35th Floor, New York, NY 10271. Internet: www.sifma.org

* North American Securities Administrator Association, 750 First St. NE, Suite 1140, Washington, DC 20002. Internet: www.nasaa.org

* Securities and Exchange Commission (SEC), 100 F St. NE, Washington, DC 20549. Internet: www.sec.gov

Data Bank

Education and Training: Bachelor's degree

Average Earnings: $45,000–$117,000

Earnings Growth Potential: Very high

Total Jobs Held: 208,000

Job Outlook: Rapid increase

Annual Job Openings: 8,500

Related Jobs: Accountants and auditors; actuaries; budget analysts; financial analysts; financial managers; insurance sales agents; insurance underwriters; real estate brokers and sales agents; securities, commodities, and financial services sales agents

Personality Types: Enterprising-Conventional-Social

Did You Know?

When advising married couples, personal financial advisors sometimes have to act as referees. That's because couples often have very different attitudes about how to handle money. Typically one spouse has a greater tolerance for risk than the other, so the financial advisor may be pulled in two different directions when trying to find the right balance between risky and safe investments. Financial advisors need to have good people skills and to be able to avoid the perception that they are ganging up with one spouse against the other.

Tax Examiners, Collectors, and Revenue Agents

At a Glance

Taxes are one of few certainties in life (see the entry on Funeral Directors for another). As long as governments collect taxes, there will be jobs for tax examiners, collectors, and revenue agents. These individuals work for the federal, state, and local governments and review tax returns to make sure people and businesses are paying the right amount. They send notices to those who have made mistakes, conduct audits, and track down those who are trying to avoid taxes altogether. Tax examiners often handle the simpler tax returns—those of individuals or small businesses. Revenue agents work on the more complex returns of large corporations. All must be trustworthy and have an eye for details.

Data Bank

Education and Training: Bachelor's degree

Average Earnings: $37,000–$67,000

Earnings Growth Potential: Medium

Total Jobs Held: 73,000

Job Outlook: Average increase

Annual Job Openings: 3,500

Related Jobs: Accountants and auditors; budget analysts; cost estimators; financial analysts; financial managers; loan officers; personal financial advisors

Personality Types: Conventional-Enterprising

Did You Know?

As far back as ancient Egypt, governments have been collecting taxes. Most ancient books, including the Torah, the Bible, and Hindu Sutras, mention paying taxes. Some kings collected animals, crops, or slaves from taxpayers; later governments demanded gold or jewels. Today, the IRS accepts money orders, personal checks, and charge cards. Contrary to popular belief, they do not take first-born children.

Career in Focus: *Tax Collector*

Tax collectors, also called revenue officers in the IRS, deal with overdue accounts. When a collector takes a case, he or she first sends the taxpayer a notice. The collector then works with the taxpayer on how to settle the debt. A big part of a collector's job at the federal level is setting and following up on payment deadlines. Collectors must maintain accurate records.

Where and When

Most of these individuals work a standard 40-hour week, though overtime may be necessary during tax season. They work in comfortable office settings, and much of their job involves using computers and managing paperwork. Tax collectors have the stressful and sometimes unpleasant job of dealing with overdue taxpayers.

For More Information

* Internal Revenue Service, 1111 Constitution Ave. NW, Washington, DC 20224. Internet: www.jobs.irs.gov

Professional and Related Occupations

Actuaries

At a Glance

Actuaries analyze risk. Most of them design insurance plans that will help their company make a profit. Actuaries estimate the probability and likely cost of events such as death, sickness, injury, disability, or loss of property. Actuaries also answer financial questions, including questions about pensions and investments. Most actuaries are employed in the insurance industry, specializing in life and health insurance or property and casualty insurance. They study statistics and social trends to decide how much money an insurance company should charge for insurance. Actuaries in other financial services industries manage credit or price investment offerings. Some actuaries are self-employed and work as consultants.

Data Bank

Education and Training: Bachelor's or higher degree plus related work experience

Average Earnings: $65,000–$121,000

Earnings Growth Potential: Medium

Total Jobs Held: 20,000

Job Outlook: Rapid increase

Annual Job Openings: 1,000

Related Jobs: Accountants and auditors; budget analysts; economists; financial analysts; insurance underwriters; market and survey researchers; mathematicians; personal financial advisors; statisticians

Personality Types: Conventional-Investigative-Enterprising

Did You Know?

Because of their knowledge of insurance, actuaries are often called as expert witnesses in lawsuits. For example, they might testify about the expected lifetime earnings of a person who was disabled or killed in an accident. This testimony is used to determine how much money an insurance company must pay the individual's family.

Career in Focus: *Pension Actuary*

Pension actuaries work under the provisions of the Employee Retirement Income Security act (ERISA) of 1974. They are primarily responsible for evaluating pension plans covered by that act and reporting on the plans' financial soundness to participants, sponsors, and federal regulators.

Where and When

Actuaries have desk jobs in comfortable office environments. Most of them work a standard 40-hour week. Travel is minimal, but still a possibility. They spend a majority of their time using a computer, so they may experience physical stress on the back, wrists, and eyes.

For More Information

* American Society of Pension Professionals & Actuaries, 4245 N. Fairfax Dr., Suite 750, Arlington, VA 22203. Internet: www.aspa.org

* Society of Actuaries (SOA), 475 N. Martingale Rd., Suite 600, Schaumburg, IL 60173-2226. Internet: www.soa.org

* Casualty Actuarial Society (CAS), 4350 N. Fairfax Dr., Suite 250, Arlington, VA 22203. Internet: www.casact.org

* The SOA and CAS jointly sponsor a Web site for those interested in pursuing an actuarial career. Internet: www.beanactuary.org

* American Academy of Actuaries, 1850 M St. NW, Suite 300, Washington, DC 20036. Internet: www.actuary.org

Computer Network, Systems, and Database Administrators

At a Glance

Computer network, systems, and database administrators help individuals and organizations share and store information through computer networks and systems, the Internet, and computer databases. Network and computer systems administrators design, install, and support an organization's computer systems. They are responsible for local area networks (LANs), wide area networks (WANs), and other data communications systems. Systems administrators are responsible for maintaining system efficiency. They ensure that the design of an organization's computer system allows all of the components, including computers, the network, and software, to work properly together. Database administrators find ways to help businesses organize and store data. Computer security specialists plan, coordinate, and maintain an organization's information security.

Career in Focus: *Webmaster and Web Designer*

The vast expansion of the Internet has prompted the need for occupations related to the design, development, and maintenance of Web sites. For example, webmasters are responsible for all technical aspects of a Web site, including the speed of accessing approved content. Web developers, also called Web designers, are responsible for day-to-day site creation and design.

Where and When

Computer network, systems, and database administrators normally work in offices or laboratories. They typically work 40 hours per week, although some of these workers may be required to be "on call" outside of normal business hours in order to resolve system failures or other problems. Telecommuting is a popular option as well, as more and more work can be done from home. Like most other jobs involving heavy computer use, eyestrain, back discomfort, and hand and wrist problems can occur.

For More Information

* The League of Professional System Administrators, 15000 Commerce Pkwy., Suite C, Mount Laurel, NJ 08054. Internet: www.lopsa.org

* Data Management International, 19239 N. Dale Mabry Hwy. #132, Lutz, FL 33548. Internet: www.dama.org

* Association for Computing Machinery (ACM), 2 Penn Plaza, Suite 701, New York, NY 10121-0701. Internet: http://computingcareers.acm.org

Data Bank

Education and Training: Associate degree to bachelor's degree

Average Earnings: $55,000–$91,000

Earnings Growth Potential: Medium

Total Jobs Held: 961,000

Job Outlook: Rapid increase

Annual Job Openings: 46,100

Related Jobs: Computer and information systems managers; computer scientists; computer software engineers and computer programmers; computer support specialists; computer systems analysts

Personality Types: Investigative-Conventional-Realistic

Did You Know?

Computer security is not just a concern for corporations and home computer users. It's also a matter of national security. The Pentagon has a Cyber Command, run by a four-star general, to shield the Defense Department's computers from attacks by hackers. Although our military defends our homes and businesses from traditional warfare, it does not defend these targets from cyber attacks. That's why every business needs the help of computer security specialists and every home computer user needs to be careful to use virus-protection software and hard-to-crack passwords.

Computer Scientists

At a Glance

Computer scientists solve complex business, scientific, and general computing problems by developing new technology or by finding new uses for existing resources. Some computer scientists work on multidisciplinary projects, collaborating with electrical engineers, mechanical engineers, and other specialists. Computer scientists conduct research on a wide array of topics. Examples include computer hardware architecture, virtual reality, and robotics. Researchers in academic settings have more flexibility to focus on pure theory, while those working in business or scientific organizations usually focus on projects that have the possibility of producing patents and profits.

Did You Know?

The Internet that is so vital to today's personal, education, and business worlds started as a military research project by computer scientists back in the 1960s. In one early experiment, one computer was programmed to make statements like a person suffering from severe mental illness. Another was programmed to react to statements in the way a psychiatrist might: "When did you start feeling this way?" The hilarious transcript of their "conversation" appears in *Where Wizards Stay Up Late*, by Katie Hafner.

Career in Focus: *Computer Hardware Architect*

Scientists who research hardware architecture discover new ways for computers to process and transmit information. They design computer chips and processors, using new materials and techniques to make them work faster and give them more computing power. They usually test their designs by writing programs that simulate how the chips will work.

Where and When

Computer scientists normally work in offices or laboratories in comfortable surroundings. Like other workers who spend long periods in front of a computer terminal typing on a keyboard, computer scientists are susceptible to eyestrain, back discomfort, and hand and wrist problems such as carpal tunnel syndrome.

For More Information

* Association for Computing Machinery (ACM), 2 Penn Plaza, Suite 701, New York, NY 10121-0701. Internet: http://computingcareers.acm.org

* Institute of Electrical and Electronics Engineers Computer Society, Headquarters Office, 2001 L St. NW, Suite 700, Washington, DC 20036-4910. Internet: www.computer.org

* National Center for Women and Information Technology, University of Colorado, Campus Box 322 UCB, Boulder, CO 80309-0322. Internet: www.ncwit.org

* National Workforce Center for Emerging Technologies, 3000 Landerholm Circle SE, Bellevue, WA 98007. Internet: www.nwcet.org

Computer Software Engineers and Computer Programmers

At a Glance

Computer software engineers research and design computers and programs. Software engineers analyze users' needs and design, construct, test, and maintain computer applications software to meet those needs. They may also identify problems in business, science, and engineering and then design specialized computer software to solve those problems. Software engineers must possess strong programming skills, but computer programmers are mainly responsible for writing, updating, testing, and maintaining the programs that make computers work. They provide detailed, step-by-step instructions for the computer. If the software does not produce the desired result, the programmer must correct the errors.

Career in Focus:
Computer Systems Software Engineer

Computer systems software engineers coordinate the construction and maintenance of a company's computer systems and plan that company's future growth. They coordinate each department's computer needs—ordering, inventory, billing, and payroll, for example—and make suggestions about the software required. They might set up the company's networks as well.

Where and When

Computer software engineers and programmers normally work in offices or laboratories. Software engineers who work for software vendors and consulting firms frequently travel to meet with customers. Telecommuting is becoming more common. Most software engineers and programmers work 40 hours a week, but some work longer hours. Like other workers who spend long periods in front of a computer terminal typing at a keyboard, engineers and programmers are susceptible to eyestrain, back discomfort, and hand and wrist problems.

For More Information

* Association for Computing Machinery, 2 Penn Plaza, Suite 701, New York, NY 10121-0701. Internet: http://computingcareers.acm.org

* Institute of Electrical and Electronics Engineers Computer Society, Headquarters Office, 2001 L St. NW, Suite 700, Washington, DC 20036-4910. Internet: www.computer.org

* National Workforce Center for Emerging Technologies, 3000 Landerholm Circle SE, Bellevue, WA 98007. Internet: www.nwcet.org

Data Bank

Education and Training: Bachelor's degree

Average Earnings: $66,000–$106,000

Earnings Growth Potential: Medium

Total Jobs Held: 1,336,000

Job Outlook: Rapid increase

Annual Job Openings: 45,200

Related Jobs: Actuaries; computer network, systems, and database administrators; computer scientists; computer support specialists; computer systems analysts; engineers; mathematicians; operations research analysts; statisticians

Personality Types: Investigative-Conventional-Realistic

Did You Know?

Computer software engineers are projected to be one of the fastest-growing occupations in the next ten years. Those with at least a bachelor's degree in computer engineering or computer science should have very good job opportunities as businesses continue to adapt to advances in technology. In addition, the continued growth of the Internet will provide more and more job possibilities for creative engineers. Jobs for programmers, however, are expected to shrink in the U.S. because much of the work can be done overseas by lower-wage workers.

Computer Support Specialists

At a Glance

What do companies do when their computers crash? They call in the computer support specialists, the troubleshooters of the computer world. These workers find and fix problems for big businesses and individual computer owners. They provide advice to users as well as the day-to-day maintenance and support of computer networks for companies. Sometimes they run automatic diagnostics programs to resolve problems. They may write training manuals and train computer users in the use of new computer hardware and software. They also install, modify, clean, and repair computer hardware and software.

Data Bank

Education and Training: Associate degree

Average Earnings: $34,000–$57,000

Earnings Growth Potential: Medium

Total Jobs Held: 566,000

Job Outlook: Above-average increase

Annual Job Openings: 23,500

Related Jobs: Broadcast and sound engineering technicians and radio operators; computer and information systems managers; computer network, systems, and database administrators; computer software engineers and computer programmers; customer service representatives

Personality Types: Realistic-Conventional-Investigative

Did You Know?

The most common computer problem of all is that performance has slowed down. Usually this is caused by a lack of maintenance. Data gets fragmented, unnecessary programs run in the background, and occasionally viruses or spyware gum up the works. Support specialists know which software tools can diagnose and fix these problems. Many such tools are readily available to home users.

Career in Focus: *Help-Desk Technician*

These workers respond to telephone calls and e-mail messages from customers looking for help with computer problems. In responding to these inquiries, help-desk technicians must listen carefully to the customer, ask questions to diagnose the nature of the problem, and then patiently walk the customer through the problem-solving steps. Help-desk technicians deal directly with customer issues, and their employers value them as a source of feedback on their products and services. They are consulted for information about what gives customers the most trouble, as well as other customer concerns.

Where and When

These individuals generally work in comfortable office settings for a standard 40-hour workweek, though they may be on call to fix unexpected technical problems. Many of these support specialists interact directly with customers and fellow employees and need good people skills. Like other workers who spend long periods of time in front of a computer, programmers are susceptible to hand and wrist problems, back discomfort, and eyestrain.

For More Information

* Association of Support Professionals, 122 Barnard Ave., Watertown, MA 02472. Internet: http://asponline.com

* HDI, 102 S. Tejon, Suite 1200, Colorado Springs, CO 80903. Internet: www.thinkhdi.com

* Association for Computing Machinery, 2 Penn Plaza, Suite 701, New York, NY 10121-0701. Internet: http://computingcareers.acm.org

* National Workforce Center for Emerging Technologies, 3000 Landerholm Circle SE, Bellevue, WA 98007. Internet: www.nwcet.org

Computer Systems Analysts

At a Glance

Computer systems analysts help businesses and organizations decide which computer systems will best help them grow. Systems analysts may plan and develop new computer systems or devise ways to apply existing systems' resources to new operations. They often set up and test the new technology as well. Many systems analysts are involved in networking, which involves connecting computers together within a company or to the Internet.

Career in Focus: *Software Quality Assurance Analyst*

While all computer systems analysts are sometimes involved in testing the programs and systems they put in place, software quality assurance analysts do more in-depth testing of products. In addition to running tests, these individuals diagnose problems, recommend solutions, and determine whether program requirements have been met.

Where and When

Computer systems analysts generally work in comfortable offices or laboratories. Though they typically work a 40-hour week, evenings or weekends may be necessary to meet deadlines. As the technology continues to change, more and more computer professionals are able to telecommute as well. Like other workers who spend long periods of time in front of a computer, programmers are susceptible to hand and wrist problems, back discomfort, and eyestrain.

For More Information

* Association for Computing Machinery (ACM), 2 Penn Plaza, Suite 701, New York, NY 10121-0701. Internet: http://computingcareers.acm.org

* Institute of Electrical and Electronics Engineers Computer Society, Headquarters Office, 2001 L St. NW, Suite 700, Washington, DC 20036-4910. Internet: www.computer.org

* National Workforce Center for Emerging Technologies, 3000 Landerholm Circle SE, Bellevue, WA 98007. Internet: www.nwcet.org

Data Bank

Education and Training: Bachelor's degree

Average Earnings: $60,000–$97,000

Earnings Growth Potential: Medium

Total Jobs Held: 532,000

Job Outlook: Rapid increase

Annual Job Openings: 22,300

Related Jobs: Actuaries; computer and information systems managers; computer network, systems, and database administrators; computer software engineers and computer programmers; engineers; management analysts; mathematicians; operations research analysts; statisticians

Personality Types: Investigative-Conventional

Did You Know?

The average functional lifespan for a personal computer is two to five years. Technology changes so rapidly that newer and faster machines are necessary to meet the demands of new software for business and personal use. Computer systems analysts have to be constantly aware of these changes in technology so they can keep businesses competitive.

Mathematicians

At a Glance

Mathematicians use mathematical theory, computation, and computers to solve economic, engineering, scientific, and business problems. Mathematicians work in two areas: theory and applications. Theoretical mathematicians look for relationships between new math principles and old ones. Most work as part of a university faculty where they teach and conduct research. Applied mathematicians use math to solve practical problems in business, government, and everyday life. Much of this work is done by individuals who aren't formally called mathematicians, such as economists, statisticians, and computer scientists.

Did You Know?

While the number of jobs that hold the formal title "mathematician" are declining, some of the hottest and best-paying fields require math as one of the most important, if not the most important skill. Increasingly, individuals graduating with a degree in mathematics are going into careers in computer science and software development, engineering, and financial analysis. Those interested in sticking with a career in pure math will likely have to earn a doctorate and compete for university jobs.

Career in Focus: *Cryptanalyst*

Some mathematicians, called cryptanalysts, analyze and decipher encryption systems designed to transmit military, political, financial, or law enforcement–related information in code. Sometimes these mathematicians are asked to crack an enemy code during times of war or keep a computer hacker from getting access to customers' credit card numbers, making this job both brainy and cool at the same time.

Where and When

Mathematicians generally work in comfortable office settings. They may need to travel to conferences or seminars as part of the job. Those who work at the university level are required to balance teaching, research, and publishing responsibilities.

For More Information

* American Mathematical Society, 201 Charles St., Providence, RI 02904-2294. Internet: www.ams.org
* Society for Industrial and Applied Mathematics, 3600 Market St., 6th Floor, Philadelphia, PA 19104-2688. Internet: www.siam.org

Operations Research Analysts

At a Glance

Operations research analysts help businesses operate efficiently by applying mathematical principles to real-world problems. Large companies search for the most effective use of their resources, and operations research analysts help these companies coordinate their money, materials, equipment, and people. First, analysts define and study the problem. Next, they gather information by talking with people and choosing which mathematical model they will use. Finally, they present their findings and recommendations to the company's management. They often specialize in one industry and are sometimes involved in top-level planning and management.

Career in Focus: *Government Operations Analyst*

Probably no other institution in America has as many resources to coordinate as the federal government. In fact, the fields of "operation research" and "management science" have been used extensively by the U.S. military. Because of its size and scope, inefficiencies in government operations are common, and analysts are often required to find and fix them. For their efforts, operations research analysts working for the federal government earn an average annual salary of nearly $90,000.

Where and When

Operations research analysts work regular hours in comfortable office settings. They may be required to work long hours to meet deadlines, and they spend much of their time using a computer to research and compile data.

For More Information

* Institute for Operations Research and the Management Sciences, 7240 Parkway Dr., Suite 300, Hanover, MD 21076. Internet: www.informs.org
* Military Operations Research Society, 1703 N. Beauregard St., Suite 450, Alexandria, VA 22311. Internet: www.mors.org

Data Bank

Education and Training: Master's degree

Average Earnings: $52,000–$94,000

Earnings Growth Potential: High

Total Jobs Held: 63,000

Job Outlook: Rapid increase

Annual Job Openings: 3,200

Related Jobs: Computer software engineers and computer programmers; computer systems analysts; economists; engineers; management analysts; market and survey researchers; mathematicians; statisticians

Personality Types: Investigative-Conventional-Enterprising

Did You Know?

One of the primary tools of operations research analysts is game theory. It is a branch of applied mathematics that studies decision making in situations where each party seeks the best course of action. It has been used to analyze everything from animal behavior to nuclear strategy. It has found its most consistent and practical use in economics. American mathematician John Nash won the Nobel Prize in economics for his work in game theory and was the subject of the film *A Beautiful Mind*.

Statisticians

At a Glance

Statistics is the application of mathematics to the collection, analysis, and presentation of data. Statisticians collect information from surveys and experiments. They decide where and how to gather the information, who to survey, and what questions to ask. They primarily use the information they collect to make predictions about the economy or to assess various social problems in order to help business and government leaders make decisions. Other fields that use statisticians include biology, engineering, medicine, public health, psychology, education, and sports.

Data Bank

Education and Training: Master's degree

Average Earnings: $51,000–$96,000

Earnings Growth Potential: High

Total Jobs Held: 23,000

Job Outlook: Average increase

Annual Job Openings: 1,000

Related Jobs: Actuaries; computer scientists; computer software engineers and computer programmers; computer systems analysts; economists; engineers; financial analysts; market and survey researchers; mathematicians; operations research analysts; personal financial advisors; social scientists, other; teachers—kindergarten, elementary, middle, and secondary; teachers—postsecondary

Personality Types: Conventional-Investigative

Did You Know?

You might know who holds the Major League record for home runs in a season (Barry Bonds, 73), but do you know who holds the record for most strikeouts in a career (Reggie Jackson, 2,597) or the most sacrifice flies (Eddie Murray, 128)? And did you know that St. Louis pitcher John Grimes hit a total of six batters with pitches during a game in July of 1897? Sports statisticians keep track of even the most obscure player and team statistics, although some devoted fans can recite the lifetime numbers of their favorite players as well.

Career in Focus: *Government Statistician*

Four out of every ten statisticians work for the federal, state, or local governments. Government statisticians measure everything from population growth to consumer confidence to unemployment. Other government statisticians work for scientific, environmental, and agricultural agencies. Statisticians are also involved in our national defense, determining the likely effectiveness of military strategies.

Where and When

Statisticians work regular hours in comfortable office environments. They are sometimes required to travel to gather data or give presentations. Those who work at colleges and universities usually have to balance teaching and research responsibilities.

For More Information

* American Statistical Association, 732 N. Washington St., Alexandria, VA 22314. Internet: www.amstat.org
* American Mathematical Society, 201 Charles St., Providence, RI 02904. Internet: www.ams.org

Architects, Except Landscape and Naval

At a Glance

Architects design buildings and other structures—everything from churches, houses, and hospitals to college campuses and industrial parks. They are not just concerned with the overall appearance of the buildings they design; they also make sure the buildings are functional, safe, and economical. They draw plans of every part of a building, including the plumbing, heating, air-conditioning, communication, and electrical systems. They also help choose a building site and decide what materials to use. They may be involved in all phases of development, from the initial discussion with the client through the entire construction process. Architects spend a great deal of time explaining their ideas, so they must have good communication skills. Most architects today use computers in their work, and many are self-employed.

Career in Focus: *Museum Architect*

Some architects end up specializing in one type of building, such as houses, office buildings, or hospitals. One field that has produced a wide range of styles is museum architecture. Like the paintings and artifacts inside them, the actual museum building acts as a kind of display, and museum architects are careful to balance the need to make the buildings functional with the desire to make them works of art.

Where and When

Architects spend most of their time in offices either developing their drawings and models or discussing them with clients. They sometimes visit the construction sites to review the building's progress. Most work a standard 40-hour week, though deadlines can cause them to work overtime.

For More Information

* The American Institute of Architects, 1735 New York Ave. NW, Washington, DC 20006. Internet: www.aia.org

* The National Architectural Accrediting Board, 1735 New York Ave. NW, Washington, DC 20006. Internet: www.naab.org

* The National Council of Architectural Registration Boards, Suite 700K, 1801 K St. NW, Washington, DC 20006. Internet: www.ncarb.org

* The American Institute of Architects and the American Institute of Architecture Students jointly sponsor a Web site: www.archcareers.org

Data Bank

Education and Training: Bachelor's degree

Average Earnings: $55,000–$94,000

Earnings Growth Potential: Medium

Total Jobs Held: 141,000

Job Outlook: Above-average increase

Annual Job Openings: 4,700

Related Jobs: Commercial and industrial designers; construction managers; engineers; graphic designers; interior designers; landscape architects; urban and regional planners

Personality Types: Artistic-Investigative

Did You Know?

Sometimes flaws in architectural design can become famous. Take the cathedral bell tower in the Italian city of Pisa, for example. Begun in 1173 and not completed until 1372, the tower had only a three-meter foundation set into unstable soil. The tower began to lean almost immediately and subsequent additions didn't help much. It is said that Benito Mussolini ordered the tower to be straightened, but pouring additional concrete into the foundation only caused it to sink further. The Leaning Tower of Pisa has been leaning for more than 800 years now, making it as much an architectural marvel as a mistake.

Landscape Architects

At a Glance

Everyone enjoys attractively designed neighborhoods, public parks, college campuses, and golf courses. Landscape architects make these areas beautiful and useful. They decide where the buildings, roads, and walkways will go and how the flower gardens and trees should be arranged. They create designs, estimate costs, and check that the plans are carried out correctly. Some landscape architects work on a variety of projects. Others specialize in a particular area, such as street and highway beautification, parks and playgrounds, or shopping centers. Increasingly, landscape architects are becoming involved with preserving and restoring natural environments and historical landscapes.

Data Bank

Education and Training: Bachelor's degree

Average Earnings: $47,000–$80,000

Earnings Growth Potential: Medium

Total Jobs Held: 27,000

Job Outlook: Rapid increase

Annual Job Openings: 1,000

Related Jobs: Architects, except landscape and naval; construction managers; engineers; environmental scientists and specialists; geoscientists and hydrologists; surveyors, cartographers, photogrammetrists, and surveying and mapping technicians; urban and regional planners

Personality Types: Artistic-Investigative-Realistic

Did You Know?

Before the widespread use of computers, architects had to draw their landscape designs by hand and build models piece by piece. Today, they use computer-aided design (CAD) systems and video simulations to let their clients see their ideas in full color and three dimensions. If the client wants to make a change, the architect can do it with the click of a mouse. Too bad it's not that easy at the actual construction site.

Career in Focus: *Park Designer and Preservationist*

Landscape architects who work for government agencies are often responsible for recreation planning and restoration in national parks and forests such as Glacier or Yellowstone. They must keep the natural environment intact for future generations while making it accessible for people to visit. For example, they may have to decide where to put a paved road that won't disrupt the wildlife.

Where and When

Though they are concerned with how to design the landscape, these architects still spend most of their time inside the office drawing plans and preparing models and reports. They do spend some time at the site doing tests and checking progress. Most work regular hours, and many are self-employed.

For More Information

* American Society of Landscape Architects, Career Information, 636 I St. NW, Washington, DC 20001-3736. Internet: www.asla.org

* Council of Landscape Architectural Registration Boards, 3949 Pender Dr., Suite 120, Vienna, VA 22030. Internet: www.clarb.org

Surveyors, Cartographers, Photogrammetrists, and Surveying and Mapping Technicians

At a Glance

These workers measure and map the earth's surface. Surveyors are primarily responsible for establishing official land, airspace, and water boundaries. They also write descriptions for deeds, leases, and other legal documents and take measurements of construction sites. Cartographers prepare maps and charts in either digital or graphic form, using information provided by geodetic surveys, aerial photographs, and satellite data. Surveying and mapping technicians assist these professionals by collecting data in the field and using it to calculate mapmaking information. Most of these workers use computers and software (such as GIS) to help them assemble, analyze, and display data.

Career in Focus: *Photogrammetrist*

Photogrammetrists measure and analyze aerial and satellite photographs to help make detailed maps. They are especially needed to map areas that are inaccessible, difficult, or more costly to survey by other methods (mountain peaks or the South Pole, for example). Some states require photogrammetrists to be licensed as surveyors.

Where and When

These workers typically work 40-hour weeks and spend a lot of time outdoors. Demands for overtime tend to be seasonal. The work of surveyors and technicians often requires physical activity—some of it strenuous—and possible exposure to extreme weather conditions. Travel is usually required to get to survey sites or to present findings.

For More Information

* American Congress on Surveying and Mapping, 6 Montgomery Village Ave., Suite 403, Gaithersburg, MD 20879. Internet: www.acsm.net

* National Society of Professional Surveyors, 6 Montgomery Village Ave., Suite 403, Gaithersburg, MD 20879. Internet: www.nspsmo.org

* American Association of Geodetic Surveying (AAGS), 6 Montgomery Village Ave., Suite 403, Gaithersburg, MD 20879. Internet: www.aagsmo.org

* ASPRS: Imaging and Geospatial Information Society, 5410 Grosvenor Lane, Suite 210, Bethesda, MD 20814-2160. Internet: www.asprs.org

Data Bank

Education and Training: Moderate-term on-the-job training to bachelor's degree

Average Earnings: $34,000–$60,000

Earnings Growth Potential: Medium

Total Jobs Held: 147,000

Job Outlook: Above-average increase

Annual Job Openings: 5,900

Related Jobs: Architects, except landscape and naval; engineers; environmental scientists and specialists; landscape architects; social scientists, other; urban and regional planners

Personality Types: Conventional-Realistic-Investigative

Did You Know?

Satellites are revolutionizing survey work. Surveyors can now use a Global Positioning System (GPS) to locate points on the earth by collecting information from several satellites at once. Theoretically, the technology is making some surveying tasks so easy that amateurs could do them. However, licensing laws restrict who can create acceptable survey documents.

Engineers

At a Glance

Engineers design machinery, buildings, and highways. They also develop new products and new ways of making them. Some engineers test the quality of products or supervise production in factories. They work in laboratories, factories, offices, and construction sites. Most engineers specialize to work in a particular industry or with particular materials: Aerospace engineers design, develop, and test aircraft, spacecraft, and missiles. Civil engineers design and supervise the construction of roads, buildings, airports, tunnels, dams, and bridges. Mechanical engineers research, develop, manufacture, and test tools, engines, and machines. Other specialties include agricultural, chemical, computer hardware, electrical, environmental, industrial, marine, materials, nuclear, and petroleum engineers. All engineers use computers extensively.

Data Bank

Education and Training: Bachelor's degree

Average Earnings: $65,000–$103,000

Earnings Growth Potential: Medium

Total Jobs Held: 1,572,000

Job Outlook: Average increase

Annual Job Openings: 53,200

Related Jobs: Agricultural and food scientists; architects, except landscape and naval; atmospheric scientists; biological scientists; chemists and materials scientists; computer and information systems managers; computer scientists; computer software engineers and computer programmers; drafters; engineering and natural sciences managers; engineering technicians; environmental scientists and specialists; geoscientists and hydrologists; mathematicians; physicists and astronomers; sales engineers; science technicians

Personality Types: Investigative-Realistic

Did You Know?

Statistics show that each year the United States produces about 60,000 engineering graduates. Although that sounds like a lot, one-third of these engineering grads go to work in unrelated fields such as finance. Economists and educators are worried that we aren't producing enough engineers to keep up with other countries, such as India and China. After all, a country needs engineers to keep its technological edge and stay innovative. So what are you waiting for?

Career in Focus: *Biomedical Engineer*

Working in one of the hottest fields in engineering, biomedical engineers develop devices and procedures that solve medical and health-related problems. They combine their knowledge of biology and medicine with engineering principles and practices. Biomedical engineers may also design devices used in various medical procedures, imaging systems such as magnetic resonance imaging (MRI), and devices for controlling body functions. This specialty combines a background in engineering with biomedical training.

Where and When

Engineers generally work in office buildings, laboratories, or industrial plants. They sometimes work outdoors on site to monitor operations and solve problems. Though most work a standard 40-hour week, deadlines can cause them to work long hours.

For More Information

* JETS, 1420 King St., Suite 405, Alexandria, VA 22314. Internet: www.jets.org

* ABET, Inc., 111 Market Place, Suite 1050, Baltimore, MD 21202. Internet: www.abet.org

* National Society of Professional Engineers, 1420 King St., Alexandria, VA 22314. Internet: www.nspe.org

* American Society for Engineering Education, 1818 N St. NW, Suite 600, Washington, DC 20036. Internet: www.asee.org

Drafters

At a Glance

Drafters prepare the technical drawings used to build everything from spacecraft to bridges. They start with the specifications, codes, and calculations previously made by engineers, surveyors, architects, or scientists. Then they produce detailed technical drawings with the information needed to create a finished product, including dimensions, materials, and procedures. Drafters use handbooks, tables, calculators, and computers to do their work.

Career in Focus: *Architectural Drafter*

Architectural drafters draw the features of buildings and other structures. These workers may specialize in a type of structure, such as residential (houses or apartments) or commercial (hospitals or department stores), or in a kind of material used, such as concrete, masonry, steel, or lumber. They make up about 43 percent of all drafters.

Where and When

Most drafters work 40 hours per week, usually in comfortable offices. Though a few may produce drawings manually, the majority use computers. Like other workers who spend long periods of time in front of a computer, drafters may be susceptible to eyestrain, backaches, and hand and wrist problems.

For More Information

* Accrediting Commission of Career Schools and Colleges, 2101 Wilson Blvd., Suite 302, Arlington, VA 22201. Internet: www.accsc.org
* American Design Drafting Association, 105 E. Main St., Newbern, TN 38059. Internet: www.adda.org

Data Bank

Education and Training: Vocational/technical training

Average Earnings: $37,000–$59,000

Earnings Growth Potential: Low

Total Jobs Held: 252,000

Job Outlook: Little change

Annual Job Openings: 6,600

Related Jobs: Architects, except landscape and naval; commercial and industrial designers; engineering technicians; engineers; landscape architects; surveyors, cartographers, photogrammetrists, and surveying and mapping technicians

Personality Types: Realistic-Conventional-Investigative

Did You Know?

Traditionally, drafters sat at drawing boards and used pencils and protractors to draw their designs manually. Most drafters today, however, use CADD (computer-aided design and drafting) systems. Consequently, some drafters may be referred to as CADD operators. CADD systems use computers to create and store drawings, which lets drafters quickly prepare variations of a design. Despite the nearly universal use of CADD systems, manual drafting and sketching are still necessary in some cases.

Engineering Technicians

At a Glance

Engineering technicians use science, engineering principles, and math to solve problems in research and development, manufacturing, sales, construction, inspection, and maintenance. They help engineers and scientists with experiments and develop models of new equipment. Some supervise production workers or check the quality of products. In manufacturing, they may also assist in designing, developing, and producing new products. Like engineers, they specialize in an area such as aeronautics, mechanics, electronics, or chemicals.

Data Bank

Education and Training: Associate degree

Average Earnings: $40,000–$63,000

Earnings Growth Potential: Medium

Total Jobs Held: 497,000

Job Outlook: Little change

Annual Job Openings: 12,500

Related Jobs: Broadcast and sound engineering technicians and radio operators; drafters; science technicians

Personality Types: Realistic-Investigative-Conventional

Did You Know?

In 1895, King C. Gillette, a Boston bottle-cap salesman, came up with an idea for a disposable razor blade. It took him eight years (and the help of engineering technicians) to develop the methods to mass-produce his razor for sale to the public. Today, the company he founded is worth millions, and most Americans have used his invention at one time or another.

Career in Focus: *Mechanical Engineering Technician*

Mechanical engineering technicians help engineers design, develop, test, and manufacture machinery, products, and other equipment. They make sketches, record and analyze data, and report on their findings. In production, mechanical engineering technicians prepare layouts and drawings of the assembly process and of parts to be manufactured. They estimate labor costs, equipment life, and plant space. Some test and inspect machines and equipment or work with engineers to eliminate production problems.

Where and When

Engineering technicians tend to work at least 40 hours per week in offices, laboratories, plants, or construction sites. Some may be exposed to hazards from equipment, chemicals, or toxic materials.

For More Information

* JETS (Junior Engineering Technical Society), 1420 King St., Suite 405, Alexandria, VA 22314. Internet: www.jets.org

* Pathways to Technology. Internet: www.pathwaystotechnology.org

* ABET, Inc., 111 Market Place, Suite 1050, Baltimore, MD 21202. Internet: www.abet.org

Agricultural and Food Scientists

At a Glance

Agricultural scientists study farm crops and animals and use the principles of biology, chemistry, physics, mathematics, and other sciences to solve problems in agriculture. They look for ways to control pests and weeds safely, increase crop yields with less labor, and save water and soil. They may specialize in plant, soil, or animal science. New research in genetics is opening up new ways for agricultural scientists to improve our food supply as well. Some agricultural scientists are consultants to business firms, private clients, or the government.

Career in Focus: *Food Scientist*

Food scientists usually work in the food processing industry, universities, or the federal government. They help meet consumer demand for foods that are healthy, safe, appetizing, and convenient. They also develop new or better ways of preserving, processing, packaging, storing, and delivering foods. Some food scientists engage in basic research, such as discovering new food sources, analyzing food products, or searching for substitutes for harmful additives. Other food scientists enforce government regulations, ensuring that sanitation, safety, and quality standards are met.

Where and When

Agricultural and food scientists tend to work in offices or laboratories. Specific work environments vary, from test kitchens to university labs. Soil and crop scientists spend much of their time outdoors doing research, and entomologists spend a lot of time hunting and studying insects in their natural habitats. These jobs generally allow for a great deal of independence. One out of every three of these workers is self-employed.

For More Information

* Institute of Food Technologists, 525 W. Van Buren, Suite 1000, Chicago, IL 60607. Internet: www.ift.org

* American Society of Agronomy, 677 S. Segoe Rd., Madison, WI 53711-1086. Internet: www.agronomy.org

* Crop Science Society of America, 677 S. Segoe Rd., Madison, WI 53711-1086. Internet: www.crops.org

* Soil Science Society of America, 677 S. Segoe Rd., Madison, WI 53711-1086. Internet: www.soils.org

Data Bank

Education and Training: Bachelor's degree to doctoral degree

Average Earnings: $44,000–$80,000

Earnings Growth Potential: High

Total Jobs Held: 31,000

Job Outlook: Above-average increase

Annual Job Openings: 1,600

Related Jobs: Biological scientists; chemists and materials scientists; conservation scientists and foresters; farmers, ranchers, and agricultural managers; medical scientists; veterinarians

Personality Types: Investigative-Realistic

Did You Know?

Did you know that the flavoring in a banana popsicle is actually isoamyl acetate? Or that the flavor in wintergreen gum is probably derived from methyl salicylate? Such are the discoveries of flavor scientists, who use their knowledge of chemistry to re-create many natural flavors in artificial forms. In fact, some artificial flavors can even be safer than their natural versions because they don't contain the traces of toxins that natural flavor compounds do. Think about that the next time you enjoy some tasty isoamyl acetate–flavored pudding.

Biological Scientists

At a Glance

Biological scientists study living things and their environments. They do research, develop new medicines, and increase crop amounts. Some study specialty areas such as viruses, ocean life, plant life, or animal life. Many biological scientists work in research and development to find solutions to human health problems and to preserve the natural environment. Some conduct experiments using laboratory animals or greenhouse plants. Recent advances in biotechnology—especially in the field of genetics—have created research opportunities with commercial applications in the food industry, agriculture, and health care. Biological scientists may work in company, college, or government labs or as high school biology teachers.

Data Bank

Education and Training: Bachelor's degree to doctoral degree

Average Earnings: $52,000–$88,000

Earnings Growth Potential: High

Total Jobs Held: 91,000

Job Outlook: Rapid increase

Annual Job Openings: 4,900

Related Jobs: Agricultural and food scientists; conservation scientists and foresters; dentists; engineering and natural sciences managers; epidemiologists; medical scientists; physicians and surgeons; teachers—postsecondary; veterinarians

Personality Types: Investigative-Realistic

Did You Know?

For those who believe we know all there is to know about the natural world, consider this: More than 6,000 new species of insects are described (discovered) each year. In total, there are about 900,000 known species of insects, and recent figures suggest that there are more than 200 million insects for every single human on the planet. If you want to become famous, one route might be to become an entomologist, travel to a tropical rainforest, and start looking under rocks and trees. The next new species of cockroach might be waiting for you.

Career in Focus: *Ecologist*

Ecologists study the relationships between living things and their environments. They examine the effects of population size, pollutants, rainfall, temperature, and altitude. Ecologists collect, study, and report data on the quality of air, food, soil, and water. This research is used by both corporate and government programs to help preserve the environment and maintain natural habitats.

Where and When

Biological scientists typically work regular hours in office and laboratory settings. Those who work with dangerous organisms or toxic chemicals follow strict safety procedures. Many biological scientists also spend time in the field doing research, which can require strenuous physical activity. Those working at colleges and universities must balance their research with their teaching responsibilities.

For More Information

* American Institute of Biological Sciences, 1444 I St. NW, Suite 200, Washington, DC 20005. Internet: www.aibs.org

* Federation of American Societies for Experimental Biology, 9650 Rockville Pike, Bethesda, MD 20814. Internet: www.faseb.org

* The Botanical Society of America, P.O. Box 299, St. Louis, MO 63166. Internet: www.botany.org

* Ecological Society of America, 1990 M St. NW, Suite 700, Washington, DC 20036. Internet: www.esa.org

* American Society for Microbiology, Career Information—Education Department, 1752 N St. NW, Washington, DC 20036. Internet: www.asm.org

Medical Scientists

At a Glance

Medical scientists research diseases in order to improve human health. Most medical scientists do basic research to learn more about viruses, bacteria, and other infectious diseases. They then use this information to develop vaccines, medicines, and treatments. Medical scientists also attempt to discover ways to prevent health problems, such as finding a link between smoking and lung cancer. Recent research in genetics and advances in biotechnology have led to the discovery of important new drugs and treatments and opened up new avenues for research for these scientists. Medical scientists also engage in clinical investigation, technical writing, and drug application review. Some work in managerial, consulting, or administrative positions.

Career in Focus:
Epidemiologist

Epidemiologists investigate and describe the causes of disease, disability, and other health problems and develop means for prevention and control. Epidemiologists may study many different diseases, such as tuberculosis, influenza, or cholera, often focusing on epidemics. Research epidemiologists work at colleges and universities, medical schools, and research firms. Clinical epidemiologists work primarily in consulting roles at hospitals, informing the medical staff of infectious outbreaks and providing containment solutions. If you find infectious diseases interesting, this may be the job for you.

Where and When

Medical scientists typically work regular hours in offices, laboratories, clinics, or hospitals. Those who work with dangerous organisms, toxic chemicals, or infectious diseases follow strict safety procedures. Those working at colleges and universities must balance their research with their teaching responsibilities.

For More Information

* Federation of American Societies for Experimental Biology, 9650 Rockville Pike, Bethesda, MD 20814. Internet: www.faseb.org

* National Association of M.D.-Ph.D. Programs. Internet: www.aamc.org/students/considering/research/mdphd

* American Association of Pharmaceutical Scientists (AAPS), 2107 Wilson Blvd., Suite 700, Arlington, VA 22201. Internet: www.aapspharmaceutica.org

* American Society for Pharmacology and Experimental Therapeutics, 9650 Rockville Pike, Bethesda, MD 20814. Internet: www.aspet.org

Data Bank

Education and Training: Doctoral degree

Average Earnings: $54,000–$103,000

Earnings Growth Potential: High

Total Jobs Held: 109,000

Job Outlook: Rapid increase

Annual Job Openings: 6,600

Related Jobs: Agricultural and food scientists; biological scientists; dentists; epidemiologists; pharmacists; physicians and surgeons; teachers—postsecondary; veterinarians

Personality Types: Investigative-Realistic-Artistic

Did You Know?

Smallpox, typhoid fever, the bubonic plague: Although some of the diseases that have wreaked havoc on humanity have been all but eradicated, others continue to spring up in their place, such as Severe Acute Respiratory Syndrome (SARS) and the Avian flu. Medical scientists continue to research ways to control or eliminate infectious diseases, such as HIV-AIDS, a pandemic that has taken more than 25 million lives in the last 25 years.

Conservation Scientists and Foresters

At a Glance

Foresters and conservation scientists manage and protect natural resources such as water, wood, and wildlife. Foresters supervise the use of timber for lumber companies, protecting the forests and managing the harvesting of trees. They may also design campgrounds and recreation areas on public lands. Conservation scientists manage, improve, and protect the country's natural resources. They work with landowners and federal, state, and local governments to devise ways to use and improve the land without damaging the environment. A growing number are advising landowners and governments on recreational uses for the land as well. Soil conservationists specifically help farmers preserve soil, water, and other natural resources.

Data Bank

Education and Training: Bachelor's degree

Average Earnings: $45,000–$70,000

Earnings Growth Potential: Medium

Total Jobs Held: 30,000

Job Outlook: Average increase

Annual Job Openings: 700

Related Jobs: Agricultural and food scientists; biological scientists; environmental scientists and specialists; farmers, ranchers, and agricultural managers; geoscientists and hydrologists

Personality Types: Realistic-Investigative-Enterprising

Did You Know?

Deforestation is an ongoing environmental concern for everyone, not just conservationists. According to the Food and Agriculture Organization of the United Nations, about 32 million acres of the world's forests are lost each year. The concern is not only for the loss of a valuable natural resource, but for the effect that it has on both the environment (including greenhouse gases) and the many species that call these forests home.

Career in Focus: *Range Manager*

Range managers—also called range conservationists, range ecologists, or range scientists—manage, improve, and protect rangelands. Rangelands cover hundreds of millions of acres of the United States and contain many natural resources, including grass and shrubs for animal grazing, wildlife habitats, water, and valuable mineral and energy resources. Range managers may inventory soils, plants, and animals; develop resource management plans; help to restore ecosystems; or simply assist in managing a ranch.

Where and When

Working conditions for foresters and conservationists vary considerably. They often split their time between field work and office work, though many spend most of their time outdoors. The work can be physically demanding, requiring extensive walking, sometimes in potentially dangerous environments.

For More Information

* Society of American Foresters, 5400 Grosvenor Ln., Bethesda, MD 20814-2198. Internet: www.safnet.org

* Forest Guild, P.O. Box 519, Santa Fe, NM 87504. Internet: www.forestguild.org

* Society for Range Management, 10030 W. 27th Ave., Wheat Ridge, CO 80215-6601. Internet: www.rangelands.org

Atmospheric Scientists

At a Glance

Atmospheric scientists, commonly called meteorologists, study the atmosphere (the blanket of air covering the earth) and its effects on our environment. The most well-known area of their work is weather forecasting. These meteorologists gather data from weather satellites, radar, sensors, and stations in many parts of the world. They study information on air pressure, temperature, humidity, and wind velocity and then apply their knowledge of math and physics to make weather predictions. Atmospheric scientists also study trends in the earth's climate and apply their research to air-pollution control, agriculture, forestry, environmental studies, air and sea transportation, and defense. About 40 percent of these workers are employed by the federal government.

Career in Focus:
Climatologist

Climatologists study changes in climate spanning hundreds or even millions of years. They collect, analyze, and interpret past records of wind, rainfall, sunshine, and temperature in specific areas or regions. Their studies are then used to design buildings, plan heating and cooling systems, and aid in farming.

Where and When

Atmospheric scientists often work nights, weekends, and holidays because weather stations operate around the clock. During weather emergencies, meteorologists might work overtime. Some atmospheric scientists work in isolated or remote areas or spend time observing weather conditions from aircraft. Those involved in broadcasting must meet the constant deadlines for weather reports.

For More Information

* American Meteorological Society. Internet: www. ametsoc.org/AMS

Data Bank

Education and Training: Bachelor's degree

Average Earnings: $59,000–$105,000

Earnings Growth Potential: High

Total Jobs Held: 9,000

Job Outlook: Above-average increase

Annual Job Openings: 300

Related Jobs: Chemists and materials scientists; engineers; environmental scientists and specialists; geoscientists and hydrologists; mathematicians; physicists and astronomers

Personality Types: Investigative-Realistic

Did You Know?

Although kids count on meteorologists mainly to spread the news about snow days, these scientists are vital for predicting potential natural emergencies. Even with advanced warning from meteorologists, however, it is sometimes difficult to avoid the destruction caused by Mother Nature. In August of 2005, Hurricane Katrina touched down in Florida, Mississippi, Alabama, and Louisiana, with particularly devastating effects on the city of New Orleans. Doing at least $125 billion in damage, it is considered to be the most destructive hurricane in American history.

Chemists and Materials Scientists

At a Glance

Everything in our environment is composed of chemicals. Chemists and materials scientists look for and use new information about chemicals and other materials. They develop new paints, fibers, adhesives, and other products. They also develop processes that save energy and reduce pollution. Materials scientists study the structures and chemical properties of materials to develop new products or improve existing ones. Chemists work with life scientists to make new medicines. Chemists also work in production and quality control in chemical manufacturing plants. Chemists often specialize in a particular field such as organic chemistry, medicinal chemistry, or biochemistry. Many teach at colleges and universities.

Data Bank

Education and Training: Bachelor's degree

Average Earnings: $51,000–$93,000

Earnings Growth Potential: High

Total Jobs Held: 94,000

Job Outlook: Little change

Annual Job Openings: 3,400

Related Jobs: Agricultural and food scientists; biological scientists; engineering and natural sciences managers; engineers; environmental scientists and specialists; geoscientists and hydrologists; medical scientists; physicists and astronomers; science technicians

Personality Types: Investigative-Realistic

Did You Know?

When chemist Wallace Carothers began his work with DuPont in the 1930s, he might not have predicted that it would lead to pantyhose and parachutes. Yet his work on polymerization (hooking small molecules together to form large ones) led to the invention of nylon, a synthetic material that has been used in products as diverse as tires, tents, ropes, and ponchos—not to mention women's stockings.

Career in Focus: *Analytical Chemist*

Analytical chemists determine the structure, composition, and nature of substances by examining and identifying their various elements. These chemists help the pharmaceutical industry by identifying the compounds that the industry hopes to turn into drugs. Analytical chemists also identify the presence and concentration of chemical pollutants in air, water, and soil in order to help preserve the environment.

Where and When

Chemists and materials scientists typically work regular hours in office or laboratory settings. They may also do some of their work in a chemical plant or outdoors. They often have to work alongside engineers and other specialists. Proper safety precautions keep them from being exposed to harmful chemicals.

For More Information

✳ American Chemical Society, Education Division, 1155 16th St. NW, Washington, DC 20036. Internet: www.acs.org

Environmental Scientists and Specialists

At a Glance

Environmental scientists and specialists study the earth and humans' impact on it. They analyze measurements or observations of air, food, water, and soil to determine the way to clean and preserve the environment. Understanding the issues involved in protecting the environment—degradation, conservation, recycling, and replenishment—is central to the work of environmental scientists. They often use this understanding to design and monitor waste disposal sites, preserve water supplies, and reclaim contaminated land and water. They also write risk assessments, describing the likely effect of construction and other environmental changes; write technical proposals; and give presentations to managers and regulators.

Career in Focus: *Environmental Ecologist*

Environmental ecologists study the relationships between organisms and their environments and the effects of factors such as population size, pollutants, rainfall, temperature, and altitude on both. They may collect, study, and report data on air, soil, and water, using their knowledge of various scientific disciplines.

Where and When

Entry-level environmental scientists and specialists spend a significant amount of their time in the field doing research, while more experienced workers spend the majority of their time in the office or laboratory. Those in the field may work in a variety of climates and conditions. The work often requires travel and physical activity. Those involved heavily in research are often under pressure to meet deadlines.

For More Information

* American Geological Institute, 4220 King St., Alexandria, VA 22302. Internet: www.agiweb.org

---

Data Bank

Education and Training: Master's degree

Average Earnings: $46,000–$82,000

Earnings Growth Potential: Medium

Total Jobs Held: 86,000

Job Outlook: Rapid increase

Annual Job Openings: 4,800

Related Jobs: Atmospheric scientists; biological scientists; chemists and materials scientists; conservation scientists and foresters; engineering technicians; engineers; epidemiologists; geoscientists and hydrologists; physicists and astronomers; science technicians; surveyors, cartographers, photogrammetrists, and surveying and mapping technicians

Personality Types: Investigative-Realistic-Conventional

Did You Know?

Most people think "environmental science" and "ecology" are the same thing. Actually, ecology is concerned only with organisms and how they interact with each other and the environment. Some environmental issues are not connected to organisms—for example, the causes of global warming. The effects of global warming, on the other hand, are of interest to ecologists.

Geoscientists and Hydrologists

At a Glance

Geoscientists study the earth, focusing on its composition and geologic past and present. Many are involved in the search for natural resources such as groundwater, metals, and petroleum, while others concern themselves with cleaning up the environment. Geoscientists also study the evolution of life by analyzing plant and animal fossils. They often specialize in a particular field of study, such as volcanologists, who investigate volcanoes and try to predict their potential danger, do. Hydrologists often specialize in either underground water or surface water. They examine the form and intensity of precipitation, its rate of infiltration into the soil, its movement through the earth, and its return to the ocean and atmosphere.

Data Bank

Education and Training: Master's degree

Average Earnings: $56,000–$113,000

Earnings Growth Potential: High

Total Jobs Held: 42,000

Job Outlook: Above-average increase

Annual Job Openings: 1,900

Related Jobs: Atmospheric scientists; biological scientists; chemists and materials scientists; engineering technicians; engineers; environmental scientists and specialists; physicists and astronomers; science technicians; surveyors, cartographers, photogrammetrists, and surveying and mapping technicians

Personality Types: Investigative-Realistic

Did You Know?

One of the hottest fields in geology is seismology—the study of earthquakes. And one of the biggest seismology experiments in history continues in Parkfield, California. This small town is known for its regular pattern of earthquakes: For the last 150 years, Parkfield has experienced a magnitude 6 earthquake every 20 to 30 years. That's why seismologists from around the world set up monitors in Parkfield, waiting for a chance to measure the next one.

Career in Focus: *Oceanographer*

Oceanographers study the world's oceans and coastal waters. They study the motion and circulation of ocean waters; the physical and chemical properties of the oceans; and how these properties affect coastal areas, climate, and weather.

Where and When

Geoscientists and hydrologists divide their time between the office or laboratory and the field. Work at remote sites is common, and travel to some locations involves strenuous activity in a variety of weather conditions. Oceanographers may spend considerable time at sea. An increasing number of geoscientists and hydrologists do their research in foreign countries.

For More Information

* American Geological Institute, 4220 King St., Alexandria, VA 22302-1502. Internet: www.agiweb.org
* American Association of Petroleum Geologists, P.O. Box 979, Tulsa, OK 74101. Internet: www.aapg.org
* American Institute of Hydrology, Engineering D–Mail Code 6603, Southern Illinois University Carbondale, 1230 Lincoln Dr., Carbondale, IL 62901. Internet: www.aihydrology.org

Physicists and Astronomers

At a Glance

Physicists study the matter that makes up the universe. They also study forces of nature, such as gravity; motion; and the nature of energy, electromagnetism, and nuclear interactions. Some use their research to answer theoretical questions, such as the nature of time or origin of the universe. Others use their studies for practical matters, such as to design medical equipment, electronic devices, and lasers. Astronomers use the principles of physics and mathematics to study the moon, sun, planets, galaxies, and stars. Their knowledge is used in space flight and exploration, satellite communications, and navigation. A small number of astronomers work in museum planetariums. Most physicists and astronomers are involved in research of one kind or another, and many teach in colleges and universities.

Career in Focus: *Nuclear Physicist*

Because of the tremendous energy that is released through nuclear fission and fusion, physicists look for ways to harness that energy. They also study the effects of radiation, which has implications for modern medicine. Though some nuclear physicists do military research, the majority concentrate on finding safe and efficient ways to use nuclear reactions as an alternative energy resource. Of course you don't have to be a nuclear physicist to know that this job requires a lot of education.

Where and When

Physicists and astronomers typically work in laboratories and offices, though some may work away from home at national or international facilities. Astronomers may spend long periods of time in observatories, and their work often involves travel to remote locations and frequent night work (for obvious reasons).

For More Information

* American Institute of Physics, Career Services Division and Education and Employment Division, One Physics Ellipse, College Park, MD 20740-3843. Internet: www.aip.org
* American Physical Society, One Physics Ellipse, College Park, MD 20740-3844. Internet: www.aps.org

Data Bank

Education and Training: Doctoral degree
Average Earnings: $79,000–$139,000
Earnings Growth Potential: High
Total Jobs Held: 17,000
Job Outlook: Above-average increase
Annual Job Openings: 800
Related Jobs: Atmospheric scientists; chemists and materials scientists; computer scientists; computer software engineers and computer programmers; computer systems analysts; engineering and natural sciences managers; engineers; environmental scientists and specialists; geoscientists and hydrologists; mathematicians; statisticians
Personality Types: Investigative-Realistic-Artistic

Did You Know?

In 1934, the Italian physicist Enrico Fermi bombarded uranium with neutrons and found his sample was then contaminated with several elements much lighter than uranium. It took five years for anyone to realize that Fermi had split the uranium atom into smaller parts. But by 1945, scientists and engineers working at a secret U.S. defense lab in Los Alamos, New Mexico, had used this technology to make an atomic bomb. Several of those scientists later regretted their work on the bomb. For better or worse, those physicists assured their place in the history books and ushered in the atomic age.

Economists

At a Glance

Economists study how people use resources such as land, labor, raw materials, and machinery to produce goods and services. They monitor inflation, interest rates, and employment levels and research issues such as energy costs and business cycles. They use sampling and modeling techniques to make economic predictions. Economists working for corporations help predict consumer demand and sales of the firm's products. They also analyze the market and advise their company on how to handle the competition. Economists working in consulting or research firms collect data; analyze historical trends; and develop models to predict growth, inflation, unemployment, or interest rates. Their analyses and forecasts are frequently published in newspapers and journal articles. Economists in the federal government collect the majority of the economic data on the United States in order to estimate the economic effects of policy changes.

Data Bank

Education and Training: Master's degree

Average Earnings: $61,000–$120,000

Earnings Growth Potential: High

Total Jobs Held: 15,000

Job Outlook: Little change

Annual Job Openings: 500

Related Jobs: Accountants and auditors; actuaries; budget analysts; cost estimators; financial analysts; financial managers; insurance underwriters; loan officers; management analysts; market and survey researchers; mathematicians; operations research analysts; personal financial advisors; purchasing managers, buyers, and purchasing agents; sociologists and political scientists; statisticians

Personality Types: Investigative-Conventional-Enterprising

Did You Know?

The Federal Reserve is the central banking system of the United States. Its Board of Governors supervises banks and controls the amount of money in circulation. They also adjust the federal funds rate, which has a direct impact on the interest rates that the rest of us pay on loans. These interest rate changes have a significant impact on the economy. Because of this important power, even a whisper of activity by the Federal Reserve Board can cause the stock market to go up or down.

Career in Focus: *Labor Economist*

Labor economists study the supply and demand for labor and how wages are determined. These economists also try to explain the reasons for unemployment and the effects of changing demographic trends, such as an aging population or increasing immigration, on the economy. This information is especially useful to the government, which is constantly reviewing and changing its labor laws and policies.

Where and When

Economists typically work in comfortable office settings and spend much of their time doing research and writing reports. Most work under the stress of deadlines. Frequent travel may be required.

For More Information

＊ National Association for Business Economics, 1233 20th St. NW, Suite 505, Washington, DC 20036. Internet: www.nabe.com

Market and Survey Researchers

At a Glance

Market and survey researchers tell businesses the best ways to sell a product based on information they gather through interviews and questionnaires. Market research analysts are concerned with the potential sales of a product or service. By gathering data on competitors and examining prices, sales, and methods of marketing and distribution, they are able to predict future sales. They then provide the information needed to make decisions on the promotion, distribution, design, and pricing. They might also develop advertising brochures and commercials, sales plans, and product promotions such as rebates and giveaways. Market research analysts use a variety of methods for obtaining the data they need. They design telephone, mail, or Internet surveys and conduct some surveys as personal interviews. They may lead focus group discussions or set up booths in public places such as shopping malls.

Career in Focus: *Survey Researcher*

Survey researchers design and conduct surveys for a variety of clients, such as corporations, government agencies, and political candidates. The surveys collect information that is used for performing research, making funding or policy decisions, or improving customer satisfaction. Survey researchers may consult with economists, statisticians, or market research analysts to design surveys. They also may have to present survey results to clients.

Where and When

Market and survey researchers generally work a standard 40-hour week, though some overtime and travel may be required. The work is often done alone and involves extensive report writing, statistical analysis, and computer use.

For More Information

* Marketing Research Association, 110 National Dr., 2nd Floor, Glastonbury, CT 06033. Internet: www.mra-net.org

* Council of American Survey Research Organizations, 170 North Country Rd., Suite 4, Port Jefferson, NY 11777. Internet: www.casro.org

Data Bank

Education and Training: Bachelor's degree

Average Earnings: $43,000–$83,000

Earnings Growth Potential: High

Total Jobs Held: 273,000

Job Outlook: Rapid increase

Annual Job Openings: 15,100

Related Jobs: Actuaries; advertising, marketing, promotions, public relations, and sales managers; cost estimators; economists; management analysts; mathematicians; operations research analysts; psychologists; public relations specialists; sociologists and political scientists; statisticians; urban and regional planners

Personality Types: Investigative-Enterprising-Conventional

Did You Know?

Market researchers have studied people's preferences for every kind of product. They've learned that dads prefer televisions over ties for Father's Day, that organic food is becoming more popular, and that (believe it or not) 60 percent of Americans are interested in traveling into outer space as a vacation. Yet despite numerous taste tests and millions of dollars in marketing research, America still hasn't given a clear indication of whether it likes Coke or Pepsi better. The answer depends on how the question is posed.

Psychologists

At a Glance

Psychologists study the way people think, feel, and act. They also work to understand, explain, and change people's behavior. They may conduct training programs, do market research, or provide counseling. Psychologists work with schools, businesses, and health-care centers to help people deal with stress and changes in their lives, such as divorce and aging. Psychologists sometimes gather information through laboratory experiments, interviews, and clinical studies. Clinical psychologists—who make up the largest specialty—work most often in counseling centers, private practices, hospitals, or clinics. They help mentally and emotionally disturbed clients adjust to life and may assist medical patients in dealing with illnesses or injuries. Others help people deal with times of personal crisis or overcome addictions. Other focused fields of interest include neuropsychology, social psychology, and developmental psychology.

Data Bank

Education and Training: Master's degree to doctoral degree

Average Earnings: $51,000–$88,000

Earnings Growth Potential: Medium

Total Jobs Held: 170,000

Job Outlook: Average increase

Annual Job Openings: 6,800

Related Jobs: Audiologists; clergy; counselors; dentists; funeral directors; human resources, training, and labor relations managers and specialists; market and survey researchers; optometrists; physicians and surgeons; radiation therapists; recreation workers; social workers; sociologists and political scientists; speech-language pathologists; teachers—special education

Personality Types: Investigative-Social-Artistic

Did You Know?

One hot avenue of research in psychology is pain management. Studies have shown that psychological factors such as mood, stress, and coping styles play important roles in increasing or decreasing levels of pain. Psychologists work with individuals who experience chronic pain to help them develop ways to manage their pain cycle. One technique, cognitive behavior therapy, involves replacing negative thoughts with more motivating ones that can lead to an increased activity level and improved functioning.

Career in Focus: *School Psychologist*

School psychologists help students in elementary and secondary schools. They work with teachers, parents, and school administrators to create safe, healthy, and supportive learning environments. They address learning and behavior problems, substance abuse, and classroom management strategies. They also assess gifted and talented students and students with learning disabilities to help determine the best way to educate them.

Where and When

Psychologists work in schools, clinics, and private offices. They often work evening or weekend hours to accommodate clients. Those employed in hospitals and health-care facilities often work in shifts.

For More Information

✳ American Psychological Association, Center for Psychology Workforce Analysis and Research and Education Directorate, 750 First St. NE, Washington, DC 20002. Internet: www.apa.org/students

✳ National Association of School Psychologists, 4340 East-West Hwy., Suite 402, Bethesda, MD 20814. Internet: www.nasponline.org

✳ Association of State and Provincial Psychology Boards, P.O. Box 241245, Montgomery, AL 36124. Internet: www.asppb.org

✳ American Board of Professional Psychology, 600 Market St., Suite 300, Chapel Hill, NC 27516. Internet: www.abpp.org

Urban and Regional Planners

At a Glance

Urban and regional planners develop programs that encourage growth in communities and regions. They make plans for the best use of land and study the area's schools, hospitals, parks, roads, and other facilities to see whether they meet the needs of the community. Planners may be involved in such issues as traffic congestion, public transportation, and the effects of growth and change on a community. They may help make plans to construct new school buildings or public housing. Some are involved in environmental issues ranging from pollution control to the location of new landfills. Planners also may be involved in legislation on environmental, social, and economic issues, such as sheltering the homeless, planning a new park, or meeting the demand for new prisons. Local governments employ the majority of urban and regional planners.

Career in Focus: *Housing Development Specialist*

Housing development specialists most often work for local governments. They are responsible for planning and developing affordable and assisted housing and revitalizing poor neighborhoods. They spend much of their time doing research and then reporting to other government departments and the legislature. They are also involved in the funding and oversight of approved projects.

Where and When

Urban and regional planners generally work a standard 40-hour week, though they may also attend evening or weekend meetings and hearings. Most work out of offices, though they travel often to inspect the regional and urban areas that concern them. They also work under the pressure of frequent deadlines and political interest groups.

For More Information

* American Planning Association, 1776 Massachusetts Ave. NW, Suite 400, Washington, DC 20036. Internet: www.planning.org

* Association of Collegiate Schools of Planning, 6311 Mallard Trace, Tallahassee, FL 32312. Internet: www.acsp.org

Data Bank

Education and Training: Master's degree

Average Earnings: $49,000–$78,000

Earnings Growth Potential: Low

Total Jobs Held: 38,000

Job Outlook: Above-average increase

Annual Job Openings: 1,500

Related Jobs: Architects, except landscape and naval; civil engineers; environmental engineers; geographers; landscape architects; market and survey researchers; property, real estate, and community association managers; surveyors, cartographers, photogrammetrists, and surveying and mapping technicians

Personality Types: Investigative-Enterprising-Artistic

Did You Know?

Some cities are planned to grow a certain way. Known as "planned communities" or "new towns," these cities are plotted in detail before the first house is built. Washington and Savannah are, in fact, planned communities, as is the fairly successful city of Reston, Virginia. In 1994, the Disney Corporation built a planned community in Florida—called Celebration—that's made to look like an old-fashioned town and to be just as walkable.

Sociologists and Political Scientists

At a Glance

Sociologists and political scientists study all aspects of human society and political systems—from social behavior and the origin of social groups to the origin, development, and operation of political systems. Their research provides insights into different ways individuals, groups, and governments make decisions, exercise power, and respond to change. Through their studies and analyses, sociologists and political scientists suggest solutions to social, business, personal, and governmental problems. In fact, many work as public policy analysts for government or private organizations.

Data Bank

Education and Training: Master's degree

Average Earnings: $61,000–$111,000

Earnings Growth Potential: High

Total Jobs Held: 9,000

Job Outlook: Rapid increase

Annual Job Openings: 500

Related Jobs: Archivists, curators, and museum technicians; counselors; economists; judges, magistrates, and other judicial workers; lawyers; market and survey researchers; news analysts, reporters, and correspondents; paralegals and legal assistants; psychologists; social scientists, other; social workers; statisticians; teachers—kindergarten, elementary, middle, and secondary; teachers—postsecondary; urban and regional planners

Personality Types: Investigative-Artistic-Social

Did You Know?

Even though social network Web sites are a new phenomenon, sociologists have already begun to research the kinds of groups and interactions that occur on the Web. For example, they study how site users share information or maintain their privacy, how they choose to project their personalities, how they feel they benefit from the contacts they make, and how they differ from people who don't use these sites.

Career in Focus: *Political Scientist*

Political scientists conduct research on a wide range of subjects, such as relations between the United States and other countries, the institutions and political life of nations, the politics of small towns or major metropolises, and the decisions of the U.S. Supreme Court. Studying and evaluating topics such as public opinion, political decision making, ideology, and public policy, they analyze the structure and operation of governments as well as various other entities.

Where and When

Most sociologists and political scientists have regular hours. Generally working behind a desk, either alone or in collaboration with other social scientists, they read and write research articles or reports. Many experience the pressures of writing and publishing, as well as those associated with deadlines and tight schedules. Some sociologists may be required to attend meetings. Political scientists on foreign assignment must adjust to unfamiliar cultures, climates, and languages.

For More Information

* American Sociological Association, 1430 K St. NW, Suite 600, Washington, DC 20005. Internet: www.asanet.org

* American Political Science Association, 1527 New Hampshire Ave. NW, Washington, DC 20036. Internet: www.apsanet.org

* National Association of Schools of Public Affairs and Administration, 1029 Vermont Ave. NW, Suite 1100, Washington, DC 20005. Internet: www.naspaa.org

Social Scientists, Other

At a Glance

Social scientists study all aspects of society—from past events to human behavior and group relationships. Their research helps us understand different ways individuals and groups make decisions and respond to change as well as suggest solutions to social, business, personal, governmental, and environmental problems. Anthropologists study the origin, development, and behavior of humans in order to analyze the customs, values, and social patterns of different cultures. Geographers study how physical geography affects politics and culture. Historians research, analyze, and interpret the past. Political scientists study the development and operation of political systems and public policy. Sociologists study society and social behavior by examining groups and their social, religious, political, and business organizations. All of these individuals are heavily involved in research.

Career in Focus: *Archaeologist*

Archaeologists recover evidence about past human cultures, such as the ruins of buildings, tools, pottery, and other objects. They study these artifacts to determine the history, customs, and living habits of earlier civilizations. Unlike Indiana Jones, most archaeologists spend most of their time at a dig site or in the library doing research and writing. Seldom, if ever, do they get to dodge bullets or boulders, and pits of poisonous snakes are uncommon.

Where and When

Most social scientists have regular work schedules and spend the majority of their time behind a desk. Sometimes they are part of a research team. Travel—including extensive international visits—is common. Some social scientists do fieldwork under rugged conditions involving strenuous physical exercise.

For More Information

* American Anthropological Association, 2200 Wilson Blvd., Suite 600, Arlington, VA 22201. Internet: www.aaanet.org
* Archaeological Institute of America, 656 Beacon St., 6th Floor, Boston, MA 02215. Internet: www.archaeological.org
* Society for American Archaeology, 900 2nd St. NE, Suite 12, Washington, DC 20002. Internet: www.saa.org
* Association of American Geographers, 1710 16th St. NW, Washington, DC 20009. Internet: www.aag.org
* American Historical Association, 400 A St. SE, Washington, DC 20003. Internet: www.historians.org

Data Bank

Education and Training: Master's degree

Average Earnings: $39,000–$75,000

Earnings Growth Potential: High

Total Jobs Held: 11,000

Job Outlook: Rapid increase

Annual Job Openings: 800

Related Jobs: Archivists, curators, and museum technicians; atmospheric scientists; computer network, systems, and database administrators; computer scientists; conservation scientists and foresters; counselors; economists; environmental scientists and specialists; geoscientists and hydrologists; market and survey researchers; psychologists; social workers; statisticians; surveyors, cartographers, photogrammetrists, and surveying and mapping technicians; teachers—kindergarten, elementary, middle, and secondary; teachers—postsecondary; urban and regional planners

Personality Types: Investigative-Artistic

Did You Know?

The Valley of the Kings in Egypt has been the site of many groundbreaking archaeological discoveries. Known for its tomb of King Tutankhamen (discovered in 1922), it was believed to have been fully explored. That is, until Egyptologist Kent Weeks began clearing out one of the outer tombs, which had been used as a dumping ground. There he found long corridors extending off into more than 120 rooms containing hundreds of artifacts. The discovery was made in 1995 and to this day archaeologists are still cataloguing everything they've found. There are always mysteries left to be uncovered.

Science Technicians

At a Glance

Science technicians use science and math to solve problems in research and development. They also invent and help improve products. They set up, operate, and maintain lab equipment; monitor experiments; and record results. Those working in production may be involved in ensuring quality by testing products for proper proportion of ingredients, for purity, or for strength and durability. Most technicians interpret data and devise solutions to problems under the direction of scientists. These technicians may specialize in agriculture, biology, chemistry, or other sciences, though their work tends to be more practical in nature than that of more traditional scientists.

Data Bank

Education and Training: Associate degree to bachelor's degree

Average Earnings: $32,000–$53,000

Earnings Growth Potential: Medium

Total Jobs Held: 271,000

Job Outlook: Average increase

Annual Job Openings: 12,400

Related Jobs: Broadcast and sound engineering technicians and radio operators; clinical laboratory technologists and technicians; diagnostic medical sonographers; drafters; engineering technicians; radiologic technologists and technicians

Personality Types: Realistic-Investigative-Conventional

Did You Know?

In the last few decades, one of the most useful innovations for forensic scientists and technicians has been DNA testing. Invented in 1985, DNA tests can be used to match potential suspects to blood, hair, saliva, or semen samples. Knowing that investigators will rely on this evidence, some criminals have planted fake DNA evidence (such as another person's blood or hair) at a crime scene to steer investigators and technicians the wrong way.

Career in Focus: *Forensic Science Technician*

Forensic science technicians investigate crimes by collecting and analyzing physical evidence. Often, they specialize in areas such as DNA analysis or firearm examination. They perform tests on weapons or on substances such as fiber, glass, hair, tissue, and body fluids to determine their significance to the investigation. Forensic science technicians also prepare reports to document their findings, and they may provide information and expert opinion to investigators. When criminal cases come to trial, forensic science technicians often give testimony as expert witnesses to their findings.

Where and When

Science technicians can work in a wide variety of settings, though most work in a laboratory during regular hours. Some work irregular hours in order to monitor experiments, and some, such as agricultural technicians, do much of their work outdoors. Science technicians may be exposed to hazards from equipment, chemicals, or other toxic materials, though proper safety precautions all but eliminate these risks.

For More Information

* Bio-Link, 1855 Folsom St., Suite 643, San Francisco, CA 94103. Internet: www.bio-link.org

* American Chemical Society, Education Division, Career Publications, 1155 16th St. NW, Washington, DC 20036. Internet: www.acs.org

* American Academy of Forensic Sciences, 410 N. 21st St., Colorado Springs, CO 80904. Internet: www.aafs.org

* Society of American Foresters, 5400 Grosvenor Ln., Bethesda, MD 20814. Internet: www.safnet.org

Counselors

At a Glance

Counselors help people with their problems, and the work they do depends on the people they serve. School counselors help students with personal, social, and behavioral problems. They also help students evaluate their abilities, interests, and talents in order to develop academic and career goals. School counselors may provide special services, including alcohol and drug prevention programs and conflict resolution classes. High school counselors specifically advise students regarding college admissions and financial aid. Career planning and placement counselors at colleges and universities help students decide on careers and find jobs. Rehabilitation counselors help people deal with the personal, social, and vocational effects of disabilities and addictions. Employment or vocational counselors help people decide what kinds of jobs they want and then help them find work. Mental health counselors work with individuals, families, and groups to treat mental and emotional disorders.

Career in Focus: *Marriage and Family Therapist*

Marriage and family therapists help individuals, families, or couples resolve emotional conflicts. They work to change people's perceptions and behaviors, enhance communication and understanding among family members, and help prevent family and individual problems. Marriage and family therapists also do research and teach college courses.

Where and When

Counselors tend to work standard hours, and school counselors often keep the same schedule as teachers (including the potential for summers off). Most work in office settings, though many therapists work evenings in order to counsel working clients. Dealing daily with the problems of others requires a lot of physical and emotional energy.

For More Information

* American Counseling Association, 5999 Stevenson Ave., Alexandria, VA 22304. Internet: www.counseling.org

* American School Counselors Association, 1101 King St., Suite 625, Alexandria, VA 22314. Internet: www.schoolcounselor.org

* American Mental Health Counselors Association, 801 N. Fairfax St., Suite 304, Alexandria, VA 22314. Internet: www.amhca.org

* American Association for Marriage and Family Therapy, 112 S. Alfred St., Alexandria, VA 22314. Internet: www.aamft.org

---

Data Bank

Education and Training: Bachelor's degree to master's degree

Average Earnings: $34,000–$56,000

Earnings Growth Potential: Medium

Total Jobs Held: 665,000

Job Outlook: Above-average increase

Annual Job Openings: 25,100

Related Jobs: Human resources, training, and labor relations managers and specialists; occupational therapists; physicians and surgeons; psychologists; registered nurses; social and human service assistants; social workers; teachers—kindergarten, elementary, middle, and secondary; teachers—special education

Personality Types: Social-Investigative-Artistic

Did You Know?

Society has always had to deal with addictions. Whether it's alcoholism or nicotine, prescription drugs or gambling, statistics show that millions of people need help. And counselors are often the ones to provide it. Substance abuse counselors are trained to deal with a wide variety of issues, from drug addictions to eating disorders. Recently they have been given a new addiction to deal with: video games. While perhaps not as dangerous as some of the others, it is still a growing concern, and counselors are being educated to deal with this trend.

Health Educators

At a Glance

Health educators work to encourage healthy lifestyles and wellness by educating individuals and communities about behaviors that can prevent diseases, injuries, and other health problems. They may organize an event, such as a lecture, class, demonstration, or health screening, or they may develop educational material, such as a video, pamphlet, or brochure. Often, these tasks require working with other people in a team or on a committee. Although programming is a large part of their job, health educators also serve as a resource on health topics. This may include locating services, reference material, and other resources and referring individuals or groups to organizations or medical professionals.

Data Bank

Education and Training: Bachelor's degree

Average Earnings: $33,000–$61,000

Earnings Growth Potential: High

Total Jobs Held: 66,000

Job Outlook: Above-average increase

Annual Job Openings: 2,600

Related Jobs: Counselors; psychologists; registered nurses; social and human service assistants; social workers; teachers—kindergarten, elementary, middle, and secondary

Personality Types: Social-Enterprising

Did You Know?

Doctors sometimes are not effective in explaining things to patients. That's why some hospitals employ health educators to work one-on-one with patients and their families, explaining the patients' diagnosis and how that may change or affect their lifestyle. They may also direct patients to outside resources, such as support groups, home health agencies, or social services. Often, health educators work closely with physicians, nurses, and other staff to create educational programs or materials, such as brochures, Web sites, and classes.

Career in Focus: *Community Health Educator*

Some health educators work for nonprofits, providing the public with information related to health and educating people about resources available in the community. While some organizations target a particular audience, others educate the community regarding one disease or health issue. Therefore, health educators may be limited in either the topics they cover, the populations they serve, or both. Work in this setting may include creating print-based material for distribution to the community, often in conjunction with organizing lectures, health screenings, and activities related to increasing health awareness.

Where and When

In public health, nonprofit organizations, corporations and businesses, colleges and universities, and medical care settings, health educators primarily work in offices. However, they may spend a lot of time away from the office implementing and attending programs, meeting with community organizers, speaking with patients, or teaching classes. Health educators in schools spend the majority of their day in classrooms. Health educators generally work 40-hour weeks. When programs, events, or meetings are scheduled, however, they may need to work evenings or weekends.

For More Information

* American Association for Health Education, 1900 Association Dr., Reston, VA 20191-1598. Internet: www.aahperd.org/aahe

* Society for Public Health Education, 10 G St. NE, Suite 605, Washington, DC 20002-4242. Internet: www.sophe.org

* The National Commission for Health Education Credentialing, Inc., 1541 Alta Dr., Suite 303, Whitehall, PA 18052-5642. Internet: www.nchec.org

Probation Officers and Correctional Treatment Specialists

At a Glance

Many people who are convicted of crimes are placed on probation instead of being sent to jail. Probation officers supervise these people, making sure they stay out of trouble. Probation and parole agencies also seek help from community organizations, such as churches, neighborhood groups, and local residents, to monitor the behavior of offenders. Probation officers may arrange for offenders to get substance abuse help or job training. They usually work with either adults or juveniles. Parole officers and pretrial services officers perform many of the same duties as probation officers. The difference is that parole officers supervise offenders who have been released from prison, whereas probation officers work with those who are sentenced to probation instead of prison. Correctional treatment specialists work in jails, prisons, or parole or probation agencies. In jails and prisons, they evaluate the progress of inmates. In addition, they plan education and training programs to improve offenders' job skills and provide them with coping skills and counseling.

Career in Focus: *Prisoner-Classification Interviewer*

Some correctional specialists have the job of classifying incoming prisoners. These interviewers obtain social and criminal histories to help assign prisoners to appropriate work and other activities. They gather data, such as work history; school, criminal, and military records; family background; habits; and religious beliefs. They also analyze the prisoner's social attitudes, mental capacity, character, and physical capabilities in order to prepare an admission summary.

Where and When

Some of the criminal offenders these individuals work with may be dangerous. In addition, probation officers and correctional treatment specialists may be assigned to work in high-crime areas or institutions where there is a risk of violence. Extensive travel may be necessary. Many of these workers may be required to carry a firearm for protection.

For More Information

❋ American Probation and Parole Association, P.O. Box 11910, Lexington, KY 40578. Internet: www.appa-net.org

Data Bank

Education and Training: Bachelor's degree

Average Earnings: $36,000–$62,000

Earnings Growth Potential: Low

Total Jobs Held: 103,000

Job Outlook: Above-average increase

Annual Job Openings: 4,200

Related Jobs: Correctional officers; counselors; firefighters; police and detectives; social and human service assistants; social workers

Personality Types: Social-Enterprising-Conventional

Did You Know?

What happens when a man commits a crime in Ohio but is captured in Florida? Or a woman is convicted in Utah but will serve her sentence in Illinois? Some prisoners are simply handcuffed and put on a regular airplane with a guard, but prisoners who are too dangerous for commercial flights have their own airline. The U.S. Marshals Service operates a fleet of planes they use to transport prisoners. The Justice Prisoner and Alien Transportation System (JPATS) operates regular flights to 40 cities around the country. Security, we assume, is pretty tight.

Social and Human Service Assistants

At a Glance

This description encompasses a wide range of job titles, from human service worker to case management aide to community outreach worker. Regardless of title, all social and human service assistants are in the business of helping people. They might work in a food bank, train mentally handicapped adults to do a job, or supervise groups of teenagers in a day program. They evaluate clients' needs, help them to get benefits, keep records, and file reports with social service agencies. They also arrange for transportation and escorts and provide emotional support. In group homes and government-supported housing programs, they assist adults who need supervision with personal hygiene and daily living skills. The amount of responsibility and supervision they are given varies a great deal.

Data Bank

Education and Training: Moderate-term on-the-job training

Average Earnings: $22,000–$36,000

Earnings Growth Potential: Low

Total Jobs Held: 352,000

Job Outlook: Rapid increase

Annual Job Openings: 15,400

Related Jobs: Child care workers; correctional officers; counselors; eligibility interviewers, government programs; health educators; home health aides and personal and home care aides; occupational therapist assistants and aides; probation officers and correctional treatment specialists; psychologists; recreational therapists; social workers

Personality Types: Conventional-Social-Enterprising

Did You Know?

The boomers are getting old. This simple fact is important for human service assistants who are interested in working with the elderly. Not only are Americans living longer, but the post–World War II generation (known collectively as the baby boomers) is nearing retirement. That means they are also nearing the age when many of the services provided by human service assistants, especially those related to health care, become necessary. This will only increase the demand for individuals willing to work in group homes or provide in-home support.

Career in Focus: *Gerontology Aide*

Gerontology aides assist the elderly with their daily living arrangements. This can include helping them with their medication, assisting them in errands, or simply helping them maintain a high quality of life. Many work in nursing care centers, retirement communities, or hospitals. Others provide assistance to the elderly as a home health aide. America's increasing elderly population guarantees this will be a growing industry.

Where and When

Working conditions for these individuals vary. Some work in offices, clinics, or hospitals while others work in group homes, shelters, and day programs. Some clients can be dangerous, though agencies do everything they can to ensure workers' safety. The work can be both satisfying and emotionally draining. Turnover is high due to stress and relatively low pay.

For More Information

* Council for Standards in Human Services Education, 1935 S. Plum Grove Rd., PMB 297, Palatine, IL 60067. Internet: www.cshse.org

* National Organization for Human Services, 5341 Old Highway 5, Suite 206, #214, Woodstock, GA 30188. Internet: www.nationalhumanservices.org

Social Workers

At a Glance

Social workers help people find solutions to their problems and improve their lives. They might help a client find housing, a job, or health care. They deal with issues like child abuse, poverty, alcohol or drug abuse, and criminal behavior. They may work in hospitals, group homes, government agencies, or schools. Child, family, and school social workers provide services to help children function socially and psychologically and to improve family well-being. Some social workers assist single parents, arrange adoptions, or help find foster homes for children. In schools, they address such problems as teenage pregnancy, misbehavior, and truancy. Mental health and substance abuse social workers help individuals with mental illness or drug abuse problems. Medical and public health social workers provide people with the support needed to cope with chronic, acute, or terminal illnesses, such as Alzheimer's disease, cancer, or AIDS.

Career in Focus: *Social Work Planner and Policymaker*

Social work planners and policymakers develop the programs needed to address such issues as child abuse, homelessness, substance abuse, and poverty. These workers research and analyze policies and programs. They identify social problems and suggest solutions. They may help raise funds or write grants to support these programs. They are usually more involved in the legal and financial aspect of social services and thus spend less time working directly with people.

Where and When

Social workers usually work a standard 40-hour week, mostly in an office environment. They sometimes work evenings or weekends to meet with clients or handle emergencies. The work can be both internally gratifying and emotionally draining.

For More Information

* National Association of Social Workers, 750 First St. NE, Suite 700, Washington, DC 20002-4241. Internet: www.socialworkers.org

* Center for Clinical Social Work, 27 Congress St., Suite 501, Salem, MA 01970. Internet: www.centercsw.org

* Council on Social Work Education, 1725 Duke St., Suite 500, Alexandria, VA 22314-3457. Internet: www.cswe.org

* Association of Social Work Boards, 400 South Ridge Pkwy., Suite B, Culpeper, VA 22701. Internet: www.aswb.org

Data Bank

Education and Training: Bachelor's degree to master's degree

Average Earnings: $33,000–$54,000

Earnings Growth Potential: Low

Total Jobs Held: 642,000

Job Outlook: Above-average increase

Annual Job Openings: 26,500

Related Jobs: Clergy; counselors; health educators; probation officers and correctional treatment specialists; psychologists; social and human service assistants

Personality Types: Social-Investigative

Did You Know?

With turnover rates for social workers ranging anywhere from 20 percent to 100 percent depending on the state, there is no question that burnout is a huge problem for workers in this field. Low pay, huge caseloads, little room for advancement, and a lack of support all contribute to increased job stress. Yet agencies are starting to realize the toll this is taking on both their employees and their clients, and many have started initiatives to improve job satisfaction.

Court Reporters

At a Glance

These workers create written transcripts of speeches, conversations, legal proceedings, meetings, and other events where words are needed as records or legal proof. They make notes using shorthand or a stenotype machine. They also use audio recordings and computer voice translation software. They often help judges and attorneys access information, and they sometimes make suggestions regarding courtroom administration and procedure. Increasingly, court reporters are providing closed-captioning and real-time translating services to the deaf and hard-of-hearing community. Sometimes they type as fast as 200 words per minute, and because they are the only ones recording what is being said, they must be accurate.

Data Bank

Education and Training: Vocational/technical training

Average Earnings: $35,000–$67,000

Earnings Growth Potential: High

Total Jobs Held: 22,000

Job Outlook: Above-average increase

Annual Job Openings: 700

Related Jobs: Data entry and information processing workers; human resources assistants, except payroll and timekeeping; interpreters and translators; medical transcriptionists; paralegals and legal assistants; receptionists and information clerks; secretaries and administrative assistants

Personality Types: Conventional-Enterprising

Did You Know?

Carpal tunnel syndrome is a painful condition that occurs when tendons in the wrist become inflamed. The syndrome is common among people who do lots of work using computer keyboards. In its worst form, it can be crippling. Health professionals recommend that individuals who are required to type for long periods of time take frequent breaks.

Career in Focus: *Stenocaptioner*

Court reporters who specialize in captioning (providing subtitles for) live television programming for people with hearing loss are commonly known as stenocaptioners. They work for television networks or cable stations captioning news, emergency broadcasts, sporting events, and other programming. In an emergency, such as a tornado or a hurricane, people's safety may depend on the accuracy of information provided in the form of captioning.

Where and When

Court reporters work in comfortable settings such as offices, courtrooms, and conventions. Many of them work from home as freelancers. As with any job that requires extensive keyboarding, court reporters are prone to backaches and eyestrain and are especially susceptible to repetitive stress injuries such as carpal tunnel syndrome.

For More Information

* American Association of Electronic Reporters and Transcribers, 2900 Fairhope Rd., Wilmington, DE 19810. Internet: www.aaert.org

* National Court Reporters Association, 8224 Old Courthouse Rd., Vienna, VA 22182. Internet: www.ncraonline.org

* National Verbatim Reporters Association, 629 N. Main St., Hattiesburg, MS 39401. Internet: www.nvra.org

* United States Court Reporters Association, 4725 N. Western Ave., Suite 240, Chicago, IL 60625-2012. Internet: www.uscra.org

Judges, Magistrates, and Other Judicial Workers

At a Glance

Judges, magistrates, and other judicial workers oversee trials and make sure that everyone follows the court rules. They preside over all types of cases, from traffic tickets to murder trials. All judicial workers must ensure that trials and hearings are conducted fairly and that the court protects the legal rights of all parties involved. Judges often hold pretrial hearings for cases where they determine whether there is enough evidence for a trial. In court cases without a jury, the judge decides the verdicts, imposes sentences, and awards compensation. All judges work for the government—either local, state, or federal. Traffic violations, misdemeanors, and small-claims cases constitute the bulk of the work of state court judges. Nearly all judges have law degrees.

Career in Focus: *Justice of the Peace*

In some states, the Justice of the Peace is a judge in a court with limited jurisdiction. They typically preside over cases involving misdemeanors, traffic violations, or petty crimes. They are often involved in small claims court proceedings. These proceedings tend to go much quicker than in other courts. A Justice of the Peace can also confer a civil union. Justices of the Peace normally don't require a law degree to be appointed.

Where and When

Judges, magistrates, and other judicial workers perform most of their duties in offices, law libraries, and courtrooms. Judges typically work a 40-hour week, though some overtime is required. Many judges work part time in order to make room for other careers.

For More Information

* National Center for State Courts, 300 Newport Ave., Williamsburg, VA 23185-4147. Internet: www.ncsc.org

* American Arbitration Association, 1633 Broadway, Floor 10, New York, NY 10019. Internet: www.adr.org

* Administrative Office of the United States Courts, One Columbus Circle NE, Washington, DC 20544. Internet: www.uscourts.gov

Data Bank

Education and Training: Bachelor's or higher degree plus related work experience

Average Earnings: $54,000–$124,000

Earnings Growth Potential: Very high

Total Jobs Held: 51,000

Job Outlook: Little change

Annual Job Openings: 1,200

Related Jobs: Counselors; law clerks; lawyers; paralegals and legal assistants; private detectives and investigators; title examiners, abstractors, and searchers

Personality Types: Enterprising-Social

Did You Know?

The United States Supreme Court is the highest court in the nation. It has ultimate authority to rule over cases that have been appealed to it. Most importantly, it is responsible for interpreting the U.S. Constitution. These decisions can have a huge impact on the rest of us. There are only nine Supreme Court justices, and each of them has to be appointed by the president. The only way justices can lose their job is to resign or be impeached. Not many jobs have that level of security.

Lawyers

At a Glance

Lawyers advise people about the law and their rights. They represent people in court, presenting evidence that supports a client's position, asking questions, and arguing their case. Lawyers must do research to support their cases. They must also have good reading, writing, and speaking skills. There are a number of areas that lawyers may specialize in. Trial lawyers must be able to think quickly and strategically and speak with authority. Most lawyers are in private practice, concentrating on criminal or civil law. In criminal law, lawyers represent individuals who have been charged with crimes. Attorneys dealing with civil law assist clients with personal lawsuits, wills, trusts, contracts, mortgages, titles, and leases. Other lawyers may specialize in bankruptcy, probate, or international law.

Data Bank

Education and Training: First professional degree

Average Earnings: $76,000–$166,400+

Earnings Growth Potential: High

Total Jobs Held: 759,000

Job Outlook: Average increase

Annual Job Openings: 24,000

Related Jobs: Judges, magistrates, and other judicial workers; law clerks; paralegals and legal assistants; title examiners, abstractors, and searchers

Personality Types: Enterprising-Investigative

Did You Know?

Though the image we get of lawyers from television and movies suggests otherwise, the vast majority of lawsuits never go before a jury. Some surveys suggest that as few as two percent of lawsuits make it to trial, meaning the rest are settled out of court. Individuals interested in becoming lawyers should be aware that the majority of their time would be spent behind a desk and not in front of a jury.

Career in Focus: *Environmental Lawyer*

Lawyers specializing in environmental law may represent interest groups, waste disposal companies, or construction firms in their dealings with the U.S. Environmental Protection Agency (EPA) and other federal and state agencies. These lawyers help clients prepare and file for licenses and applications for approval. Those working for the government help ensure that companies keep up with environmental standards.

Where and When

Lawyers spend most of their time in offices, libraries, and courtrooms. They may have to travel to attend meetings, gather evidence, appear before courts, or meet with clients. They normally have structured work schedules, though they often work 50 hours or more per week.

For More Information

❋ American Bar Association, 321 N. Clark St., Chicago, IL 60654. Internet: www.abanet.org

❋ National Association for Law Placement, 1025 Connecticut Ave. NW, Suite 1110, Washington, DC 20036. Internet: www.nalp.org

❋ Law School Admission Council, 662 Penn St., Newtown, PA 18940. Internet: www.lsac.org

Paralegals and Legal Assistants

At a Glance

Paralegals and legal assistants help lawyers prepare their cases. They do research and write reports that lawyers use to present their arguments in court. Paralegals may help prepare the legal arguments and draft pleadings and motions to be filed with the court. They also obtain affidavits and assist attorneys during trials. Paralegals organize and track files of all important case documents. Some paralegals help lawyers draft contracts, mortgages, separation agreements, and wills. They also may assist in preparing tax returns and planning estates. Paralegals may meet with clients, but they do not argue cases in court, give legal advice, or set fees. Some paralegals have a wide variety of tasks, while others specialize in one area of the law, such as tax law or publishing law.

Career in Focus: *Community Legal-Services Provider*

Community legal-service programs are designed to provide legal assistance to those who could not otherwise afford it. Often federally funded, these programs employ lawyers and paralegals to help the poor, the elderly, minorities, and middle-income families. They are often involved in consultation and are dedicated to preserving the rights of all individuals, especially those who can't pay normal attorney fees.

Where and When

Like lawyers, paralegals and legal assistants spend the majority of their time in offices or libraries. Travel is occasionally required to do research. They are increasingly dependent upon computers and other technology to do their work. Most work a standard 40-hour week.

For More Information

* Standing Committee on Paralegals, American Bar Association, 321 N. Clark St., Chicago, IL 60654. Internet: www.abanet.org/legalservices/paralegals

* National Association of Legal Assistants, Inc., 1516 S. Boston St., Suite 200, Tulsa, OK 74119. Internet: www.nala.org

* National Federation of Paralegal Associations, P.O. Box 2016, Edmonds, WA 98020. Internet: www.paralegals.org

* American Association for Paralegal Education, 19 Mantua Rd., Mt. Royal, NJ 08061. Internet: www.aafpe.org

* American Alliance of Paralegals, Inc., Suite 134-146, 4001 Kennett Pike, Wilmington, DE 19807. Internet: http://aapipara.org

---

Data Bank

Education and Training: Associate degree

Average Earnings: $37,000–$61,000

Earnings Growth Potential: Low

Total Jobs Held: 264,000

Job Outlook: Rapid increase

Annual Job Openings: 10,400

Related Jobs: Claims adjusters, examiners, and investigators; law clerks; occupational health and safety specialists; occupational health and safety technicians; title examiners, abstractors, and searchers

Personality Types: Conventional-Investigative-Enterprising

Did You Know?

The Latin phrase *pro bono* is actually short for *pro bono publico*, meaning "for the public good." Of course a more common translation would be "without charging a fee." The American Bar Association recommends that all lawyers offer at least 50 hours of pro bono service per year, and paralegals are often involved in this work.

Archivists, Curators, and Museum Technicians

At a Glance

Archivists, curators, and museum technicians acquire and care for collections of books, records, art, and other items for libraries and museums. They also may work for governments, zoos, and universities. They catalogue, analyze, exhibit, and maintain valuable objects and collections for the benefit of researchers and the public. The items might include coins, stamps, plants, paintings, sculptures, or even animals. They plan exhibits, educational programs, and tours. Although some duties of archivists and curators are similar, the types of items they deal with differ: Curators usually handle objects such as sculptures, artifacts, and paintings, while archivists handle mainly records and documents. Today, an increasing part of a curator's duties involves fundraising and promotion.

Data Bank

Education and Training: Bachelor's degree to master's degree

Average Earnings: $33,000–$58,000

Earnings Growth Potential: Medium

Total Jobs Held: 29,000

Job Outlook: Rapid increase

Annual Job Openings: 1,500

Related Jobs: Artists and related workers; librarians; social scientists, other

Personality Types: Conventional-Investigative-Realistic

Did You Know?

The national archives of the United States are held in the Smithsonian Institution in Washington, DC. The Smithsonian archives contain an estimated 7,000,000 photographs and about 50,000 cubic feet of paper documents. Add to this the Smithsonian libraries, which house more than 1.5 million books, and you have a lot of materials for the museum's archivists and curators to take care of.

Career in Focus: *Conservator*

Conservators manage and preserve artifacts and works of art that require substantial historical, scientific, and archaeological research. They use X-rays, chemical testing, microscopes, and other laboratory equipment to examine objects and determine their need for restoration and the appropriate method for preserving them. Conservators document their findings and treat items to preserve them or restore them. Conservators usually specialize in a particular group of objects such as books or paintings.

Where and When

Working conditions for these individuals vary. Many spend their time working with the public, while others spend most of their time doing research or taking care of the collection. Curators who work for large libraries and museums may have to travel extensively to evaluate potential additions to the collection or organize exhibitions.

For More Information

* Society of American Archivists, 17 N. State St., Suite 1425, Chicago, IL 60602-3315. Internet: www.archivists.org

* American Association of Museums, 1575 Eye St. NW, Suite 400, Washington, DC 20005. Internet: www.aam-us.org

* American Institute for Conservation of Historic and Artistic Works, 1156 15th St. NW, Suite 320, Washington, DC 20005-1714. Internet: www.conservation-us.org

* Academy of Certified Archivists, 1450 Western Ave., Suite 101, Albany, NY 12203. Internet: www.certifiedarchivists.org

Instructional Coordinators

At a Glance

Instructional coordinators help improve the quality of education in our classrooms. They evaluate how well a school or training program's curriculum meets students' needs. Based on their research and observations, they recommend instruction and curriculum improvements. They develop teaching materials, select textbooks, and train teachers. They also help bring new technology into the classroom. Instructional coordinators often specialize in a specific subject, such as language arts, math, or gifted and talented programs. Most work for school districts or independent consulting firms. Many instructional coordinators are former teachers and school administrators.

Career in Focus:
Curriculum Director

Many educators are given the opportunity to choose their own books and resources. However, the constant pressure to meet standards often prompts a need for a standard curriculum to be used. The curriculum director or curriculum coordinator is responsible for selecting the textbooks, equipment, and instructional supplies for a school or even an entire district. The director or coordinator sets the guidelines for teachers to follow and helps them implement any changes in their classroom.

Where and When

Instructional coordinators usually work year round in offices or classrooms. Some may spend a majority of their time traveling between schools. Though the job of improving education can be gratifying, the task of meeting standards can be stressful. It is not uncommon for people in these jobs to work long hours.

For More Information

Information on requirements and job opportunities for instructional coordinators is available from local school systems and state departments of education.

Data Bank

Education and Training: Master's degree

Average Earnings: $44,000–$76,000

Earnings Growth Potential: High

Total Jobs Held: 134,000

Job Outlook: Rapid increase

Annual Job Openings: 6,100

Related Jobs: Counselors; education administrators; human resources, training, and labor relations managers and specialists; teachers—kindergarten, elementary, middle, and secondary; teachers—postsecondary; teachers—preschool, except special education; teachers—special education

Personality Types: Social-Investigative-Artistic

Did You Know?

The No Child Left Behind Act of 2001 placed an increased emphasis on accountability, asking schools to focus on improving educational quality and student performance. This explains, in part, the increased need for instructional coordinators, especially those who specialize in reading, math, and science. In addition, the constant innovations in technology—especially with regard to computers and the Internet—suggest that more instructional coordinators will be needed to show teachers how to use that technology in their classrooms.

Librarians

At a Glance

Librarians help people find information. To do so, they must have knowledge of a wide variety of scholarly and public information sources. They follow trends related to publishing, computers, and the media in order to oversee the selection and organization of library materials. Librarians manage staff and develop and direct programs for the public, such as storytelling for children and book discussions for adults. They also conduct classes, publicize services, provide reference help, write grants, and oversee other administrative matters. Some manage other workers, prepare budgets, and order materials for their libraries. In large libraries, librarians often specialize in a single area, such as acquisitions, cataloguing, bibliography, reference, or administration.

Data Bank

Education and Training: Master's degree

Average Earnings: $43,000–$67,000

Earnings Growth Potential: Medium

Total Jobs Held: 160,000

Job Outlook: Average increase

Annual Job Openings: 5,400

Related Jobs: Archivists, curators, and museum technicians; computer scientists; computer systems analysts; teachers—kindergarten, elementary, middle, secondary; teachers—postsecondary

Personality Types: Conventional-Social-Enterprising

Did You Know?

The Royal Library of Alexandria was one of the oldest and largest libraries in history. Founded in Egypt around 300 B.C., it was believed to hold anywhere from 40,000 to 700,000 books. Housed in several buildings, it was primarily a place of scholarly research and was visited by the likes of Euclid and Archimedes. The library fell victim to several fires and was almost completely destroyed by 400 A.D.

Career in Focus: *School Librarian*

In school library media centers, librarians—often called school media specialists—help teachers develop lessons, acquire materials for classroom instruction, and sometimes team-teach. They are involved in coordinating class research projects and often develop school-wide literacy programs. Because today's students are more comfortable with computers and the Internet, school librarians must be especially aware of changes in technology.

Where and When

Librarians spend most of their time at desks or in front of computers. Some may have to lift or carry heavy stacks of books. Some public and college librarians work weekends and evenings. As with all professions that involve extensive computer use, strain on the back, wrist, and eyes can be a hazard.

For More Information

* American Library Association, Office for Human Resource Development and Recruitment, 50 E. Huron St., Chicago, IL 60611. Internet: www.ala.org/ala/educationcareers/index.cfm

* Special Libraries Association, 331 S. Patrick St., Alexandria, VA 22314-3501. Internet: www.sla.org

* American Association of Law Libraries, 105 W. Adams St., Suite 3300, Chicago, IL 60603. Internet: www.aallnet.org

* Medical Library Association, 65 E. Wacker Place, Suite 1900, Chicago, IL 60601-7246. Internet: www.mlanet.org

* Human Resources Office, Library of Congress, 101 Independence Ave. SE, Washington, DC 20540-2231. Internet: www.loc.gov/hr

Library Technicians and Library Assistants

At a Glance

Library technicians and assistants help librarians acquire, prepare, and organize materials and assist users in locating the appropriate resources. These workers usually work under the supervision of a librarian, although they sometimes work independently. In small libraries, they handle a range of duties, while those in large libraries usually specialize. In some libraries, library technicians may have more responsibilities than library assistants. Technicians may be responsible for administering library programs, working with librarians to acquire new materials, and overseeing lower-level staff. Assistants may be assigned more clerical duties, like shelving books, checking in returned material, and assisting patrons with basic questions and requests.

Career in Focus:
Bookmobile Technician

To extend library services to more patrons, many libraries operate bookmobiles, often run by library technicians. The technicians take trucks stocked with books to designated sites on a regular schedule, frequently stopping at shopping centers, apartment complexes, schools, and nursing homes. Library technicians who drive bookmobiles are responsible for answering patrons' questions, receiving and checking out books, collecting fines, maintaining the book collection, shelving materials, and occasionally operating audiovisual equipment to show slides or films.

Where and When

Library technicians and assistants generally work at desks or computer terminals. Like other workers who spend long periods of time in front of a computer, they are susceptible to hand and wrist problems, back discomfort, and eyestrain. Those who work in school libraries work regular school hours, while others may work weekends, evenings, and even some holidays. Those who drive bookmobiles may have more unusual schedules.

For More Information

✳ American Library Association, Office for Human Resource Development and Recruitment, 50 E. Huron St., Chicago, IL 60611. Internet: www.ala.org/ala/educationcareers/index.cfm

✳ Human Resources Office, Library of Congress, 101 Independence Ave. SE, Washington, DC 20540-2231. Internet: www.loc.gov/hr

Data Bank

Education and Training: Short-term on-the-job training to vocational/technical training

Average Earnings: $20,000–$34,000

Earnings Growth Potential: Low

Total Jobs Held: 243,000

Job Outlook: Average increase

Annual Job Openings: 12,900

Related Jobs: Librarians; medical records and health information technicians; receptionists and information clerks; teacher assistants

Personality Types: Conventional-Social-Realistic

Did You Know?

According to the American Library Association, there are approximately 117,500 libraries in the United States employing nearly 400,000 workers. Though the job outlook for library-related occupations is about average, most individuals interested in working in a library shouldn't have to go far to find one.

Teacher Assistants

At a Glance

Teacher assistants—also called teacher aides—support classroom teachers, giving them more time for lesson planning and instruction. They help children in the classroom and school cafeteria or on the playground and field trips. Sometimes they pay special attention to individual students or small groups who need more help with a subject. They help teachers by grading papers, keeping attendance records, typing, filing, ordering supplies, helping out in the computer lab, or preparing class lessons. While most teacher assistants work in primary and secondary schools, others work in preschools and other child care centers. Teacher assistants also work with infants and toddlers who have developmental delays or other disabilities.

Data Bank

Education and Training: Short-term on-the-job training

Average Earnings: $18,000–$29,000

Earnings Growth Potential: Low

Total Jobs Held: 1,313,000

Job Outlook: Average increase

Annual Job Openings: 41,300

Related Jobs: Child care workers; library technicians and library assistants; occupational therapist assistants and aides; teachers—kindergarten, elementary, middle and secondary; teachers—preschool, except special education; teachers—special education; teachers—vocational

Personality Types: Social-Conventional

Did You Know?

Studies have shown that smaller class sizes generally produce better educational results. Still, there are many teachers with class sizes of 25 students or more because of budget and physical space constraints. While average student-to-teacher ratios range from 12 to 20 students per teacher, depending on the state, there is no denying the impact that teacher assistants can have to help teachers manage large classes.

Career in Focus: *Special Education Teacher Assistant*

Many teacher assistants work extensively with special education students. As schools integrate special education students into general education classrooms, teacher assistants are increasingly needed to assist students with disabilities. Teacher assistants attend to a disabled student's physical needs. They also provide personal attention to students with other special needs, such as those who speak English as a second language or those who need remedial education.

Where and When

Most teacher assistants work in schools or preschools. They also work outdoors supervising recess and spend much of their time standing, walking, or kneeling. Teacher assistants who work with special education students must often perform strenuous tasks including heavy lifting. About four out of every ten teacher assistants work part time, and most work a 40-hour week or less.

For More Information

* American Federation of Teachers, Paraprofessional and School Related Personnel Division, 555 New Jersey Ave. NW, Washington, DC 20001. Internet: www.aft.org/psrp/index.html

* National Education Association, Educational Support Personnel Division, 1201 16th St. NW, Washington, DC 20036. Internet: www.nea.org/esphome

* National Resource Center for Paraprofessionals, 6526 Old Main Hill, Utah State University, Logan, UT 84322. Internet: www.nrcpara.org

Teachers—Adult Literacy and Remedial Education

At a Glance

Adult literacy and remedial education teachers teach basic skills courses, such as writing, reading, and math, to adults and out-of-school youths. They also work with people who want to update their job skills or prepare for the GED (high school equivalency) exam. Traditionally, the students in adult education classes have been those who did not graduate high school or who passed through school without learning necessary skills. Increasingly, however, students in these classes are people whose native language is not English. Because the students often are at different levels, teachers must assess each student's abilities beforehand. They must often teach students effective study skills and give them the self-confidence they need to succeed academically as well.

Career in Focus: *ESOL Teacher*

ESOL teachers (teachers of English to speakers of other languages) help adults speak, listen, read, and write in English, often in the context of real-life situations. ESOL teachers teach adults who possess a wide range of abilities and who speak a variety of languages. More advanced students may concentrate on writing and conversational skills or focus on learning more academic or job-related communication skills.

Where and When

Many of these classes are held on days and at times to meet adult students' schedules, so evening and weekend work is common. A large number of these teachers work part time, sometimes in addition to another full-time career. Most of the students are motivated to learn, which can make this job satisfying and rewarding.

For More Information

* The U.S. Department of Education, Office of Vocational and Adult Education, Potomac Center Plaza, 400 Maryland Ave. SW, Washington, DC 20202. Internet: www.ed.gov/about/offices/list/ovae/index.html

* The Center for Adult English Language Acquisition, 4646 40th St. NW, Suite 200, Washington, DC 20016. Internet: www.cal.org/caela

Data Bank

Education and Training: Bachelor's degree

Average Earnings: $35,000–$63,000

Earnings Growth Potential: High

Total Jobs Held: 96,000

Job Outlook: Above-average increase

Annual Job Openings: 2,900

Related Jobs: Counselors; interpreters and translators; social workers; teachers—kindergarten, elementary, middle, and secondary; teachers—postsecondary; teachers—preschool, except special education; teachers—special education; teachers—vocational

Personality Types: Social-Artistic-Enterprising

Did You Know?

According to the U.S. Department of Education, ESL (English as a second language) programs are the fastest-growing adult education programs in the country, accounting for close to half of the total adult enrollment. The majority of these students are native Spanish speakers. Demand for ESL and ESOL teachers will be greatest in states with large populations of nonnative speakers, including California, Florida, Texas, and New York.

Teachers–Postsecondary

At a Glance

Postsecondary teachers work at colleges, community colleges, universities, and research facilities. They specialize in one field, such as history, physics, or journalism, and most have an advanced degree. College and university faculty teach and advise more than 16 million students. They prepare lectures, exercises, and laboratory experiments; grade exams and papers; and advise and work with students individually. Most research and write articles and books in addition to their teaching duties. Faculty members at universities and four-year colleges spend more of their time doing research, while those at two-year colleges spend most of their time teaching. Most faculty members also serve on committees that deal with departmental matters, academic issues, budgets, and hiring. Graduate teaching assistants assist faculty and staff at colleges and universities by performing teaching or teaching-related duties.

Data Bank

Education and Training: Work experience in a related occupation to doctoral degree

Average Earnings: $46,000–$88,000

Earnings Growth Potential: High

Total Jobs Held: 1,391,000

Job Outlook: Above-average increase

Annual Job Openings: 55,300

Related Jobs: Authors, writers, and editors; counselors; education administrators; librarians; management analysts; public relations specialists; teachers—kindergarten, elementary, middle, and secondary; teachers—vocational

Personality Types: Social-Investigative

Did You Know?

The majority of universities and four-year colleges require their teachers to have a doctoral degree in their chosen field of study. Doctoral degrees generally take six years beyond a bachelor's degree to complete. That means students graduating high school and wanting to teach at the college level can look forward to about ten more years of schooling. Of course, the rewards are more than worth it for those who make it through and land a job. But colleges are relying more and more on adjunct teachers, who work only part time.

Career in Focus: *Postsecondary Vocational Education Teacher*

Postsecondary vocational education teachers provide instruction for occupations that require specialized training but may not require a four-year degree, such as dental hygienist, X-ray technician, auto mechanic, and cosmetologist. Classes often are taught in an industrial or laboratory setting where students can get hands-on experience.

Where and When

Postsecondary teachers usually have flexible schedules and a great deal of freedom. Some teach night and weekend classes—especially at community colleges or schools with a lot of adult students. Most of these teachers work nine months out of the year and can take advantage of school holidays as well. Travel may be required to do research, and many postsecondary teachers experience some conflict between their responsibilities as teachers and as researchers.

For More Information

❋ Council of Graduate Schools, One Dupont Circle NW, Suite 230, Washington, DC 20036-1173. Internet: www.preparing-faculty.org

Teachers–Preschool, Except Special Education

At a Glance

Preschool teachers nurture, teach, and care for children who have not yet entered kindergarten. They provide early childhood care and education through a variety of teaching strategies. They teach children, usually aged 3 to 5, both in groups and one on one. They do so by planning and implementing a curriculum that covers various areas of a child's development, such as motor skills, social and emotional development, and language development. Preschool teachers play a vital role in the development of children. They introduce children to reading and writing, expanded vocabulary, creative arts, science, and social studies. They use games, music, artwork, films, books, computers, and other tools to teach concepts and skills.

Career in Focus: *Preschool Foreign Language Teacher*

The easiest time to learn a foreign language is when you're a young child. Recognizing this opportunity, some preschools include foreign language instruction in their curriculum. One strategy is full immersion, meaning that students spend part or all of the school day learning in a foreign language. The preschool foreign language teacher may read stories, supervise art projects, lead singing, or do any of the other typical preschool activities but in the foreign language. Other schools restrict language instruction to a particular lesson. Either way, the teacher should be a fluent speaker of the language, with a good accent.

Where and When

Seeing students develop new skills and gain an appreciation of knowledge and learning can be very rewarding. Part-time schedules are common among preschool teachers. Many teachers work the traditional ten-month school year with a two-month vacation during the summer. Preschool teachers working in day care settings often work year round.

For More Information

* National Association for the Education of Young Children, 1313 L St. NW, Suite 500, Washington, DC 20005. Internet: www.naeyc.org
* Council for Professional Recognition, 2460 16th St. NW, Washington, DC 20009-3575. Internet: www.cdacouncil.org

---

Data Bank

Education and Training: Vocational/technical training

Average Earnings: $19,000–$32,000

Earnings Growth Potential: Low

Total Jobs Held: 457,000

Job Outlook: Above-average increase

Annual Job Openings: 17,800

Related Jobs: Child care workers; teachers assistants; teachers—kindergarten, elementary, middle, secondary; teachers—special education

Personality Types: Social-Artistic

Did You Know?

For preschool children, play is one of the most important learning activities. Effective preschool teachers find ways to make learning playful: encouraging language and vocabulary development by using storytelling, rhyming games, and acting games; improving social skills by having the children work together to build a neighborhood in a sandbox; and introducing scientific and mathematical concepts by showing the children how to balance and count blocks when building a bridge or how to mix colors when painting.

Teachers–Kindergarten, Elementary, Middle, and Secondary

At a Glance

Teachers plan lessons, prepare tests, grade papers, and write reports of students' progress. They encourage group learning and problem solving and prepare students for advanced education and the world of work. They meet with parents and school staff to talk about grades and problems. Kindergarten and elementary school teachers introduce children to mathematics, language, science, and social studies. They use games, music, artwork, films, books, computers, and other tools to teach basic skills. Most elementary school teachers instruct one class of children in several subjects. Middle school teachers and secondary school teachers help students delve more deeply into subjects introduced in elementary school. Middle and secondary school teachers specialize in a specific subject, such as English, Spanish, mathematics, history, or biology. In addition to conducting classroom activities, teachers oversee study halls and homerooms, supervise extracurricular activities, and accompany students on field trips.

Data Bank

Education and Training: Bachelor's degree

Average Earnings: $41,000–$64,000

Earnings Growth Potential: Low

Total Jobs Held: 3,476,000

Job Outlook: Average increase

Annual Job Openings: 132,300

Related Jobs: Athletes, coaches, umpires, and related workers; child care workers; counselors; education administrators; librarians; social workers; teacher assistants; teachers—postsecondary; teachers—preschool, except special education; teachers—special education; teachers—vocational

Personality Types: Social-Artistic

Did You Know?

Although private schools certainly have their appeal, including smaller class sizes and more freedom for teachers to design their own classes, teacher turnover is actually higher in private schools than in public schools. In general, public schools pay better and offer solid benefit packages, but they also all require a teaching license. While licenses are recommended for most private school teaching positions, they often are not required. Future teachers should weigh all the pros and cons before deciding whether to go public or private.

Career in Focus: *Math Teacher*

Math teachers often can find jobs easily when other kinds of teachers can't. That's because math is an essential skill and schools are under pressure to raise test scores for math, yet many people who are skilled with math choose careers in science, business, or other fields rather than teaching. Like all teachers, math teachers need people skills and an understanding of how young people learn.

Where and When

Teaching is considered one of the most frustrating and rewarding careers. Accountability standards, unruly students, heavy workloads, and a lack of control can lead to feelings of stress. Including duties performed outside of the class, such as lesson planning and grading, most teachers work more than 40 hours per week. The majority of them work a standard ten-month school year.

For More Information

* American Federation of Teachers, 555 New Jersey Ave. NW, Washington, DC 20001. Internet: www.aft.org

* National Education Association, 1201 16th St. NW, Washington, DC 20036. Internet: www.nea.org

* National Council for Accreditation of Teacher Education, 2010 Massachusetts Ave. NW, Suite 500, Washington, DC 20036-1023. Internet: www.ncate.org

* National Center for Alternative Certification, 4401A Connecticut Ave. NW, Suite 212, Washington, DC 20008. Internet: www.teach-now.org

Teachers—Self-Enrichment Education

At a Glance

Self-enrichment teachers are usually specialists in a certain subject who are willing to share what they know with mostly adult students who are eager to learn. Some teach classes that provide students with life skills, such as personal finance, cooking, and time management classes. Others teach subjects purely for recreation, such as photography, painting, or ballroom dancing. Most self-enrichment classes are designed for individuals who just want to improve themselves, enrich their lives, or learn more about a topic. The courses seldom lead to a particular degree, and student attendance is voluntary. Some classes, such as pottery or sewing, may be largely hands-on. All self-enrichment teachers must prepare lessons beforehand and stay current in their fields. Many are self-employed.

Career in Focus: *Art, Music, or Dance Instructor*

Many self-enrichment teachers provide one-on-one lessons to students or teach classes on their own as part of a studio, particularly in the arts. Whether it's teaching someone to play the piano, paint *a fresco*, or dance *en pointe*, most of these instructors teach subjects they are passionate about and skilled in. In the case of one-on-one instruction, the teacher may work with each student for only an hour or two per week. Many instructors work with the same students on a weekly basis for years, however, and find satisfaction in helping them mature and gain expertise.

Where and When

Few of these teachers are full-time salaried workers. Most either work part time or are self-employed. Although pay for these jobs is generally low, most teachers enjoy sharing what they know with others, which leads to high job satisfaction. Many self-enrichment classes for adults are held in the evenings and on weekends. Those for children are almost always after school or on weekends. Most of the teaching is done in comfortable classroom, laboratory, or workshop settings.

For More Information

For information on employment of self-enrichment teachers, contact schools or local companies that offer self-enrichment programs.

Data Bank

Education and Training: Work experience in a related occupation

Average Earnings: $27,000–$52,000

Earnings Growth Potential: High

Total Jobs Held: 254,000

Job Outlook: Rapid increase

Annual Job Openings: 12,000

Related Jobs: Artists and related workers; athletes, coaches, umpires, and related workers; dancers and choreographers; musicians, singers, and related workers; recreation workers; teachers—kindergarten, elementary, middle, and secondary; teachers—preschool, except special education

Personality Types: Social-Artistic-Enterprising

Did You Know?

"Lifelong learning" is a phrase growing in popularity. Retirees provide one of the larger groups of students in self-enrichment education because they have more time to take classes. The impending retirement of baby boomers should provide self-enrichment teachers increased opportunity to share their talents, whether it's working with wood or doing the cha-cha.

Teachers—Special Education

At a Glance

Special education teachers work with students who have disabilities. Most work in elementary, middle, or high schools, but some work with toddlers and preschoolers. The majority work with children with mild to moderate disabilities, modifying the general curriculum to meet the child's individual needs. A small number of special education teachers work with students with mental retardation or autism, primarily teaching them life skills and basic literacy. Early identification of a child with special needs is an important part of a special education teacher's job. Special education teachers also help to develop an Individualized Education Program (IEP) for each special education student. The IEP sets personalized goals for each student and is tailored to the student's individual needs and ability. Special education teachers communicate frequently with parents, social workers, school psychologists, occupational and physical therapists, school administrators, and other teachers.

Data Bank

Education and Training: Bachelor's degree

Average Earnings: $42,000–$65,000

Earnings Growth Potential: Low

Total Jobs Held: 473,000

Job Outlook: Above-average increase

Annual Job Openings: 20,400

Related Jobs: Audiologists; counselors; occupational therapists; psychologists; recreational therapists; social workers; speech-language pathologists; teacher assistants; teachers—kindergarten, elementary, middle, and secondary; teachers—preschool, except special education; teachers—vocational

Personality Types: Social-Artistic

Did You Know?

Special education is not restricted to students with learning disabilities, although more and more students are being diagnosed with such disabilities. Special education covers classes for students with mental handicaps, physical disabilities, and emotional problems. It also includes classes for gifted and talented students. Special education classes spread from preschool and early-intervention programs to continuing education classes for disabled adults. It's a wide and growing field.

Career in Focus: *Inclusion Aide*

As schools become more inclusive, special education teachers and general education teachers are increasingly working together in general education classrooms. Inclusion aides provide one-to-one instruction for students with special needs as part of a general education classroom. They help general educators adapt class materials and teaching techniques to specifically meet the needs of students with disabilities.

Where and When

Although helping students with disabilities can be highly rewarding, the work is often emotionally and physically draining. Heavy workloads and lots of paperwork can lead to stress. The majority of special education teachers work a standard ten-month school schedule during regular school hours. Some heavy lifting may be required.

For More Information

* The Council for Exceptional Children, 1110 N. Glebe Rd., Suite 300, Arlington, VA 22201. Internet: www.cec.sped.org

* National Center for Special Education Personnel and Related Service Providers, National Association of State Directors of Special Education, 1800 Diagonal Rd., Suite 320, Alexandria, VA 22314. Internet: www.personnelcenter.org

Teachers—Vocational

At a Glance

Vocational education teachers—commonly called career and technical education (CTE) teachers or career-technology teachers—instruct and train students to work in a wide variety of fields. In middle and secondary schools, they may be introducing students to a trade or skill for the first time. They often teach courses that are in high demand by area employers, who often provide input into the curriculum and offer internships or apprenticeships to students at the secondary school level. Many vocational teachers play an active role in building and overseeing these partnerships.

Career in Focus: *Agricultural Science Teacher*

In agricultural science, students learn a wide variety of subjects related to the science and business of agriculture. Classes may cover topics like agricultural production; agricultural-related business; horticulture; agri-science; small animal care; veterinary science; and plant, animal, and food systems. Teachers in this subject may have students plant and care for crops or tend to animals to apply what they have learned in the classroom.

Where and When

Helping students develop new skills and gain an appreciation of knowledge and learning can be very rewarding. CTE teachers often spend part of the school day in the community, working with their business and industry partners. Including school duties performed outside the classroom, many teachers work more than 40 hours a week. Most middle and secondary school CTE teachers work the traditional ten-month school year with a two-month vacation during the summer. CTE teachers with active work-based learning programs may be on twelve-month contracts to provide time for them to engage in job development for current and future students.

For More Information

✳ Association for Career and Technical Education, 1410 King St., Alexandria, VA 22314. Internet: www.acteonline.org

---

Data Bank

Education and Training: Bachelor's or higher degree plus related work experience

Average Earnings: $43,000–$64,000

Earnings Growth Potential: Low

Total Jobs Held: 115,000

Job Outlook: Average increase

Annual Job Openings: 4,300

Related Jobs: Counselors; education administrators; librarians; teachers—kindergarten, elementary, middle, and secondary school; teachers—preschool, except special education; teachers—special education

Personality Types: Social-Artistic

Did You Know?

CTE teachers have to deal with more frequent changes in curriculum than do most other teachers. Unlike the principles of mathematics or punctuation, the skills that industry requires are constantly changing, often rapidly. CTE teachers have to keep up with these changes, mastering new skills that are required in the workplace even though the teachers' main workplace is in schools.

Artists and Related Workers

At a Glance

Artists communicate ideas, thoughts, or feelings through art. They might use oil paints, watercolors, pencils, clay, chalk, or even scrap metal to create their work. Art directors develop designs and review material for periodicals, newspapers, and other media. Craft artists hand-make a wide variety of objects that are sold in their own studios, in retail outlets, or at arts-and-crafts shows. Craft artists work with many different materials, including ceramics, glass, wood, metal, and paper.

Visual artists are usually either graphic artists or fine artists. Graphic artists use art to meet the needs of business clients, such as stores, ad agencies, and publishing firms. Fine artists create artwork to sell and display in museums or galleries. More than half of all artists are self-employed and must use good business skills to be successful.

Data Bank

Education and Training: Long-term on-the-job training to bachelor's or higher degree plus related work experience

Average Earnings: $44,000–$87,000

Earnings Growth Potential: High

Total Jobs Held: 222,000

Job Outlook: Average increase

Annual Job Openings: 7,600

Related Jobs: Archivists, curators, and museum technicians; commercial and industrial designers; computer software engineers and computer programmers; desktop publishers; fashion designers; graphic designers; jewelers and precious stone and metal workers; photographers; woodworkers

Personality Types: Artistic-Realistic-Enterprising

Did You Know?

Scholars, artists, critics, and audiences have debated for centuries over what is and isn't art. Though most agree that art incorporates creativity, expression, and even a sense of beauty, it still holds true that one person's masterpiece is another person's garbage. One famous piece that called the definition of art into question was Marcel Duchamp's Fountain. Displayed in a museum in 1917, it was simply a urinal with "R. Mutt 1917" written on it. It has since been voted the "most influential artwork of the 20th century" by a panel of art world professionals.

Career in Focus: *Illustrator*

Illustrators create pictures for books, magazines, and other publications and for commercial products such as stationery, greeting cards, and calendars. Medical and scientific illustrators combine drawing skills with knowledge of biology or other sciences. Medical illustrators draw illustrations of human anatomy and surgical procedures. Scientific illustrators draw illustrations of animal and plant life, atomic and molecular structures, and geologic and planetary formations. Increasingly, illustrators are doing all their work directly on a computer.

Where and When

Most artists work in studios located in office buildings, in warehouses, or in the privacy of their own home. Artists employed by publishing companies, advertising agencies, and design firms generally work a standard 40-hour workweek. Self-employed artists can set their own schedule, but spend much of their time meeting potential customers and building a reputation.

For More Information

* National Association of Schools of Art and Design, 11250 Roger Bacon Dr., Suite 21, Reston, VA 20190. Internet: http://nasad.arts-accredit.org

* American Craft Council Library, 72 Spring St., 6th Floor, New York, NY 10012. Internet: www.craftcouncil.org

* Society of Illustrators, 128 E. 63rd St., New York, NY 10065. Internet: www.societyillustrators.org

* Association of Medical Illustrators, P.O. Box 1897, Lawrence, KS 66044. Internet: www.ami.org

* Art Directors Club, 106 W. 29th St., New York, NY 10001. Internet: www.adcglobal.org

Commercial and Industrial Designers

At a Glance

These individuals are responsible for the look, feel, function, quality, and safety of most of the products we use every day. They combine their knowledge of art, engineering, and business to create sketches and models that are then used in production. When creating a new design, they often begin by researching how the product will be used. Many designers use computer-aided design (CAD) tools to create and visualize the final product. Designers then present the designs and prototypes to their client or managers and incorporate any changes and suggestions. Often, commercial and industrial designers specialize in one product or another, from automobiles to appliances, toys to tools. Designers also work with engineers, accountants, and cost estimators to determine whether a product could be made safer, easier to use, or cheaper to produce.

Career in Focus: *Furniture Designer*

Commercial and industrial designers may specialize in any number of products. Furniture designers do exactly what their name suggests, designing everything from conference tables to microwave carts for industrial, commercial, and individual clients. Furniture designers must always balance the function of their design with its form or appearance. Sometimes the most beautiful chairs are the least comfortable and the ugliest couches offer the best naps. Being a furniture designer requires business skills as well. Many of them are self-employed.

Where and When

Working conditions vary. Designers employed by large corporations or design firms generally work regular hours in comfortable settings. Self-employed consultants and designers may work longer hours to meet deadlines. Some travel may be required to meet clients.

For More Information

* Industrial Designers Society of America, 45195 Business Court, Suite 250, Dulles, VA 20166. Internet: www.idsa.org

* National Association of Schools of Art and Design, 11250 Roger Bacon Dr., Suite 21, Reston, VA 20190. Internet: http://nasad.arts-accredit.org

Data Bank

Education and Training: Bachelor's degree

Average Earnings: $42,000–$77,000

Earnings Growth Potential: High

Total Jobs Held: 44,000

Job Outlook: Average increase

Annual Job Openings: 1,800

Related Jobs: Architects, except landscape and naval; artists and related workers; computer software engineers and computer programmers; desktop publishers; drafters; engineers; fashion designers; floral designers; graphic designers; interior designers

Personality Types: Artistic-Enterprising-Realistic

Did You Know?

Not all products are created on purpose. Post-it Notes—those colored, sticky pieces of paper—were created almost by accident. A researcher at 3M set out to make a stronger adhesive but ultimately developed a weaker one that just barely stuck. Three years later, a fellow researcher at the company discovered he could coat scraps of paper with the stuff and use them as bookmarks. They would stick, but could be lifted off with ease. Now you can find them in almost every office.

Fashion Designers

At a Glance

Fashion designers create the clothing, shoes, and accessories worn by millions of people. They research fashion trends, sketch designs, select materials, create samples, and oversee the production of their items. The process from initial design to final production takes between 18 and 24 months. Once the design is finished and samples of the article are sewn, they are marketed to clothing retailers. Many designs are shown at fashion and trade shows a few times a year. Retailers will then place orders for the items they want to sell. Computer-aided design (CAD) is increasingly being used in the fashion design industry, meaning designers must be aware of trends in technology as well as trends in fashion.

Data Bank

Education and Training: Associate degree

Average Earnings: $44,000–$90,000

Earnings Growth Potential: High

Total Jobs Held: 23,000

Job Outlook: Little change

Annual Job Openings: 700

Related Jobs: Artists and related workers; commercial and industrial designers; demonstrators and product promoters; floral designers; graphic designers; interior designers; jewelers and precious stone and metal workers; models; photographers; purchasing managers, buyers, and purchasing agents; retail salespersons; textile, apparel, and furnishings occupations

Personality Types: Artistic-Enterprising-Realistic

Did You Know?

Two-thirds of fashion designers work in either New York or California, the fashion capitals of the United States. This is an important consideration for anyone interested in pursuing fashion design as a career, especially given the cost of living in these states' major cities. Of course if you'd rather go international, you'll always have Paris.

Career in Focus: *Costume Designer*

Some fashion designers specialize in costume design for plays, movies, and television shows. The work of costume designers is similar to other fashion designers. Costume designers research the styles worn during the period in which the performance takes place or work with directors to select the right attire. They make sketches of designs, select fabric and other materials, and oversee the production of the costumes. They also must stay within the costume budget. At least they are given their own Academy Award category.

Where and When

Fashion designers generally work regular hours in comfortable settings. Freelancers who work on a contract basis must frequently adjust their schedules to meet their clients' needs. Regardless of their work setting, all fashion designers must occasionally work long hours in order to meet deadlines or prepare for fashion shows. Travel can be frequent.

For More Information

* National Association of Schools of Art and Design, 11250 Roger Bacon Dr., Suite 21, Reston, VA 20190. Internet: http://nasad.arts-accredit.org

* Fashion Group International, 8 W. 40th St., 7th Floor, New York, NY 10018. Internet: www.fgi.org

Floral Designers

At a Glance

Floral designers use flowers, greenery, ribbons, and containers to produce arrangements for decoration and special occasions. They are skilled at making bouquets, corsages, table centerpieces, and wreaths. Most work independently or in small shops creating designs for special events such as weddings and funerals. Others work in the wholesale floral business or in the floral departments in grocery stores. Some designers also assist interior designers in creating live or silk floral displays for hotels, restaurants, and private residences. Self-employed floral designers must handle the various aspects of running their own businesses, such as selecting and purchasing flowers, hiring and supervising staff, and maintaining financial records. Floral designers often work under deadlines (the flowers need to be fresh, after all) and must have a good sense of visual design.

Career in Focus: *Wedding Florist*

Because of the wide variety of designs involved—from boutonnières to the bride's bouquet—some florists choose to focus only on weddings. The average cost of wedding flowers ranges from $500 to $1,500, though at more elaborate weddings they can cost as much as $5,000 or $10,000. As long as people continue to get married (and spend lots of money on weddings), floral designers will always have some job security.

Where and When

Most floral designers work in comfortable settings, though work outdoors is sometimes required. Designers may have to make frequent trips to deliver or pick up flowers or to set up arrangements. Because fresh flowers are perishable, orders cannot be completed too far in advance. Many designers often work long hours before or during holidays, plus nights and weekends to complete large orders for weddings and other events. They can be susceptible to allergic reactions from flower pollens.

For More Information

* American Institute of Floral Designers, 720 Light St., Baltimore, MD 21230. Internet: www.aifd.org
* Society of American Florists, 1601 Duke St., Alexandria, VA 22314. Internet: www.safnow.org

Data Bank

Education and Training: Short-term on-the-job training

Average Earnings: $19,000–$30,000

Earnings Growth Potential: Low

Total Jobs Held: 76,000

Job Outlook: Declining

Annual Job Openings: 2,300

Related Jobs: Agricultural and food scientists; agricultural workers, other; artists and related workers; commercial and industrial designers; fashion designers; graphic designers; interior designers; landscape architects

Personality Types: Artistic-Enterprising-Realistic

Did You Know?

Can you guess what the biggest holiday is for floral designers? Despite the dramatic increase in the sale of roses in February, it's not Valentine's Day. And though geraniums are common in May, it's not Mother's Day either. It's Christmas. In fact, flowers are becoming more and more popular as a holiday gift.

Graphic Designers

At a Glance

Otherwise known as graphic artists, these designers decide the best way to communicate a message in print, film, or electronic media. Some graphic designers develop the layout of newspapers, journals, and magazines, while others work in advertising, designing packaging and logos and making signs. Perhaps the hottest trend in graphic designing is developing material for Web pages and other interactive multimedia environments. In creating their designs, graphic artists first gather relevant information by meeting with clients or art directors. Graphic designers then prepare sketches or layouts to illustrate the vision for the design. Finally, they present the completed design to their clients or to the art director for approval. Graphic designers use computer software to assist in their designs and so are expected to be familiar with the latest technology.

Data Bank

Education and Training: Bachelor's degree

Average Earnings: $33,000–$58,000

Earnings Growth Potential: Medium

Total Jobs Held: 286,000

Job Outlook: Average increase

Annual Job Openings: 12,500

Related Jobs: Advertising, marketing, promotions, public relations, and sales managers; artists and related workers; authors, writers, and editors; commercial and industrial designers; computer software engineers and computer programmers; desktop publishers; drafters; fashion designers; floral designers; interior designers; photographers; prepress technicians and workers

Personality Types: Artistic-Enterprising-Realistic

Did You Know?

The Nike "swoosh" is one of the most recognizable symbols in the world and can be found on hats, shirts, socks, towels, bags, posters, and of course, shoes. The logo was originally created by a graphic design student named Carolyn Davidson, who sold it to the company founder, Phil Knight, for a modest sum of $35. Rumor has it that Knight wasn't thrilled with the design, but went with it anyway. Since then the "swoosh" has become an icon, and Davidson has been justly rewarded for her contributions to the company.

Career in Focus: *Graphic Designer—Marketing*

Marketing and advertising departments are one of the chief employers of graphic designers. These designers develop catalogs and brochures, create print and Web-based graphics, create promotional and event materials, and design Web sites. The job requires a mix of artistic vision and business savvy. Those with degrees or experience in both marketing and design should have the best chances at such jobs.

Where and When

Graphic designers employed by large advertising, publishing, or design firms usually work regular hours in comfortable settings. Freelancers or those working at smaller firms may frequently adjust their schedules to meet their clients' needs. They also may work longer hours in smaller, more congested environments. Designers frequently spend a lot of time in front of a computer, which can result in strain on the eyes, back, and wrists.

For More Information

* National Association of Schools of Art and Design, 11250 Roger Bacon Dr., Suite 21, Reston, VA 20190-5248. Internet: http://nasad.arts-accredit.org

* American Institute of Graphic Arts, 164 Fifth Ave., New York, NY 10010. Internet: www.aiga.org

* Art Directors Club, 106 W. 29th St., New York, NY 10001. Internet: www.adcglobal.org

Interior Designers

At a Glance

These workers design and arrange the physical space within buildings, whether it's a home, hospital, theater, restaurant, or office. They experiment with colors, textures, furniture, lighting, and space to create a safe, functional, and pleasing atmosphere. Traditionally, most interior designers focused on decorating: choosing a style and colors and then selecting appropriate furniture, floor and window coverings, artwork, and lighting. However, an increasing number of designers are becoming involved in the architectural details, helping to determine the location of windows, stairways, escalators, and walkways. Designers frequently work with architects, electricians, and building contractors to ensure that their designs are safe and meet construction requirements.

Career in Focus: *In-Store Designer*

Those who work as in-store designers for furniture or home and garden stores offer their design services in addition to selling the store's products. In-store designers help customers select a style and color scheme that fits their needs or find suitable accessories and lighting. However, in-store designers rarely visit a customer's home or business and are limited in using only their store's products.

Where and When

Interior designers employed by large corporations or firms usually work regular hours in comfortable settings. Those in smaller firms or who work on a freelance basis may have irregular schedules and work in more cramped environments. Interior designers may work under stress to meet deadlines, stay under budget, and please clients.

For More Information

* American Society of Interior Designers, 608 Massachusetts Ave. NE, Washington, DC 20002. Internet: www.asid.org

* Council for Interior Design Accreditation, 206 Granville Ave., Suite 350, Grand Rapids, MI 49503. Internet: www.accredit-id.org

* National Association of Schools of Art and Design, 11250 Roger Bacon Dr., Suite 21, Reston, VA 20190. Internet: http://nasad.arts-accredit.org

* National Council for Interior Design Qualification, 1602 L St. NW, Suite 200, Washington, DC 20036. Internet: www.ncidq.org

* National Kitchen and Bath Association, 687 Willow Grove St., Hackettstown, NJ 07840. Internet: www.nkba.org/student

Data Bank

Education and Training: Associate degree

Average Earnings: $35,000–$64,000

Earnings Growth Potential: Medium

Total Jobs Held: 72,000

Job Outlook: Above-average increase

Annual Job Openings: 3,600

Related Jobs: Architects, except landscape and naval; artists and related workers; commercial and industrial designers; fashion designers; floral designers; graphic designers; landscape architects

Personality Types: Artistic-Enterprising

Did You Know?

Three areas of design that are becoming increasingly popular are ergonomic design, elder design, and environmental—or green—design. Ergonomic design involves designing work spaces and furniture that emphasize good posture and minimize muscle strain on the body. Elder design involves planning interiors to aid in the movement of the elderly and disabled, such as widening passageways to accommodate wheelchairs. Green design involves selecting furniture and carpets that are free of chemicals and using construction materials that are energy efficient. So your environmentally conscious grandfather with bad posture can now have the living room of his dreams.

Actors, Producers, and Directors

At a Glance

Actors, producers, and directors make words come alive through plays, TV shows, and films. Actors perform in stage, radio, television, video, or movie productions. They also work in nightclubs, theme parks, commercials, and training and educational films. Directors are responsible for the creative decisions in a production. They interpret scripts, advise set and costume designers, audition and select cast members, conduct rehearsals, and direct the work of cast and crew. Producers arrange the financing and decide the size of the production and the budget. Directors and producers often work under tight deadlines and stressful conditions. Although the most famous actors, producers, and directors work in film or network television, far more work in local or regional television studios, theaters, or film production companies preparing independent, small-scale productions.

Data Bank

Education and Training: Long-term on-the-job training to bachelor's or higher degree plus related work experience

Average Earnings: $43,000–$111,000 (for Producers and Directors)

Earnings Growth Potential: Very high (for Producers and Directors)

Total Jobs Held: 155,000

Job Outlook: Average increase

Annual Job Openings: 6,100

Related Jobs: Announcers; dancers and choreographers; fashion designers; makeup artists, theatrical and performance; musicians, singers, and related workers; set and exhibit designers; top executives

Personality Types: Enterprising-Artistic

Did You Know?

Actors have some of the best-paying and worst-paying jobs in the country. While movie stars can make upwards of $20 million per picture, many extras barely make minimum wage. The key is to speak up for yourself—literally. Motion picture and television actors with speaking parts are guaranteed a minimum daily rate of $716. Of course, once the production is done filming, these actors aren't guaranteed anything. For most it is an uphill struggle, and it's rare to find an actor who doesn't have another job on the side.

Career in Focus: *Talent Director*

Sometimes called casting directors, talent directors audition and interview performers in order to select the most appropriate person for parts in stage, television, radio, or film productions. They arrange screen tests and find and hire extras, stand-ins, and photo and stunt doubles. They also negotiate contracts and maintain talent files.

Where and When

All of these individuals work under the constant pressure of deadlines and schedules. Many of them are under pressure to find their next job as well. Acting assignments are usually short-term, which often results in periods of unemployment. Actors and directors usually work long, irregular hours when filming or performing. Extensive travel may be necessary for those filming or recording in other locations or touring with a show.

For More Information

✷ National Association of Schools of Theater, 11250 Roger Bacon Dr., Suite 21, Reston, VA 20190. Internet: http://nast.arts-accredit.org

✷ Actors' Equity Association, 165 W. 46th St., New York, NY 10036. Internet: www.actorsequity.org

✷ Screen Actors Guild, 5757 Wilshire Blvd., 7th Floor, Los Angeles, CA 90036-3600. Internet: www.sag.org

✷ Producers Guild of America. Internet: www.producersguild.org

Athletes, Coaches, Umpires, and Related Workers

At a Glance

Athletes compete in organized sports events to entertain spectators. They spend many hours each day practicing and improving teamwork under the guidance of a coach. Because competition is intense and job security is questionable, many athletes train year round to stay in peak physical condition. Coaches organize, lead, teach, and referee indoor and outdoor games. Along with refining athletes' skills, coaches are responsible for instilling good sportsmanship, a competitive spirit, and teamwork and for managing their teams. During competition, coaches may call specific plays and substitute players. Umpires, referees, and other sports officials officiate at competitive athletic and sporting events. They observe the play and make sure everyone follows the established rules and regulations.

Career in Focus: *Sports Instructor*

Sports instructors train professional and nonprofessional athletes on a one-to-one basis. They organize, instruct, and lead athletes in indoor and outdoor sports such as bowling, tennis, golf, and swimming. Because activities are as diverse as weight lifting, gymnastics, scuba diving, and karate, instructors tend to specialize in one or a few activities. Like coaches, sports instructors also may hold daily practice sessions and be responsible for equipment and supplies.

Where and When

Because of the intense physical nature of most sports, professional athletes are highly prone to injury. Athletes, coaches, and sports officials work irregular hours, often working weekends, evenings, and holidays. They may work longer hours during the regular season, but will continue to practice in the off-season as well. Travel by bus or airplane can be frequent. Sports officials regularly encounter verbal abuse from fans, coaches, and players.

For More Information

✳ National Association of Sports Officials, 2017 Lathrop Ave., Racine, WI 53405. Internet: www.naso.org

Data Bank

Education and Training: Long-term on-the-job training

Average Earnings: $19,000–$46,000

Earnings Growth Potential: High

Total Jobs Held: 258,000

Job Outlook: Rapid increase

Annual Job Openings: 10,900

Related Jobs: Dietitians and nutritionists; fitness workers; physical therapists; recreation workers; recreational therapists; teachers—kindergarten, elementary, middle, and secondary

Personality Types: Realistic-Enterprising-Social

Did You Know?

We are a sports-loving nation. Many who participate in amateur sports dream of becoming paid professional athletes, coaches, or sports officials, but very few beat the odds of making a living from it. Only about 1 out of every 5,000 high school athletes ever signs a professional sports contract. Those athletes who do make it to professional levels find that careers are short and jobs are insecure. Even though the chances of employment as a professional athlete are slim, there are many opportunities for at least a part-time job as a coach, instructor, referee, or umpire in amateur athletics or in high school, college, or university sports.

Dancers and Choreographers

At a Glance

Dancers express ideas and tell stories through the movement of their bodies. Dance styles include classical ballet, modern dance, tap, jazz, and different folk dances. Dancers perform in musicals, operas, TV shows, movies, music videos, and commercials. Dancers must be strong, coordinated, and dedicated. Choreographers create dances and teach dancers. In addition, choreographers usually are involved in auditioning performers. They may work for one company or on a freelance basis. Those who operate their own studios must have good business skills.

Data Bank

Education and Training: Long-term on-the-job training to work experience in a related occupation

Average Earnings: $25,000–$56,000 (for Choreographers)

Earnings Growth Potential: Very high (for Choreographers)

Total Jobs Held: 29,000

Job Outlook: Little change

Annual Job Openings: 1,500

Related Jobs: Actors, producers, and directors; athletes, coaches, umpires, and related workers; barbers, cosmetologists, and other personal appearance workers; fashion designers; musicians, singers, and related workers; set and exhibit designers

Personality Types: Artistic-Social-Realistic

Did You Know?

To dance *en pointe* means to dance on the tips of one's toes, and it is a notoriously difficult skill to master. *Pointe* ballet training traditionally starts at the age of 12, although regular ballet classes usually start much earlier. Most dancers have their first professional auditions by the time they are 17 or 18. But the training and practice for professional ballet dancers never ends. By the time they are 30, most ballet dancers are done with their performing days and move into teaching and choreography.

Career in Focus: *Dance Instructor*

While the opportunities to dance on Broadway may be few, thousands of kids across the country enroll in dance classes each year. Dance instructors primarily teach children and youth from kindergarten up through high school various forms of dance, including ballet, tap, and jazz. They are responsible for creating a safe and fun environment for the participants as well as for coordinating performances and working with parents. Many dance instructors work out of studios, school, or gyms.

Where and When

Dancing is strenuous exercise. Few dancers can continue performing in their forties or fifties due to the stress on the body. Daily rehearsals require long hours, and many dance companies usually tour for part of the year. Dancers in musical productions spend much of their time on the road, and others work in nightclubs or on cruise ships.

For More Information

* National Association of Schools of Dance, 11250 Roger Bacon Dr., Suite 21, Reston, VA 20190. Internet: http://nasd.arts-accredit.org

* Dance/USA, 1111 16th St. NW, Suite 300, Washington, DC 20036. Internet: www.danceusa.org

Musicians, Singers, and Related Workers

At a Glance

Musicians and singers play instruments and perform vocal music. They may perform alone or in groups, before live audiences or in recording studios. Venues may include nightclubs, concert halls, and theaters. Regardless of the setting, musicians and singers spend considerable time practicing. Music directors conduct, direct, plan, and lead instrumental or vocal performances by musical groups such as orchestras, choirs, and glee clubs. Conductors specifically lead instrumental music groups, such as symphony orchestras, dance bands, and show bands. These leaders audition and select musicians, choose appropriate music, and direct rehearsals and performances. Composers create original music such as symphonies, operas, sonatas, radio and television jingles, film scores, and popular songs. Most musicians work nights and weekends and must travel to perform. Because it's so hard to support themselves with music, many take other jobs as well.

Career in Focus: *Arranger*

Arrangers adapt musical compositions to a particular style for orchestras, bands, choral groups, or individuals. For example, a piece written specifically for a full orchestra may be adapted to be played by a small band, or another piece written for a musical may be changed to become a pop song. Many arrangers use computer software to make changes.

Where and When

Working conditions vary dramatically. Musicians typically perform at night and on weekends. Those who work in nightclubs or perform solo or in small groups may travel extensively. The stress of constantly looking for work leads many musicians to find full-time jobs in other occupations while working part time as musicians. Most professional singers work in cities with major recording studios, such as New York, Los Angeles, Chicago, and Nashville. Composers and conductors may hold positions as teachers in high schools and colleges as well.

For More Information

* National Association of Schools of Music, 11250 Roger Bacon Dr., Suite 21, Reston, VA 20190. Internet: http://nasm.arts-accredit.org

---

Data Bank

Education and Training: Long-term on-the-job training to bachelor's or higher degree plus related work experience

Average Earnings: $32,000–$62,000 (for Music Directors and Composers)

Earnings Growth Potential: High (for Music Directors and Composers)

Total Jobs Held: 240,000

Job Outlook: Average increase

Annual Job Openings: 6,800

Related Jobs: Actors, producers, and directors; announcers; dancers and choreographers; musical instrument repairers and tuners

Personality Types: Artistic-Enterprising

Did You Know?

If you want to be a singer but can't find a job in Nashville or New York, consider the Caribbean. Cruise ships hire hundreds of entertainers each year for everything from lounge acts to big musical productions. It won't pay as much as a recording contract, but you get to travel to exotic places and the food is plentiful. And believe it or not, there are books, trade magazines, and Web sites dedicated to helping performers land jobs on cruise ships.

Announcers

At a Glance

Radio announcers (or disc jockeys) plan and perform radio programs. They may choose and play music, interview guests, and write program material. Television announcers and newscasters prepare and present the news, weather, and sports, although most specialize in one of these areas. When emergency situations arise, newscasters must be there to cover them. Show hosts may specialize in a certain area of interest, such as politics, personal finance, sports, or health. Most announcers help prepare the program's content; interview guests; and discuss issues with viewers, listeners, or the studio audience. Some announcers provide commentary for the audience during sporting events, at parades, and on other special occasions. Announcers may make promotional appearances and do remote broadcasts for their stations.

Data Bank

Education and Training: Moderate-term on-the-job training to long-term on-the-job training

Average Earnings: $19,000–$42,000

Earnings Growth Potential: High

Total Jobs Held: 67,000

Job Outlook: Declining

Annual Job Openings: 2,000

Related Jobs: Actors, producers, and directors; authors, writers, and authors; broadcast and sound engineering technicians and radio operators; interpreters and translators; musicians, singers, and related workers; news analysts, reporters, and correspondents; public relations specialists

Personality Types: Enterprising-Social-Artistic

Did You Know?

There were several famous radio announcers before Rush Limbaugh and Howard Stern took to the air. Most notable was a man by the name of Robert Smith, who became famous as a disc jockey in the 1960s and '70s for his gravelly voice and his signature howl. Taking the name Wolfman Jack, Smith created an on-air persona that was known worldwide. He was also noted for playing whatever music he wanted, regardless of the ethnicity of the performer, which caused quite a bit of scandal in those times.

Career in Focus: *Mobile Disc Jockey*

Some DJs announce and play music at clubs, dances, restaurants, weddings, private parties, and other special occasions. They generally have their own equipment, including a huge library of music, and they rent their services out on a job-by-job basis. At special events, they may act as an MC (Master of Ceremonies), keeping the guests informed about everything from the cutting of the cake at a wedding to the last call at the bar.

Where and When

Most announcers work in well-lighted, comfortable, sound-proof studios. Most radio and television stations broadcast for 24 hours a day, so announcers can expect to work unusual schedules.

For More Information

* National Association of Broadcasters, 1771 N St. NW, Washington, DC 20036. Internet: www.nab.org

Authors, Writers, and Editors

At a Glance

Writers and authors write novels and nonfiction books, articles, movies, plays, poems, and ads. Nonfiction writers must establish their credibility through strong research and the use of appropriate sources. Freelance writers sell their work to publishers, manufacturing firms, public relations departments, or advertising agencies. Sometimes, they contract with publishers to write a book or an article. Editors choose the stories and books that publishing houses will print. Magazine editors choose articles for publication and assign stories to writers. They review, rewrite, and edit the work of writers and may also do original writing themselves. Most authors, writers, and editors regularly use personal computers, desktop or electronic publishing systems, and scanners.

Career in Focus: *Advertising Copywriter*

Advertising copywriters prepare advertising copy for use in publications or for broadcasting and they write other materials to promote the sale of a product or service. They often must work with the client to produce advertising themes or slogans and may be involved in the marketing of the product or service. They may also collaborate with an art director, who is responsible for the visual images used in the campaign.

Where and When

Environments range from offices to laboratories to noisy newsrooms. Many authors, writers, and editors work from home or on the road. Freelance writers and editors enjoy flexible hours and creative freedom, but are also usually working under deadlines and are often unsure where their next paycheck will come from. Most salaried editors work in busy offices much of the time and have to deal with production deadline pressures and the stresses of ensuring that the information they publish is accurate. Because of pressure from deadlines, authors, writers, and editors often work overtime or evening and weekend hours. The extensive computer and keyboard work can cause back pain, eyestrain, and fatigue.

For More Information

* American Society of Journalists and Authors, 1501 Broadway, Suite 302, New York, NY 10036. Internet: www.asja.org

* The Association of Writers and Writing Programs, George Mason University, MS 1E3, Fairfax, VA 22030-4444. Internet: www.awpwriter.org

Data Bank

Education and Training: Bachelor's degree

Average Earnings: $38,000–$72,000

Earnings Growth Potential: High

Total Jobs Held: 281,000

Job Outlook: Average increase

Annual Job Openings: 8,800

Related Jobs: Announcers; interpreters and translators; news analysts, reporters, and correspondents; technical writers

Personality Types: Artistic-Enterprising

Did You Know?

The market for fiction is very hard for new writers to break into. The novel *Dune,* by Frank Herbert, may be the best-selling science fiction novel of all time, but it was rejected by more than 20 publishers. One of America's all-time best-selling authors, Stephen King, sold his first novel, *Carrie,* to the publishers at Doubleday for a $2,500 advance. The paperback rights were later sold for $400,000.

Broadcast and Sound Engineering Technicians and Radio Operators

At a Glance

Broadcast and sound engineering technicians and radio operators set up, operate, and maintain the electrical and electronic equipment involved in almost any radio or television broadcast, concert, musical recording, or movie. They operate, install, and repair microphones, TV cameras, digital recorders, projectors, monitors, mixing boards, and antennas. Many technicians also work in program production. The transition to digital recording, editing, and broadcasting has greatly changed this work, making it much easier for these operators and technicians to do their jobs, though it has forced them to learn more computer skills.

Data Bank

Education and Training: Moderate-term on-the-job training to associate degree

Average Earnings: $27,000–$55,000

Earnings Growth Potential: High

Total Jobs Held: 115,000

Job Outlook: Average increase

Annual Job Openings: 4,400

Related Jobs: Communications equipment operators; computer support specialists; electrical and electronics installers and repairers; engineering technicians; science technicians

Personality Types: Realistic-Conventional

Did You Know?

Did you ever wonder how a moviemaker gets a certain sound—maybe the hum of a spacecraft engine or the blast of a car exploding? The soundtrack in a movie is made by sound mixers, using everything from explosives to corn flakes. In the movie *Star Wars*, for example, the sound of a TIE Fighter soaring by is actually just an altered elephant roar, and the sound of a laser blast is simply the bang of a hammer on an antenna tower wire.

Career in Focus: *Sound Engineering Technician*

Sound engineering technicians operate machines and equipment to record, synchronize, mix, or reproduce music, voices, or sound effects in recording studios, sporting arenas, theater productions, or movie and video productions. More specifically, sound mixers or rerecording mixers produce soundtracks for movies or television programs. After filming or recording is complete, these workers may use a process called "dubbing" to insert sounds.

Where and When

This work is usually done indoors in comfortable environments. Those broadcasting news from locations outside the studio may have to work in all types of weather. Technicians may also be required to climb poles or towers and do heavy lifting. Evening, weekend, and holiday work is common because most stations are on the air most hours of the day, seven days a week. Technicians, especially those who work on motion pictures, may be required to travel extensively.

For More Information

* National Association of Broadcasters, 1771 N St. NW, Washington, DC 20036. Internet: www.nab.org
* Society of Broadcast Engineers, 9102 N. Meridian St., Suite 150, Indianapolis, IN 46260. Internet: www.sbe.org
* InfoComm International, 11242 Waples Mill Rd., Suite 200, Fairfax, VA 22030. Internet: www.infocomm.org

Interpreters and Translators

At a Glance

Interpreters and translators convert spoken and written words from one language into another. They must thoroughly understand the subject in order to convert information from one language into another. In addition, they must remain sensitive to the cultures associated with those languages. While interpreters often work into *and* from both languages, translators generally work only *into* their native language. For interpreters, strong research and analytical skills, mental dexterity, and a good memory are important. Translators, who convert written materials from one language into another, must have excellent writing and analytical ability, plus good editing skills. Interpreters and translators may specialize in one of several fields, including conference interpreters, travel guides, and literary translators.

Career in Focus: *Sign Language Interpreter*

Sign language interpreters help people who are deaf or hard of hearing communicate with people who can hear. Sign language interpreters must be fluent in English and in American Sign Language (ASL). ASL has its own grammatical rules, sentence structure, and idioms. Thus sign language interpreting involves more than simply replacing a word of spoken English with a sign representing that word.

Where and When

Interpreters work in a variety of settings, such as hospitals, conference centers, and courtrooms. They are often required to travel. Some work in a school setting or in call centers. Translators often work in office settings or from their own home. Many interpreters and translators freelance.

For More Information

* American Translators Association, 225 Reinekers Ln., Suite 590, Alexandria, VA 22314. Internet: www.atanet.org

* American Literary Translators Association, University of Texas at Dallas, 800 W. Campbell Rd., Mail Station JO51, Richardson, TX 75080-3021. Internet: www.utdallas.edu/alta

* International Medical Interpreters Association, 800 Washington St., Box 271, Boston, MA 02111-1845. Internet: www.imiaweb.org

* National Association of Judiciary Interpreters and Translators, 1707 L St. NW, Suite 570, Washington, DC 20036. Internet: www.najit.org

* Registry of Interpreters for the Deaf, 333 Commerce St., Alexandria, VA 22314. Internet: www.rid.org

Data Bank

Education and Training: Long-term on-the-job training

Average Earnings: $30,000–$57,000

Earnings Growth Potential: High

Total Jobs Held: 51,000

Job Outlook: Rapid increase

Annual Job Openings: 2,300

Related Jobs: Authors, writers, and editors; court reporters; medical transcriptionists; teachers—adult literacy and remedial education; teachers—kindergarten, elementary, middle, and secondary; teachers—postsecondary; teachers—self-enrichment education; teachers—special education

Personality Types: Artistic-Social

Did You Know?

Some experts believe that as many as 800 languages are spoken in New York City, including Aramaic, Bukhari, Chamorro, Kashubian, and Vlashki. Some of these languages have more speakers in New York than in the country of origin. You can imagine the growing need for people who can translate and interpret between English and these other languages. In fact, many businesses and government agencies have an urgent need for translators to help them communicate with their customers both at home and abroad.

News Analysts, Reporters, and Correspondents

At a Glance

News analysts, reporters, and correspondents gather information and write articles or deliver reports about local, state, national, and international events. News analysts—also called newscasters or news anchors—interpret and broadcast news received from various sources. News anchors present news stories and introduce videotaped news or live transmissions from on-the-scene reporters. Newscasters at large stations and networks usually specialize in a particular type of news, such as sports or weather. In covering a story, reporters investigate leads, look at documents, observe events at the scene, and interview people. Reporters take notes and may take photographs or shoot videos. Radio and television reporters often report "live" from the scene of crimes or disasters. Commentators or columnists interpret the news or offer opinions to readers, viewers, or listeners.

Data Bank

Education and Training: Bachelor's degree

Average Earnings: $26,000–$55,000

Earnings Growth Potential: High

Total Jobs Held: 69,000

Job Outlook: Declining

Annual Job Openings: 1,900

Related Jobs: Announcers; authors, writers, and editors; interpreters and translators; public relations specialists; retail salespersons; teachers—kindergarten, elementary, middle, and secondary; teachers—postsecondary

Personality Types: Artistic-Enterprising-Investigative

Did You Know?

Though every precaution is taken to ensure their safety, war correspondents often find themselves in potentially deadly situations. The war in Iraq, begun in March of 2003, had claimed the lives of 131 journalists and media specialists three years later. That's more than the number of journalists killed in the entire Vietnam conflict.

Career in Focus: *News Correspondent*

News correspondents report on news occurring in the U.S. and foreign cities where they are stationed. The job requires more than just a willingness to travel. Correspondents must be comfortable with other cultures and often speak more than one language. They report from dangerous locations and often risk their lives to get the story right. Covering everything from wars and political uprisings to fires and floods, correspondents are often in more danger than most other reporters and analysts.

Where and When

The work of news analysts, reporters, and correspondents is often hectic. Deadlines provide constant stress because broadcasts are sometimes aired with little or no time for preparation. Most work in large, noisy rooms. Working hours vary dramatically, and travel can be quite frequent.

For More Information

* National Association of Broadcasters, 1771 N St. NW, Washington, DC 20036. Internet: www.nab.org

* Dow Jones Newspaper Fund, Inc., P.O. Box 300, Princeton, NJ 08543-0300. Internet: https://www.newspaperfund.org

* Accrediting Council on Education in Journalism and Mass Communications, University of Kansas School of Journalism and Mass Communications, Stauffer-Flint Hall, 1435 Jayhawk Blvd., Lawrence, KS 66045. Internet: www.ku.edu/~acejmc/STUDENT/STUDENT.SHTML

Photographers

At a Glance

Photographers use cameras to record people, places, and events on film. Their images often paint a picture or tell a story. Commercial photographers take pictures of various subjects, such as buildings, models, merchandise, and landscapes. These photographs are then used in books, reports, advertisements, and catalogs. Portrait photographers work in studios, taking pictures of people for special occasions. Some specialize in weddings, religious ceremonies, or school photographs. Many work on location. News photographers—also called photojournalists—photograph newsworthy people, places, and sporting, political, and community events for newspapers, journals, magazines, or television. Today, most photographers use digital cameras instead of traditional film cameras.

Career in Focus: *Scientific Photographer*

Scientific photographers take pictures to illustrate or record scientific or medical phenomena. Their images are used for measurement or analysis or to accompany reports, articles, and other research. They use infrared, time-lapse, ultraviolet, and other kinds of specialized photography to take pictures that a normal camera can't. They might photograph a virus attacking a cell or the moons of Saturn. They typically possess additional knowledge in areas such as engineering, medicine, biology, or chemistry.

Where and When

Working conditions for photographers vary. Those employed by studios usually work a standard 40-hour week. On the flipside, photojournalists must be able to go to work on a moment's notice. News photographers especially can work in uncomfortable and dangerous surroundings. They also work under strict deadlines. Most photographers spend only a small portion of their time taking the photographs—more often they are developing or editing those pictures.

For More Information

＊ Professional Photographers of America, Inc., 229 Peachtree St. NE, Suite 2200, Atlanta, GA 30303. Internet: www.ppa.com

＊ National Press Photographers Association, Inc., 3200 Croasdaile Dr., Suite 306, Durham, NC 27705. Internet: www.nppa.org

＊ American Society of Media Photographers, Inc., 150 N. Second St., Philadelphia, PA 19106. Internet: www.asmp.org

---

Data Bank

Education and Training: Long-term on-the-job training

Average Earnings: $21,000–$44,000

Earnings Growth Potential: High

Total Jobs Held: 152,000

Job Outlook: Average increase

Annual Job Openings: 4,800

Related Jobs: Architects, except landscape and naval; artists and related workers; commercial and industrial designers; desktop publishers; fashion designers; graphic designers; news analysts, reporters, and correspondents; prepress technicians and workers; television, video, and motion picture camera operators and editors

Personality Types: Artistic-Realistic

Did You Know?

The Pulitzer Prize is the most distinguished award in journalism. In addition to awards for reporting, commentary, and even cartoons, the Pulitzer committee gives two awards for photography: one for breaking-news photography and another for feature photography. Many of the most haunting and tragic images that help us to remember history have won the award.

Public Relations Specialists

At a Glance

Public relations specialists serve as advocates for businesses, nonprofit associations, universities, hospitals, and other organizations. They work to present a good public image of their clients. Their job is to spread the clients' good news far and wide and to put a positive "spin" on the bad news. Public relations specialists do more than "tell the organization's story." They must understand the attitudes and concerns of community, consumer, employee, and public interest groups and maintain cooperative relationships with them. They write press releases and speeches and set up "photo opportunities" of their clients doing good things.

Data Bank

Education and Training: Bachelor's degree

Average Earnings: $39,000–$72,000

Earnings Growth Potential: Medium

Total Jobs Held: 275,000

Job Outlook: Rapid increase

Annual Job Openings: 13,100

Related Jobs: Advertising, marketing, promotions, public relations, and sales managers; demonstrators and product promoters; lawyers; market and survey researchers; news analysts, reporters, and correspondents; sales representatives, wholesale and manufacturing

Personality Types: Enterprising-Artistic-Social

Career in Focus: *Press Secretary*

In government, public relations specialists are also called press secretaries, information officers, public affairs specialists, or communication specialists. Their job is to keep the public informed about the activities of agencies and officials. For example, public affairs specialists in the U.S. Department of State keep the public informed of the government's positions on foreign issues. A press secretary for a member of Congress keeps potential voters aware of the representative's accomplishments (especially as elections get closer).

Where and When

Public relations specialists generally work a standard 40-hour workweek, but overtime is common, especially if there is an emergency or crisis. Public relations offices are busy places, and workers are commonly under pressure to meet deadlines, give speeches, and attend meetings.

For More Information

* Public Relations Society of America, Inc., 33 Maiden Lane, New York, NY 10038-5150. Internet: www.prsa.org

* International Association of Business Communicators, 601 Montgomery St., Suite 1900, San Francisco, CA 94111.

Did You Know?

When people are being skeptical, they might refer to a public relations specialist as a "spin doctor." The phrase originated in the 1980s and refers most often to government press secretaries and public affairs specialists, though it can apply to anyone in public relations who tries to give a persuasive slant to information. Though people disagree whether the origin of the phrase goes back to "spinning a yarn" or the "spin" you might put on a ball when playing pool, the idea is that the public doesn't get the whole truth—just the prettiest version of it.

Technical Writers

At a Glance

Technical writers put technical information into easily understandable language. They prepare operating and maintenance manuals, catalogs, parts lists, assembly instructions, sales promotion materials, and project proposals. They plan and edit technical materials and oversee the preparation of illustrations, photographs, diagrams, and charts. Many technical writers work directly with engineers and should have some knowledge of the product or process they are writing about.

Career in Focus: *Business Writer*

Although most technical writers specialize in making sense of information technology, some specialize in communicating business ideas. For example, they may help the manager of a startup firm by writing a business plan that explains to potential investors how the company will make profits. This kind of work requires an understanding of how businesses function, in addition to skill with writing that informs and persuades.

Where and When

Laptop computers and wireless communications permit technical writers to work from home, an office, or on the road. The ability to use the Internet to e-mail, transmit, and download information and assignments, conduct research, or review materials allows them greater flexibility in where and how they complete assignments. Some freelance writers are paid on a project basis and routinely face the pressures of juggling multiple projects and the continual need to find new work. Technical writers may be expected to work evenings, nights, or weekends to coordinate with those in other time zones, meet deadlines, or produce information that complies with project requirements and is acceptable to the client.

For More Information

* Society for Technical Communication, Inc., 9401 Lee Highway, Suite 300, Fairfax, VA 22031. Internet: www.stc.org

---

Data Bank

Education and Training: Bachelor's degree

Average Earnings: $48,000–$80,000

Earnings Growth Potential: Medium

Total Jobs Held: 49,000

Job Outlook: Above-average increase

Annual Job Openings: 1,700

Related Jobs: Announcers; authors, writers, and editors; interpreters and translators; public relations specialists

Personality Types: Artistic-Investigative-Conventional

Did You Know?

Technical writers are sometimes called technical communicators because they often use nonverbal material along with their writing. To produce their documents, they may work with graphic design, page layout, and multimedia software. Increasingly, they are preparing documents by using the interactive technologies of the Web to blend text, graphics, multidimensional images, and sound.

Television, Video, and Motion Picture Camera Operators and Editors

At a Glance

Television, video, and motion picture camera operators produce images that tell a story, inform or entertain an audience, or record an event. Camera operators work behind the scenes on TV shows, documentaries, motion pictures, and industrial films. They shoot the film you see on screen, sometimes from high up on scaffolding or flat on the ground. Producing successful images requires choosing interesting material, selecting appropriate equipment, and applying a good eye and a steady hand to ensure smooth, natural movement of the camera. Film and video editors edit soundtracks, film, and video for the motion picture, cable, and television industries. Making commercial-quality movies and videos requires both creativity and technical expertise.

Data Bank

Education and Training: Bachelor's degree

Average Earnings: $31,000–$70,000

Earnings Growth Potential: High

Total Jobs Held: 52,000

Job Outlook: Average increase

Annual Job Openings: 1,800

Related Jobs: Artists and related workers; broadcast and sound engineering technicians and radio operators; graphic designers; photographers

Personality Types: Artistic-Realistic

Did You Know?

Film editors are responsible for taking reels of footage and cutting the best parts together to make a story that audiences can enjoy in the span of an evening or afternoon. One effect that editors try to create is pacing—for example, a fast pace of cutting during a high-action scene. They sometimes put on music while they work and try to match the pace of the cutting to the pace of the music, which may or may not be the score that's used in the final soundtrack.

Career in Focus: *Director of Photography*

The director of photography (also called a cinematographer) on a film set is responsible for planning and coordinating the actual filming of a motion picture. The DP, as he or she is called for short, determines the lighting requirements and other kinds of equipment needed, decides on the right camera angles, distance, and depth of focus, and then instructs camera operators during the filming process. The DP also views the film after processing in order to make any adjustments.

Where and When

Conditions for these workers vary considerably. Those employed by television and cable networks and advertising agencies usually work a standard 40-hour week, though production schedules may require them to work overtime. Those who work in the movie industry face long, irregular hours. They may have to travel extensively to film on location.

For More Information

❋ International Cinematographer's Guild, 80 Eighth Ave., 14th Floor, New York, NY 10011.

❋ National Association of Broadcast Employees and Technicians, 501 Third St. NW, 6th Floor, Washington, DC 20001. Internet: www.nabetcwa.org

Audiologists

At a Glance

Audiologists work with people who have hearing, balance, and other ear problems. They examine individuals of all ages and identify those with the symptoms of hearing loss and other problems using audiometers, computers, and other testing devices. They assess the nature and extent of the problems and help patients manage them. Treatment may include examining and cleaning the ear canal, fitting for hearing aids, and programming cochlear implants. In hearing clinics, audiologists may develop and carry out treatment programs. In other settings, audiologists may work with other health and education providers as part of a team.

Career in Focus: *Clinic Director*

Directors of speech-and-hearing clinics oversee the daily operations of their programs. They consult with medical and professional staff of other departments to coordinate joint patient care. They conduct conferences and plan training programs to maintain the proficiency of their staff. They also decide whether to use new methods and equipment to meet patients' needs. They often set the work schedule for personnel and may coordinate research projects to develop new approaches to therapy.

Where and When

Audiologists usually work in clean, comfortable surroundings. While the job is not physically demanding, it does require intense concentration. Most full-time audiologists work a 40-hour week, which may include some weekends and evenings to meet the needs of patients.

For More Information

* American Speech-Language-Hearing Association, 2200 Research Blvd., Rockville, MD 20850. Internet: www.asha.org

* Audiology Foundation of America, 8 N. 3rd St., Suite 301, Lafayette, IN 47901. Internet: www.audfound.org

Data Bank

Education and Training: First professional degree

Average Earnings: $51,000–$79,000

Earnings Growth Potential: Low

Total Jobs Held: 13,000

Job Outlook: Rapid increase

Annual Job Openings: 600

Related Jobs: Occupational therapists; optometrists; physical therapists; psychologists; speech-language pathologists

Personality Types: Investigative-Social

Did You Know?

One of the most common side effects of aging is hearing loss. In the United States, it's estimated that only 5 percent of children have some degree of hearing loss, but that it affects as much as 80 percent of adults over the age of 65. It also has been shown to affect men more frequently than women. Studies show that as people age, they particularly lose their ability to hear high-pitched noises, which many elderly husbands use as an excuse for not listening to their wives.

Chiropractors

At a Glance

Chiropractors help people who have problems with their muscles, nerves, or skeleton, especially the spine. Chiropractors believe that problems with these systems keep the body from functioning normally and lower its resistance to disease. Like other medical professionals, they examine patients, order tests, and take X-rays. Chiropractors provide natural health treatments and rely on the body's inherent healing abilities, without the use of drugs or surgery. They primarily treat patients by massaging or adjusting the spinal column. Some chiropractors use water, light, ultrasound, electric, acupuncture, and heat therapy. They may also apply supports such as straps and braces. Well over half of all chiropractors are self-employed.

Data Bank

Education and Training: First professional degree

Average Earnings: $46,000–$97,000

Earnings Growth Potential: Very high

Total Jobs Held: 49,000

Job Outlook: Above-average increase

Annual Job Openings: 1,800

Related Jobs: Athletic trainers; massage therapists; occupational therapists; physical therapists; physicians and surgeons; podiatrists; veterinarians

Personality Types: Social-Investigative-Realistic

Did You Know?

Headaches can result from poor posture, tension, or a misalignment of the spinal cord. Using massage, heat therapy, and realignment exercises and techniques, chiropractors can help people who suffer from persistent or chronic headaches. They also teach people how to prevent headaches in the first place. Whether the bill for your treatment gives you a new headache is a different story.

Career in Focus: *Chiropractic Assistant*

Chiropractic assistants are involved in both patient and office management. They may interview new patients, teach them about treatments, perform exams, or take X-rays. They also may be responsible for answering the phone and making appointments, handling billing, and keeping track of patient files. They generally do not treat patients, though those studying to become a licensed chiropractor can learn a great deal by being an assistant.

Where and When

Chiropractors work in clean, comfortable offices and generally work a standard 40-hour week. Solo practitioners set their own hours but may work evenings and weekends to accommodate patients. Like most health practitioners, chiropractors are on their feet for most of the day.

For More Information

* American Chiropractic Association, 1701 Clarendon Blvd., Arlington, VA 22209. Internet: www.acatoday.org

* International Chiropractors Association, 1110 N. Glebe Rd., Suite 650, Arlington, VA 22201. Internet: www.chiropractic.org

* Council on Chiropractic Education, 8049 N. 85th Way, Scottsdale, AZ 85258-4321. Internet: www.cce-usa.org

* Federation of Chiropractic Licensing Boards, 5401 W. 10th St., Suite 101, Greeley, CO 80634-4400. Internet: www.fclb.org

* National Board of Chiropractic Examiners, 901 54th Ave., Greeley, CO 80634. Internet: www.nbce.org

Dentists

At a Glance

Dentists remove decay, fill cavities, examine X-rays, and straighten and repair teeth. They also perform corrective surgery on gums and supporting bones to treat gum diseases. Dentists extract teeth and make models and measurements for dentures to replace missing teeth. They provide instruction on diet, brushing, flossing, and other aspects of dental care. They also administer anesthetics and write prescriptions for antibiotics and other medications. Dentists use a variety of equipment, including drills, probes, forceps, brushes, and scalpels. They wear masks, gloves, and safety glasses to protect themselves and their patients from infectious diseases. Many are self-employed. Most are general practitioners, handling a variety of dental needs, though there are several specialties ranging from those who specialize in root canals to those who focus on replacing lost teeth.

Career in Focus: *Orthodontist*

As children grow, their teeth may form improperly, which can cause problems later in life. That's when they need to see an orthodontist. Orthodontists are the largest group of dental specialists (and the ones most feared by kids). They specialize in straightening teeth by applying pressure to them with braces, space fillers, or retainers. Thankfully, technology has dramatically improved the appearance of such devices, making kids a little less afraid of braces (though parents still fear paying for them).

Where and When

Dentists work four or five days a week, though many work evenings and weekends to accommodate their patients' schedules. Most own their own business and work alone or with a small staff or a partner. They take every precaution to keep their work environment clean and safe.

For More Information

* American Dental Association, Commission on Dental Accreditation, 211 E. Chicago Ave., Chicago, IL 60611. Internet: www.ada.org

* American Dental Education Association, 1400 K St. NW, Suite 1100, Washington, DC 20005. Internet: www.adea.org

* Academy of General Dentistry, 211 E. Chicago Ave., Suite 900, Chicago, IL 60611. Internet: www.agd.org

Data Bank

Education and Training: First professional degree

Average Earnings: $106,000–$166,400+

Earnings Growth Potential: High

Total Jobs Held: 142,000

Job Outlook: Above-average increase

Annual Job Openings: 6,200

Related Jobs: Chiropractors; optometrists; physicians and surgeons; podiatrists; veterinarians

Personality Types: Investigative-Realistic-Social

Did You Know?

Dentists have been practicing for nearly 7,000 years, although treatments have changed dramatically over the millennia. In ancient Babylon, for example, "dentists" used worms, prayers, and herbs to treat tooth decay. In the Middle Ages, dentists were considered the first surgeons—although about all they could do was remove teeth, which they did to treat nearly every condition you can think of, and without the use of anesthetics (unless brandy counts).

Dietitians and Nutritionists

At a Glance

Dietitians and nutritionists plan, prepare, and serve meals in clinics, schools, nursing homes, and hospitals. They help prevent and treat illnesses by teaching clients to eat properly. Some specialize in helping overweight or critically ill patients, or in caring for kidney or diabetic patients. In addition, clinical dietitians in nursing care facilities, small hospitals, or correctional facilities may manage the food service department. Some are self-employed and act as consultants. Increased public interest in nutrition has led to job opportunities in food manufacturing and marketing. In these areas, dietitians analyze foods, prepare literature for distribution, or report on issues such as nutritional content.

Data Bank

Education and Training: Bachelor's degree

Average Earnings: $42,000–$63,000

Earnings Growth Potential: Low

Total Jobs Held: 60,000

Job Outlook: Average increase

Annual Job Openings: 2,600

Related Jobs: Dietetic technicians; food service managers; health educators; registered nurses

Personality Types: Investigative-Social

Did You Know?

According to the National Health and Nutrition Examination Survey, more than 60 percent of American adults are overweight, and more than 30 percent of them are obese. Obesity has become the number one risk factor for many diseases in the United States, including heart disease. Dietitians and nutritionists are on the frontlines battling this trend by educating Americans on how to eat healthy.

Career in Focus: *Community Dietitian*

Community dietitians counsel the public on nutritional practices designed to prevent disease and promote health. Working in places such as public health clinics, home health agencies, and health maintenance organizations, community dietitians evaluate individual needs, develop nutritional care plans, and instruct people on how to eat properly. Dietitians working in home health agencies also provide instruction on grocery shopping and food preparation to the elderly, individuals with special needs, and children.

Where and When

Dietitians and nutritionists generally work a regular 40-hour week, though about one in four works part time. They usually work in clean, comfortable settings, though those involved directly in food preparation work in warm, busy kitchens. Most of them are on their feet for much of the workday.

For More Information

* The American Dietetic Association, 120 S. Riverside Plaza, Suite 2000, Chicago, IL 60606-6995. Internet: www.eatright.org

* The Commission on Dietetic Registration, 120 S. Riverside Plaza, Suite 2000, Chicago, IL 60606-6995. Internet: www.cdrnet.org

Occupational Therapists

At a Glance

Occupational therapists help individuals who have mental, physical, developmental, or emotional disabilities to become independent and productive in their work and daily life. Occupational therapists assist clients in performing activities of all types, ranging from using a computer to caring for daily needs such as dressing, cooking, and eating. They may help a patient learn to use a wheelchair or develop a new skill. They also help patients find jobs. They usually work in hospitals, schools, or rehab centers, and some provide home health care as well.

Career in Focus: *School Occupational Therapist*

Occupational therapists may work exclusively with individuals in a particular age group or with particular disabilities. In schools, for example, therapists evaluate children's abilities, recommend and provide therapy, modify classroom equipment, and help children participate in school activities. A therapist may work with children individually, lead small groups in the classroom, consult with a teacher, or serve on a committee.

Where and When

Occupational therapists generally work a 40-hour week, though more than 25 percent of them work part time. The work can be exhausting; therapists are on their feet much of the time, and some lifting and moving may be required.

For More Information

❋ American Occupational Therapy Association, 4720 Montgomery Lane, P.O. Box 31220, Bethesda, MD 20824-1220. Internet: www.aota.org

---

Data Bank

Education and Training: Master's degree

Average Earnings: $57,000–$84,000

Earnings Growth Potential: Low

Total Jobs Held: 104,000

Job Outlook: Rapid increase

Annual Job Openings: 4,600

Related Jobs: Athletic trainers; physical therapists; recreational therapists; respiratory therapists; speech-language pathologists

Personality Types: Social-Investigative

Did You Know?

Beginning in 2007, a master's degree or higher will be the minimum education requirement in order to be a licensed therapist. In addition to a master's degree, individuals must pass a national certification exam to become a registered occupational therapist.

Optometrists

At a Glance

Optometrists examine people's eyes to diagnose vision problems and eye diseases. They prescribe glasses and contact lenses. They also prescribe drugs to treat some eye diseases. Optometrists often provide preoperative and postoperative care to cataract patients, as well as to patients who have had laser vision or other eye surgery. Some optometrists work especially with the elderly or children. Others develop ways to protect workers' eyes from on-the-job strain or injury. A few teach optometry, perform research, or do consulting.

Data Bank

Education and Training: First professional degree

Average Earnings: $71,000–$126,000

Earnings Growth Potential: High

Total Jobs Held: 35,000

Job Outlook: Rapid increase

Annual Job Openings: 2,000

Related Jobs: Chiropractors; dentists; physicians and surgeons; podiatrists; psychologists; veterinarians

Personality Types: Investigative-Social-Realistic

Did You Know?

Famous American inventor Benjamin Franklin was both near-sighted and far-sighted. Tired of having to switch back and forth between two pairs of glasses, he invented bifocals in 1784. The top half of the lenses allowed him to see far away, and the bottom half allowed him to see up close. He soon became recognizable by his glasses alone, and many depictions of him show him with his invention perched on his nose.

Career in Focus: *Ophthalmologist*

Ophthalmologists are physicians who perform eye surgery, as well as diagnose and treat eye diseases and injuries. Like optometrists, they also examine eyes and prescribe eyeglasses and contact lenses; however, the education requirements for becoming an ophthalmologist are more intense. For more information about the requirements and earnings for ophthalmologists and other physicians, see the section on physicians and surgeons.

Where and When

Optometrists work in clean, comfortable offices and labs. Most work a 40-hour week, though many work weekends and evenings to meet the needs of their patients. Most are self-employed in their own private practice.

For More Information

* Association of Schools and Colleges of Optometry, 6110 Executive Blvd., Suite 420, Rockville, MD 20852. Internet: www.opted.org

* American Optometric Association, Educational Services, 243 N. Lindbergh Blvd., St. Louis, MO 63141. Internet: www.aoa.org

Pharmacists

At a Glance

Pharmacists measure and sell medication prescribed by physicians and provide information to patients about the medications and their use. They also provide information about over-the-counter drugs and make recommendations to patients. Pharmacists must understand the use, effects, and composition of drugs in order to inform patients about reactions and possible side effects. Most pharmacists work in a community setting, such as a retail drugstore, or in a health-care facility, such as a hospital, nursing home, or mental health institution. Most pharmacists keep confidential records of patients' drug therapies to prevent harmful interactions. Pharmacists are responsible for the accuracy of every prescription that is filled, but they often rely upon pharmacy technicians and pharmacy aides to assist them in dispensing drugs.

Career in Focus: *Geriatric Pharmacist*

Geriatric pharmacy is an area experiencing rapid job growth. These pharmacists specialize in administering drug regiments to the elderly in hospitals, nursing homes, assisted-living facilities, and home care settings. Because many of today's elderly are taking more than one prescription drug, these pharmacists must be particularly aware of possible drug interactions.

Where and When

Pharmacists work in clean, well-ventilated areas. Because many of the medications need to be kept sterile or are dangerous, pharmacists wear gloves and masks and use other special equipment. Some pharmacists may work extended hours, nights, or weekends, and they tend to spend a lot of time on their feet. About one in five works part time.

For More Information

* American Association of Colleges of Pharmacy, 1727 King St., Alexandria, VA 22314. Internet: www.aacp.org

* American Society of Health-System Pharmacists, 7272 Wisconsin Ave., Bethesda, MD 20814. Internet: www.ashp.org

* National Association of Chain Drug Stores, 413 N. Lee St., Alexandria, VA 22313. Internet: www.nacds.org

* Academy of Managed Care Pharmacy, 100 N. Pitt St., Suite 400, Alexandria, VA 22314. Internet: www.amcp.org

* American Pharmacists Association, 2215 Constitution Ave. NW, Washington, DC 20037. Internet: www.pharmacist.com

Data Bank

Education and Training: First professional degree

Average Earnings: $96,000–$123,000

Earnings Growth Potential: Low

Total Jobs Held: 270,000

Job Outlook: Above-average increase

Annual Job Openings: 10,600

Related Jobs: Biological scientists; medical scientists; pharmacy technicians and aides; physicians and surgeons; registered nurses

Personality Types: Investigative-Conventional-Social

Did You Know?

Though statistics vary, current studies suggest that Americans fill more than 3.5 billion prescriptions per year, which is an average of 14 prescriptions per person. While this certainly provides added job security for pharmacists, it has led some physicians and policy makers to wonder if we aren't overmedicated as a society. It has also led some people to consider alternative cures to their ailments, such as acupuncture or herbal medicines.

Physical Therapists

At a Glance

Physical therapists work with accident victims, stroke patients, and people with disabilities to restore function, improve mobility, and relieve pain. They also promote overall fitness and health. Treatment often includes exercise for patients who lack flexibility, strength, or endurance. Therapists may also use electricity, heat, or cold to relieve pain, reduce swelling, or increase flexibility. Therapists sometimes teach patients to use assistive devices, such as crutches, prostheses, and wheelchairs. They often show patients exercises to do at home to speed up their recovery.

Data Bank

Education and Training: Master's degree

Average Earnings: $62,000–$88,000

Earnings Growth Potential: Low

Total Jobs Held: 186,000

Job Outlook: Rapid increase

Annual Job Openings: 7,900

Related Jobs: Audiologists; chiropractors; occupational therapists; recreational therapists; speech-language pathologists

Personality Types: Social-Investigative-Realistic

Did You Know?

You've probably heard of limb reattachment—where a hand, arm, foot, or leg that has been cut off is replaced—but have you ever heard of a limb transplant? This somewhat controversial procedure first began in 1998 and involves taking someone else's limb and attaching it to the patient. Such procedures are dangerous, as the body may reject the new tissue, which can cause a serious infection. In order to avoid rejection, patients with transplants of any kind must take drugs to suppress a reaction. Those with transplanted limbs must also undergo rigorous physical therapy as well, often for several hours every day.

Career in Focus:
Orthopedic Therapist

While some physical therapists treat a wide range of ailments, others specialize in areas such as pediatrics, geriatrics, or neurology. One of the most common forms of physical therapy is orthopedic therapy. It is designed to help patients who have problems or limitations with their muscles, ligaments, tendons, and bones. This could include people with arthritis, those recovering from surgery or sports-related injuries, or people with spinal dysfunction that restricts their muscle control. Several hospitals and institutes across the country have programs specializing in orthopedic therapy.

Where and When

Physical therapists work in hospitals, clinics, and private offices. Some of them treat patients in their own homes. Most work a standard 40-hour week, though one in four works part time. The job can be physically demanding as therapists must stoop, kneel, crouch, and stand for long periods, in addition to lifting patients and helping them move.

For More Information

❋ American Physical Therapy Association, 1111 N. Fairfax St., Alexandria, VA 22314-1488. Internet: www.apta.org

Physician Assistants

At a Glance

Physician assistants always work under the supervision of a physician. They handle many of the routine but time-consuming tasks physicians do, such as taking medical records, examining patients, ordering X-rays and tests, and making diagnoses. They also treat minor injuries by suturing, splinting, and casting. In most states, physician assistants may prescribe medications. PAs also may order medical supplies or equipment and supervise other technicians and assistants. PAs may be the principal care providers in rural or inner city clinics, where a physician is present for only one or two days each week.

Career in Focus: *Surgical Physician Assistant*

Physician assistants specializing in surgery provide preoperative and postoperative care and may work as first or second assistants during major surgery, helping with the prepping, positioning, and transportation of the patient as well. They are often responsible for providing labs and records to the surgeon, managing patient issues during preop, and organizing follow-up care. These are in addition to the duties they share with other physician assistants.

Where and When

Physician assistants spend much of their time standing or walking, and their schedules vary considerably. Those working at hospitals may work weekends, nights, or early mornings and may also be on call. Most physician assistants in clinics usually work a 40-hour week.

For More Information

* American Academy of Physician Assistants Information Center, 950 N. Washington St., Alexandria, VA 22314. Internet: www.aapa.org
* Accreditation Review Commission on Education for the Physician Assistants, 12000 Findley Rd., Suite 240, Johns Creek, Georgia 30097. Internet: www.arc-pa.org
* National Commission on Certification of Physician Assistants, Inc., 12000 Findley Rd., Suite 200, Duluth, GA 30097. Internet: www.nccpa.net

Data Bank

Education and Training: Master's degree

Average Earnings: $71,000–$100,000

Earnings Growth Potential: Low

Total Jobs Held: 75,000

Job Outlook: Rapid increase

Annual Job Openings: 4,300

Related Jobs: Audiologists; occupational therapists; physical therapists; registered nurses; speech-language pathologists

Personality Types: Social-Investigative-Realistic

Did You Know?

According to the U.S. Department of Labor, physician assistant is one of the fastest-growing fields in the nation. The rising cost of health care is forcing hospitals and clinics to use more and more PAs to cut down the cost of hiring physicians. The occupation pays quite well, considering that the educational requirements for becoming a PA are not nearly as rigorous as those for physicians. The profession hasn't yet agreed on what title to use for the few physician assistants who earn a Ph.D. degree. Although people with doctoral degrees in other fields commonly use the title "Doctor," it could cause confusion in a medical setting.

Physicians and Surgeons

At a Glance

Physicians help people who are sick or have been hurt. They examine patients, perform tests, diagnose illnesses, prescribe and administer treatments, and teach people about health care. Family and general practitioners are often the first point of contact for people seeking health care. Acting as the traditional family doctor, they treat a wide range of ailments and injuries. General internists diagnose and provide treatment for diseases and injuries of internal organs such as the stomach or liver. General pediatricians are concerned with the health of infants, children, and teenagers. Obstetricians and gynecologists focus on women's health. They also provide care related to pregnancy and the reproductive system. Psychiatrists assess and treat mental illnesses through a combination of therapy, hospitalization, and medication. Surgeons perform operations on patients with life-threatening illnesses and injuries. Most physicians work in hospitals, clinics, and private practice.

Data Bank

Education and Training: First professional degree

Average Earnings: $116,000–$166,400+ (does not include Surgeons)

Earnings Growth Potential: Very high

Total Jobs Held: 568,000

Job Outlook: Rapid increase

Annual Job Openings: 26,000

Related Jobs: Chiropractors; dentists; optometrists; physician assistants; podiatrists; registered nurses; veterinarians

Personality Types: Investigative-Social-Realistic

Did You Know?

In 2008, 43 percent of all physicians and surgeons worked 50 or more hours a week, and only 9 percent worked part time. Physicians have been known to work long shifts and go for 20 hours or more without sleep. They are often on call as well, making a doctor's workweek one of the most demanding of any job on the market.

Career in Focus: *Anesthesiologist*

Anesthesiologists focus on the care of surgical patients and pain relief. Anesthesiologists are responsible for maintaining the patient's heart rate, body temperature, blood pressure, and breathing throughout surgery, while at the same time administering medications for pain. They often work outside the operating room as well, providing pain relief in the intensive care unit, during labor and delivery, and for those who suffer from chronic pain.

Where and When

Many physicians work in small private offices or clinics, often assisted by a staff. More physicians are practicing in groups or health-care organizations as part of a team, which allows for more time off. Most physicians work long, irregular hours, and travel can be quite frequent.

For More Information

* Association of American Medical Colleges, Section for Student Services, 2450 N St. NW, Washington, DC 20037. Internet: www.aamc.org/students

* Federation of State Medical Boards, P.O. Box 619850, Dallas, TX 75261-9850. Internet: www.fsmb.org

* American Medical Association, 515 N. State St., Chicago, IL 60654. Internet: www.ama-assn.org/go/becominganmd

* American Osteopathic Association, Department of Communications, 142 E. Ontario St., Chicago, IL 60611. Internet: www.osteopathic.org

Podiatrists

At a Glance

Podiatrists diagnose and treat diseases and injuries of the foot and lower leg. They may treat corns, calluses, ingrown toenails, bunions, heel spurs, and arch problems. They also treat ankle and foot injuries, deformities, and infections. They take care of foot problems caused by diseases such as diabetes or arthritis. They prescribe medications, set fractures, perform surgery, and order physical therapy. They also fit for corrective shoe inserts, make plaster casts, and design custom-made shoes.

Career in Focus: *Orthotic Practitioner*

These certified specialists examine patients and assess their needs for orthotics—mechanical devices designed to help control or correct limb movements. They examine patients, decide what kinds of devices are necessary, fit and adjust the devices, and instruct patients on their use. Because many foot problems are cured by inserts and special shoes, orthotic practitioners spend much of their time doing the work of podiatrists.

Where and When

Podiatrists spend most of their time in their own offices, though they may also visit patients in nursing homes or perform surgery at hospitals. Those who work in private practice set their own hours, but still may work evenings and weekends to accommodate patients.

For More Information

* American Podiatric Medical Association, 9312 Old Georgetown Rd., Bethesda, MD 20814-1621. Internet: www.apma.org

* American Association of Colleges of Podiatric Medicine, 15850 Crabbs Branch Way, Suite 320, Rockville, MD 20855. Internet: www.aacpm.org

---

Data Bank

Education and Training: First professional degree

Average Earnings: $78,000–$166,400+

Earnings Growth Potential: Very high

Total Jobs Held: 12,000

Job Outlook: Average increase

Annual Job Openings: 300

Related Jobs: Athletic trainers; chiropractors; massage therapists; occupational therapists; orthotists and prosthetists; physical therapists; physicians and surgeons

Personality Types: Investigative-Social-Realistic

Did You Know?

The human foot is a complex structure. It contains 26 bones, plus muscles, nerves, ligaments, and blood vessels. The 52 total bones in your two feet make up about one-fourth of all the bones in your body. As people become more physically active across all age groups, openings for podiatrists will continue to grow. Another factor is the increasing number of patients with obesity and diabetes, both of which can cause problems with the lower extremities.

Radiation Therapists

At a Glance

Radiation therapists use machines to administer radiation treatment to cancer patients. The machines, called linear accelerators, project high-energy X-rays that shrink and sometimes destroy cancerous cells. Therapists both advise patients and perform the treatment. Because many patients are under stress, it is important for the therapist to maintain a positive attitude and provide emotional support. Treatment can take anywhere from 10 to 30 minutes and is usually administered once a day, five days a week, for a period of several weeks. Radiation therapists most often work in hospitals and cancer treatment centers.

Data Bank

Education and Training: Associate degree

Average Earnings: $61,000–$91,000

Earnings Growth Potential: Low

Total Jobs Held: 15,000

Job Outlook: Rapid increase

Annual Job Openings: 700

Related Jobs: Cardiovascular technologists and technicians; dental hygienists; diagnostic medical sonographers; nuclear medicine technologists; nursing and psychiatric aides; physical therapist assistants and aides; radiologic technologists and technicians; registered nurses

Personality Types: Social-Realistic-Conventional

Did You Know?

Cancer is the cause of death for nearly 500,000 people per year and more than a million new cases are discovered each year, according to the American Cancer Society. Yet most cancers are preventable with exercise and a healthy diet, not to mention routine checkups. And, of course, it pays not to smoke, as one-third of cancer cases are the result of tobacco use.

Career in Focus:
Dosimetrist

Dosimetrists are technicians who calculate the amount of radiation that will be needed for treating each patient. The process involves complex mathematical calculations. They often prepare the treatment devices and work closely with the radiation oncologist (the physician) and the radiation therapist to ensure that the patient is getting just the right amount of treatment. After each session, dosimetrists review records to ensure that the treatment plan is working and to keep unwanted side effects to a minimum.

Where and When

Radiation therapists work in clean, well-ventilated environments, and great care is taken to limit their exposure to dangerous levels of radiation. They work on their feet most of the time, and may be required to do considerable lifting and maneuvering in order to get patients on and off treatment tables. Unlike other medical professionals, therapists generally only work a 40-hour week, mostly during the day.

For More Information

* American Registry of Radiologic Technologists, 1255 Northland Dr., St. Paul, MN 55120. Internet: www.arrt.org

* American Society of Radiologic Technologists, 15000 Central Ave. SE, Albuquerque, NM 87123. Internet: www.asrt.org

Recreational Therapists

At a Glance

Recreational therapists help people with disabilities or illnesses improve their health and well-being. They teach patients games, arts and crafts, dance, music, and sports activities and take them on community outings. These activities help patients regain skills they've lost because of illness or injury, and also improve their state of mind. More specifically, recreational therapy helps individuals reduce depression, stress, and anxiety. It also helps them recover basic motor functioning and reasoning abilities. Recreational therapy helps people build confidence so that they can enjoy greater independence. In addition, therapists teach people how to use community resources. They work closely with medical staff in hospitals and nursing homes, and are careful to document each patient's progress.

Career in Focus: *Community-Based Recreational Therapist*

Community-based recreational therapists may work in park and recreation departments, special-education programs for school districts, or programs for older adults and people with disabilities. In these programs, therapists use activities and outings to develop specific skills, while providing opportunities for exercise, creativity, and fun.

Where and When

Recreational therapists work primarily in special activity rooms, though they spend some time in offices planning activities and doing paperwork. They may be required to travel locally, and often accompany their clients to public areas such as swimming pools and theaters. Therapists often lift and carry heavy equipment, and can lead recreational activities that require physical exercise. They sometimes work evenings, weekends, and holidays.

For More Information

* American Therapeutic Recreation Association, 629 N. Main St., Hattiesburg, MS 39401. Internet: http://atra-online.com

* National Therapeutic Recreation Society, 22377 Belmont Ridge Rd., Ashburn, VA 20148-4501. Internet: www.nrpa.org

* National Council for Therapeutic Recreation Certification, 7 Elmwood Dr., New City, NY 10956. Internet: www.nctrc.org

Data Bank

Education and Training: Bachelor's degree

Average Earnings: $31,000–$50,000

Earnings Growth Potential: Medium

Total Jobs Held: 23,000

Job Outlook: Above-average increase

Annual Job Openings: 1,200

Related Jobs: Counselors; occupational therapists; physical therapists; speech-language pathologists; teachers—special education

Personality Types: Social-Artistic

Did You Know?

Individuals in nursing homes account for less than 10 percent of the total population over the age of 65. The majority of retirees are living in their own homes (perhaps Florida condos). Yet many of them will still take advantage of some of the services recreational therapists offer through community outreach programs.

Registered Nurses

At a Glance

Registered nurses (RNs) care for the sick and injured and help people stay healthy. In clinics, hospitals, and nursing homes, they provide much of the day-to-day care for patients. Under a doctor's supervision, they take patient histories, help perform tests, give treatments and medications, and help with patient follow-up and rehabilitation. RNs teach patients and their families how to manage their illness or injury, including post-treatment home care needs, diet and exercise programs, and self-administration of medication. RNs also might run general health screening or immunization clinics, blood drives, and public seminars on health issues.

Data Bank

Education and Training: Associate degree

Average Earnings: $53,000–$78,000

Earnings Growth Potential: Low

Total Jobs Held: 2,619,000

Job Outlook: Rapid increase

Annual Job Openings: 103,900

Related Jobs: Dental hygienists; diagnostic medical sonographers; emergency medical technicians and paramedics; licensed practical and licensed vocational nurses; physician assistants

Personality Types: Social-Investigative

Did You Know?

Nurses save lives. Though this might seem obvious, studies have been done to show the effect that nurses have on overall patient care. According to several studies, hospitals with more registered nurses have lower death rates following surgeries than those with fewer nurses. That's because it's often a nurse who notices whether a patient has a bad reaction to a drug, complications from surgery, or other problems. After all, nurses are the medical professionals whom patients see the most.

Career in Focus: *Nurse Practitioner*

Most RNs work as staff nurses, providing critical healthcare services along with physicians and surgeons. However, some RNs choose to become nurse practitioners, who work independently or in collaboration with physicians. Nurse practitioners provide basic health care to patients and increasingly serve as primary care providers as well. The most common areas of specialty for nurse practitioners include family practice, adult practice, women's health, and pediatrics. In most states, nurse practitioners can prescribe medications.

Where and When

Registered nurses have demanding jobs. They may spend considerable time walking and standing, and they are often required to work nights, weekends, and holidays (in addition to being on call). Nurses also confront health hazards because of the conditions they treat and the equipment they use, though strict guidelines help guard against potential dangers.

For More Information

* National League for Nursing, 61 Broadway, 33rd Floor, New York, NY 10006. Internet: www.nln.org

* American Association of Colleges of Nursing, 1 Dupont Circle NW, Suite 530, Washington, DC 20036. Internet: www.aacn.nche.edu

* American Nurses Association, 8515 Georgia Ave., Suite 400, Silver Spring, MD 20910. Internet: http://nursingworld.org

* National Council of State Boards of Nursing, 111 E. Wacker Dr., Suite 2900, Chicago, IL 60601. Internet: www.ncsbn.org

* National Association of Clinical Nurse Specialists, 2090 Linglestown Rd., Suite 107, Harrisburg, PA 17110. Internet: www.nacns.org

Respiratory Therapists

At a Glance

Respiratory therapists evaluate, treat, and care for patients with breathing problems, from premature babies to heart attack victims. They perform tests, connect patients to machines that help them breathe, and teach patients how to use these machines at home. Respiratory therapists provide temporary relief to patients with chronic asthma or emphysema. They also provide emergency care to patients who are victims of a heart attack, stroke, drowning, or shock. Therapists may also help in surgery by removing mucus from a patient's lungs so that he or she can breathe more easily. In some hospitals, therapists perform tasks that fall outside their traditional role, such as disease prevention, case management, and polysomnography—the diagnosis of breathing disorders during sleep.

Career in Focus: *Respiratory Therapy Technician*

Respiratory therapy technicians follow specific care procedures under the direction of respiratory therapists and physicians. In clinical practice, many of the daily duties of therapists and technicians overlap. Furthermore, the two have the same education and training requirements. However, therapists generally have greater responsibility than technicians. It is likely that an individual may start as a technician and work his or her way up to the level of therapist.

Where and When

Respiratory therapists generally work 40 hours per week, though those hours may include evenings, nights, and weekends. They often spend long periods standing and walking. In emergency situations they are required to be cool under pressure. Those employed in home health care must travel frequently.

For More Information

* American Association for Respiratory Care, 9425 N. MacArthur Blvd., Suite 100, Irving, TX 75063. Internet: www.aarc.org

* Commission on Accreditation for Allied Health Education Programs, 1361 Park St., Clearwater, FL 33756. Internet: www.caahep.org

* Committee on Accreditation for Respiratory Care, 1248 Harwood Rd., Bedford, TX 76021.

* National Board for Respiratory Care, Inc., 18000 W. 105th St., Olathe, KS 66061. Internet: www.nbrc.org

Data Bank

Education and Training: Associate degree

Average Earnings: $45,000–$63,000

Earnings Growth Potential: Low

Total Jobs Held: 106,000

Job Outlook: Rapid increase

Annual Job Openings: 4,100

Related Jobs: Athletic trainers; cardiovascular technologists and technicians; diagnostic medical sonographers; nuclear medicine technologists; occupational therapists; physical therapists; radiation therapists; radiologic technologists and technicians; registered nurses

Personality Types: Social-Investigative-Realistic

Did You Know?

While we don't recommend going without it for any length of time, it's true that too much oxygen can be harmful. Pulmonary oxygen toxicity can occur if an individual takes in too much oxygen. The lungs can begin to bleed internally and then thicken and scar, sometimes causing irreversible damage. Therefore, respiratory therapists are careful to ensure that a patient is getting just the right amount of oxygen.

Speech-Language Pathologists

At a Glance

Speech-language pathologists, also called speech therapists, help people who cannot produce speech sounds clearly and those with speech rhythm and fluency problems, such as stuttering. They help people with voice disorders or problems understanding language. They may work with people who wish to improve their communication skills or people with attention, memory, and problem-solving disorders. They may also work with people who have swallowing difficulties. Speech-language pathologists use assessments such as standardized tests and other special instruments to diagnose the nature of the problem. They then develop a plan of care tailored to each patient's needs. They may teach sign language to nonspeaking patients as well.

Data Bank

Education and Training: Master's degree

Average Earnings: $52,000–$82,000

Earnings Growth Potential: Low

Total Jobs Held: 119,000

Job Outlook: Above-average increase

Annual Job Openings: 4,400

Related Jobs: Audiologists; occupational therapists; physical therapists; psychologists; recreational therapists

Personality Types: Social-Investigative-Artistic

Did You Know?

Researchers have found that people who stutter can often express words smoothly while singing or while speaking as part of a group, such as when reciting the Pledge of Allegiance. Scientists used this fact to invent a device that helps people who stutter. It looks like a small hearing aid that is worn in the ear. The aid makes it sound to the person as if he or she is speaking in a group, so he or she can speak more fluently.

Career in Focus: *School Speech Therapist*

Most speech-language pathologists provide clinical services to individuals with communication problems. Speech-language pathologists in schools, however, also collaborate with teachers, interpreters, other school personnel, and parents to develop and run programs, provide counseling, and support classroom activities. They may work with one particular student or several, helping them function normally in a regular classroom environment.

Where and When

Speech-language pathologists usually work in comfortable surroundings, in hospital rooms or classrooms, or in a client's home. The job requires intense concentration and can be emotionally demanding. Most pathologists work 40 hours per week, though one in five works part time.

For More Information

＊ American Speech-Language-Hearing Association, 2200 Research Blvd., Rockville, MD 20850. Internet: www.asha.org

Veterinarians

At a Glance

Veterinarians care for pets, farm animals, zoo residents, and laboratory animals. They diagnose health problems, treat injuries, prescribe medicine, perform surgery, and vaccinate animals against diseases such as rabies. They also advise owners about animal feeding, behavior, and breeding. Some veterinarians use their skills to protect humans against diseases carried by animals and conduct clinical research on human and animal health problems. A small number of veterinarians work exclusively with large animals, mostly horses or cows. These veterinarians test for and vaccinate against diseases and consult with farm or ranch owners and managers regarding animal production, feeding, and housing issues. Veterinarians euthanize (put to sleep) animals when necessary.

Career in Focus: *Small-Animal Practitioner*

More than half of all clinical veterinarians are small-animal practitioners. They usually care for companion animals, such as dogs and cats, but they also treat birds, reptiles, rabbits, and other animals that can be kept as pets. Most work out of their own clinic and supervise a staff of assistants and technicians as well.

Where and When

Most veterinarians treat animals in private clinics or hospitals and work 50 hours or more per week. They may work nights and weekends. Those treating large animals travel to farms or ranches to see their patients. The work environment can be noisy, and veterinarians run the risk of being bitten, kicked, or scratched by hurt or frightened animals.

For More Information

* American Veterinary Medical Association, 1931 N. Meacham Rd., Suite 100, Schaumburg, IL 60173. Internet: www.avma.org

* Association of American Veterinary Medical Colleges, 1101 Vermont Ave. NW, Suite 301, Washington, DC 20005. Internet: www.aavmc.org

---

Data Bank

Education and Training: First professional degree

Average Earnings: $63,000–$105,000

Earnings Growth Potential: Medium

Total Jobs Held: 60,000

Job Outlook: Rapid increase

Annual Job Openings: 3,000

Related Jobs: Animal care and service workers; biological scientists; chiropractors; dentists; medical scientists; optometrists; physicians and surgeons; podiatrists; veterinary technologists and technicians

Personality Types: Investigative-Realistic

Did You Know?

Veterinarians contribute to human as well as animal health. They work with physicians and scientists researching ways to prevent and treat various human health problems. For example, veterinarians contributed greatly in conquering malaria and yellow fever, solved the mystery of botulism, produced a medicine used to treat people with heart disease, and developed surgical techniques.

Athletic Trainers

At a Glance

Athletic trainers specialize in the prevention and treatment of injuries to the muscular and skeletal system. These injuries are most often caused by playing sports, training, or exercising. Athletic trainers are often the first heath-care providers on the scene when these injuries occur, and therefore must provide immediate care when needed. They are also heavily involved in the rehabilitation process. Athletic trainers work under the supervision of a licensed physician and in cooperation with other health-care providers. Athletic trainers also may have administrative responsibilities. These may include regular meetings with an athletic director to deal with budgets, purchasing, policy implementation, and other business-related issues.

Data Bank

Education and Training: Bachelor's degree

Average Earnings: $34,000–$51,000

Earnings Growth Potential: Medium

Total Jobs Held: 16,000

Job Outlook: Rapid increase

Annual Job Openings: 1,200

Related Jobs: Chiropractors; emergency medical technicians and paramedics; licensed practical and licensed vocational nurses; massage therapists; occupational therapists; physical therapists; physician assistants; physicians and surgeons; podiatrists; recreational therapists; registered nurses; respiratory therapists

Personality Types: Social-Realistic-Investigative

Did You Know?

A study by the National Football League found that Alzheimer's disease and similar memory-related disorders are vastly more frequent among the league's former players. Among those ages 30–49, the occurrence is 19 times the normal rate. As a result, athletic trainers are paying much more attention to on-field concussions. After a serious head impact, players are being sidelined more often.

Career in Focus: *School Athletic Trainer*

Athletic trainers are as much teachers as they are treaters. Their first mission is to prevent injuries from ever occurring. Those who are more interested in the teaching aspect, however, should consider working as an athletic trainer in a high school or college. They will not only have the opportunity to assist athletes at all levels, but are often given the chance to teach classes in health, physical education, or a sport or activity that interests them.

Where and When

Athletic trainers work both indoors and outdoors, and their job may require extensive exercise. Schedules vary dramatically, especially for those who work and travel with college and professional sports teams. Those in high school settings who also teach can expect to work 50 to 60 hours per week or more.

For More Information

* National Athletic Trainers' Association, 2952 Stemmons Freeway, Suite 200, Dallas, TX 75247. Internet: www.nata.org

* Board of Certification, Inc., 1415 Harney St., Suite 200, Omaha, NE 68102. Internet: www.bocatc.org

Cardiovascular Technologists and Technicians

At a Glance

These workers help doctors diagnose and treat heart and blood vessel diseases. They administer a variety of tests, check the results, prepare patients for procedures, and sometimes assist in surgery. Those specializing in surgical procedures are called cardiology technologists. They help physicians guide a small tube, or catheter, through a patient's artery to determine whether a problem exists and to help treat it. Cardiovascular technologists who specialize in echocardiography run tests using ultrasound. Those who use ultrasound to examine the heart chambers, valves, and vessels are referred to as cardiac sonographers. Vascular technologists help physicians diagnose disorders affecting circulation. All of these workers may also schedule patient appointments, type doctors' reports, keep patient files, and care for equipment.

Career in Focus:
Cardiographic Technician

Cardiovascular technicians who specialize in electrocardiograms (EKGs) and stress testing are known as cardiographic technicians, or EKG technicians. An EKG traces electrical impulses transmitted by the heart. By examining these readings, doctors and specialists can determine whether the person has a heart condition and decide on a treatment. Stress tests involve monitoring the patient's EKG during exercise to examine the effects of physical activity on the heart.

Where and When

Technologists and technicians usually work a standard 40-hour week, though it might include evenings and weekends. They may also be on call. They spend a lot of time walking or standing, and some heavy lifting may be involved. Because many cardiovascular problems are life-threatening, the job can be stressful.

For More Information

* Alliance of Cardiovascular Professionals, P.O. Box 2007, Midlothian, VA 23113. Internet: www.acp-online.org

* Committee on Accreditation for Allied Health Education Programs, 1361 Park St., Clearwater, FL 33756. Internet: www.caahep.org

* Society for Vascular Ultrasound, 4601 Presidents Dr., Suite 260, Lanham, MD 20706. Internet: www.svunet.org

* Cardiovascular Credentialing International, 1500 Sunday Dr., Suite 102, Raleigh, NC 27607. Internet: www.cci-online.org

Data Bank

Education and Training: Associate degree

Average Earnings: $34,000–$63,000

Earnings Growth Potential: High

Total Jobs Held: 49,000

Job Outlook: Rapid increase

Annual Job Openings: 1,900

Related Jobs: Diagnostic medical sonographers; nuclear medicine technologists; radiation therapists; radiologic technologists and technicians; respiratory therapy technicians

Personality Types: Investigative-Realistic-Social

Did You Know?

One out of every five deaths in the United States is caused by coronary heart disease (CHD), and Americans only continue to increase their risk. The good news is that CHD is mostly preventable with a balanced diet and daily exercise. Though this prescription has been repeated over and over in television ads and news reports, the statistics show that people still aren't hearing it. As a result, we are unfortunately keeping cardiovascular technologists and technicians busier than ever.

Clinical Laboratory Technologists and Technicians

At a Glance

These workers perform medical tests to help detect, diagnose, and treat diseases. They match blood types; test for drug levels; and look for abnormal cells, bacteria, and parasites. They analyze test results of body fluids and cells and send the results to doctors to aid in diagnoses and treatment. They use automated equipment and computerized instruments capable of performing a number of tests at the same time. They also use microscopes, cell counters, and other sophisticated laboratory equipment.

Data Bank

Education and Training: Associate degree to bachelor's degree

Average Earnings: $38,000–$56,000

Earnings Growth Potential: Low

Total Jobs Held: 328,000

Job Outlook: Above-average increase

Annual Job Openings: 10,800

Related Jobs: Chemists and materials scientists; science technicians; veterinary technologists and technicians

Personality Types: Investigative-Realistic-Conventional

Did You Know?

Technology has developed many forms of home testing, such as home pregnancy tests, while also expanding the work that trained technologists and technicians do. For example, genetic testing is becoming more important as medical scientists are learning about new genetic disorders and about how people's genes affect the way they respond to medicines.

Career in Focus: *Blood Bank Technologist*

Blood bank technologists collect, type, and prepare blood and its components for transfusions. They are responsible for finding any abnormalities in the blood that might cause problems in a transfusion. They are also involved in selecting blood donors, performing screening, preparing blood for storage, and confirming tests to ensure patient safety. They may work at a hospital or a blood bank.

Where and When

In large hospitals or labs, these individuals may work day, evening, or night shifts, including weekends and holidays. In some facilities, laboratory personnel are on call several nights per week in case of emergency. Clinical laboratory personnel are trained to work with dangerous samples and infectious diseases. They follow strict procedures for keeping their environment sterile and safe.

For More Information

* National Accrediting Agency for Clinical Laboratory Sciences, 5600 N. River Rd., Suite 720, Rosemont, IL 60018. Internet: www.naacls.org

* American Association of Bioanalysts, Board of Registry, 906 Olive St., Suite 1200, St. Louis, MO 63101. Internet: www.aab.org

* American Medical Technologists, 10700 W. Higgins Rd., Suite 150, Rosemont, IL 60018. Internet: www.amt1.com

* American Society for Clinical Pathology, 33 W. Monroe St., Suite 1600, Chicago, IL 60603. Internet: www.ascp.org

* National Credentialing Agency for Laboratory Personnel, P.O. Box 15945-289, Lenexa, KS 66285. Internet: www.nca-info.org

Dental Hygienists

At a Glance

Dental hygienists examine patients' teeth and gums to find disease. They help dentists by cleaning patients' teeth, taking and developing X-rays, and applying fluoride treatments and sealants. They teach patients how to brush and floss correctly. Hygienists sometimes work chairside with the dentist during treatment. Dental hygienists use hand and rotary instruments and ultrasonics to clean and polish teeth, syringes to administer local anesthetics, and models of teeth to explain oral hygiene.

Career in Focus: *Advanced Dental Hygienist*

Even though the job titles are the same, state regulations that define what dental hygienists can do vary considerably. As a result, some dental hygienists have a wider variety of tasks to perform than others, and thus more responsibility. In some states, for example, hygienists administer anesthetics; place and carve filling materials, temporary fillings, and periodontal dressings; remove sutures; and smooth and polish metal restorations. For lack of a better title, we'll just call these workers *advanced* dental hygienists.

Where and When

Dental hygienists generally have flexible schedules, though some may work evenings and weekends. They work in clean, well-lighted offices. Important safety precautions are taken to ensure their safety, including the use of surgical masks, gloves, and safety glasses.

For More Information

* American Dental Hygienists Association, 444 N. Michigan Ave., Suite 3400, Chicago, IL 60611. Internet: www.adha.org
* Commission on Dental Accreditation, American Dental Association, 211 E. Chicago Ave., Chicago, IL 60611. Internet: www.ada.org/prof/ed/accred/commission/index.asp

Data Bank

Education and Training: Associate degree

Average Earnings: $56,000–$80,000

Earnings Growth Potential: Low

Total Jobs Held: 174,000

Job Outlook: Rapid increase

Annual Job Openings: 9,800

Related Jobs: Dental assistants; medical assistants; occupational therapist assistants and aides; physical therapist assistants and aides; physician assistants; radiation therapists; registered nurses

Personality Types: Social-Realistic-Conventional

Did You Know?

Ancient Egyptians had their own toothpaste made of ox hooves and burnt eggshells, among other things. Later toothpastes used oyster shells, charcoal, and honey. The 19th century saw common additions of brick, chalk, and salt. It wasn't until the 20th century that the fluoride toothpaste we use today was invented. As for flavors, one can only imagine what ox hooves taste like, though ancient peoples were known to chew on mint leaves to freshen their breath at least.

Diagnostic Medical Sonographers

At a Glance

Sonography, or ultrasonography, is the use of sound waves to generate an image for diagnosing various medical conditions. Sonographers use special machines called transducers to look for signs of unhealthy tissue. They take measurements and analyze the results to prepare reports for physicians. Doctors use these results to find tumors, check growing fetuses, and make medical decisions. In addition to working directly with patients, diagnostic medical sonographers keep patient records and adjust and maintain equipment. They also may prepare work schedules, evaluate equipment purchases, or manage an entire diagnostic imaging department.

Data Bank

Education and Training: Associate degree

Average Earnings: $53,000–$74,000

Earnings Growth Potential: Low

Total Jobs Held: 50,000

Job Outlook: Above-average increase

Annual Job Openings: 1,600

Related Jobs: Cardiovascular technologists and technicians; clinical laboratory technologists and technicians; nuclear medicine technologists; radiologic technologists and technicians

Personality Types: Investigative-Social-Realistic

Did You Know?

What makes ultrasound ultra? Ultrasound is actually any sound with a frequency high enough to be outside the range of human hearing (over 20,000 Hz). But just because we can't hear it doesn't mean it goes unheard. Animals with sensitive hearing, such as dogs, mice, dolphins, and bats, can hear ultrasounds. So unless you want to confuse it, don't take your pet poodle to an ultrasound appointment with you.

Career in Focus: *Obstetric and Gynecologic Sonographer*

Obstetric and gynecologic sonographers specialize in the study of the female reproductive system. Included in this field is one of the more well-known uses of sonography: examining the fetus of a pregnant woman to track the baby's growth and health. Advances in sonography have helped doctors improve the quality of prenatal care dramatically, including treating a baby for illnesses and medical problems before it is even born.

Where and When

Sonographers work about 40 hours per week, though they may work evenings and weekends and may also be on call. A growing number of sonographers work as contract employees and may have to travel to different hospitals. Sonographers are on their feet for long periods and may have to lift and turn patients.

For More Information

* Society of Diagnostic Medical Sonography, 2745 Dallas Pkwy., Suite 350, Plano, TX 75093-8730. Internet: www.sdms.org

* American Registry for Diagnostic Medical Sonography, 51 Monroe St., Plaza East One, Rockville, MD 20850-2400. Internet: www.ardms.org

* American Registry of Radiologic Technologists, 1255 Northland Dr., St. Paul, MN 55120-1155. Internet: www.arrt.org

* American Institute of Ultrasound in Medicine, 14750 Sweitzer Lane, Suite 100, Laurel, MD 20707. Internet: www.aium.org

* Joint Review Committee on Education in Diagnostic Medical Sonography, 2025 Woodlane Dr., St. Paul, MN 55125-2998. Internet: www.jrcdms.org

Emergency Medical Technicians and Paramedics

At a Glance

Automobile accidents, heart attacks, drownings, childbirth, and gunshot wounds all require immediate medical attention. Emergency medical technicians (EMTs) and paramedics drive ambulances and provide emergency medical care on the scene and on the way to the hospital. In an emergency, EMTs and paramedics typically are dispatched by a 911 operator and often work with police and fire department personnel. They give appropriate emergency care and, when necessary, transport the patient. Usually, one EMT or paramedic drives while the other monitors the patient's vital signs and gives additional care as needed. Some EMTs work as part of the flight crew of helicopters that transport critically ill or injured patients to hospital trauma centers.

Career in Focus: *Paramedic*

Beyond the general duties discussed above, the specific responsibilities of EMTs depend on their level of qualification and training. The National Registry of Emergency Medical Technicians registers emergency medical service providers at four levels. The highest level, the EMT-Paramedics (EMT-4), provide the most extensive prehospital care. In addition to giving intravenous fluids, using defibrillators to give lifesaving shocks to a stopped heart, and opening a patient's airway, paramedics may also administer drugs, interpret electrocardiograms (EKGs), and use monitors and other complex equipment.

Where and When

EMTs and paramedics work both indoors and out, in all types of weather. They do considerable kneeling, bending, and heavy lifting, and they may be exposed to diseases, as well as violence from patients. Because many of the situations are life or death, the work can be stressful and challenging. Many work more than 50 hours per week, and some of them are on call for extended periods.

For More Information

* National Association of Emergency Medical Technicians, P.O. Box 1400, Clinton, MS 39060-1400. Internet: www.naemt.org

* National Highway Traffic Safety Administration, Office of Emergency Medical Services, 1200 New Jersey Ave. SE, NTI-140, Washington, DC 20590. Internet: www.ems.gov

* National Registry of Emergency Medical Technicians, Rocco V. Morando Bldg., 6610 Busch Blvd., P.O. Box 29233, Columbus, OH 43229. Internet: www.nremt.org

Data Bank

Education and Training: Vocational/technical training

Average Earnings: $24,000–$39,000

Earnings Growth Potential: Low

Total Jobs Held: 211,000

Job Outlook: Average increase

Annual Job Openings: 6,200

Related Jobs: Air traffic controllers; fire fighters; physician assistants; police and detectives; registered nurses

Personality Types: Social-Investigative-Realistic

Did You Know?

Though its origins may date back to Napoleon and horse-drawn carts filled with wounded soldiers, the Emergency Medical Service (EMS) system as we know it today is relatively new. The movement for it began in the 1960s and gained wider acceptance in the decades to come (yes, there were people opposed to the idea of an emergency medical service system). Before the 1960s, patients were often transported in vehicles owned and operated by mortuary services rather than ambulances. Modified station wagons were a popular choice.

Licensed Practical and Licensed Vocational Nurses

At a Glance

Licensed practical nurses (LPNs) and Licensed Vocational Nurses (LVNs)—as LPNs are known in Texas and California—take care of sick, injured, and disabled people. They are supervised by physicians or registered nurses. Most LPNs provide basic bedside care, taking vital signs such as temperature, blood pressure, and pulse. They also prepare and give injections, monitor catheters, apply dressings, and treat bedsores. LPNs monitor their patients and report reactions to medications or treatments. They collect samples for testing, perform routine laboratory tests, feed patients, and record food and fluid intake and output. To help keep patients comfortable, LPNs assist with bathing, dressing, and personal hygiene. In states where the law allows, they may administer medication.

Data Bank

Education and Training: Vocational/technical training

Average Earnings: $34,000–$47,000

Earnings Growth Potential: Low

Total Jobs Held: 754,000

Job Outlook: Rapid increase

Annual Job Openings: 39,100

Related Jobs: Athletic trainers; emergency medical technicians and paramedics; home health aides and personal and home care aides; medical assistants; nursing and psychiatric aides; registered nurses

Personality Types: Social-Realistic

Did You Know?

Some LPNs work as private-duty nurses. Instead of working for a hospital, clinic, or nursing care facility, these nurses provide in-home care to patients. They may work 8 to 12 hours per day caring for a single patient. In some cases, their duties involve cooking meals and caring for other members of the patient's family as well. At night, most return to their own homes and families, but some actually live with their patients' families while they provide care.

Career in Focus: *Nursing Care Facility LPN*

About 25 percent of LPNs work in nursing care facilities. Their responsibilities are much the same as those nurses working in hospitals, though they generally spend more time with their residents and get to know them better. LPNs in nursing care facilities help determine residents' needs, develop care plans, and supervise other nursing aides.

Where and When

Most LPNs work 40-hour weeks, but they often work nights, weekends, and holidays. They stand for long periods of time and sometimes must help patients move. LPNs may face hazards from chemicals, radiation, and infectious diseases. They often have heavy workloads and spend much of their time interacting directly with patients.

For More Information

* National Association for Practical Nurse Education and Service, Inc., 1940 Duke St., Suite 200, Alexandria, VA 22314. Internet: www.napnes.org

* National Federation of Licensed Practical Nurses, Inc., 605 Poole Dr., Garner, NC 27529. Internet: www.nflpn.org

* National League for Nursing, 61 Broadway, 33rd Floor, New York, NY 10006. Internet: www.nln.org

* National Council of State Boards of Nursing, 111 E. Wacker Dr., Suite 2900, Chicago, IL 60601. Internet: www.ncsbn.org

Medical Records and Health Information Technicians

At a Glance

These workers organize and keep track of patients' medical records, including medical histories, exam results, reports of X-rays and laboratory tests, and treatment plans. They make sure all the right forms have been signed, input the information into a computer file, and code the information so that it can be pulled up easily. Some technicians also use computer programs to analyze data to improve patient care, control costs, or use in legal actions or research studies. Health information technicians must be computer literate and pay close attention to details.

Career in Focus: *Medical Record Coder*

Some medical records and health information technicians specialize in coding patients' medical information for insurance purposes. Technicians who specialize in coding are often called health information coders or medical record coders. These technicians assign a code to each diagnosis and procedure. Technicians then use computer software to assign the patient to one of several hundred "diagnosis-related groups," or DRGs. These programs determine the amount for which the hospital will be reimbursed if the patient is covered by insurance.

Where and When

These technicians usually work a 40-hour week. In hospitals where health information departments are open around the clock, technicians may work day, evening, and night shifts. They work in comfortable offices and have little contact with patients. They spend long periods of time in front of a computer and are susceptible to eyestrain and muscle fatigue.

For More Information

* The Commission on Accreditation for Health Informatics and Information Management Education, 233 N. Michigan Ave., 21st Floor, Chicago, IL 60601-5800. Internet: www.cahiim.org

* American Health Information Management Association, 233 N. Michigan Ave., 21st Floor, Chicago, IL 60601-5809. Internet: www.ahima.org or http://himcareers.ahima.org

* American Academy of Professional Coders, 2480 S. 3850 W., Suite B, Salt Lake City, UT 84120. Internet: www.aapc.com

* Professional Association of Healthcare Coding Specialists, 218 E. Bearss Ave., #354, Tampa, FL 33613. Internet: www.pahcs.org

Data Bank

Education and Training: Associate degree

Average Earnings: $25,000–$41,000

Earnings Growth Potential: Low

Total Jobs Held: 173,000

Job Outlook: Rapid increase

Annual Job Openings: 7,000

Related Jobs: Medical and health services managers; medical transcriptionists

Personality Types: Conventional-Enterprising

Did You Know?

What happens if someone gets hold of your medical records? If your family has a history of cancer, for example, a business might decide not to hire you because you are at risk for high medical bills. Thankfully, the Federal Health Insurance Portability and Accountability Act (HIPAA) sets a national standard for privacy of health information kept by health-care providers and insurance companies.

Nuclear Medicine Technologists

At a Glance

Nuclear medicine technologists give radioactive drugs to patients. These drugs help doctors diagnose and treat diseases. Using a camera, the technologist follows the drug as it enters the patient's body and records the drug's effects using magnetic resonance imaging (MRI). Abnormal areas show higher-than-expected or lower-than-expected concentrations of radioactivity. The images are produced on a computer screen or on film for a physician to interpret. Technologists must keep accurate, detailed patient records.

Data Bank

Education and Training: Associate degree

Average Earnings: $58,000–$80,000

Earnings Growth Potential: Low

Total Jobs Held: 22,000

Job Outlook: Above-average increase

Annual Job Openings: 700

Related Jobs: Cardiovascular technologists and technicians; clinical laboratory technologists and technicians; diagnostic medical sonographers; radiation therapists; radiologic technologists and technicians

Personality Types: Investigative-Realistic-Social

Did You Know?

The work of nuclear medicine technologists is highly related to that of radiologic technologists and medical sonographers. So related, in fact, that many schools offer one-year certificate programs for individuals with an associate degree in one of these other two fields, letting them specialize in nuclear medicine. Whether you would rather work with X-rays, sound waves, or radioactive elements may just be a matter of personal preference, though specialists in nuclear medicine do make more money on average.

Career in Focus: *Chief Technologist*

Chief technologists in nuclear medicine assign workers to prepare treatments, perform research studies and conduct laboratory tests, and monitor procedures to ensure accuracy. They develop guidelines for new procedures and train department workers in the use of equipment. They also implement safety procedures. This is all in addition to performing the regular duties of a nuclear medicine technologist when needed.

Where and When

Nuclear medicine technologists typically work a 40-hour week, though this might include evening or weekend hours. In addition, they may be on call on a rotational basis. Technologists are on their feet most of the day and are often required to lift and turn patients. Though the potential for radiation exposure exists, it is kept to a minimum through protective devices and strict safety guidelines.

For More Information

* Society of Nuclear Medicine Technologists, 1850 Samuel Morse Dr., Reston, VA 20190. Internet: www.snm.org

* Joint Review Committee on Educational Programs in Nuclear Medicine Technology, 2000 W. Danforth Rd., Suite 130 #203, Edmond, OK 73003. Internet: www.jrcnmt.org

* Nuclear Medicine Technology Certification Board, 3558 Habersham at Northlake, Building 1, Tucker, GA 30084. Internet: www.nmtcb.org

* American Registry of Radiologic Technologists, 1255 Northland Dr., St. Paul, MN 55120-1155. Internet: www.arrt.org

Occupational Health and Safety Specialists

At a Glance

Also known as occupational health and safety inspectors, these specialists help keep workplaces safe and workers healthy. Nearly half work for federal, state, or local government agencies to enforce rules on health and safety. The rest work for companies to ensure that their workplaces are operating safely. They analyze work environments and design programs to control, eliminate, and prevent disease or injury caused by chemical, physical, radiological, and biological factors. They may conduct inspections and inform the management about areas that may not be in compliance with laws and policies. They advise management on the cost and effectiveness of safety and health programs.

Career in Focus: *Environmental Protection Officer*

Environmental protection officers evaluate and coordinate programs that impact the environment, such as storing and handling hazardous waste or cleaning up contaminated soil or water. Many of them work for the federal government, although most companies that deal with hazardous wastes and chemicals have their own inspectors to make sure they are following the rules.

Where and When

Occupational health and safety specialists work in a variety of environments. Their jobs often require fieldwork, so they may travel frequently and work long, irregular hours. In addition, they may be exposed to the same potentially hazardous conditions as industrial employees.

For More Information

* American Industrial Hygiene Association, 2700 Prosperity Ave., Suite 250, Fairfax, VA 22031. Internet: www.aiha.org

* American Board of Industrial Hygiene, 6015 W. St. Joseph Hwy., Suite 102, Lansing, MI 48917. Internet: www.abih.org

* Board of Certified Safety Professionals, 208 Burwash Ave., Savoy, IL 61874. Internet: www.bcsp.org

* Health Physics Society, 1313 Dolley Madison Blvd., Suite 402, McLean, VA 22101. Internet: www.hps.org

* U.S. Department of Health and Human Services, Center for Disease Control and Prevention, National Institute of Occupational Safety and Health, 395 E St. SW, Suite 9200, Patriots Plaza Building, Washington, DC 20201. Internet: www.cdc.gov/niosh

Data Bank

Education and Training: Bachelor's degree

Average Earnings: $48,000–$79,000

Earnings Growth Potential: Medium

Total Jobs Held: 56,000

Job Outlook: Average increase

Annual Job Openings: 2,500

Related Jobs: Agricultural inspectors; construction and building inspectors; fire inspectors and investigators; occupational health and safety technicians

Personality Types: Investigative-Conventional

Did You Know?

On September 11, 2001, the U.S. suffered the most devastating terrorist attack in history. Months later, New York occupational health and safety inspectors were still working at the scene of the World Trade Center collapse, testing air and soil samples and collecting blood samples from rescue and cleanup workers. Their findings were grim. Fire fighters, paramedics, construction workers, and others who spent much time at Ground Zero showed signs of asbestos poisoning—which means that the 9/11 attacks might be claiming more victims for years to come.

Occupational Health and Safety Technicians

At a Glance

Occupational health and safety technicians work with occupational health and safety specialists to help prevent harm to workers, property, the environment, and the general public. For example, they might help design safe work spaces, inspect machines, or test air quality. In addition to making workers safer, technicians work with specialists to increase worker productivity by reducing absenteeism and equipment downtime, and to save money by lowering insurance premiums and workers' compensation payments, and preventing government fines. Some technicians work for governments, conducting safety inspections and imposing fines.

Data Bank

Education and Training: Associate degree

Average Earnings: $35,000–$57,000

Earnings Growth Potential: Medium

Total Jobs Held: 11,000

Job Outlook: Above-average increase

Annual Job Openings: 500

Related Jobs: Agricultural inspectors; construction and building inspectors; fire inspectors and investigators; occupational health and safety specialists

Personality Types: Conventional-Realistic

Did You Know?

One way manufacturers in developing countries compete with American manufacturers is by avoiding the costs of workplace safety measures. In response, American labor unions have pressured American employers to insist that foreign suppliers meet the same industrial safety standards that are commonplace here. This requirement raises the costs of foreign-made goods, thus preserving American jobs. It also has the benefit of improving the foreign workers' quality of life.

Career in Focus: *Mine Examiner*

Mine examiners are technicians who inspect mines for proper air flow and health hazards such as the buildup of methane or other noxious gases. When they detect hazardous conditions, they post "keep out" marks or signs. They investigate complaints from miners and maintain records of their inspections. They usually are certified and often are required to have work experience in underground mining.

Where and When

Occupational health and safety technicians work in a variety of settings, from offices and factories to mines. Their jobs often involve considerable fieldwork, and some require frequent travel. Occupational health and safety technicians may be exposed to many of the same strenuous, dangerous, or stressful conditions faced by industrial employees. Sometimes they need to go head-to-head with managers who disagree with their recommendations.

For More Information

* American Industrial Hygiene Association, 2700 Prosperity Ave., Suite 250, Fairfax, VA 22031. Internet: www.aiha.org

* Board of Certified Safety Professionals, 208 Burwash Ave., Savoy, IL 61874. Internet: www.bcsp.org

* Council on Certification of Health, Environmental, and Safety Technologists, 208 Burwash Ave., Savoy, IL 61874. Internet: www.cchest.org

* Health Physics Society, 1313 Dolley Madison Blvd., Suite 402, McLean, VA 22101. Internet: www.hps.org

* U.S. Department of Health and Human Services, Center for Disease Control and Prevention, National Institute of Occupational Safety and Health, 395 E St. SW, Suite 9200, Patriots Plaza Building, Washington, DC 20201. Internet: www.cdc.gov/niosh

Opticians, Dispensing

At a Glance

Dispensing opticians work for optometrists, making glasses and contact lenses according to the doctors' orders. They also keep customer records, track inventory, and help customers find frames that fit them well. They write up work orders that include the prescription for lenses and information on their size, material, color, and style. After the glasses are made, dispensing opticians verify that the lenses have been ground to specifications. Then they may reshape or bend the frame so that the eyeglasses fit the customer properly. Some also fix, adjust, and refit broken frames. After additional education and training, dispensing opticians may specialize in fitting contacts, artificial eyes, or cosmetic shells to cover blemished eyes.

Career in Focus: *Laboratory Technician*

Laboratory technicians cut, grind, edge, and finish lenses according to specifications provided by the optometrist. They then insert the lenses into frames to produce finished glasses. However, some dispensing opticians do this work themselves. For more information about this job and other technicians in the health-care fields, see the entry on medical, dental, and ophthalmic laboratory technicians.

Where and When

Dispensing opticians work indoors in comfortable surroundings. They may work in medical offices or stores, and they spend a fair amount of time on their feet. Most work 40 hours per week, but those who work in stores may work evenings and weekends.

For More Information

* Opticians Association of America, 4064 E. Fir Hill Dr., Lakeland, TN 38002. Internet: www.oaa.org

* American Board of Opticianry, 6506 Loisdale Rd., Suite 209, Springfield, VA 22150. Internet: www.abo.org

* National Contact Lens Examiners, 6506 Loisdale Rd., Suite 209, Springfield, VA 22150. Internet: www.abo-ncle.org

* National Federation of Opticianry Schools, 2800 Springport Rd., Jackson, MI 49202. Internet: www.nfos.org

Data Bank

Education and Training: Long-term on-the-job training

Average Earnings: $26,000–$42,000

Earnings Growth Potential: Medium

Total Jobs Held: 60,000

Job Outlook: Average increase

Annual Job Openings: 2,000

Related Jobs: Jewelers and precious stone and metal workers; ophthalmic laboratory technicians; orthotists and prosthetists

Personality Types: Enterprising-Conventional-Social

Did You Know?

While Lasik eye surgery is a relatively new phenomenon, eye surgery itself is ancient. Long before glasses were invented, ancient surgeons were removing cataracts from people's eyes. Evidence indicates that this surgery was performed in India more than 3,000 years ago—though the evidence doesn't say whether the patient was knocked unconscious first.

Pharmacy Technicians and Aides

At a Glance

Pharmacy technicians and aides help licensed pharmacists prepare prescription medications, provide customer service, and perform administrative duties within a pharmacy setting. Pharmacy technicians generally are responsible for receiving prescription requests, counting tablets, and labeling bottles. Once the prescription is filled, technicians price and file the prescription, which must be checked by a pharmacist before it is given to the patient. Pharmacy aides work closely with pharmacy technicians, performing administrative functions such as answering phones, stocking shelves, and operating cash registers.

Data Bank

Education and Training: Short-term on-the-job training to moderate-term on-the-job training

Average Earnings: $22,000–$33,000

Earnings Growth Potential: Low

Total Jobs Held: 381,000

Job Outlook: Rapid increase

Annual Job Openings: 18,800

Related Jobs: Dental assistants; medical assistants; medical records and health information technicians; medical transcriptionists; pharmacists

Personality Types: Conventional-Realistic

Did You Know?

It's a good time to be a pharmacy technician or aide. As the population ages, demand for prescription drugs will increase dramatically (the older you get, the fuller your medicine chest). Advances in science and research will increase the number of medications available on the market. Add to this the fact that insurers, pharmacies, and health systems will attempt to keep costs down by hiring technicians and aides to handle tasks that used to be done by pharmacists, and you have a field with tremendous potential for job growth.

Career in Focus: *Pharmacy Technician—Nonretail*

In hospitals, nursing homes, and assisted-living facilities, pharmacy technicians have added responsibilities. In addition to other technician responsibilities, they may also read patients' charts and prepare and deliver the medicine to patients. Still, the pharmacist must check the order before it is delivered. Technicians also may assemble a 24-hour supply of medicine for every patient or client. The job requires close attention to detail.

Where and When

Pharmacy technicians and aides work in clean, comfortable environments. Most of their workday is spent on their feet, and they may do some lifting. They may be required to work evenings, nights, weekends, and holidays, particularly in facilities that are open 24 hours a day, such as hospitals and some retail pharmacies.

For More Information

* Pharmacy Technician Certification Board, 2215 Constitution Ave. NW, Washington, DC 20037-2985. Internet: www.ptcb.org

* Institute for the Certification of Pharmacy Technicians, 2536 S. Old Hwy. 94, Suite 224, St. Charles, MO 63303. Internet: www.nationaltechexam.org

* American Society of Health-System Pharmacists, 7272 Wisconsin Ave., Bethesda, MD 20814. Internet: www.ashp.org

* National Pharmacy Technician Association, P.O. Box 683148, Houston, TX 77268. Internet: www.pharmacytechnician.org

Radiologic Technologists and Technicians

At a Glance

Radiologic technologists and technicians work in hospitals and clinics. They operate the machines that take X-rays or magnetic resolution pictures of people's bones and internal organs for diagnosing medical problems. Some specialize in diagnostic imaging technologies, such as computerized tomography (CT) and magnetic resonance imaging (MRI). Radiologic technologists and technicians must follow physicians' orders precisely. They must also conform to regulations concerning the use of radiation in order to protect themselves, their patients, and their co-workers from unnecessary exposure. In addition to preparing patients and taking pictures, radiologic technologists and technicians keep patient records and adjust and maintain equipment.

Career in Focus: *CT Technologist*

Experienced radiographers may perform more complex imaging procedures. Some radiographers, called CT technologists, operate CT scanners to produce cross-sectional images of patients. CT stands for computerized tomography, and uses several X-rays to create a three-dimensional image. In addition to operating the equipment and recording the images, CT technologists may schedule patients for procedures and provide training to new technologists. They often have to calm patients who are nervous about being scanned.

Where and When

Radiologic technologists and technicians work about 40 hours per week, though some may work evenings or weekends or be on call. They are on their feet for long periods and may be required to lift and position disabled patients. Radiation hazards are minimized by using shielding devices and badges that monitor the amount of radiation in the area.

For More Information

* American Society of Radiologic Technologists, 15000 Central Ave. SE, Albuquerque, NM 87123. Internet: www.asrt.org

* Joint Review Committee on Education in Radiologic Technology, 20 N. Wacker Dr., Suite 2850, Chicago, IL 60606-3182. Internet: www.jrcert.org

* American Registry of Radiologic Technologists, 1255 Northland Dr., St. Paul, MN 55120-1155. Internet: www.arrt.org

Data Bank

Education and Training: Associate degree

Average Earnings: $44,000–$64,000

Earnings Growth Potential: Low

Total Jobs Held: 215,000

Job Outlook: Above-average increase

Annual Job Openings: 6,800

Related Jobs: Cardiovascular technologists and technicians; diagnostic medical sonographers; nuclear medicine technologists; radiation therapists

Personality Types: Realistic-Social

Did You Know?

The first X-ray ever taken was by a German scientist named Conrad Roentgen, who discovered them quite by accident. He called them X-rays (rather than Roentgen rays as his colleagues suggested) because the type of radiation was unknown. The first X-ray of the human body was actually a picture of his wife's hand, ring and all.

Surgical Technologists

At a Glance

Surgical technologists assist in operations under the supervision of surgeons and registered nurses. They set up equipment, prepare patients for surgery, and take patients to and from the operating room. They help the surgical team "scrub" and put on gloves, masks, and surgical clothing. During an operation, they help with supplies and instruments and operate lights and equipment. Surgical technologists help prepare, care for, and dispose of specimens taken for laboratory analysis and help apply dressings. After the operation, they restock the operating room. Surgical technicians must be able to stay calm and steady in stressful circumstances.

Data Bank

Education and Training: Vocational/technical training

Average Earnings: $33,000–$47,000

Earnings Growth Potential: Low

Total Jobs Held: 92,000

Job Outlook: Rapid increase

Annual Job Openings: 4,600

Related Jobs: Clinical laboratory technologists and technicians; dental assistants; licensed practical and licensed vocational nurses; medical assistants

Personality Types: Realistic-Social-Conventional

Did You Know?

Would you believe that one of the oldest forms of surgery, in fact one of the first acts of practiced medicine, was brain surgery? Scientists have uncovered evidence of brain surgery (using bronze and stone instruments) dating back as far as 7,000 B.C. The Egyptians, Greeks, and Romans all produced writings discussing brain surgery, and some even had notable surgeons. Archeologists have found ancient skulls with healed incisions, proving that many of these operations were actually successful—or at least not fatal.

Career in Focus: *First Assistant*

With additional training, some technologists advance to first assistants. These vital members of the surgical team help with retracting, sponging, suturing, cauterizing, and closing and treating wounds. In other words, they spend more of their time getting their hands dirty. The increased responsibility generally comes with a pay increase as well.

Where and When

Surgical technologists work in clean, comfortable environments. They must stand for long periods and pay close attention to detail. They may be exposed to communicable diseases and must be prepared for the sights and smells of the operating room. Most work a 40-hour week, though they may be on call or work nights, weekends, and holidays.

For More Information

* Association of Surgical Technologists, 6 W. Dry Creek Circle, Suite 200, Littleton, CO 80120. Internet: www.ast.org

* Liaison Council on Certification for the Surgical Technologist, 6 W. Dry Creek Circle, Suite 100, Littleton, CO 80120. Internet: www.lcc-st.org

* National Center for Competency Testing, 7007 College Blvd., Suite 705, Overland Park, KS 66211.

Veterinary Technologists and Technicians

At a Glance

Veterinary technologists and technicians perform many of the same duties for a veterinarian that a nurse would for a physician. For example, they may perform laboratory tests, assist with cleaning teeth, or take blood samples. Some veterinary technicians obtain and record case histories, expose and develop X-rays, and provide specialized nursing care. Experienced veterinary technicians may discuss a pet's condition with its owners and train new clinic personnel. Veterinary technologists and technicians assisting small-animal practitioners usually care for companion animals, such as cats and dogs, but also may help with mice, rats, sheep, pigs, cattle, monkeys, birds, fish, and frogs. Some veterinary technologists vaccinate newly admitted animals.

Career in Focus: *Veterinary Research Technologist*

Besides working in private clinics and animal hospitals, veterinary technologists and technicians may work in research facilities. There they may administer medications; prepare samples for laboratory examinations; and record information on an animal's diet, weight, medications, and signs of pain and distress. Some may be required to sterilize laboratory and surgical equipment and provide routine postoperative care.

Where and When

Some of this work can be unpleasant and physically demanding or dangerous, even for animal lovers. These workers may be required to clean cages and restrain animals, risking exposure to bites and scratches. Those who witness abused or unwanted animals may experience emotional stress, and those who work for humane societies and animal shelters often have to deal with the public. In research centers, night shifts are not uncommon.

For More Information

* American Association for Laboratory Animal Science, 9190 Crestwyn Hills Dr., Memphis, TN 38125. Internet: www.aalas.org

* American Veterinary Medical Association, 1931 N. Meacham Rd., Suite 100, Schaumburg, IL 60173-4360. Internet: www.avma.org

Data Bank

Education and Training: Associate degree

Average Earnings: $24,000–$36,000

Earnings Growth Potential: Low

Total Jobs Held: 80,000

Job Outlook: Rapid increase

Annual Job Openings: 4,800

Related Jobs: Animal care and service workers; veterinarians; veterinary assistants and laboratory animal caretakers

Personality Types: Realistic-Investigative

Did You Know?

Veterinary technologists and technicians often have to help put sick or dangerous animals to sleep. This is usually done by means of a lethal injection, which provides a quick and almost pain-free death. Even knowing that it is usually the kindest thing that can be done for an animal in distress, it can still be emotionally trying. These workers often help the pet's owners deal with the loss as well.

Service Occupations

Dental Assistants

At a Glance

Dental assistants help dentists examine and treat patients. They make patients as comfortable as possible, prepare them for treatment, and obtain their records. Assistants hand instruments to dentists and keep patients' mouths dry and clear by using suction or other devices. Assistants also sterilize instruments and equipment, and they teach patients how to take proper care of their teeth. Those with lab duties clean removable dentures and make temporary crowns for teeth.

Data Bank

Education and Training: Moderate-term on-the-job training

Average Earnings: $28,000–$40,000

Earnings Growth Potential: Low

Total Jobs Held: 295,000

Job Outlook: Rapid increase

Annual Job Openings: 16,100

Related Jobs: Dental hygienists; medical assistants; occupational therapist assistants and aides; pharmacy technicians and aides; physical therapist assistants and aides; surgical technologists

Personality Types: Conventional-Realistic-Social

Did You Know?

Most assistants learn their skills from on-the-job training. However, an increasing number are being trained in dental-assistant programs offered by community and junior colleges, trade schools, and technical schools. Most programs take a year or less to complete, though all require a high school diploma.

Career in Focus: *Dentist Office Assistant*

In some dentists' offices, dental assistants are responsible for a wide variety of tasks, from suctioning saliva to scheduling a filling. In other offices they might specialize. Dental assistants with primarily office duties spend little time by the dentist chair. Instead, they schedule appointments, keep patient records, handle billing, and order supplies.

Where and When

Dental assistants work in clean, comfortable environments. Those who work chairside must wear gloves, masks, and eyewear to protect themselves and their patients from infectious diseases. Their work schedule may include weekends or evenings to accommodate patients' needs.

For More Information

* Commission on Dental Accreditation, American Dental Association, 211 E. Chicago Ave., Suite 1900, Chicago, IL 60611. Internet: www.ada.org/prof/ed/accred/commission/index.asp

* Dental Assisting National Board, Inc., 444 N. Michigan Ave., Suite 900, Chicago, IL 60611. Internet: www.danb.org

* American Dental Assistants Association, 35 E. Wacker Dr., Suite 1730, Chicago, IL 60601. Internet: www.dentalassistant.org

Home Health Aides and Personal and Home Care Aides

At a Glance

Home health aides and personal and home care aides help elderly, disabled, and seriously ill patients live at home instead of in a nursing home. Others help recently discharged hospital patients who have relatively short-term needs. They clean, do laundry, prepare meals, and help with personal hygiene. Some accompany clients to doctors' appointments or on other errands. Home health aides and personal and home care aides provide instruction and psychological support to their patients. They may advise families and patients on nutrition, cleanliness, and household tasks. Aides keep records of each patient's condition and progress. They often work with registered nurses, therapists, and other medical staff to ensure the best possible care.

Career in Focus: *Personal Aide for the Blind*

Personal and home health care aides perform a variety of duties, depending on the level of care and assistance needed. While some individuals may need help only with cooking and cleaning, others may need help with bathing and grooming. Those aides who work with blind individuals may provide transportation; assist in dressing, cooking, and moving around; or teach their clients how to use specialized equipment.

Where and When

Working conditions vary. Aides may go to the same home every day for months, even years, or they may work with a client for only a week. Aides sometimes visit four or five clients on the same day. The stress of the job often varies with the personality and mood of the client. Most aides work independently, and some work weekends and evenings to accommodate their clients' needs. Some heavy lifting and moving may be required.

For More Information

✳ National Association for Home Care and Hospice, 228 Seventh St. SE, Washington, DC 20003. Internet: www.nahc.org

Data Bank

Education and Training: Short-term on-the-job training

Average Earnings: $17,000–$24,000

Earnings Growth Potential: Very low

Total Jobs Held: 1,739,000

Job Outlook: Rapid increase

Annual Job Openings: 103,000

Related Jobs: Child care workers; licensed practical and licensed vocational nurses; medical assistants; nursing and psychiatric aides; occupational therapist assistants and aides; physical therapist assistants and aides; radiation therapists; registered nurses; social and human service assistants

Personality Types: Social-Realistic

Did You Know?

Many people require some form of assistance to help them with their daily routines, but increasingly that assistance doesn't have to be human. We all know about seeing-eye dogs, but what about trained monkeys? Today, many people who use wheelchairs have trained monkeys to help them live independently. These little animals perform simple household tasks, fetch items for their owners, and are even trained to call for help in an emergency.

Massage Therapists

At a Glance

These therapists use massage to treat muscle pain and fatigue, relieve stress, rehabilitate sport injuries, and promote general health. Some massage therapy is done simply for relaxation and rejuvenation. Massage therapists can specialize in 80 different types of massage, including Swedish massage, deep tissue massage, acupressure, and sports massage. A massage can be as long as two hours or as short as five minutes. Some therapists work in hospitals, nursing homes, or sports facilities, although a good number operate out of private offices or travel to homes and businesses. Massage can be a delicate issue for some clients. For this reason—and also for general business risks—about half of all massage therapists have liability insurance.

Data Bank

Education and Training: Vocational/technical training

Average Earnings: $24,000–$52,000

Earnings Growth Potential: Very high

Total Jobs Held: 122,000

Job Outlook: Above-average increase

Annual Job Openings: 4,000

Related Jobs: Athletic trainers; chiropractors; physical therapist assistants and aides; physical therapists

Personality Types: Social-Realistic

Did You Know?

Massage has been around for 5,000 years. Ancient Chinese texts from about 3,000 B.C. discuss the merits of moving energy around the body. The medical benefits of what they called "friction" were first documented in Western culture by the Greek physician Hippocrates around 400 B.C. Since then, the techniques have varied considerably, but much of the philosophy behind the practice has remained the same.

Career in Focus: *Sports Massage Therapist*

Massage therapy is common in the world of sports. Sports massage therapists specialize in the kinds of massage most beneficial to athletes. Because athletes tend to overwork their muscles, the buildup of tension can cause joint, ligament, tendon, and muscle problems. Sports massage therapists are trained to detect potential problems in the muscles and work them out. The services they provide are key to preventing more serious injuries.

Where and When

Massage therapists work in a wide variety of settings, from offices to hospitals, nursing homes to shopping malls. Many travel to clients' homes and offices. The work can be physically demanding, and therapists spend the majority of their time on their feet. Because of these demands, most therapists work less than 40 hours per week.

For More Information

* Associated Bodywork & Massage Professionals, 25188 Genesee Trail Rd., Suite 200, Golden, CO 80401. Internet: www.massagetherapy.com/careers/index.php

* American Massage Therapy Association, 500 Davis St., Suite 900, Evanston, IL 60201. Internet: www.amtamassage.org

* Accrediting Commission of Career Schools and Colleges, 2101 Wilson Blvd., Suite 302, Arlington, VA 22201. Internet: www.accsc.org

* Commission on Massage Therapy Accreditation, 5335 Wisconsin Ave. NW, Suite 440, Washington, DC 20015. Internet: www.comta.org

* Federation of State Massage Therapy Boards, 7111 W. 151st St., Suite 356, Overland Park, KS 66223. Internet: www.fsmtb.org

Medical Assistants

At a Glance

Medical assistants help keep a doctor's office running smoothly. They should not be confused with physician assistants, who examine, diagnose, and treat patients under the direct supervision of a physician. Medical assistants answer phones, greet patients, schedule appointments, arrange for tests, handle billing, and file records. Clinical duties vary according to state law and include taking medical histories, recording vital signs, explaining procedures, preparing patients for examination, and assisting the physician during the exam. Medical assistants also may arrange equipment, purchase and maintain supplies, and keep waiting and examining rooms neat and clean.

Career in Focus: *Ophthalmic Medical Assistant*

Ophthalmic medical assistants are specialized assistants who help ophthalmologists provide eye care. They might measure and record vision and test eye muscle function. They show patients how to insert, remove, and care for contact lenses. They also apply eye dressings. Under the direction of the physician, ophthalmic medical assistants may administer eye medications. They also maintain instruments and may assist the ophthalmologist in surgery.

Where and When

Medical assistants work in clean, comfortable environments. They are in constant contact with people and must handle several responsibilities at once. Most work 40 hours per week. Many work evenings and weekends.

For More Information

* American Association of Medical Assistants, 20 N. Wacker Dr., Suite 1575, Chicago, IL 60606. Internet: www.aama-ntl.org

* American Medical Technologists, 10700 W. Higgins Rd., Suite 150, Rosemont, IL 60018. Internet: www.amt1.com

* Accrediting Bureau of Health Education Schools, 7777 Leesburg Pike, Suite 314 N, Falls Church, VA 22043. Internet: www.abhes.org

* Commission on Accreditation of Allied Health Education Programs, 1361 Park St., Clearwater, FL 33756. Internet: www.caahep.org

Data Bank

Education and Training: Moderate-term on-the-job training

Average Earnings: $24,000–$34,000

Earnings Growth Potential: Low

Total Jobs Held: 484,000

Job Outlook: Rapid increase

Annual Job Openings: 21,800

Related Jobs: Dental assistants; dental hygienists; licensed practical and licensed vocational nurses; medical records and health information technicians; medical secretaries; medical transcriptionists; nursing and psychiatric aides; occupational therapist assistants and aides; pharmacy technicians and aides; physical therapist assistants and aides; surgical technologists

Personality Types: Conventional-Social-Realistic

Did You Know?

This is projected to be one of the fastest-growing occupations over the next 8 to 10 years. Why? It's because medical assistants are able to handle both clerical and clinical duties—answering phones and taking pulses. Because of an increasing need to give them more responsibilities, medical assistants with some formal training or certification will have the best job prospects.

Medical Transcriptionists

At a Glance

Medical transcriptionists listen to recordings made by doctors and transcribe them into documents such as discharge summaries, medical histories, progress notes, and various reports. Such documents eventually become part of patients' permanent files and must be accurate. Using a foot pedal to pause the tape when necessary, transcriptionists type the material into a computer, editing it for grammar and clarity. To transcribe clearly and effectively, medical transcriptionists must understand medical terminology, anatomy and physiology, medical procedures, and other medical jargon.

Data Bank

Education and Training: Vocational/technical training

Average Earnings: $27,000–$39,000

Earnings Growth Potential: Low

Total Jobs Held: 105,000

Job Outlook: Average increase

Annual Job Openings: 2,400

Related Jobs: Court reporters; human resources assistants, except payroll and timekeeping; medical assistants; medical records and health information technicians; receptionists and information clerks; secretaries and administrative assistants

Personality Types: Conventional-Realistic

Did You Know?

Do you know what it means to have chronic stromal inflammation or what the squamous metaplasia of the trigone is? Neither do we, but we aren't medical transcriptionists either. The job isn't simply a matter of being a fast typist. To check for errors, medical transcriptionists need to know medical terminology and procedures. That's why most employers prefer transcriptionists who have completed a two-year associate degree or a one-year certification program.

Career in Focus: *Physician's Office Transcriptionist*

Because the need for transcription may be limited on a given day, medical transcriptionists who work in physicians' offices may have other duties. They may receive patients, schedule appointments, answer the phone, and handle incoming and outgoing mail.

Where and When

Medical transcriptionists work in comfortable settings in hospitals and doctors' offices. Many are subcontracted out and telecommute from home. Like other jobs that require extended typing and computer use, these workers can suffer wrist, back, neck, or eye problems. Many work 40-hour weeks, though those who are self-employed may work irregular hours.

For More Information

* Association for Healthcare Documentation Integrity, 4230 Kiernan Ave., Suite 130, Modesto, CA 95356. Internet: www.ahdionline.org

Nursing and Psychiatric Aides

At a Glance

Nursing and psychiatric aides care for physically or mentally ill, injured, or disabled individuals in hospitals, nursing homes, and mental health clinics. They feed, bathe, and dress patients; help them get in and out of bed; take vital signs; and set up equipment. They report any changes to doctors or nurses. Aides employed in nursing care facilities often are the primary caregivers, having far more contact with residents than other members of the staff. Because some residents may stay in a nursing care facility for months or even years, aides develop positive, caring relationships with their patients.

Career in Focus: *Psychiatric Aide*

Psychiatric aides care for mentally impaired or emotionally disturbed individuals. They work under a team that may include psychiatrists, psychologists, psychiatric nurses, social workers, and therapists. In addition to helping patients dress, bathe, and eat, psychiatric aides lead them in activities such as playing cards or taking field trips. Because they have such close contact, psychiatric aides can have a great deal of influence on their patients' outlook and treatment.

Where and When

Most aides work 40 hours per week, though many work evenings, nights, weekends, and holidays. About one in four works part time. They spend much of their time standing and walking and may have to lift and move patients as well. Some of the work can be unpleasant or stressful. While the work can be emotionally demanding, many aides get satisfaction from helping those in need.

For More Information

* National Association of Health Care Assistants, 1201 L St. NW, Washington, DC 20005. Internet: www.nahcacares.org

* National Network of Career Nursing Assistants, 3577 Easton Rd., Norton, OH 44203. Internet: www.cna-network.org

* American Health Care Association, 1201 L St. NW, Washington, DC 20005. Internet: www.ahca.org

Data Bank

Education and Training: Short-term on-the-job training to vocational/technical training

Average Earnings: $20,000–$29,000

Earnings Growth Potential: Low

Total Jobs Held: 1,532,000

Job Outlook: Above-average increase

Annual Job Openings: 43,200

Related Jobs: Child care workers; home health aides and personal and home care aides; licensed practical and licensed vocational nurses; medical assistants; occupational therapist assistants and aides; registered nurses; social and human service assistants

Personality Types: Social-Realistic-Conventional

Did You Know?

The education and training requirements for being an aide are minimal—a high school degree is usually sufficient. Being an aide is a good stepping stone to better-paying jobs. Experience as an aide can help people decide whether to pursue a career in health care. Then, with some additional training or education, they may become nurses or medical assistants.

Occupational Therapist Assistants and Aides

At a Glance

Occupational therapist assistants and aides help therapists in clinics, rehab centers, nursing homes, and home health-care programs. The ultimate goal is to improve clients' quality of life and ability to perform daily activities. Assistants help injured patients regain use of damaged muscles. They might help patients learn to use wheelchairs or other devices. They also help mentally disabled patients with living skills such as cooking and keeping a checkbook. The assistant is responsible for reporting the client's progress to the therapist and helping him or her decide on the best course of action.

Data Bank

Education and Training: Short-term on-the-job training to associate degree

Average Earnings: $36,000–$54,000

Earnings Growth Potential: Low

Total Jobs Held: 34,000

Job Outlook: Rapid increase

Annual Job Openings: 1,500

Related Jobs: Dental assistants; medical assistants; occupational therapists; pharmacy technicians and aides; physical therapist assistants and aides

Personality Types: Social-Realistic

Did You Know?

Though the principles behind it had been around for centuries, the formal practice behind occupational therapy is less than a century old. The National Society for the Promotion of Occupational Therapy was founded in 1917 to help World War I veterans recover from their injuries and reenter the workforce. The momentum behind OT (as it is called) increased again after World War II. America's need to help its returning veterans has created a practice that helps many other kinds of people with disabilities.

Career in Focus: *Occupational Therapist Aide*

Occupational therapist aides typically prepare materials and assemble equipment used during treatment. They are also responsible for a range of office tasks, including scheduling appointments, answering the telephone, ordering supplies, and filling out insurance forms or other paperwork. Aides are not licensed, so the law does not allow them to perform as wide a range of tasks as occupational therapist assistants.

Where and When

These assistants and aides work in a variety of settings. Many offices and clinics have evening and weekend hours to meet patients' personal schedules. These workers are often required to lift and help move patients, and the constant kneeling, stooping, and standing require the assistant or aide to be in good shape.

For More Information

* American Occupational Therapy Association, 4720 Montgomery Lane, P.O. Box 31220, Bethesda, MD 20824-1220. Internet: www.aota.org

Physical Therapist Assistants and Aides

At a Glance

Physical therapist assistants and aides help physical therapists care for patients in hospitals, nursing homes, and home health-care programs. They help patients recovering from injuries or disease improve their mobility, relieve pain, and regain muscle use. They may help with exercises, traction, ultrasound, and electrical stimulation. They also may give massages and apply hot/cold packs. Physical therapist assistants record the patient's responses to treatment and report the results to the physical therapist.

Career in Focus: *Physical Therapist Aide*

Physical therapist aides help make therapy sessions productive. They usually are responsible for keeping the treatment area clean and organized and for preparing for each patient's therapy. Because they are not licensed, aides do not perform the clinical tasks of a physical therapist assistant. Instead, the duties of aides include some clerical tasks, such as ordering supplies, answering the phone, and filling out insurance forms.

Where and When

These assistants and aides generally work in offices and clinics, and many have evening and weekend hours. About 30 percent work part time. Like physical therapists, their assistants and aides need moderate strength to assist patients with their treatment. Lifting, kneeling, stooping, and standing for long periods of time are all part of the job.

For More Information

* The American Physical Therapy Association, 1111 N. Fairfax St., Alexandria, VA 22314-1488. Internet: www.apta.org

Data Bank

Education and Training: Short-term on-the-job training to associate degree

Average Earnings: $31,000–$46,000

Earnings Growth Potential: Low

Total Jobs Held: 110,000

Job Outlook: Rapid increase

Annual Job Openings: 5,400

Related Jobs: Dental assistants; medical assistants; nursing and psychiatric aides; occupational therapist assistants and aides; pharmacy technicians and aides

Personality Types: Social-Realistic

Did You Know?

When LeBron James pulls a muscle, who does he turn to for help? A sports medicine specialist is a physical therapist specializing in sports-related injuries. These workers help athletes prepare for competition, and they are available during sporting events to help in emergencies. After an injury or illness, they work with an athlete to help him or her rebuild muscle tone and agility. Of course, with LeBron's salary, he could probably hire the Surgeon General if he wanted to.

Correctional Officers

At a Glance

Correctional officers guard people who are awaiting trial and those who have been convicted and sentenced to serve time. They keep order and enforce rules in jails or prisons. They also assign and supervise inmates' work, help inmates with personal problems, and report any bad behavior. Sometimes, officers must search inmates and their living quarters for weapons or drugs, settle disputes between inmates, and enforce discipline. If necessary, they help law enforcement authorities investigate crimes. Some correctional officers oversee individuals being held by the U.S. Immigration and Naturalization Service pending release or deportation. Others work for correctional institutions that are run by private for-profit organizations. Most of the jails in the United States are operated by county governments, with about three-quarters of all jails under the jurisdiction of an elected sheriff.

Data Bank

Education and Training: Moderate-term on-the-job training to work experience in a related occupation

Average Earnings: $32,000–$54,000

Earnings Growth Potential: Low

Total Jobs Held: 518,000

Job Outlook: Average increase

Annual Job Openings: 16,900

Related Jobs: Police and detectives; probation officers and correctional treatment specialists; security guards and gaming surveillance officers

Personality Types: Realistic-Enterprising-Conventional

Did You Know?

Most correctional officers are employed in state and federal prisons, watching over about 1.4 million offenders. Correctional officers in local jails admit and process about 12 million people per year, with about 700,000 offenders in jail at any given time. When individuals are first arrested, the jail staff may not know their true identity or criminal record, and violent detainees may be placed alongside everyone else. This is the most dangerous phase of the incarceration process.

Career in Focus: *Bailiff*

Bailiffs, also known as marshals or court officers, maintain safety and order in courtrooms. Their duties include enforcing courtroom rules, assisting judges, guarding juries from outside contact, delivering court documents, and providing general security for courthouses.

Where and When

Obviously working in a correctional institution can be stressful and hazardous. Each year correctional officers are injured in confrontations with inmates. Some prisons can be overcrowded, hot, and noisy. Most correctional officers work 40 hours per week on rotating shifts. However, night, weekend, and holiday work is common. Some officers may carry firearms for protection.

For More Information

* American Correctional Association, 206 N. Washington St., Suite 200, Alexandria, VA 22314. Internet: www.aca.org

* American Jail Association, 1135 Professional Ct., Hagerstown, MD 21740. Internet: www.corrections.com/aja

* Information on entrance requirements, training, and career opportunities for correctional officers at the federal level may be obtained from the Federal Bureau of Prisons. Internet: www.bop.gov

Fire Fighters

At a Glance

Every year, fires and other emergencies take thousands of lives and destroy billions of dollars' worth of property. Fire fighters help protect the public against these dangers. They are frequently the first emergency personnel at the scene. They put out fires, rescue victims, treat injuries, and attempt to salvage the contents of buildings. Because fighting fires is dangerous, it requires organization and teamwork. Fire fighters sometimes remain at the site of a disaster for several days, rescuing trapped survivors and assisting with medical treatment. In fact, 65 percent of all fire departments provide emergency medical service. Between alarms, fire fighters clean and maintain equipment, conduct practice drills and fire inspections, and participate in physical fitness activities. They also prepare written reports on fire incidents and review fire science literature to stay informed about technological developments and changing administrative practices and policies.

Career in Focus: *Forest Fire Fighter*

Workers specializing in forest fires utilize methods and equipment different from those of other fire fighters. When fires break out, crews of fire fighters are brought in to suppress the blaze with heavy equipment and water hoses. One of the most effective means of fighting a forest fire is creating fire lines—cutting down trees and digging out grass and all other combustible vegetation in the path of the fire in order to deprive it of fuel. Elite fire fighters called smoke jumpers parachute from airplanes to reach otherwise inaccessible areas. This tactic, however, can be extremely hazardous.

Where and When

While fire fighters spend much of their time at stations, their working conditions can change on a moment's notice. Fire fighting involves risk of death or injury from cave-ins; traffic accidents; exposure to flames and smoke; and contact with poisonous, flammable, or explosive gases. They wear heavy protective gear, and the work is incredibly demanding, both emotionally and physically. Most work more than 50 hours per week and many work extra-long shifts with several days off in between.

For More Information

* International Association of Fire Fighters, 1750 New York Ave. NW, Washington, DC 20006. Internet: www.iaff.org

* U.S. Fire Administration, 16825 S. Seton Ave., Emmitsburg, MD 21727. Internet: www.usfa.dhs.gov

---

Data Bank

Education and Training: Long-term on-the-job training to work experience in a related occupation

Average Earnings: $35,000–$64,000

Earnings Growth Potential: High

Total Jobs Held: 366,000

Job Outlook: Above-average increase

Annual Job Openings: 18,500

Related Jobs: Emergency medical technicians and paramedics; fire inspectors and investigators; police and detectives

Personality Types: Realistic-Enterprising-Social

Did You Know?

Fire fighting is one of the most dangerous jobs in the U.S. economy. Each year, about 100 fire fighters lose their lives in the line of duty. On September 11, 2001, more than 300 fire fighters died attempting to rescue victims. Individuals in this profession are so committed to helping others that they are willing to risk their lives every day.

Police and Detectives

At a Glance

Police, detectives, and special agents protect people from crime and violence. They patrol highways, issue traffic tickets, and help accident victims. They also collect evidence and investigate crimes. Uniformed police officers maintain regular patrols and respond to calls for service. They may direct traffic at the scene of an accident, investigate a burglary, or give first aid to an accident victim. During their shift, they may identify, pursue, and arrest suspected criminals; resolve problems within the community; and enforce traffic laws. Sheriffs and deputy sheriffs enforce the law on the county level. State police officers arrest criminals statewide and patrol highways to enforce motor vehicle laws. Regardless of job duties or location, police officers and detectives at all levels must write reports and maintain accurate records.

Data Bank

Education and Training: Long-term on-the-job training to associate degree

Average Earnings: $44,000–$73,000

Earnings Growth Potential: Medium

Total Jobs Held: 884,000

Job Outlook: Average increase

Annual Job Openings: 32,400

Related Jobs: Correctional officers; emergency medical technicians and paramedics; fire fighters; private detectives and investigators; probation officers and correctional treatment specialists; security guards and gaming surveillance officers

Personality Types: Realistic-Enterprising-Conventional

Did You Know?

Federal Bureau of Investigation (FBI) agents are the federal government's main detectives, responsible for investigating violations of federal law and national security. The FBI investigates organized crime, public corruption, fraud, bribery, civil rights violations, bank robbery, extortion, kidnapping, terrorism, espionage, drug trafficking, and other violations. Other government positions with related job skills and responsibilities include U.S. Drug Enforcement Administration (DEA) agents, U.S. marshals and deputy marshals, Federal Air Marshals, and U.S. Secret Service special agents.

Career in Focus: *Detective*

Detectives are investigators who gather facts and collect evidence for criminal cases. They conduct interviews, examine records, observe the activities of suspects, and participate in raids or arrests. Detectives usually specialize in investigating one kind of crime, such as homicide or fraud. They are assigned cases on a rotating basis and work on them until an arrest and conviction occur or until the case is dropped.

Where and When

This line of work can obviously be very dangerous and stressful. Law enforcement officers witness death and suffering. Most of these individuals work 40-hour weeks, though paid overtime is common and shift work is a necessity. Nearly all officers are expected to be armed at all times. The jobs of some federal agents require extensive travel.

For More Information

* National Law Enforcement Recruiters Association, P.O. Box 17132, Arlington, VA 22216. Internet: www.nlera.org

* National Sheriffs' Association, 1450 Duke St., Alexandria, VA 22314. Internet: www.sheriffs.org

* International Association of Chiefs of Police, 515 N. Washington St., Alexandria, VA 22314. Internet: www.theiacp.org

* Information about qualifications for employment as a Federal Bureau of Investigation (FBI) Special Agent is available from the nearest state FBI office. The address and phone number are listed in the local telephone directory. Internet: www.fbi.gov

Private Detectives and Investigators

At a Glance

Private detectives and investigators work for lawyers, insurance companies, businesses, and individuals. They gather information for trials, track down people who owe companies money, search for missing persons, and conduct background checks. They also investigate computer crimes and are sometimes hired to prove or disprove infidelity. Corporate investigators conduct internal and external investigations for corporations, looking for things such as drug use in the workplace or theft of company assets. Financial investigators may be hired to develop confidential profiles of individuals involved in large financial transactions. All of these investigators may spend long hours doing surveillance, hunting for clues, and interviewing people, though much of a private detective's work can now be done via computer.

Career in Focus: *Store Detective*

Detectives who work for retail stores or hotels are responsible for preventing theft. Store detectives arrest anyone attempting to steal merchandise or destroy store property. Store detectives also conduct periodic inspections of stock areas, dressing rooms, and restrooms, and sometimes assist in opening and closing the store. They may prepare security reports for management and testify in court against people they catch.

Where and When

Private detectives and investigators often work irregular hours in order to conduct surveillance and interviews. Though much of the time is spent behind a desk, working conditions outside the office vary considerably. Some of this work involves possible confrontation, making the job stressful and dangerous. For this reason, some detectives and investigators are licensed to carry handguns.

For More Information

* National Association of Legal Investigators, NALI World Headquarters, 235 N. Pine St., Lansing, MI 48933. Internet: www.nalionline.org

* ASIS International, 1625 Prince St., Alexandria, VA 22314-2818. Internet: www.asisonline.org

Data Bank

Education and Training: Work experience in a related occupation

Average Earnings: $32,000–$58,000

Earnings Growth Potential: High

Total Jobs Held: 45,000

Job Outlook: Rapid increase

Annual Job Openings: 1,900

Related Jobs: Accountants and auditors; bill and account collectors; claims adjusters, appraisers, examiners, and investigators; financial analysts; personal financial advisors; police and detectives; security guards and gaming surveillance officers

Personality Types: Enterprising-Conventional

Did You Know?

Watching Humphrey Bogart or a private-eye TV show gives the impression that being a private detective is an action-packed career full of mischief and mayhem, but it is seldom that exciting. Most private detectives spend the majority of their time on the phone, running computer searches, recording statements, or watching people from afar. They prefer avoiding confrontation, and they don't all wear trenchcoats.

Security Guards and Gaming Surveillance Officers

At a Glance

Security guards, who are also called security officers, patrol and inspect property to protect against fire, theft, and vandalism. They use radios and telephones to call for assistance from police, fire, or emergency medical services when necessary. They also may interview witnesses or victims, prepare case reports, and testify in court. The security guard's job responsibilities vary with the employer. In office buildings, banks, and hospitals, for example, guards maintain order and protect the property, staff, and customers. At air, sea, and rail terminals, guards protect people and freight, and they screen passengers and baggage using metal detectors and high-tech equipment. Guards working at universities, parks, and sports stadiums perform crowd control and direct traffic. All security officers must use good judgment and common sense.

Data Bank

Education and Training: Short-term on-the-job training to moderate-term on-the-job training

Average Earnings: $19,000–$31,000

Earnings Growth Potential: Low

Total Jobs Held: 1,086,000

Job Outlook: Above-average increase

Annual Job Openings: 37,700

Related Jobs: Correctional officers; gaming services occupations; police and detectives; private detectives and investigators

Personality Types: Realistic-Conventional-Enterprising

Did You Know?

Imagine having to put on a bulletproof vest every time you got out of your car. If it were an armored car carrying hundreds of thousands, even millions of dollars in cash, the effort might be worth the trouble. When an armored car arrives at the door of a business, an armed guard enters, signs for the money, and returns to the truck with the valuables in hand. Carrying money just the few steps between the truck and the door can be extremely hazardous.

Career in Focus: *Gaming Surveillance Officer*

Gaming surveillance officers act as security agents for casino managers and patrons. Using primarily audio and video equipment, they observe casino operations for irregular activities, such as cheating or theft, by either employees or patrons. They keep recordings that are sometimes used as evidence in police investigations. So don't go counting cards the next time you're in Vegas. You are being watched, after all.

Where and When

Most security guards and gaming surveillance officers spend most of their time on their feet or behind a desk. While the work is usually routine, guards must be constantly on alert. They usually work in shifts, though most still work a standard 40-hour week.

For More Information

* ASIS International, 1625 Prince St., Alexandria, VA 22314-2818. Internet: www.asisonline.org

Chefs, Head Cooks, and Food Preparation and Serving Supervisors

At a Glance

Chefs and head cooks are usually responsible for directing cooks in the kitchen, dealing with food-related concerns, and providing leadership. They are also the most skilled cooks in the kitchen and use their creativity and knowledge of food to develop and prepare recipes. Food preparation and serving supervisors oversee the kitchen and nonkitchen staff in a restaurant or food service facility. They may also oversee food preparation workers in fast food, cafeteria, or casual dining restaurants, where the menu is fairly standard from day to day, or in more formal restaurants, where a chef provides specific guidelines and exacting standards on how to prepare each item. All of these workers hire, train, and supervise staff, prepare cost estimates for food and supplies, set work schedules, order supplies, and ensure that the food service establishment runs efficiently and profitably.

Career in Focus: *Research Chef*

Research chefs combine cooking skills with knowledge of food science to develop recipes, test new formulas, and experiment with the flavors and appeal of foods. They also may test new products and equipment for chain restaurants, food growers, manufacturers, and marketers. The education requirements for research chefs tend to be higher than other chefs, however, and often include a college degree.

Where and When

Kitchens can be crowded and hot and filled with potential dangers, such as hot ovens and slippery floors. Job hazards include slips and falls, cuts, and burns, but these injuries are seldom serious. The pace of work can be hectic during peak dining times. Work hours in restaurants may include early mornings, late evenings, holidays, and weekends. Many executive chefs regularly work 12-hour days because they oversee the delivery of foodstuffs early in the day, plan the menu, and prepare those menu items that require the most skill.

For More Information

* National Restaurant Association, 1200 17th St. NW, Washington, DC 20036. Internet: www.restaurant.org
* American Culinary Federation, 180 Center Place Way, St. Augustine, FL 32095. Internet: www.acfchefs.org

Data Bank

Education and Training: Work experience in a related occupation

Average Earnings: $24,000–$40,000

Earnings Growth Potential: Low

Total Jobs Held: 942,000

Job Outlook: Little change

Annual Job Openings: 14,500

Related Jobs: Cooks and food preparation workers; food and beverage serving and related workers; food processing occupations; food service managers

Personality Types: Enterprising-Realistic-Conventional

Did You Know?

While traditional colleges and universities do offer degrees in hospitality or the culinary arts, many chefs and cooks prefer to attend independent cooking schools and culinary arts institutes. There they can focus on their training and earn their certification much faster. The American Culinary Federation accredits more than 100 formal training programs, including the prestigious Le Cordon Bleu schools, which will teach you how to make more than chicken cordon bleu (like veal cordon bleu, for example).

Cooks and Food Preparation Workers

At a Glance

Cooks and food preparation workers prepare, season, and cook a wide range of foods—from soups, snacks, and salads to entrees, side dishes, and desserts—in a variety of restaurants and other food services establishments. Cooks measure, mix, and cook ingredients according to recipes, using a variety of equipment, including pots, pans, cutlery, ovens, broilers, grills, slicers, grinders, and blenders. Food preparation workers perform routine, repetitive tasks under the direction of chefs, head cooks, or food preparation and serving supervisors. They peel and cut vegetables, trim meat, prepare poultry, keep work areas clean, and monitor the temperatures of ovens and stovetops.

Data Bank

Education and Training: Short-term on-the-job training to long-term on-the-job training

Average Earnings: $17,000–$24,000

Earnings Growth Potential: Very low

Total Jobs Held: 2,044,000

Job Outlook: Little change

Annual Job Openings: 73,500

Related Jobs: Bakers; butchers and meat cutters; chefs, head cooks, and food preparation and serving supervisors; food and beverage serving and related workers; food service managers

Personality Types: Realistic-Conventional

Did You Know?

Americans are eating more meals than ever away from home. It's expected that in the next decade, more than half the average household's food budget will go to such meals. (Compare that to 25 percent in 1955.) This has created many opportunities for businesses, ranging from drive-up taco vans to upscale restaurants, all of which will require cooks and food preparation workers.

Career in Focus: *Institution or Cafeteria Cook*

These cooks work in the kitchens of schools, cafeterias, businesses, hospitals, and other institutions. For each meal, they prepare a large quantity of a limited number of entrees, vegetables, and desserts according to preset menus. Meals are generally prepared in advance so diners seldom get the opportunity to special-order a meal.

Where and When

Working conditions for cooks and food preparation workers vary considerably, from large, air-conditioned kitchens to cramped, steamy ones. These workers spend most of their time on their feet and are usually under constant pressure to keep up with orders. Job hazards include slips and falls, cuts, and burns. Work hours can vary from early morning shifts to late nights, including holidays and weekends. Part-time work is very common.

For More Information

* National Restaurant Association, 1200 17th St. NW, Washington, DC 20036. Internet: www.restaurant.org

* American Culinary Federation, 180 Center Place Way, St. Augustine, FL 32095. Internet: www.acfchefs.org

Food and Beverage Serving and Related Workers

At a Glance

These workers deal with customers in restaurants, coffee shops, and other places that serve food. Most work as part of a team, helping to improve customer service. Waiters and waitresses, the largest group of these workers, take customers' orders, serve food and beverages, prepare bills, and sometimes accept payment. Their specific duties vary considerably depending on the establishment. Hosts and hostesses welcome guests, maintain reservation or waiting lists, and assign guests to tables. Dining room and cafeteria attendants and helpers assist waiters, waitresses, and bartenders by cleaning tables, removing dirty dishes, and keeping serving areas stocked with supplies. Counter attendants take orders and serve food in cafeterias, coffee shops, and carryout eateries.

Career in Focus: *Bartender*

Bartenders fill drink orders. Bartenders must know a wide range of drink recipes and be able to mix drinks accurately, quickly, and without waste. Besides mixing and serving drinks, bartenders stock and prepare garnishes; maintain an adequate supply of ice, glasses, and other bar supplies; and keep the bar area clean for customers. Bartenders should be friendly and enjoy talking with customers. They also need to know when a patron has had one too many.

Where and When

Food and beverage service workers spend most of their time on their feet and are often under pressure to serve customers quickly. Part-time work is more common among these workers than in almost any other occupation. In fact, half of all waiters and waitresses work part time. Because of long dining hours, work schedules vary and often include weekends and holidays.

For More Information

* National Restaurant Association, 1200 17th St. NW, Washington, DC 20036. Internet: www.restaurant.org

* International Council on Hotel, Restaurant, and Institutional Education, 2810 N. Parham Rd., Suite 230, Richmond, VA 23294. Internet: www.chrie.org

Data Bank

Education and Training: Short-term on-the-job training

Average Earnings: $16,000–$21,000

Earnings Growth Potential: Very low

Total Jobs Held: 7,652,000

Job Outlook: Average increase

Annual Job Openings: 391,600

Related Jobs: Cashiers; chefs, head cooks, and food preparation and serving supervisors; cooks and food preparation workers; flight attendants; retail salespersons

Personality Types: Realistic-Conventional-Enterprising

Did You Know?

Working in a restaurant is a time-honored first job for many people. About 25 percent of these workers are 16 to 19 years old. That's about six times the proportion for all workers. In fact, about one in ten Americans will end up working at a McDonald's at some point in their lives. The variable schedules make restaurant work an ideal job for high-school and college students, and if the tips are good, it can help pay the tuition.

Building Cleaning Workers

At a Glance

Building cleaning workers include janitors, maids, housekeepers, window washers, and rug shampooers. They keep office buildings, hospitals, stores, hotels, and residences clean and in good condition. Some do only cleaning, while others have a wide range of duties. Janitors and cleaners perform a variety tasks. In addition to general cleaning they may fix leaky faucets, empty trash cans, do painting and carpentry, mow lawns, and see that heating and air-conditioning equipment works properly. Maids and housekeeping cleaners perform light cleaning duties to keep private households, hotels, restaurants, or hospitals clean and orderly. Those in private households dust and polish furniture; sweep, mop, and wax floors; vacuum; and clean ovens, refrigerators, and bathrooms. They also may wash dishes and clothes and change and make beds.

Data Bank

Education and Training: Short-term on-the-job training to work experience in a related occupation

Average Earnings: $18,000–$28,000

Earnings Growth Potential: Low

Total Jobs Held: 4,139,000

Job Outlook: Little change

Annual Job Openings: 95,100

Related Jobs: Dishwashers; grounds maintenance workers

Personality Types: Realistic-Conventional-Enterprising

Did You Know?

Families are becoming more and more pressed for time. Between soccer practice, school meetings, and ballet, families with single parents or two working parents are finding it difficult to keep the house clean. This is good news for those who clean residential properties, many of whom are self-employed.

Career in Focus: *Cleaning Supervisor*

Cleaning supervisors coordinate, schedule, and supervise the activities of janitors and cleaners. They assign tasks and inspect areas to see that work has been done properly. They also manage supplies and equipment. Supervisors screen and hire job applicants; train new and experienced employees; and recommend promotions, transfers, or dismissals. Some also perform cleaning duties as the need arises.

Where and When

Most of these workers perform their duties in the evening, though some, such as school and hospital custodians, work in the daytime. Most full-time building cleaners work 40 hours per week. Both indoor and outdoor work is common. Janitors may suffer cuts, bruises, and burns from machines, hand tools, and chemicals. Many cleaning tasks require constant bending, stooping, and stretching, which can result in back injuries and sprains.

For More Information

* Information about janitorial jobs may be obtained from state employment service offices.

* International Executive Housekeepers Association, Inc., 1001 Eastwind Dr., Suite 301, Westerville, OH 43081-3361. Internet: www.ieha.org

Grounds Maintenance Workers

At a Glance

Grounds maintenance workers care for lawns, trees, gardens, and other plants and keep the grounds free of litter. They may prune, feed, and water gardens and cut, fertilize, and water lawns at private homes and public places. In addition to caring for sod, plants, and trees, they rake and mulch leaves and clear snow from walkways and parking lots. They maintain and repair sidewalks, parking lots, pools, fountains, fences, and benches. They also maintain athletic fields, golf courses, cemeteries, and parks. Some care for indoor gardens and plants in malls, hotels, and botanical gardens. They may specialize in using pesticides, often working for chemical lawn service companies. Tree trimmers and pruners cut away dead or excess branches from trees or shrubs either to maintain rights-of-way for roads, sidewalks, or utilities or to improve the appearance and health of trees. Grounds maintenance workers use hand tools such as shovels and saws, as well as power lawnmowers, chain saws, snow-blowers, and electric clippers.

Career in Focus:
Greenskeeper

Workers who maintain golf courses are called greens-keepers. Greenskeepers do many of the same things as other groundskeepers, spending a great deal of time mowing and trimming. In addition, greenskeepers periodically relocate the holes on putting greens to eliminate uneven wear of the turf and to add interest and challenge to the game. Greens-keepers also keep canopies, benches, ball washers, and tee markers repaired and freshly painted.

Where and When

Many of these jobs are in demand only in the spring, summer, and fall. Most of the work is done outdoors in all kinds of weather. The work is physically demanding and repetitive, involving lots of bending, lifting, pushing, and shoveling. Those who work with pesticides, fertilizers, and other chemicals, as well as dangerous equipment such as chain saws, must exercise safety precautions.

For More Information

* Tree Care Industry Association, 136 Harvey Rd., Suite 101, Londonderry, NH 03053. Internet: www.treecareindustry.org

* Professional Grounds Management Society, 720 Light St., Baltimore, MD 21230. Internet: www.pgms.org

* Professional Landcare Network, 950 Herndon Pkwy., Suite 450, Herndon, VA 20170. Internet: www.landcarenetwork.org

Data Bank

Education and Training: Short-term on-the-job training to work experience in a related occupation

Average Earnings: $21,000–$33,000

Earnings Growth Potential: Low

Total Jobs Held: 1,521,000

Job Outlook: Above-average increase

Annual Job Openings: 45,000

Related Jobs: Agricultural workers, other; farmers, ranchers, and agricultural managers; forest and conservation workers; landscape architects; logging workers

Personality Types: Realistic-Conventional-Enterprising

Did You Know?

Groundskeepers don't always work with Mother Nature. Those who are responsible for keeping athletic fields in top condition may work with artificial turf (or Astroturf) instead. Instead of mowing, watering, and fertilizing it, they vacuum and disinfect it to prevent bacteria from growing. In addition, they sometimes must remove the turf and replace the cushioning pad underneath.

Pest Control Workers

At a Glance

Unwanted creatures that infest households, buildings, or surrounding areas are pests that can pose serious risks to human health and safety. Pest control workers find and exterminate roaches, rats, mice, spiders, termites, ants, bees, and many other pests. They use chemicals, poisonous fumes, traps, and electrical equipment. They travel to homes and offices, often crawling and climbing into tight places. Because many of the chemicals they use pose a threat to other living creatures and the environment, all pest control workers are licensed according to state and federal law.

Data Bank

Education and Training: Moderate-term on-the-job training

Average Earnings: $25,000–$37,000

Earnings Growth Potential: Low

Total Jobs Held: 68,000

Job Outlook: Above-average increase

Annual Job Openings: 3,400

Related Jobs: Building cleaning workers; construction laborers; grounds maintenance workers; heating, air-conditioning, and refrigeration mechanics and installers

Personality Types: Realistic-Conventional

Did You Know?

Pest control workers use a combination of techniques known as "integrated pest management." This involves ensuring there is proper sanitation; creating physical barriers; setting traps; and using baits, some of which destroy the pests and others that prevent them from reproducing. Integrated pest management is becoming popular for several reasons. First, it cuts down on the amount of pesticides used. Second, some pests are becoming more resistant to pesticides and thus require a more comprehensive solution. How else are you going to take out those mutated, hard-to-kill super-roaches?

Career in Focus: *Pest Control Supervisor*

Also known as operators, pest control supervisors manage service technicians and certified applicators. While they are licensed to apply pesticides, they usually are more involved in running the business. Supervisors are responsible for ensuring that employees obey rules regarding pesticide use, and they must resolve any problems that arise with government officials or angry customers. Most states require each pest control establishment to have a supervisor. Self-employed pest control workers usually fill that position themselves.

Where and When

Pest control workers often wear heavy protective gear and spend much of their time kneeling, bending, reaching, and crawling, sometimes in dark, restrictive areas. They often work evenings and weekends, and about 25 percent of them work more than 40 hours per week. Despite the training and the precautions taken by pest control workers, pesticides still pose a health risk.

For More Information

* National Pest Management Association, 10460 North St., Fairfax, VA 22030. Internet: www.pestworld.org/Looking-for-a-Career-in-Pest-Management

Animal Care and Service Workers

At a Glance

Animal care and service workers feed, water, bathe, and exercise animals in clinics, kennels, and zoos. They play with the animals, watch them for illness or injury, and clean and repair their cages. Kennel staff care for cats and dogs. They may also sell pet food and supplies, assist in obedience training, and help with breeding. Caretakers in animal shelters perform a variety of duties. In addition to meeting the basic needs of the animals, caretakers also keep health and admittance records. Some vaccinate newly admitted animals and euthanize (painlessly put to death) seriously ill, severely injured, or unwanted animals. Stable workers groom, exercise, and care for horses. In zoos, keepers prepare the diets and clean the enclosures of animals. Keepers also may answer questions and ensure that the public behaves responsibly. Animal trainers train animals for riding, security, performance, obedience, or assisting persons with disabilities.

Career in Focus: *Groomer*

Animal caretakers who specialize in grooming or maintaining a pet's appearance (usually a dog or cat) are called groomers. Groomers also answer telephones and schedule appointments. Some groomers work in kennels, veterinary clinics, animal shelters, or pet-supply stores. Others run their own business at a salon or by making house calls. Mobile services are growing rapidly, as they offer convenience for pet owners and flexible hours for groomers.

Where and When

This work may be unpleasant (cleaning cages), physically and emotionally demanding (putting a cat to sleep), and dangerous (convincing a crocodile to get a vaccination). The work often involves kneeling, crawling, bending, and heavy lifting. Those working with humane societies and animal shelters often deal with the public, which may have its own challenges. Work conditions vary—much of it may be outdoors, and hours are irregular. Still, animal lovers find a lot of satisfaction in these careers.

For More Information

* National Animal Control Association, P.O. Box 480851, Kansas City, MO 64148-0851. Internet: www.nacanet.org

* Pet Care Services Association, 2760 N. Academy Blvd., Suite 120, Colorado Springs, CO 80917. Internet: www.petcareservices.org

* National Dog Groomers Association of America, P.O. Box 101, Clark, PA 16113. Internet: www.nationaldoggroomers.com

Data Bank

Education and Training: Short-term on-the-job training to moderate-term on-the-job training

Average Earnings: $17,000–$25,000

Earnings Growth Potential: Very low

Total Jobs Held: 220,000

Job Outlook: Rapid increase

Annual Job Openings: 9,300

Related Jobs: Agricultural workers, other; animal control workers; biological scientists; farmers, ranchers, and agricultural managers; veterinarians; veterinary assistants and laboratory animal caretakers; veterinary technologists and technicians

Personality Types: Realistic-Conventional

Did You Know?

An adult lion can eat as much as 40 pounds of meat in one sitting. An adult elephant usually eats between 300 and 600 pounds of vegetables per day. Feeding the animals in a zoo can be a challenge. Zookeepers must know what kind of food the animals need, how much they need, and when to feed them. Exotic animals, such as the koala, which only eats eucalyptus, might need foods that must be specially ordered or grown.

Barbers, Cosmetologists, and Other Personal Appearance Workers

At a Glance

These workers—also called hairdressers and hairstylists—help people look their best. They cut, shampoo, style, color, and perm hair. They may fit customers for hairpieces, shave male customers, and give facial massages or advice on makeup. In addition to working with clients, personal appearance workers are expected to clean their work areas and instruments. They may make appointments and keep records. A growing number actively sell hair care products and other cosmetic supplies. Those who operate their own salons have managerial duties that may include hiring, supervising, and firing workers, as well as keeping inventory, ordering supplies, and arranging for advertising.

Data Bank

Education and Training: Short-term on-the-job training to vocational/technical training

Average Earnings: $18,000–$31,000

Earnings Growth Potential: Low

Total Jobs Held: 822,000

Job Outlook: Rapid increase

Annual Job Openings: 28,600

Related Jobs: Fitness workers; makeup artists, theatrical and performance; massage therapists

Personality Types: Realistic-Enterprising-Social

Did You Know?

Entrepreneurship is alive and well in the personal appearance industry. Nearly half of all barbers, cosmetologists, and other personal appearance workers are self-employed. Many own their own salons, but those who can't afford it can lease booth space or a chair from another salon's owner. Self-employed stylists with a good reputation can usually charge much more than someone working out of a chain establishment.

Career in Focus: *Manicurist and Pedicurist*

A number of workers offer specialized services. Manicurists and pedicurists work exclusively on nails and provide manicures, pedicures, coloring, and nail extensions to clients. They may also treat nails to repair them or improve their strength, as well as provide hand massages. Many of these workers are self-employed.

Where and When

These workers are on their feet most of their shift in clean, pleasant surroundings. Prolonged exposure to some hair and nail chemicals can cause irritation, so protective clothing is usually worn. Work schedules are variable, often including evenings and weekends.

For More Information

* National Accrediting Commission of Cosmetology Arts and Sciences, 4401 Ford Ave., Suite 1300, Alexandria, VA 22302. Internet: www.naccas.org

* National Cosmetology Association, 401 N. Michigan Ave., Chicago, IL 60611. Internet: www.ncacares.org

* National Association of Barber Boards of America, 2703 Pine St., Arkadelphia, AR 71923. Internet: www.nationalbarberboards.com

Child Care Workers

At a Glance

Child care workers nurture and care for children under the age of five. They also may work with older children in before- and after-school situations. Those caring for infants and toddlers may change diapers, heat bottles, teach basic skills, and rock children to sleep. Those caring for preschoolers serve meals, play games, read stories, and organize activities to help the children socialize and learn new skills. These workers are responsible for helping children grow physically, emotionally, intellectually, and socially. They help children explore individual interests, develop independence, build self-esteem, and learn how to get along with others. Those working at before- and after-school programs watch over school-aged children during the gap between school hours and their parents' work hours. They help students with their homework or engage them in other activities.

Career in Focus: *Nanny*

While many child care workers work out of their own homes, some work at the parents' home. Nannies work full or part time for a single family. They generally take care of children from birth to age 10 or 12, tending to the child's early education, nutrition, health, and other needs. They may also perform the duties of a housekeeper, including cleaning and laundry. Because they generally spend so much time with one or two children, they often develop close bonds and are sometimes treated as part of the family.

Where and When

Child care work can be physically and emotionally demanding. Workers stand, walk, bend, stoop, and lift to attend to each child's interests and needs. Work hours vary, though child care is usually open year round. Most centers employ both full-time and part-time staff. A third of all child care workers run child care services out of their homes.

For More Information

* National Child Care Information Center, 10530 Rosehaven St., Suite 400, Fairfax, VA 22030. Internet: www.nccic.org

* National Child Care Association, 1325 G St. NW, Suite 500, Washington, DC 20005. Internet: www.nccanet.org

* National Association for the Education of Young Children, 1313 L St. NW, Suite 500, Washington, DC 20005. Internet: www.naeyc.org

* International Nanny Association, P.O. Box 1299, Hyannis, MA 02601. Internet: www.nanny.org

Data Bank

Education and Training: Short-term on-the-job training

Average Earnings: $17,000–$24,000

Earnings Growth Potential: Very low

Total Jobs Held: 1,302,000

Job Outlook: Average increase

Annual Job Openings: 52,300

Related Jobs: Teacher assistants; teachers—kindergarten, elementary, middle, and secondary; teachers—preschool, except special education; teachers—special education

Personality Types: Social-Artistic

Did You Know?

Research suggests that 75 percent of human brain development occurs in the first 3–5 years. Whether it's learning how to drink out of a cup, forming a first sentence, or learning shapes and colors, the pace at which toddlers and preschoolers learn is startling. Child care workers have a tremendous responsibility when it comes to shaping a young mind, and many of them enjoy the process.

Fitness Workers

At a Glance

Fitness workers help people exercise and get healthy. They teach proper exercise methods and activities including cardiovascular exercise, strength training, and stretching. They work in commercial and nonprofit health clubs, country clubs, hospitals, universities, resorts, and clients' homes. Personal trainers work one-on-one with individuals to help them reach their fitness goals. Group exercise instructors, on the other hand, lead sessions focusing on a particular activity like yoga or aerobics. Naturally these workers must be in good shape. They are sometimes required to do other tasks, such as tending the front desk, signing up new members, giving tours, and supervising the weight training and cardiovascular equipment areas.

Data Bank

Education and Training: Vocational/technical training

Average Earnings: $20,000–$46,000

Earnings Growth Potential: High

Total Jobs Held: 261,000

Job Outlook: Rapid increase

Annual Job Openings: 12,400

Related Jobs: Athletes, coaches, umpires, and related workers; dietitians and nutritionists; physical therapists; recreation workers

Personality Types: Social-Realistic-Enterprising

Did You Know?

Yoga began as a spiritual practice in India more than 7,000 years ago. However, in Western culture, it is much more popular as a form of exercise designed to improve health, reduce stress, and keep fit. The interest in yoga has exploded in recent years, and many programs have sprung up to train yoga instructors. For more information, visit the Yoga Alliance at www.yogaalliance.org.

Career in Focus: *Fitness Director*

Fitness directors oversee the daily programs of a health club or fitness center. They create and maintain programs to meet the needs of the club's members, including new member orientations, fitness assessments, and workout incentive programs. They also select fitness equipment; coordinate personal training and group exercise programs; and hire, train, and supervise fitness staff.

Where and When

Most of these workers spend their time indoors at fitness centers and health clubs. Hours vary but may include evenings, weekends, and even holidays. Naturally the physical exercise required presents some risk for injury. Fitness workers generally have the freedom to design their own classes and their clients' routines.

For More Information

* National Strength and Conditioning Association, 1885 Bob Johnson Dr., Colorado Springs, CO 80906. Internet: www.nsca-lift.org

* American College of Sports Medicine, P.O. Box 1440, Indianapolis, IN 46206-1440. Internet: www.acsm.org

* American Council on Exercise, 4851 Paramount Dr., San Diego, CA 92123. Internet: www.acefitness.org

* National Academy of Sports Medicine, 26632 Agoura Rd., Calabasas, CA 91302. Internet: www.nasm.org

* NSCA Certification Commission, 1885 Bob Johnson Dr., Colorado Springs, CO 80906. Internet: www.nsca-cc.org

Flight Attendants

At a Glance

Flight attendants help keep airline passengers safe and comfortable. In an emergency, they help passengers react calmly and quickly. They also stock the plane with food, drinks, blankets, first-aid kits, and other supplies. Before takeoff they greet passengers, check their tickets, help them store their baggage, and instruct them on safety procedures. During the flight, they serve food and drinks and answer questions. They may administer first aid to passengers who become injured or ill. All flight attendants must be able to remain calm in emergencies.

Career in Focus: *Lead Flight Attendant*

Lead, or first, flight attendants oversee the work of the other attendants aboard the aircraft, while performing most of the same duties. They are responsible for coordinating and directing all in-flight services on board and ensuring that each flight attendant has a working knowledge of his or her position. Lead flight attendants tend to be better paid for their added responsibilities. They usually earn the position through years of experience.

Where and When

Flight attendants may be expected to work evenings, nights, weekends, and holidays. Most work a maximum of 12 hours a day, and attendants usually work anywhere from 65 to 90 hours a month. When they are away from their home base, the airline provides accommodations. The work can be strenuous and tiring. Flight attendants spend most of their time on their feet, and must often deal with demanding, nervous, or irritated passengers. Contrary to what Hollywood might suggest, flight attendants do not have to deal with snakes on their planes.

For More Information

❊ Association of Flight Attendants-CWA, 501 Third St. NW, Washington, DC 20001. Internet: www.afanet.org

---

Data Bank

Education and Training: Long-term on-the-job training

Average Earnings: $31,000–$51,000

Earnings Growth Potential: Low

Total Jobs Held: 99,000

Job Outlook: Average increase

Annual Job Openings: 3,000

Related Jobs: Emergency medical technicians and paramedics; fire fighters; food and beverage serving and related workers; reservation and transportation ticket agents and travel clerks

Personality Types: Enterprising-Social-Conventional

Did You Know?

Being a flight attendant is hard work, but it does have its benefits. Attendants receive discounted travel on many airlines (often between 50 and 90 percent) and sometimes travel free on their company airline. They are often granted 10–15 days off each month, and the benefits packages for flight attendants are usually good. Also, it provides the possibility of meeting rock stars, athletes, and politicians (the ones who don't own their own jet, at least).

Gaming Services Occupations

At a Glance

Legalized gambling in the United States today includes casino gaming, state lotteries, betting on contests such as horse or dog racing, and charitable gaming, all of which provide unique job opportunities. Most gaming services workers are employed by casinos. Some positions are concerned with supervision, surveillance, and investigation. Others involve working with the games or patrons themselves, such as tending slot machines, handling money, and dealing cards. Supervisors oversee the gaming tables and workers. Slot attendants watch over the slot machines, making sure everything is working smoothly. Gaming and sports book writers and runners run games such as bingo and keno, in addition to taking bets on sporting events. All gaming workers must be licensed and have good customer-relations skills.

Data Bank

Education and Training: Vocational/technical training

Average Earnings: $28,000–$48,000

Earnings Growth Potential: Medium

Total Jobs Held: 26,000

Job Outlook: Declining

Annual Job Openings: 400

Related Jobs: Cashiers; gaming cage workers; retail salespersons; sales worker supervisors; security guards and gaming surveillance officers; tellers

Personality Types: Artistic-Investigative-Conventional

Did You Know?

Don't want or can't afford to go to college? Try dealing school. These are schools all across the country that teach students how to run games like blackjack, poker, craps, and roulette. Programs generally take between three and six weeks, and some even offer job placement assistance. Places like the Casino Career Institute in New Jersey or the Casino College in California can teach you everything you need to know. Naturally, the majority of dealing schools are in Las Vegas.

Career in Focus: *Gaming Dealer*

Gaming dealers operate table games such as craps, blackjack, and roulette. Standing or sitting behind the table, dealers provide dice, deal cards to players, or run the equipment. Some dealers also watch the patrons for cheating. Dealers determine winners, calculate and pay winning bets, and collect losing bets. Most gaming dealers are competent in at least two games, usually blackjack and craps. All gaming dealers must be skilled in customer service to ensure that patrons are having a good time, even when they are losing.

Where and When

Casino work can be physically demanding. Most workers stand for long periods, and some may be required to do heavy lifting. Smoking is still permitted in many casinos, which can also be noisy and chaotic places. In addition, casinos are generally open 24 hours a day, 7 days a week, so a variety of shifts are possible.

For More Information

✳ American Gaming Association, 555 13th St. NW, Suite 1010 East, Washington, DC 20004. Internet: www.americangaming.org

Recreation Workers

At a Glance

Recreation workers often work as camp counselors or coaches, organizing leisure activities at parks, health clubs, camps, tourist sites, community centers, and theme parks. They may also work in state and national parks, health clubs, or even on cruise ships. Activities vary but often include dance, drama, crafts, games, and sports. They organize events and direct participants, teach people how to use recreation equipment, and schedule the use of facilities. Directors develop and manage recreation programs in parks, playgrounds, and other settings. Directors usually serve as technical advisors to state and local recreation and park commissions and may be responsible for budgets.

Career in Focus: *Camp Counselor*

Camp counselors lead and instruct children and teenagers in activities such as swimming, hiking, horseback riding, and camping. In addition, counselors teach subjects such as archery, boating, music, drama, gymnastics, tennis, and computers. In resident camps, counselors also provide guidance and supervise daily living. This often makes an ideal summer job for high school and college students, especially those who want long-term careers helping people or working with kids.

Where and When

The setting for recreation workers can range from a woodland park to an urban playground to a cruise ship on the Caribbean. Regardless of setting, most recreation work is physically demanding, requiring workers to spend the majority of their time on their feet. Many recreation workers work a 40-hour week, though night and weekend hours are common and schedules vary tremendously. Many of these jobs are seasonal as well.

For More Information

* National Recreation and Park Association, Division of Professional Services, 22377 Belmont Ridge Rd., Ashburn, VA 20148-4501. Internet: www.nrpa.org

* American Camping Association, 5000 State Road 67 North, Martinsville, IN 46151-7902. Internet: www.acacamps.org

Data Bank

Education and Training: Short-term on-the-job training

Average Earnings: $18,000–$29,000

Earnings Growth Potential: Low

Total Jobs Held: 328,000

Job Outlook: Above-average increase

Annual Job Openings: 10,700

Related Jobs: Athletes, coaches, umpires, and related workers; counselors; fitness workers; probation officers and correctional treatment specialists; psychologists; recreational therapists; social workers; teachers—self-enrichment education

Personality Types: Social-Enterprising-Artistic

Did You Know?

People from all walks of life can get a taste of the wilderness with Outward Bound expeditions. Teenagers, senior citizens, school groups, and business groups can take two-week treks into the mountains. There, they go hiking, white-water rafting, rock climbing, and back-country skiing. Outward Bound trainers help the adventurers build their self-confidence and their teamwork, while making sure they are safe.

Sales and Related Occupations

Advertising Sales Agents

At a Glance

Advertising sales agents do exactly what the name suggests—they sell advertising, including space in publications, signs and billboards, and television and radio time. Some work with businesses to decide what forms of advertising will work best for them. Others work for media companies to sell the space they have for advertising. In fact, most of the revenue for magazines, newspapers, and broadcasters is generated from advertising. Sales agents gather background information and explain how specific types of advertising will help promote a client's products or services. They prepare an advertising proposal, which includes sample advertisements and estimates of the cost. Advertising sales agents serve as the main contact between the client and the firm. They also analyze sales statistics, prepare reports, and handle the scheduling of their appointments. The good ones read about new and existing products and monitor the prices and products of their competitors.

Data Bank

Education and Training: Moderate-term on-the-job training

Average Earnings: $31,000–$65,000

Earnings Growth Potential: High

Total Jobs Held: 167,000

Job Outlook: Average increase

Annual Job Openings: 4,500

Related Jobs: Advertising, marketing, promotions, public relations, and sales managers; insurance sales agents; real estate brokers and sales agents; sales engineers; sales representatives, wholesale and manufacturing; securities, commodities, and financial services sales agents

Personality Types: Enterprising-Conventional-Artistic

Did You Know?

Advertising is everywhere. It's on our radios and televisions, in our magazines and newspapers, on billboards, on our shirts and shoes, in our schools, as part of our movie previews, and now as part of our bodies. Some advertisers pay individuals to wear temporary tattoos on their foreheads pitching a particular product. Some people have even gone so far as to sell their forehead space on eBay.

Career in Focus: *Local Sales Agent*

Local sales agents work for local publications (such as a newspaper) or radio and television stations. They are generally responsible for sales in a specific territory. For these sales agents, obtaining new accounts is an important part of the job, and they may spend much of their time visiting advertisers and current clients. They are often under constant pressure to meet quotas.

Where and When

Because income and job security are often dependent on the worker's results, selling can be stressful. The need to meet monthly quotas often causes sales agents to work more than 40 hours per week, though most have the freedom to set their own schedule. More and more of an advertising sales agent's business can be done over the phone and Internet, making telecommuting more popular.

For More Information

✳ The Newspaper Association of America, 4401 Wilson Boulevard, Suite 900, Arlington, VA 22203. Internet: www.naa.org

Cashiers

At a Glance

Supermarkets, department stores, gasoline service stations, movie theaters, restaurants, and many other businesses employ cashiers. Cashiers add up customers' bills, take their money, and give change. They also fill out charge forms for credit cards, give receipts, and handle returns and exchanges. Cashiers are responsible for the money they collect during their shift, and they cannot leave their cash drawers without permission from their supervisor. At the end of the day they compare the cash in their drawers with their sales totals. In many establishments, repeated shortages are grounds for dismissal. Cashiers use cash registers, scanners, and computers regularly.

Career in Focus: *Booth Cashier*

In casinos, booth cashiers exchange coins, chips, and tokens and may issue payoffs. They may also operate a booth in the slot-machine area or count and audit money in drawers. Unlike most cashiers in stores, booth cashiers in casinos generally operate behind protective enclosures and are at much less risk for robbery.

Where and When

Cashiers spend most of their day on their feet, doing repetitive work in mostly comfortable environments. The job requires constant interaction with the public, which can sometimes be stressful. In addition, most places employing cashiers are open nights and weekends, which means schedules may vary. Being a cashier can also be dangerous work: Cashiers' risk from robberies and homicides is much higher than most other occupations.

For More Information

* Food Marketing Institute, 2345 Crystal Dr., Suite 800, Arlington, VA 22202. Internet: www.fmi.org

* The Association for Convenience and Petroleum Retailing, 1600 Duke St., Alexandria, VA 22314. Internet: www.nacsonline.com

* United Food and Commercial Workers International Union, Education Office, 1775 K St. NW, Washington, DC 20006.

Data Bank

Education and Training: Short-term on-the-job training

Average Earnings: $16,000–$20,000

Earnings Growth Potential: Very low

Total Jobs Held: 3,550,000

Job Outlook: Little change

Annual Job Openings: 172,000

Related Jobs: Counter and rental clerks; food and beverage serving and related workers; gaming cage workers; Postal Service clerks; retail salespersons; tellers

Personality Types: Conventional-Enterprising

Did You Know?

Cashiers used to have to look at the price tag of an item and ring it up manually (and still do in some stores). In 1974, however, the business of cashiering changed forever. That was the year the first UPC (Uniform Product Code) scanner was installed at a Marsh supermarket in Troy, Ohio. The first product to have a bar code: a pack of Wrigley's gum. Now advances in scanner and checkout technology could begin to put cashiers out of business. More and more grocery stores are using new self-checkout lanes where customers scan, bag, and pay for their items themselves.

Demonstrators and Product Promoters

At a Glance

Demonstrators and product promoters create public interest in products such as clothing, cosmetics, food, and housewares. Demonstrators show products to customers, either in retail stores or in private homes. Product promoters try to convince stores to carry new products. They may set up displays in stores or host special events to show off their products. Some demonstrations are intended to generate immediate sales through impulse buying, while others are designed to generate future sales and increase brand awareness. Demonstrations and product promotions are conducted in stores, shopping malls, trade shows, and outdoor fairs. A demonstrator's presentation may include visuals, models, case studies, testimonials, test results, and surveys.

Data Bank

Education and Training: Moderate-term on-the-job training

Average Earnings: $19,000–$30,000

Earnings Growth Potential: Low

Total Jobs Held: 103,000

Job Outlook: Average increase

Annual Job Openings: 3,700

Related Jobs: Insurance sales agents; models; real estate brokers and sales agents; reservation and transportation ticket agents and travel clerks; retail salespersons; sales representatives, wholesale and manufacturing

Personality Types: Enterprising-Conventional-Realistic

Did You Know?

Cartoons often show a frantic salesworker demonstrating a kitchen gadget on somebody's doorstep. Nowadays, manufacturers often try to reach a wider audience by using TV infomercials for these promotions: "It slices, it dices, it juliennes!" Nevertheless, human contact and firsthand experience of a product can be more convincing than television. That's why demonstrators are still sent to places that attract large flows of potential customers: trade shows, state fairs, even airports.

Career in Focus: *Trade Show Exhibitor*

Some of the best-known trade shows invite the public to see new models of automobiles or boats, but countless other trade shows are aimed at buyers for businesses. Exhibitors who staff the booths at these shows attract the attention of passers-by and demonstrate the wares being exhibited. These workers need to be well informed about the products, have outgoing personalities, and be unafraid of rejection. Most of them do other kinds of demonstration work between shows.

Where and When

About half of all demonstrators and product promoters work part time, and many positions last six months or less. Demonstrators may work long hours while standing and walking, and many of them travel frequently. However, many enjoy the opportunity to interact with a variety of people.

For More Information

✳ Association for Integrated Marketing, 257 Park Ave. S., Suite 1102, New York, NY 10010. Internet: www.pmalink.org

✳ Promotional Products Association International, 3125 Skyway Circle N., Irving, TX 75038. Internet: www.ppa.org

Insurance Sales Agents

At a Glance

Insurance agents sell insurance policies to people and businesses, protecting them against losses. Common policies include health, life, and car insurance. Insurance agents and brokers help people choose the policies that best meet their needs. Captive agents work for a single insurance company, while insurance brokers and independent agents sell insurance for several different companies. All of these workers prepare reports, maintain records, and seek out new clients. In the event of a loss, they help policyholders settle their insurance claims. Increasingly, some are also offering their clients financial advice. The Internet has made the insurance industry much more efficient, reducing the amount of time agents spend actively seeking new clients and allowing them to take on more work.

Career in Focus: *Life Insurance Agent*

Life insurance agents specialize in selling policies that pay beneficiaries when a policyholder dies. The policy can be designed to provide retirement income, funds for the education of children, or other benefits. Selling life insurance can be difficult: The money is only paid out under certain conditions, and if you are the person being covered, odds are you won't be around to spend it.

Where and When

Most insurance sales agents work out of small offices, but much of their time may be spent traveling to meet with clients or to investigate insurance claims. Agents usually set their own hours, though most work at least 40 hours per week, and some can work as many as 60.

For More Information

* National Association of Professional Insurance Agents, 400 N. Washington St., Alexandria, VA 22314. Internet: www.pianet.org

* National Association of Health Underwriters, 2000 N. 14th St., Suite 450, Arlington, VA 22201. Internet: www.nahu.org

* Insurance Information Institute, 110 William St., New York, NY 10038. Internet: www.iii.org

* The American Institute for Chartered Property and Casualty Underwriters/Insurance Institute of America, 720 Providence Rd., Suite 100, Malvern, PA 19355-3433. Internet: www.aicpcu.org

* The American College, 270 S. Bryn Mawr Ave., Bryn Mawr, PA 19010-2195. Internet: www.theamericancollege.edu

Data Bank

Education and Training: Vocational/technical training

Average Earnings: $33,000–$70,000

Earnings Growth Potential: High

Total Jobs Held: 435,000

Job Outlook: Average increase

Annual Job Openings: 15,300

Related Jobs: Advertising sales agents; claims adjusters, appraisers, examiners, and investigators; customer service representatives; financial analysts; financial managers; insurance underwriters; personal financial advisors; real estate brokers and sales agents; sales representatives, wholesale and manufacturing; securities, commodities, and financial services sales agents

Personality Types: Enterprising-Conventional-Social

Did You Know?

People buy insurance to protect their assets. But not all assets are cars or houses. The famous insurance group Lloyd's of London has issued some odd insurance policies in recent years. Some of these policies include accident insurance for Russian cosmonauts traveling to the MIR space station; coverage in case of a crocodile attack; and insuring a famous model's legs, a singer's vocal cords, and a food critic's taste buds. One London-based insurance company has sold 30,000 policies that cover the risk of alien abduction.

Models

At a Glance

Models pose for photos or as subjects for paintings or sculptures. They display clothing for a variety of audiences and in various types of media. They model accessories, such as handbags, shoes, and jewelry, and promote beauty products, including fragrances and cosmetics. The most successful models, called supermodels, hold celebrity status and often use their image to sell other products (including *lots* of calendars). Almost all models work through agents, who provide a link between models and clients.

Data Bank

Education and Training: Moderate-term on-the-job training

Average Earnings: $20,000–$37,000

Earnings Growth Potential: Medium

Total Jobs Held: 2,000

Job Outlook: Above-average increase

Annual Job Openings: 100

Related Jobs: Actors, producers, and directors; demonstrators and product promoters

Personality Types: Artistic-Enterprising-Realistic

Did You Know?

Models spend a considerable amount of time promoting and developing themselves. They assemble and maintain portfolios, print composite cards, and travel to check out potential clients, or "go-sees." A portfolio is a collection of a model's previous work that is carried to all go-sees and bookings. A composite card contains the best photographs from a model's portfolio, along with his or her measurements. The self-promotion is a little like what artists do, only the artworks are images of yourself.

Career in Focus: *Parts Model*

Parts models have a body part, such as a hand or foot, that is particularly well suited to model products such as fingernail polish or shoes. For example, Ellen Sirot is not nearly as recognizable as Kate Moss or Tyra Banks, but you've probably seen her hands holding everything from soft drinks to cell phones. The modeling industry also uses foot models, leg models, hair models, and even lip models.

Where and When

Many models work part time, often with variable work schedules. They may work in a comfortable, climate-controlled studio or outdoors in adverse weather conditions. Frequent travel may be required.

For More Information

For information about modeling schools and agencies in your area, contact a local consumer affairs organization such as the Better Business Bureau.

Real Estate Brokers and Sales Agents

At a Glance

Real estate agents and brokers help people buy and sell homes and rental properties. Real estate agents show homes, help buyers get financing, and make sure the contract conditions are met. Brokers may sell houses and rent and manage properties. Both know which neighborhoods will best fit clients' needs and budgets. They are familiar with local zoning and tax laws and know where to obtain financing. Agents and brokers also help in price negotiations between buyers and sellers. Agents and brokers spend lots of time obtaining listings—agreements by owners to place properties for sale with the firm. After the property is sold, both the agent who sold it and the agent who obtained the listing receive a portion of the profit.

Career in Focus: *Real Estate Broker— Nonresidential*

Most real estate brokers and sales agents sell houses. However, a small number—usually employed in large or specialized firms—sell commercial, industrial, agricultural, or other types of real estate. Each specialty requires knowledge of that particular type of property. For example, selling or leasing business property requires an understanding of leasing practices, business trends, and the location of the property. Likewise, agents who sell or lease industrial properties must know about the region's transportation, utilities, and labor supply.

Where and When

Most real estate brokers and sales agents work out of their home or office, though much of their time is spent meeting with clients, showing properties, or doing research. They often work more than 40 hours per week, and evenings and weekends are common. However, they also get to set their own schedule.

For More Information

* National Association of Realtors. Internet: www.realtor.org

---

Data Bank

Education and Training: Work experience in a related occupation to vocational/technical training

Average Earnings: $29,000–$71,000

Earnings Growth Potential: Very high

Total Jobs Held: 518,000

Job Outlook: Above-average increase

Annual Job Openings: 15,900

Related Jobs: Appraisers and assessors of real estate; insurance sales agents; property, real estate, and community association managers; sales representatives, wholesale and manufacturing; securities, commodities, and financial services sales agents

Personality Types: Enterprising-Conventional

Did You Know?

Real estate sales agents often don't have the privilege of a steady paycheck. Not only is the housing market seasonal (more people buy in the spring and summer), but it is highly sensitive to swings in the economy. When economic activity declines and interest rates go up, people are much less likely to buy a new home. This means real estate brokers and sales agents may be eating filet mignon one month and Spam-on-toast the next.

Retail Salespersons

At a Glance

Consumers spend millions of dollars every day on merchandise and often form their impression of a store based on its employees. That's why retailers stress the importance of providing courteous and efficient service. Retail salespersons help customers choose and buy all kinds of items, from sweaters and makeup to lumber and plumbing. Their primary job is to interest customers in the products they are selling. They describe a product's features, demonstrate its use, or show various models and colors. They also fill out sales checks, take payment, bag purchases, and give change and receipts. Most sales workers are responsible for keeping track of the money in their cash registers. In addition, they may help stock shelves, mark price tags, take inventory, and prepare displays.

Data Bank

Education and Training: Short-term on-the-job training

Average Earnings: $17,000–$27,000

Earnings Growth Potential: Low

Total Jobs Held: 4,489,000

Job Outlook: Average increase

Annual Job Openings: 162,700

Related Jobs: Cashiers; counter and rental clerks; customer service representatives; gaming cage workers; insurance sales agents; real estate brokers and sales agents; sales engineers; sales representatives, wholesale and manufacturing; securities, commodities, and financial services sales agents

Personality Types: Enterprising-Conventional

Did You Know?

Internet sales have exploded in the last few years. Whether they are buying a book from Amazon or a plane ticket to Tahiti, more and more people are shopping online. Contrary to expectations, however, this has not decreased the need for retail salespersons. Retail salespersons provide a specialized service that Internet services can't: face-to-face human interaction with a smile.

Career in Focus:
Automobile Salesperson

For some sales jobs, particularly those involving expensive items, retail salespersons need special knowledge or skills. Salespersons who sell automobiles must be able to explain the features of various models, the manufacturers' specifications, the types of options and financing available, and the warranty. They frequently negotiate or "haggle" with the consumer for the price, and they spend more time than most other retail salespersons filling out paperwork. Many of them work at least partly on commission and make considerably more than most other workers in retail sales.

Where and When

Most salespersons in retail work in clean, comfortable stores. They often stand for the majority of their time. Some may work outdoors selling cars, plants, or construction materials. Most salespersons work evenings and weekends, and they may not be allowed to take vacation during the holiday season.

For More Information

* National Retail Federation, 325 7th St. NW, Suite 1100, Washington, DC 20004. Internet: www.nrf.com

* National Automobile Dealers Association, Public Relations Department, 8400 Westpark Dr., McLean, VA 22102-3591. Internet: www.nada.org

Sales Engineers

At a Glance

Sales engineers work for companies that produce complex products, such as chemicals or technical tools. Sales engineers work with the production or research and development departments of their companies, or with independent sales firms, to determine how products and services could be designed or modified to suit customers' needs. Selling is an important part of the job, but sales engineers also help their customers learn to use the products they buy. They also may help companies produce better materials based on customer feedback. Most sales engineers have a bachelor's degree in engineering, and many have previous work experience in an engineering specialty.

Career in Focus: *Technical Sales Engineer*

Technology is constantly changing, and it can be difficult for businesses to keep up. Technical sales engineers combine their technical knowledge with sales experience to find products that will meet each client's technology needs, whether it's a new computer mainframe or the control systems of an airplane. Those sales engineers who specialize in keeping up with innovations in technology should have good job prospects over the next ten years.

Where and When

Many sales engineers work more than 40 hours per week to satisfy their clients' needs. Some may be required to travel extensively, often for days or weeks at a time. Though hours may be long and irregular, many sales engineers have the freedom to set their own schedules.

For More Information

* Manufacturers' Agents National Association, 16 A Journey, Suite 200, Aliso Viejo, CA 92656-3317. Internet: www.manaonline.org
* Manufacturers' Representatives Educational Research Foundation, 8329 Cole St., Arvada, CO 80005. Internet: www.mrerf.org

Data Bank

Education and Training: Bachelor's degree

Average Earnings: $63,000–$110,000

Earnings Growth Potential: High

Total Jobs Held: 78,000

Job Outlook: Average increase

Annual Job Openings: 3,500

Related Jobs: Advertising sales agents; engineers; insurance sales agents; purchasing managers, buyers, and purchasing agents; real estate brokers and sales agents; retail salespersons; sales representatives, wholesale and manufacturing; sales worker supervisors; securities, commodities, and financial services sales agents

Personality Types: Enterprising-Realistic-Investigative

Did You Know?

Why does an engineer become a sales worker? Given that the vast majority of sales engineers have a bachelor's degree in engineering, one might wonder why they pursue a career with so much focus on selling and all the pressures that come with it. Some do it for the added challenge, others because it allows them to pursue two interests at once, and still others because of the larger paychecks that commissions and bonuses bring in. Sales engineers get to experience the best and the worst of two worlds.

Sales Representatives, Wholesale and Manufacturing

At a Glance

These sales representatives sell products to manufacturers, wholesale and retail stores, construction contractors, government agencies, and other institutions. They answer questions about their products and show how the products can meet clients' needs. Sales representatives may help install new equipment and train employees to use it. They also take orders and resolve problems or complaints about the merchandise. Sales representatives follow leads from other clients, participate in trade shows and conferences, and may visit potential clients unannounced.

Data Bank

Education and Training: Work experience in a related occupation

Average Earnings: $39,000–$80,000

Earnings Growth Potential: High

Total Jobs Held: 1,973,000

Job Outlook: Average increase

Annual Job Openings: 60,000

Related Jobs: Advertising sales agents; insurance sales agents; purchasing managers, buyers, and purchasing agents; real estate brokers and sales agents; retail salespersons; sales engineers; sales worker supervisors; securities, commodities, and financial services sales agents

Personality Types: Enterprising-Conventional

Did You Know?

While the minimum requirement to become a sales representative is on-the-job training, more and more companies are looking for college graduates. Firms selling complex, technical products especially look for individuals with a degree in a technical field. There are also several certification programs available. Though either of these routes will increase your chances of landing a career in this field, some companies will still hire people who lack a college degree, provided they have sales experience and the right personality.

Career in Focus: *Manufacturers' Agent*

Manufacturers' agents are self-employed sales workers or independent firms who contract their services to all types of manufacturing companies. Manufacturers' agents might sell several similar products made by different manufacturers. They also take orders and resolve any problems with the merchandise. Manufacturers' agents who operate a sales agency also must manage their business. This requires organizational and general business skills, as well as knowledge of accounting, marketing, and administration.

Where and When

Sales representatives with large territories travel considerably. Because of the travel and the nature of the work, many sales representatives work more than 40 hours per week. Though the hours are long and irregular, most sales representatives have the freedom to set their own schedule. Sales representatives are under constant pressure to make their clients happy, expand their client base, and meet sales goals.

For More Information

* Manufacturers' Agents National Association, 16 A Journey, Suite 200, Aliso Viejo, CA 92656-3317. Internet: www.manaonline.org

* Manufacturers' Representatives Educational Research Foundation, 8329 Cole St., Arvada, CO 80005. Internet: www.mrerf.org

Sales Worker Supervisors

At a Glance

Sales worker supervisors oversee the work of retail salespersons, cashiers, customer service representatives, stock clerks and order fillers, and others. They work in all kinds of businesses—dress shops, toy stores, department stores, and bakeries, just to name a few. They hire, train, and supervise workers and set the work schedule. They order supplies, make bank deposits, and often wait on customers themselves. In retail establishments, supervisors ensure that customers receive satisfactory service. They also deal with complaints, and sometimes handle purchasing, budgeting, and accounting. All sales worker supervisors must have good management skills.

Career in Focus: *Sales Worker Supervisor—Nonretail*

Supervisors in nonretail establishments supervise and coordinate the activities of sales workers who sell industrial products, automobiles, or services such as advertising or Internet service. They may prepare budgets, make hiring and firing decisions, create sales-incentive programs, assign sales territories, and approve sales contracts. They generally have less direct contact with customers than the sales workers they supervise, though they often deal with problems and complaints.

Where and When

Sales worker supervisors in retail spend a majority of their time on the sales floor (and on their feet). Most supervisors have offices as well. Work hours vary because work schedules depend on customers' needs. Most supervisors work at least 40 hours per week, and long irregular hours, evenings, and weekends are common.

For More Information

* National Retail Federation, 325 7th St. NW, Suite 1100, Washington, DC 20004. Internet: www.nrf.com

* National Automobile Dealers Association, Public Relations Dept., 8400 Westpark Dr., McLean, VA 22102-3591. Internet: www.nada.org

Data Bank

Education and Training: Work experience in a related occupation

Average Earnings: $31,000–$55,000

Earnings Growth Potential: High

Total Jobs Held: 2,192,000

Job Outlook: Little change

Annual Job Openings: 58,000

Related Jobs: Administrative services managers; advertising, marketing, promotions, public relations, and sales managers; food service managers; lodging managers; office and administrative support worker supervisors and managers

Personality Types: Enterprising-Conventional-Social

Did You Know?

Many sales worker supervisors are promoted from within. Most begin their careers on the sales floor and work their way up the ladder through years of service, establishing a record of success. Promotion generally occurs more quickly in larger companies, though this can sometimes result in relocation. Those who become sales worker supervisors often use that experience to start their own business later. In fact, about one-third of all supervisors are self-employed.

Securities, Commodities, and Financial Services Sales Agents

At a Glance

Securities and commodities sales agents–also called brokers, account executives, or financial consultants—buy and sell stocks, bonds, and other financial products for clients who want to invest in the stock market. They explain the advantages and disadvantages of different investments. They also supply the latest price quotes on any securities and information on the financial positions of the corporations issuing the securities. In addition, many agents provide advice on investments, insurance, tax planning, estate planning, and other financial matters. Most securities and commodities sales agents help individual investors. Others specialize in institutional investors, such as banks. The most important part of a sales representative's job is finding clients and building a customer base.

Data Bank

Education and Training: Bachelor's degree

Average Earnings: $39,000–$119,000

Earnings Growth Potential: Very high

Total Jobs Held: 317,000

Job Outlook: Average increase

Annual Job Openings: 12,700

Related Jobs: Financial analysts; insurance sales agents; loan officers; personal financial advisors; real estate brokers and sales agents

Personality Types: Enterprising-Conventional

Did You Know?

Have you heard of the Dow Jones Industrial Average or the *Wall Street Journal*? The same person was the driving force behind both. Charles Dow published the first daily paper that gave financial information about companies. That paper grew into the *Wall Street Journal*. Dow also developed the first stock market average, which became the Dow Jones Industrial Average. Interestingly, Charles Dow never finished high school, though the vast majority of agents working on Wall Street today have a college degree.

Career in Focus: *Financial Services Sales Agent*

Financial services sales agents usually work for banks. They contact potential customers to sell their bank's services, which might include loans, mutual funds, deposit accounts, retirement planning, and other investment services. They also may ask businesses to participate in consumer credit card programs. Financial services sales agents who serve all the financial needs of a single person or business often are called private bankers.

Where and When

Though most securities and commodities sales agents work in comfortable offices, they are almost always working under stressful conditions. Sales activity fluctuates daily, and sales agents have to constantly keep up with these shifts. Most of them work a standard 40-hour week, though beginning sales agents may spend more time meeting potential customers. Many accommodate customers by meeting with them in the evenings or on weekends.

For More Information

* American Academy of Financial Management, 245 Glendale Dr., Suite 1, Metairie, LA 70001. Internet: www.financialanalyst.org

* Securities Industry and Financial Markets Association, 120 Broadway, 35th Floor, New York, NY 10271. Internet: www.sifma.org

* Financial Industry Regulatory Authority (FINRA), 1735 K St. NW, Washington, DC 20006. Internet: www.finra.org

* CFA Institute, P.O. Box 3668, 560 Ray C. Hunt Dr., Charlottesville, VA 22903. Internet: www.cfainstitute.org

Travel Agents

At a Glance

Travel agents make hotel, airline, car-rental, and cruise reservations for people and businesses. They also plan group tours and conferences. They tell clients which documents they will need for foreign travel and help them plan their trip. They must be up-to-date on cultural and political issues, restaurants, and tourist attractions. Travel agents consult published and computer-based sources for information on departure and arrival times, fares, and hotel ratings and accommodations. They may also visit hotels, resorts, and restaurants so that they can base recommendations on their own travel experiences. Many cruise lines, resorts, and specialty travel groups use travel agents to promote travel packages to millions of people every year.

Career in Focus:
Adventure Travel Agent

While the majority of travel agents plan getaways to the Bahamas or family cruises, some specialize in more exotic and unusual destinations. Whether it's planning a climb up Mount Kilimanjaro or tracking gorillas through the Bwindi Impenetrable Forest, there are agents out there who specialize in exotic trips. These agents not only plan complex (and sometimes risky) vacations, many of them also act as tour guides. Most are experts at the activity in question, such as mountain climbing, or on the kind of vacation, such as an African safari. The trips they offer tend to be all-inclusive and *very* expensive.

Where and When

Travel agents spend most of their time behind their desks in comfortable office environments. Pressure and hours may increase during peak vacation periods and holidays. Advances in computer systems and telecommunications make it easier than ever for travel agents to work from home.

For More Information

✳ American Society of Travel Agents, Education Department, 1101 King St., Suite 200, Alexandria, VA 22314. Internet: www.asta.org

Data Bank

Education and Training: Vocational/technical training

Average Earnings: $24,000–$38,000

Earnings Growth Potential: Medium

Total Jobs Held: 105,000

Job Outlook: Declining

Annual Job Openings: 800

Related Jobs: Hotel, motel, and resort desk clerks; reservation and transportation ticket agents and travel clerks; tour guides and escorts; travel guides

Personality Types: Enterprising-Conventional

Did You Know?

Two important factors have contributed to the decline in the number of travel agent jobs. First, airlines have stopped offering commissions to travel agencies. Perhaps even more powerful is the effect of the Internet. Travel accommodations account for a large percent of online business, and many people find it easier to just point and click to get plane tickets and hotel reservations. However, because some people want more information or want someone else to do the work, travel agents who specialize in specific destinations or luxury travel will have an easier time combating the competition offered by the Internet.

Office and Administrative Support Occupations

Bill and Account Collectors

At a Glance

These workers keep track of accounts that are overdue and try to collect payment on them. Some are employed by third-party collection agencies. Others work directly for companies like stores, hospitals, or banks. First they track down and notify customers who owe money. Where feasible, they offer the customer advice on how to pay off the debts. If a customer fails to respond, collectors notify the credit department of the establishment. In more extreme cases, collectors may initiate repossession proceedings, disconnect the customer's service, or hand the account over to an attorney for legal action. Collectors use computers and special software to keep track of clients. They spend a lot of time on the phone and must have good communication skills.

Data Bank

Education and Training: Short-term on-the-job training

Average Earnings: $25,000–$38,000

Earnings Growth Potential: Low

Total Jobs Held: 411,000

Job Outlook: Above-average increase

Annual Job Openings: 15,700

Related Jobs: Credit authorizers, checkers, and clerks; customer service representatives; interviewers, except eligibility and loan; loan officers; sales representatives, wholesale and manufacturing

Personality Types: Conventional-Enterprising

Did You Know?

According to American Consumer Credit Counseling, about half of all credit card holders pay only their minimum monthly balance. The rest of what they owe is not paid and continues to rack up interest charges. Given that there are more than a billion credit and retail cards in North America, that means some potentially big bills getting even bigger. The United States is a nation that relies on credit for its spending and thus a nation that relies on its bill collectors to make sure lenders and companies get that money back.

Career in Focus: *Skip Tracer*

When customers move without leaving a forwarding address, collectors may check with the post office, telephone companies, credit bureaus, or former neighbors to obtain the new address. The attempt to find the new address is called "skip tracing," and some collectors specialize in this kind of research. New computer systems assist in tracing by automatically tracking when customers change their contact information on any of their open accounts. Skip tracers are like private investigators in some respects, except they track down missing persons who would usually prefer to *stay* missing.

Where and When

Bill and account collectors work in a comfortable office or call-center environment. They spend most of their time on the phone. The work can be stressful as some customers get confrontational when asked about debts and overdue payments. Bill and account collectors often have to work evenings and weekends, when it is easier to reach people at home. Most still work a 40-hour week.

For More Information

* ACA International, The Association of Credit and Collection Professionals, P.O. Box 390106, Minneapolis, MN 55439. Internet: www.acainternational.org

Bookkeeping, Accounting, and Auditing Clerks

At a Glance

Bookkeeping and accounting clerks keep records of all the money their company spends and receives. They might be full-charge bookkeepers who maintain an entire company's books, or clerks who handle specific accounts. All of these clerks make numerous computations each day and must be comfortable using computers. They prepare reports, post bank deposits, and pay bills. They also may handle payroll, make purchases, prepare invoices, and keep track of overdue accounts. In small establishments, bookkeeping clerks handle all financial transactions and recordkeeping. They produce financial statements and prepare reports and summaries for supervisors and managers. In large offices and accounting departments, accounting clerks have more specialized tasks. Most bookkeeping, accounting, and auditing clerks use specialized accounting software to do their work.

Career in Focus: *Auditing Clerk*

Auditing clerks verify records of transactions posted by other workers *within* a company. They check figures, postings, and documents for accuracy. They also correct or note errors for accountants or other workers to adjust. The work is crucial to ensure that the company is operating within the boundaries of local, state, and federal law.

Where and When

Bookkeeping, accounting, and auditing clerks work in comfortable office settings. They typically work a 40-hour week, though many choose to work part time. They may work longer hours at the end of the fiscal year, during tax time, or when audits are performed. Having to sit and use a computer for extended periods can cause eye and muscle strain, head- and backaches, and hand and wrist problems.

For More Information

* American Institute of Professional Bookkeepers, 6001 Montrose Rd., Suite 500, Rockville, MD 20852. Internet: www.aipb.org

Data Bank

Education and Training: Moderate-term on-the-job training

Average Earnings: $27,000–$41,000

Earnings Growth Potential: Low

Total Jobs Held: 2,064,000

Job Outlook: Average increase

Annual Job Openings: 46,000

Related Jobs: Accountants and auditors; billing and posting clerks and machine operators; brokerage clerks; credit authorizers, checkers, and clerks; payroll and timekeeping clerks; procurement clerks

Personality Types: Conventional-Enterprising

Did You Know?

The history of financial record keeping goes back thousands of years, but the history of modern bookkeeping begins in Italy in the 1400s with a mathematician named Fra Luca Bartolomeo de Pacioli. He wrote a math textbook that was the first to detail the debit/credit system still used by accountants today. He included a warning that a bookkeeper should not go to sleep at night until the debits equaled the credits.

Gaming Cage Workers

At a Glance

Gaming cage workers, also called cage cashiers, work in casinos and other gaming establishments. The "cage" they work in is the central depository for money, chips, and paperwork. They do checks on people who want to open a casino credit account and sell gambling chips, tokens, and tickets. They use cash registers, adding machines, and computers. At the end of their shift, cage cashiers must balance their books. Because gaming establishments are closely watched, cage workers must follow a number of rules and regulations related to handling money. For example, they must report all large cash transactions to the Internal Revenue Service for tax purposes.

Data Bank

Education and Training: Short-term on-the-job training

Average Earnings: $19,000–$29,000

Earnings Growth Potential: Low

Total Jobs Held: 39,000

Job Outlook: Declining

Annual Job Openings: 1,300

Related Jobs: Cashiers; credit authorizers, checkers, and clerks; gaming services occupations; retail salespersons; sales worker supervisors; tellers

Personality Types: Conventional-Enterprising-Realistic

Did You Know?

Las Vegas pulls in more than 30 billion dollars a year in revenue from tourists. More than 7 billion of that comes from gambling. Gaming cage workers are used to seeing big dollar amounts taken in and cashed out. To them, thousands of dollars won or lost is just part of a day's work.

Career in Focus: *Gaming Cage Worker—Riverboat and Cruise*

While there isn't a lot of variety in the career of a gaming cage worker, there is some variety in terms of location. While the majority of cage cashiers work in Las Vegas and Atlantic City, gaming establishments are popping up all across the nation, and not always on land. Riverboats and large cruise ships offer gambling as well. Gaming cage workers working on cruise ships may be away for long periods of time.

Where and When

Gaming cage workers stand for long periods, often doing repetitive work. The casino atmosphere exposes workers to cigarette, cigar, and pipe smoke, in addition to noise pollution. Because most casinos are open around the clock, cage workers are expected to work in shifts, including nights, weekends, and holidays.

For More Information

* American Gaming Association, 1299 Pennsylvania Ave. NW, Suite 1175, Washington, DC 20004. Internet: www.americangaming.org

Customer Service Representatives

At a Glance

These representatives work directly with customers, answering questions, taking orders, and solving problems. They make sure customers are satisfied. They may handle billing mistakes, arrange for customers to have services switched on or off, and listen to lots of complaints. In handling customers' complaints, customer service representatives attempt to resolve the problem according to guidelines established by the company. In some cases, they are required to follow up with a customer until an issue is resolved. Some customer service representatives even help people decide what types of products or services would best suit their needs. Many work for banks, insurance companies, and utilities, such as electric, gas, or cable companies. These workers spend a lot of time on the phone or replying to e-mail.

Career in Focus: *Customer Service in Insurance*

Customer service representatives in insurance interact with agents, other insurance companies, and policyholders. They handle much of the paperwork related to insurance policies, such as applications and renewals. They answer questions regarding policy coverage and help with reporting claims. Although they know as much as insurance agents about insurance products and have the credentials required to sell products and make changes to policies, they are not responsible for actively seeking potential customers.

Where and When

Customer service representatives tend to work in clean, comfortable environments, usually in their own workstation or cubicle. Many of these positions require early morning, evening, or late night shifts as well as weekend or holiday work. The work may be repetitious and stressful, and conversations may be monitored by supervisors. For nearly all of these workers, dealing with irate customers can be difficult. Nearly one out of every five customer service representatives works part time.

For More Information

* International Customer Service Association, 24 Wernik Pl., Metuchen, NJ 08840. Internet: www.icsatoday.org

---

Data Bank

Education and Training: Moderate-term on-the-job training

Average Earnings: $24,000–$38,000

Earnings Growth Potential: Low

Total Jobs Held: 2,252,000

Job Outlook: Above-average increase

Annual Job Openings: 110,800

Related Jobs: Bill and account collectors; computer support specialists; insurance sales agents; retail salespersons; securities, commodities, and financial services sales agents; tellers

Personality Types: Social-Enterprising-Conventional

Did You Know?

The customer wasn't always "always right." In fact, the phrase "the customer is always right" wasn't coined until the early 1900s, when it became the working policy of American entrepreneur Harry Selfridge in his department stores. Since then, the idea has become the mantra of customer service representatives. However, many customer service representatives can probably make you a list of the customers who have been wrong (though the customers were probably *told* they were right anyway).

Receptionists and Information Clerks

At a Glance

Receptionists greet customers on the phone and in person and refer them to the proper person or department. Making a good impression is an important part of this job. Some receptionists are responsible for the coordination of all mail into and out of the office as well. In addition, they contribute to security by monitoring visitor access. When they are not busy with callers, most receptionists perform a variety of office duties, including opening and sorting mail, transmitting and delivering faxes, updating appointment calendars, and performing basic bookkeeping, word processing, and filing.

Data Bank

Education and Training: Short-term on-the-job training

Average Earnings: $21,000–$30,000

Earnings Growth Potential: Low

Total Jobs Held: 1,139,000

Job Outlook: Above-average increase

Annual Job Openings: 48,000

Related Jobs: Customer service representatives; dispatchers, except police, fire, and ambulance; secretaries and administrative assistants

Personality Types: Conventional-Enterprising-Social

Did You Know?

While this job may not have the best pay or the most perks, it does have its own day. The second Wednesday in May is the unofficial National Receptionists Day. Employers are urged to treat their receptionists to lunch or buy them flowers or candy. This is not to be confused with Administrative Professionals Day, which is celebrated during the last week of April.

Career in Focus: *Medical Receptionist*

Receptionists in hospitals and doctors' offices perform most of the same duties as any other receptionist. In addition, they are expected to gather patients' personal and financial information and direct them to the proper waiting rooms. They answer questions regarding charges and insurance coverage, schedule patient appointments, explain clinic or hospital policy, schedule hospital admissions, pull patient charts, and even code diagnoses and procedures. Some schools offer special certification or two-year degree programs for medical receptionists.

Where and When

Receptionists usually work in areas that are designed to make a good impression, so they are usually clean, comfortable, and relatively quiet. The work can be tiring, repetitious, and stressful, especially for those who answer the phone all day and encounter angry callers. The majority work a standard 40-hour week.

For More Information

State employment offices can provide information on job openings for receptionists.

* International Association of Administrative Professionals, P.O. Box 20404, Kansas City, MO 64195-0404. Internet: www.iaap-hq.org

Cargo and Freight Agents

At a Glance

Cargo and freight agents work for air and railroad carriers, trucking services, and department stores. They sort cargo by destination, determine shipping rates, and then track the shipments. They take orders from customers and arrange for pickup of items or delivery to loading platforms. They also check on missing or damaged items. For imported or exported freight, they verify that the proper customs paperwork is in order. Cargo and freight agents often track shipments electronically using bar codes and computers, and they must be able to answer customers' questions on the status of their shipments.

Career in Focus: *Transportation Agent*

Cargo and freight agents working in airline services are sometimes called transportation agents. They oversee and assist in the movement of freight, mail, baggage, and passengers through airline terminals. They report the arrival of air freight and record data on the airplane's flight papers. They oversee or participate in loading cargo, and they may be required to operate a forklift or other heavy machinery.

Where and When

Cargo and freight agents work in a variety of businesses and industries. Some may work in warehouses or stockrooms, others in cold storage rooms or outside on loading platforms. Most jobs require frequent standing, bending, walking, and stretching. The work can by physically strenuous, even with the automated devices used to lift heavy materials. While the typical workweek is Monday through Friday, evening and weekend hours are common.

For More Information

✳ Transportation Intermediaries Association (TIA), 1625 Prince St., Suite 200, Alexandria, VA 22314. Internet: www.tianet.org

---

Data Bank

Education and Training: Moderate-term on-the-job training

Average Earnings: $28,000–$48,000

Earnings Growth Potential: Medium

Total Jobs Held: 86,000

Job Outlook: Rapid increase

Annual Job Openings: 4,000

Related Jobs: Postal Service clerks; Postal Service mail sorters, processors, and processing machine operators; shipping, receiving, and traffic clerks; weighers, measurers, checkers, and samplers, recordkeeping

Personality Types: Conventional-Enterprising

Did You Know?

While cargo traffic is expected to increase, the number of jobs for cargo and freight agents will decrease. Technology has improved the process of tracking shipments to the point of cutting jobs in this part of the economy. The use of bar codes, online forms, and Internet tracking procedures make it possible to automate most of this process, which explains the decline in the number of new jobs.

Couriers and Messengers

At a Glance

Messengers and couriers drive, walk, or ride bicycles to pick up and deliver letters and packages that must be delivered quickly—usually within a single city. Most work for courier services, although some work for law firms and many others are self-employed. By sending an item by courier or messenger, the sender ensures that it reaches its destination the same day or even within the hour. Couriers and messengers also deliver very important items such as legal or financial documents, passports, airline tickets, or medical samples. Some messengers are paid by how many deliveries they make and how far they travel.

Data Bank

Education and Training: Short-term on-the-job training

Average Earnings: $19,000–$30,000

Earnings Growth Potential: Low

Total Jobs Held: 122,000

Job Outlook: Declining

Annual Job Openings: 2,800

Related Jobs: Cargo and freight agents; Postal Service mail carriers; shipping, receiving, and traffic clerks; truck drivers and driver/sales workers

Personality Types: Realistic-Conventional-Enterprising

Did You Know?

If you have a desire to act or sing and want to be a messenger as well, there is a job for you. Believe it or not, there are a few companies out there that still specialize in delivering "singing telegrams." First started by Western Union in 1933, the "singing telegram" involves a performer, often dressed in costume, delivering a message in song or rhyme. Whereas telegrams were first designed to inform people of emergencies or death, the singing variety tend to be given as gifts on happy occasions such as birthdays and anniversaries.

Career in Focus: *Medical Courier*

Although e-mail and fax machines can deliver information faster than couriers and messengers, some things, such as medical samples, simply can't be faxed. (Imagine trying to send a liver tissue sample through a fax machine.) Medical couriers are trained to handle medical samples and specimens, keeping them safe as they deliver them from one medical facility to another. Some work within hospitals or health-care networks, while others work for special medical courier services. Such companies generally have specialized insurance plans in case something (or part of some*body*) should get lost or damaged in delivery.

Where and When

Couriers and messengers spend most of their time on their own making deliveries. They are sometimes required to lift heavy loads and are exposed to all weather conditions. The pressure to make as many deliveries as possible in a given day can be stressful. The typical workweek is Monday through Friday, though evening and weekend hours are common.

For More Information

* Messenger Courier Association of the Americas, 750 National Press Building, 529 14th St. NW, Washington, DC 20045. Internet: www.mcaa.com

Postal Service Mail Carriers

At a Glance

Postal Service mail carriers deliver mail to residences and businesses in cities, towns, and rural areas. They travel established routes, delivering and collecting mail. They start work at the post office early in the morning, when they arrange the mail in delivery sequence. Automated equipment has reduced the time that carriers need to sort the mail, allowing them to spend more of their time delivering it. They cover their routes on foot, by vehicle, or by a combination of both. They deliver mail to houses, to roadside mailboxes, and to large buildings such as offices or apartments, which generally have all of their tenants' mailboxes in one location.

Career in Focus: *Rural Mail Carrier*

In comparison with city carriers, rural carriers perform a wider range of postal services, in addition to delivering and picking up mail. For example, rural carriers may sell stamps and money orders and register, certify, and insure parcels and letters. Most rural carriers use their own vehicles for deliveries and are reimbursed for that use.

Where and When

Most carriers begin work early in the morning. Overtime hours are frequently required for urban carriers. Carriers spend most of their time outdoors, delivering mail in all kinds of weather. The work also may cause injuries to various joints and muscles, because it requires repetitive arm and hand movements, as well as constant lifting and bending.

For More Information

Information on job requirements, entrance examinations, and specific employment opportunities for Postal Service mail carriers is available from local post offices and state employment service offices. This information also is available from the United States Post Office online at www.usps.com.

Data Bank

Education and Training: Short-term on-the-job training

Average Earnings: $44,000–$54,000

Earnings Growth Potential: Low

Total Jobs Held: 343,000

Job Outlook: Declining

Annual Job Openings: 10,700

Related Jobs: Couriers and messengers; truck drivers and driver/sales workers

Personality Types: Conventional-Realistic

Did You Know?

Although e-mail uses less paper than "snail mail," the U.S. Postal Service is very active in trying to conserve resources. It runs the nation's largest fleet of alternative-fuel vehicles, including many that are powered by compressed natural gas. It also recycles more than one million tons of materials each year.

Shipping, Receiving, and Traffic Clerks

At a Glance

Shipping, receiving, and traffic clerks keep records of all goods shipped and received. In smaller companies, a clerk also prepares shipments and accepts deliveries. Shipping clerks keep records on all outgoing shipments. Sometimes they fill the order themselves, obtaining merchandise from the stockroom and wrapping or packing the goods themselves. They also address and label packages, compute freight or postal rates, and record the weight and cost of each shipment. They may be responsible for directing the workers who load products onto trucks. Receiving clerks check materials coming into the warehouse, make sure they are in good condition, and send them to the right departments. In many companies, receiving clerks use hand-held scanners to record barcodes on incoming products.

Data Bank

Education and Training: Short-term on-the-job training

Average Earnings: $23,000–$36,000

Earnings Growth Potential: Low

Total Jobs Held: 751,000

Job Outlook: Declining

Annual Job Openings: 18,600

Related Jobs: Cargo and freight agents; material moving occupations; Postal Service clerks; production, planning, and expediting clerks; stock clerks and order fillers

Personality Types: Conventional-Realistic-Enterprising

Did You Know?

Today's warehouses look like something out of yesterday's science fiction novels. Computerized conveyor belts, robots, computer-directed trucks, and automated data storage systems are commonplace, not to mention the hand-held scanners used by the clerks who monitor all of these gadgets and machines. Despite all the automation, a human being is still needed to make sure everything in the shipment checks out—and to keep the robots from taking over the world.

Career in Focus: *Traffic Clerk*

Traffic clerks keep track of shipments in transit. They maintain records on the destination, weight, and charges of all incoming and outgoing freight. The information they gather is used by the accounting department or other departments. Traffic clerks also keep a file of claims for overcharges and for damage to goods in transit.

Where and When

Most of these jobs require frequent standing, bending, walking, and stretching. Some lifting and carrying of smaller items may also be necessary. Most work a typical 40-hour week, Monday through Friday, though evening and weekend hours may be required for some jobs.

For More Information

Information about job opportunities may be obtained from local employers and offices of the state employment service.

Desktop Publishers

At a Glance

Desktop publishers use computers to format text, photos, charts, and other graphics in order to produce newsletters, magazines, calendars, business cards, newspapers, and books. Depending on the project, desktop publishers may write and edit text, create graphics, convert photographs and drawings into digital images, and design page layouts. They may also create proposals, develop presentations and advertising campaigns, and translate electronic information onto film. With the use of specialized software, an entire newspaper, catalog, or book can be created on the screen exactly as it will appear in print. Most desktop publishers work for newspapers or in companies that handle commercial printing. This is one of the fastest-growing jobs in the United States.

Career in Focus: *Web Publications Designer*

Although desktop publishers must be familiar with a variety of computer applications, most of them use computers to produce materials on real paper. Web publications designers, on the other hand, specialize in creating, formatting, and developing materials for the Internet. These may be anything from online newsletters to Web-based instructional materials. Like all desktop publishing jobs, this career combines a love of creative arts and a love of (or at least a tolerance for) computers.

Where and When

Desktop publishers typically work in comfortable office environments. Most work a standard 40-hour week, though some night shifts, weekends, and holidays may be required. The job can be stressful given the pressure of deadlines and tight work schedules. Like others who work in front of a computer for extended periods, desktop publishers are susceptible to eyestrain, back discomfort, and wrist problems.

For More Information

* Graphic Arts Education and Research Foundation, 1899 Preston White Dr., Reston, VA 20191-4367. Internet: www.gaerf.org

* Graphic Arts Information Network, 200 Deer Run Rd., Sewickley, PA 15143-2324. Internet: www.gain.net

Data Bank

Education and Training: Short-term on-the-job training

Average Earnings: $26,000–$38,000

Earnings Growth Potential: Low

Total Jobs Held: 529,000

Job Outlook: Above-average increase

Annual Job Openings: 16,800

Related Jobs: Artists and related workers; commercial and industrial designers; graphic designers; prepress technicians and workers

Personality Types: Conventional-Enterprising

Did You Know?

One of the keys to landing a job as a desktop publisher is a degree in graphic arts, graphic communications, or graphic design. Both associate and bachelor's degree programs teach everything from typography to packaging to Web site design. Many employers prefer these graduates because their training helps them learn the company's processes and software faster.

Office Clerks, General

At a Glance

General office clerks work in all kinds of businesses, from doctors' offices to banks, from big law firms to small companies. Clerks' duties vary by industry and level of experience. These workers generally file, type, keep records, prepare mailings, and proofread documents. Depending on the organization, they may sort checks, keep payroll records, take inventory, access information, or fill orders. Part-time and temporary positions are common in this field.

Data Bank

Education and Training: Short-term on-the-job training

Average Earnings: $20,000–$33,000

Earnings Growth Potential: Low

Total Jobs Held: 3,024,000

Job Outlook: Average increase

Annual Job Openings: 77,100

Related Jobs: Bookkeeping, accounting, and auditing clerks; cashiers; communications equipment operators; counter and rental clerks; customer service representatives; data entry and information processing workers; food and beverage serving and related workers; order clerks; receptionists and information clerks; secretaries and administrative assistants; stock clerks and order fillers; tellers

Personality Types: Conventional-Enterprising-Realistic

Did You Know?

Don't let the job outlook data fool you. While employment of office clerks will grow more slowly than average over the next ten years, the number of job openings is still huge, primarily because of high turnover. Those who know how to use basic office equipment—computers, telephones, fax machines, copiers, and scanners—and have good communication skills will have the best opportunities.

Career in Focus: *Senior Office Clerk*

When is an office clerk more than an office clerk? When he gets promoted to senior clerk. Despite the fact that office clerk is traditionally an entry-level job, there *is* room for advancement. Senior office clerks are generally responsible for more complicated or sensitive work tasks, such as maintaining financial records, setting up spreadsheets, or handling customer complaints. In addition, senior clerks may be expected to monitor and direct the work of lower-level clerks.

Where and When

Most office clerks work in comfortable office settings. Those who are full-time work a standard 40-hour week, though some work shifts or overtime during busy periods. About 16 percent of clerks work part time.

For More Information

✳ International Association of Administrative Professionals, P.O. Box 20404, Kansas City, MO 64195-0404. Internet: www.iaap-hq.org

✳ American Management Association, 1601 Broadway, New York, NY 10019. Internet: www.amanet.org

✳ Association of Professional Office Managers, P.O. Box 1926, Rockville, MD 20849. Internet: www.apomonline.org

Secretaries and Administrative Assistants

At a Glance

Secretaries and administrative assistants help keep offices organized and running smoothly. In their role as information and communication managers, they schedule appointments, maintain files, type correspondence, greet visitors, and answer telephone calls. They also may manage projects, conduct research, and send out company information by telephone, mail, and e-mail. They work with office equipment such as computers, fax machines, and copiers. In addition, secretaries and administrative assistants do tasks previously handled by managers and professionals: create spreadsheets; manage databases; and create presentations, reports, and other documents. They may supervise clerks and other office workers as well.

Career in Focus: *Legal Secretary*

In addition to many of the tasks performed by other kinds of secretaries, legal secretaries have special job responsibilities. For example, they prepare correspondence and legal papers such as complaints, motions, responses, and subpoenas under the supervision of an attorney or a paralegal. They also may review legal journals and assist with legal research, such as verifying quotes and citations in legal briefs.

Where and When

Secretaries and administrative assistants work in schools, hospitals, government agencies, and legal, medical, and corporate offices. Their jobs often involve sitting for long periods in front of a computer, which can cause eyestrain, stress, backaches, and wrist problems. Though one in five secretaries works part time, the majority work a standard 40-hour week.

For More Information

✳ International Association of Administrative Professionals, P.O. Box 20404, Kansas City, MO 64195-0404. Internet: www.iaap-hq.org

✳ Association of Executive and Administrative Professionals, 900 S. Washington St., Suite G-13, Falls Church, VA 22046. Internet: www.theaeap.com

✳ Legal Secretaries International, Inc., 2302 Fannin St., Suite 500, Houston, TX 77002-9136. Internet: www.legalsecretaries.org

✳ National Association of Legal Secretaries, Inc., 8159 E. 41st. St., Tulsa, OK 74145. Internet: www.nals.org

✳ International Virtual Assistants Association, 561 Keystone Ave., Suite 309, Reno, NV 89503. Internet: www.ivaa.org

Data Bank

Education and Training: Moderate-term on-the-job training to associate degree

Average Earnings: $28,000–$43,000

Earnings Growth Potential: Low

Total Jobs Held: 4,348,000

Job Outlook: Average increase

Annual Job Openings: 105,800

Related Jobs: Administrative services managers; bookkeeping, accounting, and auditing clerks; communications equipment operators; computer and information systems managers; computer operators; court reporters; data entry and information processing workers; human resources assistants, except payroll and timekeeping; human resources, training, and labor relations managers and specialists; medical assistants; medical records and health information technicians; office and administrative support worker supervisors and managers; paralegals and legal assistants; receptionists and information clerks

Personality Types: Conventional-Enterprising

Did You Know?

In the past, people thought of secretaries as low-level workers: young women who typed, answered phones, and made coffee. Today's reality is much different. Changes in organization and technology have prompted secretaries and administrative assistants to assume responsibilities formerly reserved for managers and professional staff. A secretary now acts as a kind of junior executive, the keeper of the office schedules and key information.

Farming, Fishing, and Forestry Occupations

Fishers and Fishing Vessel Operators

At a Glance

Fishers and fishing vessel operators catch and trap fish and seafood for the country's restaurants and grocery stores. The boat's captain plans and oversees the fishing, hires crew members, and arranges for the day's catch to be sold. The first mate is the captain's assistant and is in charge when the captain is not on duty. The deckhands carry out the sailing and fishing operations. Large fishing vessels that operate in deep water may have facilities on board where the fish are processed and prepared for sale. Fishers on small boats work in relatively shallow waters, often in sight of land. A very small proportion of commercial fishing is conducted as diving operations. Although most fishers are involved in commercial fishing, some captains and deckhands use their fishing expertise for sport or recreational purposes, often hiring themselves out as guides to tourists.

Data Bank

Education and Training: Moderate-term on-the-job training

Average Earnings: $19,000–$33,000

Earnings Growth Potential: Medium

Total Jobs Held: 36,000

Job Outlook: Declining

Annual Job Openings: 900

Related Jobs: Fish and game wardens; meat, poultry, and fish cutters and trimmers; water transportation occupations

Personality Types: Realistic

Did You Know?

American fisheries are in a state of recovery. Destruction of natural habitats and excessive fish harvesting have dramatically hampered the fishing industry. As a result of government regulations designed to allow fish populations to replenish naturally, many fishers are forced to limit their catches, which in turn means limited paychecks. For these reasons, and because of the dangerous and seasonal nature of the job, many fishers and fishing vessel operators are leaving the occupation.

Career in Focus: *Boatswain*

The boatswain is a highly experienced deckhand who supervises the other deckhands as they carry out the sailing and fishing operations. Before departure, the boatswain directs the deckhands to load equipment and supplies. When necessary, boatswains repair fishing gear, equipment, nets, and accessories. Their supervisory roles usually earn them a slightly better percentage of the sale of the catch.

Where and When

Fishers and fishing vessel operators work under some of the most hazardous conditions of any occupation. Storms, fog, wind, potentially dangerous gear, slippery decks, and a host of other problems make this job one of the most dangerous. In addition, the work is physically demanding and requires workers to be away from home for weeks or even months. The job can be seasonal as well.

For More Information

* National Maritime Center, Coast Guard Headquarters, 2100 2nd St. SW, Washington, DC 20593-0005. Internet: www.uscg.mil/nmc

* Commanding Officer (MSC), 2100 2nd St. SW, Stop 7102, Washington, DC 20593-7102. Internet: www.uscg.mil/hq/msc

Forest and Conservation Workers

At a Glance

Forest and conservation workers help develop, maintain, and protect the nation's forests by growing and planting new seedlings, fighting insects and diseases that attack trees, and helping to control soil erosion. Forest workers also remove diseased or undesirable trees with power saws or handsaws and apply herbicides on undesirable brush to reduce competing vegetation. Some clear away brush and debris from camp trails, roadsides, and camping areas. Others work in forest nurseries, sorting out tree seedlings and discarding those not meeting standards of root formation, stem development, and condition of foliage. Still other forest workers gather products from the woodlands, such as decorative greens, tree cones and barks, moss, and other wild plant life.

Career in Focus: *Tree Farmer*

Some forest workers are employed on tree farms, where they plant, cultivate, and harvest many different kinds of trees. Those who work on specialty farms, such as farms growing Christmas or ornamental trees for nurseries, are responsible for shearing treetops and limbs to control the growth of the trees under their care, to increase the density of limbs, and to improve the shapes of the trees. In addition, these workers' duties include planting the seedlings, spraying to control surrounding weed growth and insects, and harvesting the trees.

Where and When

Most of these jobs are physically demanding. Workers spend all their time outdoors, sometimes in poor weather and often in isolated areas. Workers must be careful and use proper safety measures and equipment such as hardhats, eye protection, safety clothing, and boots to reduce the risk of injury.

For More Information

* Forest Resources Association, Inc., 600 Jefferson Plaza, Suite 350, Rockville, MD 20852-1157. Internet: www.forestresources.org

* American Forest and Paper Association, 1111 19th St. NW, Suite 800, Washington, DC 20036-3652. Internet: www.afandpa.org

---

Data Bank

Education and Training: Moderate-term on-the-job training

Average Earnings: $21,000–$36,000

Earnings Growth Potential: Very low

Total Jobs Held: 13,000

Job Outlook: Average increase

Annual Job Openings: 400

Related Jobs: Conservation scientists and foresters; forest and conservation technicians; grounds maintenance workers

Personality Types: Realistic-Conventional-Investigative

Did You Know?

Forest workers have been tapping trees for their sweet sap since before the Europeans came to North America. Nowadays, most commercial tree-tapping operations don't hang buckets from the sides of trees; they run plastic pipes downhill from trees to the sugar house or a central collection tank. It takes about 10 gallons of sap to make one quart of maple syrup. In Quebec, which leads the world in production of maple syrup, they call the imitation products "pole syrup"—joking that it is made by tapping telephone poles.

Logging Workers

At a Glance

Logging workers harvest thousands of acres of forests each year for the timber that provides the raw material for countless consumer and industrial products. The timber-cutting and logging process is carried out by a logging crew. A typical crew might consist of one or two tree fallers or one tree harvesting machine operator to cut down trees, one bucker to cut logs, two logging skidder operators to drag cut trees to the loading deck, and one equipment operator to load the logs onto trucks. These jobs require various levels of skill, ranging from the unskilled task of manually moving logs, branches, and equipment to skillfully using chain saws or heavy equipment. To keep costs down, many timber-cutting and logging workers maintain and repair the equipment they use.

Data Bank

Education and Training: Moderate-term on-the-job training

Average Earnings: $26,000–$39,000

Earnings Growth Potential: Low

Total Jobs Held: 66,000

Job Outlook: Little change

Annual Job Openings: 2,200

Related Jobs: Conservation scientists and foresters; construction equipment operators; forest and conservation workers; grounds maintenance workers; material moving occupations

Personality Types: Realistic-Conventional

Did You Know?

The paper that you are holding comes at a cost. Logging is dangerous work. In fact, in 1997, logging surpassed fishing as the most dangerous job in the nation. Every year more than 100 workers lose their lives in this industry, despite all of the safety precautions that are taken. Some common *non*lethal hazards are poisonous plants, brambles, insects, heat, humidity, and extreme cold.

Career in Focus: *Log Grader*

Log graders inspect logs for defects, measure logs to determine their volume, and estimate their value on the market. These workers often use hand-held computers to enter data about individual trees. Later, the data can be downloaded or sent from the scaling area to a central computer for processing.

Where and When

Logging jobs are physically demanding and can be hazardous. Workers spend all their time outdoors, sometimes in poor weather and often in isolated areas. The use of hearing protection devices is required on logging operations because of the high noise level of felling and skidding operations. Workers must be careful and use proper safety measures and equipment such as hardhats, eye and ear protection, safety clothing, and boots to reduce the risk of injury.

For More Information

* Forest Resources Association, Inc., 600 Jefferson Plaza, Suite 350, Rockville, MD 20852-1157. Internet: www.forestresources.org

* American Loggers Council, P.O. Box 966, Hemphill, TX 75948-0966. Internet: www.americanloggers.org

* American Forest & Paper Association, 1111 19th St. NW, Suite 800, Washington, DC 20036-3652. Internet: www.afandpa.org

Agricultural Workers, Other

At a Glance

Agricultural workers play a large role in getting food, plants, and other agricultural products to market. Working mostly on farms or ranches, but also in nurseries and slaughterhouses, these workers have numerous and diverse duties. Farmworkers grow grains, fruits, vegetables, nuts, and other crops. They also operate heavy machinery for plowing, harvesting, and sorting. They apply pesticides, herbicides, and fertilizers to crops and repair fences and some farm equipment. Nursery and greenhouse workers grow trees, plants, and flowers in controlled environments. Animal farmworkers care for live farm, ranch, or water animals that may include cattle, sheep, swine, goats, horses, poultry, finfish, shellfish, and bees.

Career in Focus: *Animal Breeder*

Animal breeders select and breed animals, using their knowledge of genetics and animal science to produce offspring with desired characteristics, such as chickens that lay more eggs and pigs that produce leaner meat. To know which animals to breed and when, animal breeders keep detailed records, including the health of the animals, their size and weight, and the amount and quality of the product produced by them. They also keep track of the traits of the offspring.

Where and When

Much of this work takes place outdoors on farms and ranches. The work tends to be physically demanding, especially for farmworkers, and much of it is seasonal in nature. Many farmers work six or seven days per week. Agricultural workers involved in crop production risk exposure to pesticides and other hazardous chemicals. Those who work on mechanized farms must take precautions to avoid injury when working with tools and heavy equipment. Those who work directly with animals risk being bitten or kicked.

For More Information

* United Farm Workers, P.O. Box 62, Keene, CA 93531-0062. Internet: www.ufw.org

* New England Small Farm Institute, 275 Jackson St., Belchertown, MA 01007-9818. Internet: www.growingnewfarmers.org

Data Bank

Education and Training: Work experience in a related occupation

Average Earnings: $18,000–$22,000

Earnings Growth Potential: Very low

Total Jobs Held: 15,000

Job Outlook: Little change

Annual Job Openings: 500

Related Jobs: Animal care and service workers; fishers and fishing vessel operators; forest and conservation workers; grounds maintenance workers; veterinarians; veterinary technologists and technicians

Personality Types: Realistic

Did You Know?

Many of the laborers working in farms today are migrant farmworkers; they move from one farm to the next to keep up with various harvests. Many times the entire family works on the farm, though children must be 12 years old according to federal law. Most migrant farmworkers struggle to find permanent housing, and the pay is quite low. About two-thirds of these workers are immigrants, and their life expectancy of around 50 years is much less than that of the average American.

Construction Trades and Related Workers

Boilermakers

At a Glance

Boilermakers build, install, and repair boilers, vats, and other large tanks used for storing liquids and gases. Boilers supply steam for electric engines and for heating and power systems in buildings, factories, and ships. Tanks and vats are used to store and process everything from oil to beer. Because most boilers last for 35 years or more, repairing and maintaining them is a big part of a boilermaker's job. They inspect tubes, fittings, valves, and controls; clean the boilers; and repair or replace broken parts.

Did You Know?

While the term *boilermaker* used to refer only to workers who actually made boilers (and graduates of Purdue University), today members of the boilermakers' union do a wide variety of jobs in construction, ship-building, and manufacturing. Some work at power plants and oil refineries. Others make heavy machinery, heaters, or even golf balls. Some produce cement, wallboard, and bricks, while others mine coal and other minerals.

Career in Focus: *Boilermaker Apprentice*

While there are many technical school programs available to teach the same skills, many boilermakers learn the trade through a formal apprenticeship. An apprenticeship usually consists of four or more years of on-the-job training, plus a hundred-plus hours of classroom instruction each year. Apprentices generally start at about half of what journey-level boilermakers earn. Apprenticeships are usually advertised by local unions when they are available.

Where and When

Boilermaker work is physically demanding, and workers often use potentially dangerous equipment such as torches and power grinders. Work may be done in cramped quarters or at high elevations. Extended periods of overtime are common, and boilermakers often may find themselves in between jobs.

For More Information

✳ International Brotherhood of Boilermakers, Iron Ship Builders, Blacksmiths, Forgers, and Helpers, 753 State Ave., Suite 570, Kansas City, KS 66101. Internet: www.boilermakers.org

Brickmasons, Blockmasons, and Stonemasons

At a Glance

These workers lay sidewalks and patios, build fireplaces, and install ornamental exteriors on buildings. Brickmasons work with (you guessed it) bricks. Blockmasons work with concrete blocks. Both brickmasons and blockmasons—who often are just called bricklayers—build and repair walls, floors, partitions, chimneys, and other structures. Stonemasons build stone walls and set stone exteriors and floors. They work with two types of stone: natural-cut stone, such as marble, granite, and limestone, and artificial stone, made from concrete, marble chips, or other materials. They often work on churches, office buildings, and hotels. Many masons are self-employed.

Career in Focus: *Refractory Mason*

A refractory mason is a brickmason who specializes in installing firebrick and refractory tile in high-temperature boilers, furnaces, ovens, and ladles for industrial companies. Most of these workers are employed in steel mills, where molten materials flow on refractory beds from furnaces to rolling machines. Work in such places can literally be hot and heavy.

Where and When

These individuals usually work outdoors in a variety of weather conditions. The work can be physically demanding. Masons stand, kneel, bend, and lift heavy materials. Injuries from tools and falls from scaffolds can be avoided with proper safety precautions and equipment.

For More Information

* Mason Contractors Association of America, 33 South Roselle Rd., Schaumburg, IL 60193. Internet: www.masoncontractors.org

* National Association of Home Builders, Home Builders Institute, 1201 15th St. NW, Washington, DC 20005. Internet: www.hbi.org

* International Union of Bricklayers and Allied Craftworkers, 620 F St. NW, Washington, DC 20004. Internet: www.bacweb.org

* National Center for Construction Education and Research, 3600 NW 43rd St., Bldg. G, Gainesville, FL 32606. Internet: www.nccer.org

* International Masonry Institute National Training Center, The James Brice House, 42 East St., Annapolis, MD 21401. Internet: www.imiweb.org

* Associated General Contractors of America, Inc., 2300 Wilson Blvd., Suite 400, Arlington, VA 22201. Internet: www.agc.org

Data Bank

Education and Training: Long-term on-the-job training

Average Earnings: $35,000–$59,000

Earnings Growth Potential: Medium

Total Jobs Held: 160,000

Job Outlook: Average increase

Annual Job Openings: 5,900

Related Jobs: Carpenters; carpet, floor, and tile installers and finishers; cement masons, concrete finishers, segmental pavers, and terrazzo workers; drywall and ceiling tile installers, tapers, plasterers, and stucco masons

Personality Types: Realistic-Conventional

Did You Know?

You may have heard of Boy Scout camp and church camp, but have you heard of masonry camp? Each year, the International Masonry Institute sponsors a masonry camp on Swan's Island in Maine. For one week each summer, architects, engineers, and masonry apprentices spend a week working together to design and build a challenging new project. This way, workers from several fields learn how building plans go from paper to actual bricks and mortar.

Carpenters

At a Glance

Carpenters do all kinds of construction work, including woodworking, concrete work, drywall work, and many other jobs. They frame walls; build stairs; replace doors, windows, and locks; repair wooden furniture; and hang kitchen cabinets. They work with hand and power tools such as saws, drills, and levels, and they must be able to read blueprints. Most work in new construction or remodeling. Carpenters who remodel homes and other structures need a broad range of carpentry skills. These carpenters can switch from residential building to commercial construction or remodeling work, depending on which offers the best work opportunities.

Data Bank

Education and Training: Long-term on-the-job training

Average Earnings: $30,000–$54,000

Earnings Growth Potential: Medium

Total Jobs Held: 1,285,000

Job Outlook: Average increase

Annual Job Openings: 32,500

Related Jobs: Brickmasons, blockmasons, and stonemasons; cement masons, concrete finishers, segmental pavers, and terrazzo workers; construction equipment operators; drywall and ceiling tile installers, tapers, plasterers, and stucco masons; electricians; plumbers, pipelayers, pipefitters, and steamfitters

Personality Types: Realistic-Conventional-Investigative

Did You Know?

What do Han Solo, Jack Ryan, and Indiana Jones have in common? They were all former carpenters. Or at least they were played by one. Actor Harrison Ford was working as a carpenter when he got his role in the first *Star Wars* film. It's not surprising, because carpenters make up the largest building-trade occupation with more than a million workers. Of course, we imagine Mr. Ford earned a bit more as an actor (though the vast majority of actors would be better off financially as carpenters).

Career in Focus: *Brattice Builder*

Brattice builders are specialized carpenters who build tunnel bracing, or brattices, in underground passageways and mines. Brattices control the circulation of air through the passageways and to work sites. Brattice builders might also drill and blast obstructing boulders to reopen ventilation shafts. This is probably not a job for the claustrophobic.

Where and When

Carpentry work can be strenuous because of the prolonged standing, climbing, bending, and kneeling required. Work is done both indoors and out, and carpenters risk injury working with sharp tools and equipment or in situations where they might slip or fall. Many carpenters are self-employed and set their own schedules, although others work for contractors who set their hours for them.

For More Information

* Associated Builders and Contractors, 4250 N. Fairfax Dr., 9th Floor, Arlington, VA 22203-1607. Internet: www.trytools.org

* Associated General Contractors of America, Inc., 2300 Wilson Blvd., Suite 400, Arlington, VA 22201-5426. Internet: www.agc.org

* National Center for Construction Education and Research, 3600 NW 43rd St., Bldg. G, Gainesville, FL 32606-8134. Internet: www.nccer.org

* National Association of Home Builders, Home Builders Institute, 1201 15th St. NW, Washington, DC 20005-2842. Internet: www.hbi.org

* United Brotherhood of Carpenters and Joiners of America, Carpenters Training Fund, 101 Constitution Ave. NW, Washington, DC 20001-2192. Internet: www.carpenters.org

Carpet, Floor, and Tile Installers and Finishers

At a Glance

Carpet installers put carpet in new or old buildings and houses. Floor layers install flooring foundation materials such as rubber, laminate, vinyl, and linoleum. Tilesetters use grout to apply ceramic tiles to floors and walls, primarily in kitchens and bathrooms. Marble setters cut and set marble slabs in floors and walls of buildings. All of these workers use a wide variety of specialized tools. They do installations in homes, offices, hospitals, stores, restaurants, and many other types of buildings.

Career in Focus: *Floor Sander and Finisher*

After a carpenter installs a new hardwood floor or when a customer wants to refinish an old wood floor, floor sanders and finishers are called in. They smooth any imperfections in the wood, using power sanders, wood chisels, and even sandpaper. Afterwards, they apply finish coats of varnish or polyurethane to both protect the floor and give it a glossy finish.

Where and When

Carpet, floor, and tile installers and finishers usually work indoors during regular daytime hours. Work done in stores and offices generally requires evening and weekend work. This work can be physically demanding. Workers spend much of their time bending, kneeling, pulling, and reaching, as well as lifting heavy rolls of carpet and moving heavy furniture.

For More Information

* Finishing Trades Institute International, 7230 Parkway Dr., Hanover, MD 21076. Internet: www.finishingtradesinstitute.org

* National Association of Home Builders, Home Builders Institute, 1201 15th St. NW, Washington, DC 20005. Internet: www.hbi.org and www.nahb.org

* National Tile Contractors Association, P.O. Box 13629, Jackson, MS 39236. Internet: www.tile-assn.com

Data Bank

Education and Training: Moderate-term on-the-job training to long-term on-the-job training

Average Earnings: $28,000–$51,000

Earnings Growth Potential: High

Total Jobs Held: 160,000

Job Outlook: Average increase

Annual Job Openings: 5,400

Related Jobs: Brickmasons, blockmasons, and stonemasons; carpenters; cement masons, concrete finishers, segmental pavers, and terrazzo workers; drywall and ceiling tile installers, tapers, plasterers, and stucco masons; painters and paperhangers; roofers; sheet metal workers

Personality Types: Realistic-Conventional

Did You Know?

Do you know what a "knee kicker" is? It's actually not an angry four-year-old who is about to get into even more trouble. Instead, it is a tool used by carpet installers to stretch carpet into place. Contrary to the name, it is not actually kicked with the knee (which is a hard enough thing to do), but is pushed with the leg. Now can you guess what a "power stretcher" does? (Hint: It has nothing to do with aerobics.)

Cement Masons, Concrete Finishers, Segmental Pavers, and Terrazzo Workers

At a Glance

Cement masons and concrete finishers use a mixture of cement, gravel, sand, and water to build home patios, huge dams, and miles of roads. They pour the concrete and smooth the finished surface. Segmental pavers lay out flat pieces of masonry to form paths, patios, playgrounds, and driveways. These workers need a thorough knowledge of concrete's characteristics so that they can determine what is happening to the concrete and prevent defects. Many workers get their training through three- or four-year apprenticeship programs.

Data Bank

Education and Training: Moderate-term on-the-job training to long-term on-the-job training

Average Earnings: $28,000–$48,000

Earnings Growth Potential: Low

Total Jobs Held: 208,000

Job Outlook: Average increase

Annual Job Openings: 7,900

Related Jobs: Brickmasons, blockmasons, and stonemasons; carpet, floor, and tile installers and finishers; drywall and ceiling tile installers, tapers, plasterers, and stucco masons; grounds maintenance workers

Personality Types: Realistic

Did You Know?

The ancient Romans were serious road builders. Only Roman men of the highest rank were allowed to build and maintain roads. Those cement-block roads were so well constructed that in many places they have lasted for more than 2,000 years. At the height of the Roman Empire, 29 different roads led from Rome to Northern Europe and the Middle East and even into parts of Africa. Hence the expression, "All roads lead to Rome."

Career in Focus: *Terrazzo Worker*

Terrazzo workers create attractive walkways, floors, patios, and panels by exposing marble chips on the surface of finished concrete. Much of the preliminary work of terrazzo workers is similar to that of cement masons. Terrazzo requires workers to add marble chips of various colors into concrete panels. They then grind, clean, polish, and seal the dry surface for a lustrous and decorative finish.

Where and When

This work can be physically strenuous, as most of it is done at floor level, requiring much bending and kneeling. Many jobs are outdoors and are generally stopped during bad weather. Workers wear kneepads and water-repellent boots when working with concrete. Most of these workers are employed by specialty trade contractors who set their hours. Overtime is sometimes needed to finish a job on schedule.

For More Information

* Associated Builders and Contractors, Workforce Development Division, 4250 N. Fairfax Dr., 9th Floor, Arlington, VA 22203-1607. Internet: www.trytools.org

* Associated General Contractors of America, Inc., 2300 Wilson Blvd., Suite 400, Arlington, VA 22201-5426. Internet: www.agc.org

* International Union of Bricklayers and Allied Craftworkers, International Masonry Institute, The James Brice House, 42 East St., Annapolis, MD 21401-1731. Internet: www.imiweb.org

* National Center for Construction Education and Research, 3600 NW 43rd St., Bldg. G, Gainesville, FL 32606-8127. Internet: www.nccer.org

* National Concrete Masonry Association, 13750 Sunrise Valley Dr., Herndon, VA 20171-4662. Internet: www.ncma.org

* National Terrazzo and Mosaic Association, 201 N. Maple, Suite 208, Purcellville, VA 20132-6102. Internet: www.ntma.com

Construction and Building Inspectors

At a Glance

Construction and building inspectors make sure that the country's buildings, roads, sewers, dams, and bridges are safe. They may check electrical or plumbing systems, elevators, or the beams and girders on skyscrapers. In the United States, building construction is regulated by building codes. To monitor compliance with these codes, inspectors make an initial inspection during the first phase of construction and follow up with further inspections throughout the project. In areas where natural disasters—such as earthquakes or hurricanes—are more common, inspectors check for compliance with additional safety regulations. If necessary, inspectors notify the contractor, superintendent, or supervisor when they discover a violation. If the problem is not corrected, government inspectors have the authority to issue a "stop-work" order.

Career in Focus: *Home Inspector*

Home inspectors conduct inspections of newly built or previously owned homes, condominiums, town homes, and apartments. Typically, inspectors are hired by prospective home buyers to inspect and report on the condition of a home. In addition to examining structural quality, inspectors evaluate all home systems and features, including roofing as well as the exterior, garage or carport, foundation, interior, plumbing, electrical, and heating and cooling systems. Home inspection has become a standard practice in the home-buying process.

Where and When

Construction and building inspectors spend considerable time inspecting work sites, which pose their own dangers. They also spend a lot of time in a field office, reviewing blueprints, answering calls, and writing reports. Inspectors normally work regular hours, though if an accident occurs, they must respond immediately.

For More Information

* International Code Council, 500 New Jersey Ave. NW, 6th Floor, Washington, DC 20001-2070. Internet: www.iccsafe.org

* National Fire Protection Association, 1 Batterymarch Park, Quincy, MA 02169-7471. Internet: www.nfpa.org

* Association of Construction Inspectors, 810N Farrell Dr., Palm Springs, CA 92262. Internet: www.aci-assoc.org

* International Association of Electrical Inspectors, 901 Waterfall Way, Suite 602, Richardson, TX 75080-7702. Internet: www.iaei.org

Data Bank

Education and Training: Work experience in a related occupation

Average Earnings: $40,000–$65,000

Earnings Growth Potential: Medium

Total Jobs Held: 106,000

Job Outlook: Above-average increase

Annual Job Openings: 4,000

Related Jobs: Appraisers and assessors of real estate; architects, except landscape and naval; carpenters; construction managers; cost estimators; electricians; engineering technicians; engineers; plumbers, pipelayers, pipefitters, and steamfitters; surveyors, cartographers, photogrammetrists, and surveying and mapping technicians

Personality Types: Realistic-Conventional-Investigative

Did You Know?

About 45 percent of all construction and building inspectors are employed by local governments. These local governments employ large staffs, including plan examiners or inspectors who specialize in steel, concrete, electrical, and elevator inspection. Getting a job working for state or local government almost always requires some type of certification, but the benefits are usually worth it.

Construction Equipment Operators

At a Glance

Construction equipment operators drive and operate the huge machinery used in building construction, road building and repair, and demolition. They might operate cranes, tractors, backhoes, pavers, cement mixers, tamping machines, or hoists, just to name a few. They work at construction sites, shipping docks, airports, mines, and on the nation's highways. They clear land, dig trenches, apply asphalt, and may even work on oil rigs. The pay for these jobs can be high, but the work may slow down in bad weather, reducing earnings.

Data Bank

Education and Training: Moderate-term on-the-job training

Average Earnings: $31,000–$53,000

Earnings Growth Potential: Low

Total Jobs Held: 469,000

Job Outlook: Average increase

Annual Job Openings: 13,600

Related Jobs: Agricultural equipment operators; logging equipment operators; material moving occupations; truck drivers, heavy and tractor-trailor

Personality Types: Realistic-Conventional

Did You Know?

A piledriver is more than a professional wrestling move. Piledrivers are large machines, mounted on skids, barges, or cranes, that hammer long, heavy beams of wood or steel (known as piles) into the ground. These beams are used to support retaining walls, bridges, piers, or building foundations. These machines are common in the oil industry. In fact, some piledriver operators work on offshore oil rigs.

Career in Focus: *Operating Engineer*

Operating engineers generally operate excavation and loading machines equipped with scoops, shovels, or buckets that dig sand, gravel, or earth, and load it into trucks or onto conveyors. Sometimes, they may drive and control industrial trucks or tractors equipped with forklifts or booms for lifting materials or with hitches for pulling trailers. They also may operate and maintain air compressors, pumps, and other power equipment at construction sites.

Where and When

Most construction equipment operators work outdoors in all kinds of conditions, though operations are usually stopped in the winter and during extremely wet weather. Operating heavy construction equipment can be dangerous, and it is usually dirty work. Operators may have irregular hours if work on the project continues around the clock, including late night and early morning shifts.

For More Information

❋ Associated General Contractors of America, 2300 Wilson Blvd., Suite 400, Arlington, VA 22201-5426. Internet: www.agc.org

❋ International Union of Operating Engineers, 1125 17th St. NW, Washington, DC 20036-4786. Internet: www.iuoe.org

❋ National Center for Construction Education and Research, 3600 NW 43rd St., Building G, Gainesville, FL 32606-8134. Internet: www.nccer.org

❋ Pile Driving Contractors Association, P.O. Box 66208, Orange Park, FL 32065-0021. Internet: www.piledrivers.org

Construction Laborers

At a Glance

Construction laborers do a wide range of physically demanding jobs. They build skyscrapers and houses, roads and mine shafts. They remove waste materials and help tear down buildings. They load, unload, and distribute building materials; mix concrete; and use a variety of tools including jackhammers and torches. Construction laborers often help other craftworkers, including carpenters, plasterers, and masons. At other times, construction laborers may work alone, reading and following construction plans with little or no supervision. Many of the jobs they perform require physical strength and some specialized training and experience.

Career in Focus: *Road Construction Worker*

A good percentage of construction laborers are employed in highway, street, and bridge construction. These workers clear and prepare highway work zones, installing traffic barricades and markers. They also dig trenches; install sewer, water, and storm drain pipes; place concrete and asphalt on roads; and are responsible for the installation and maintenance of traffic control devices. This work can be dangerous because of the number of passing motorists.

Where and When

All of the lifting, carrying, stooping, kneeling, crouching, and crawling makes this a physically demanding job. Some laborers work at great heights or outdoors in all kinds of weather. Some jobs expose workers to harmful chemicals, loud noises, or dangerous equipment. To avoid injury, workers wear special gear and take safety precautions. Construction laborers generally work eight-hour shifts, though longer shifts are common and overnight work may be required, especially when working on highways. The work often stops due to bad weather.

For More Information

* LIUNA Training and Education Fund, 37 Deerfield Rd., Pomfret Center, CT 06259. Internet: www.liunatraining.org

* National Center for Construction Education and Research, 3600 NW 43rd St., Bldg. G, Gainesville, FL 32606. Internet: www.nccer.org

Data Bank

Education and Training: Moderate-term on-the-job training

Average Earnings: $23,000–$40,000

Earnings Growth Potential: Low

Total Jobs Held: 1,249,000

Job Outlook: Rapid increase

Annual Job Openings: 33,900

Related Jobs: Assemblers and fabricators; brickmasons, blockmasons, and stonemasons; forest and conservation workers; grounds maintenance workers; highway maintenance workers; logging workers; material moving occupations; refractory materials repairers, except brickmasons; roustabouts, oil and gas

Personality Types: Realistic-Conventional

Did You Know?

Who built the great pyramids of Egypt? Certainly, the pharaohs funded the projects, but it was the estimated 30,000 construction laborers who did the actual building. Using only the technology of ancient times, these workers cut huge stones from quarries, shaped them into building blocks, moved them from the quarries to the building sites, then raised them hundreds of feet, layer upon layer. It's a spectacular building feat, even by modern standards.

Drywall and Ceiling Tile Installers, Tapers, Plasterers, and Stucco Masons

At a Glance

Drywall and ceiling tile installers and tapers work indoors, installing wallboards to ceilings or to interior walls of buildings. Installers fasten drywall panels to the inside framework of houses and other buildings. Tapers prepare these panels for painting by taping and finishing joints and imperfections. In addition to drywall workers, ceiling tile installers also help to build walls and ceilings. Plasterers and stucco masons work both indoors and outdoors—applying plaster to interior walls and cement or stucco to exterior walls. When plasterers work with hard interior surfaces, they first apply a brown coat of gypsum plaster that provides a base, which is followed by a white finish coat.

Data Bank

Education and Training: Moderate-term on-the-job training to long-term on-the-job training

Average Earnings: $30,000–$51,000

Earnings Growth Potential: Medium

Total Jobs Held: 238,000

Job Outlook: Average increase

Annual Job Openings: 5,700

Related Jobs: Brickmasons, blockmasons, and stonemasons; carpenters; carpet, floor, and tile installers and finishers; cement masons, concrete finishers, segmental pavers, and terrazzo workers; insulation workers

Personality Types: Realistic-Conventional

Did You Know?

In part we have the military to thank for the drywall in our houses. During World War II, the government was looking for ways to build military barracks and bases faster and cheaper. Using lath and plaster took too long and was too expensive. Enter the United States Gypsum Company and its "Sheetrock" panels—later to become drywall. The subsequent housing boom after the war only increased drywall's popularity. Now it is the most common method for building interior walls.

Career in Focus: *Lather*

Lathers fasten lath—strips of metal or other material—to walls, ceilings, and partitions of buildings. Lath forms the support for plaster, fireproofing, or other materials. Using hand tools and portable power tools, lathers nail, screw, staple, or wire-tie the lath directly to the framework. Due to the popularity of drywall, the lath and plaster method is not near as common as it used to be, and the number of lathers is dwindling.

Where and When

Most of this work is done indoors, though the work is sometimes strenuous. Drywall installers, ceiling tile installers, and tapers spend most of the day standing, bending, or kneeling. Some tapers even use stilts. Falls from ladders and scaffolds and injuries from power tools are the most common hazards. Many wear masks to keep from breathing in too much dust. Most of them work for contractors, though nearly 20 percent of them are self-employed and set their own schedule.

For More Information

* Associated Builders and Contractors, 4250 N. Fairfax Dr., 9th Floor, Arlington, VA 22203. Internet: www.abc.org

* Association of Wall and Ceiling Industries International, 513 W. Broad St., Suite 210, Falls Church, VA 22046. Internet: www.awci.org

* Finishing Trades Institute, International Union of Painters and Allied Trades, 1750 New York Ave. NW, Washington, DC 20006. Internet: www.finishingtradesinstitute.org

* National Center for Construction Education and Research, 3600 NW 43rd St., Building G, Gainesville, FL 32606. Internet: www.nccer.org

Electricians

At a Glance

Electricians work with the systems that provide electricity to homes and businesses. They may install, test, maintain, and repair wiring, heating, and air-conditioning systems. Electricians generally specialize in construction or maintenance work, though some do both. Electricians in construction work primarily install wiring systems into new homes, businesses, and factories. Electricians specializing in maintenance work primarily upgrade existing electrical systems and repair electrical equipment. Electricians may install wiring for telephones, intercoms, and fire alarm and security systems as well. Electricians also may install coaxial or fiber-optic cable for computers and other telecommunications equipment. All electricians must follow government codes to ensure their own safety and the safety of the buildings they work on.

Career in Focus:
Maintenance Electrician

Maintenance work for electricians varies. Electricians who specialize in residential work may rewire a home and replace an old fuse box with a new circuit breaker box or install new lighting and ceiling fans. Those who work in factories may repair motors, transformers, generators, and electronic controllers on machine tools and industrial robots. Maintenance electricians in factories, hospitals, and other institutional settings may install new equipment.

Where and When

Electricians work at construction sites and in homes, businesses, and factories. The work can be physically demanding, involving standing, stooping, kneeling, and lifting heavy objects. Some electricians may commute long distances to job sites, and all electricians run some risk of injury from electrical shock, falls, and cuts. Most work a standard 40-hour week, and those in maintenance may work nights and weekends.

For More Information

* National Joint Apprenticeship Training Committee, 301 Prince George's Blvd., Upper Marlboro, MD 20774-7410. Internet: www.njatc.org

* National Electrical Contractors Association, 3 Bethesda Metro Center, Suite 1100, Bethesda, MD 20814-6302. Internet: www.necanet.org

* International Brotherhood of Electrical Workers, 900 Seventh St. NW, Washington, DC 20001-3886. Internet: www.ibew.org

* Independent Electrical Contractors, Inc., 4401 Ford Ave., Suite 1100, Alexandria, VA 22302-1464. Internet: www.ieci.org

Data Bank

Education and Training: Long-term on-the-job training

Average Earnings: $36,000–$63,000

Earnings Growth Potential: Medium

Total Jobs Held: 695,000

Job Outlook: Average increase

Annual Job Openings: 25,100

Related Jobs: Computer, automated teller, and office machine repairers; electrical and electronics drafters; electrical and electronics engineering technicians; electrical and electronics installers and repairers; electronic home entertainment equipment installers and repairers; elevator installers and repairers; heating, air-conditioning, and refrigeration mechanics and installers; line installers and repairers

Personality Types: Realistic-Conventional-Investigative

Did You Know?

Many of us learn in elementary school that Thomas Edison invented the light bulb in 1879, but the truth is much more complicated. In fact, an English chemist named Humphry Davy invented the first electric light almost 70 years earlier. In addition, Edison's light bulb was actually based on one developed by Henry Woodward in 1875. On top of that, a year before Edison's bulb, Sir Joseph Swan, an English physicist, invented a bulb that lasted for more than 13 hours. Just how many inventors does it take to make a light bulb?

Elevator Installers and Repairers

At a Glance

Elevator installers and repairers assemble, install, repair, and replace elevators and escalators. They update older equipment and install new equipment. They also test the equipment to make sure it works properly. To install, repair, and maintain modern elevators, these workers must have a thorough knowledge of electronics, electricity, and hydraulics. Installers and repairers also install other moving devices such as dumbwaiters and material lifts, which are similar to elevators in design. They also build and maintain moving walkways, stair lifts, and wheelchair lifts.

Data Bank

Education and Training: Long-term on-the-job training

Average Earnings: $53,000–$82,000

Earnings Growth Potential: High

Total Jobs Held: 25,000

Job Outlook: Average increase

Annual Job Openings: 900

Related Jobs: Boilermakers; electrical and electronics installers and repairers; electricians; industrial machinery mechanics and millwrights; sheet metal workers; structural and reinforcing iron and metal workers

Personality Types: Realistic-Investigative-Conventional

Did You Know?

Many people have an intense fear of riding in elevators, so much so that they would rather take the stairs (which is generally a healthier option anyway). But did you know that escalators are actually more dangerous than elevators? According to some studies, escalator accidents are 15 times more likely than elevator accidents. The majority of escalator injuries come from falls, though there have been cases of individuals losing fingers and toes in the combs at the top and bottom of the escalator. Something to remember the next time you're at the mall.

Career in Focus: *Adjuster*

The most highly skilled elevator installers and repairers, called adjusters, specialize in fine-tuning all the equipment after installation. Adjusters make sure that an elevator works according to specifications and stops correctly at each floor within a specified time. Adjusters must be good troubleshooters, and often have a better understanding of electricity and electronics than other elevator installation workers.

Where and When

Most elevator installers and repairers work a standard 40-hour week, though some repairers are on call. Workers who specialize in maintenance are on their own most of the day and often service the same set of elevators according to a schedule. Elevator installers lift and carry heavy equipment and work in cramped spaces. Dangers include falls, electric shock, and muscle strain. Predictably, most of the work is done indoors.

For More Information

* International Union of Elevator Constructors, 7154 Columbia Gateway Dr., Columbia, MD 21046. Internet: www.iuec.org

* National Association of Elevator Contractors, 1298 Wellbrook Circle, Conyers, GA 30012. Internet: www.naec.org

Glaziers

At a Glance

Glaziers select, cut, install, and remove all kinds of glass in doors, windows, showers, and baths. Residential glaziers replace glass in home windows; install glass mirrors, shower doors, and bathtub enclosures; and fit glass for tabletops and display cases. Commercial glaziers install decorative room dividers or security windows and replace storefront windows for supermarkets, auto dealerships, or banks. In large buildings, glaziers build the metal framework and install glass panels or curtain walls. Besides working with glass, glaziers also may work with plastics, granite, marble, and other glass substitutes. They may use cranes to lift large, heavy pieces into place. After the glass is mounted, glaziers secure it with bolts, cement, metal clips, or wood molding.

Career in Focus: *Window Repairer*

While they may not always be called glaziers, workers who install and repair windows in homes across the country do much of the same work. Window repairers fix and adjust metal and wooden casement windows, storm windows, and doors, using hand tools and portable power tools. They may also repair or replace locks, hinges, and cranks and cut and install glass. Much of their work involves upgrading older windows to newer, more energy efficient ones.

Where and When

Glaziers often work outdoors, sometimes in bad weather. The work can result in injuries because they work with sharp tools and sometimes need to remove broken glass. Lifting and manipulating heavy glass panels while working on scaffolding or ladders can't be easy either. All of the kneeling, bending, and standing only adds to the physical demands of the job. Most glaziers work a standard 40-hour week. Almost two-thirds of them work for contractors in new construction and repair.

For More Information

* International Union of Painters and Allied Trades, 1750 New York Ave. NW, Washington, DC 20006. Internet: www.iupat.org

* Associated Builders and Contractors, Workforce Development Department, 4250 N. Fairfax Dr., 9th Floor, Arlington, VA 22203-1607. Internet: www.trytools.org

* National Glass Association, Education and Training Department, 8200 Greensboro Dr., Suite 302, McLean, VA 22102-3881. Internet: www.glass.org

Data Bank

Education and Training: Long-term on-the-job training

Average Earnings: $28,000–$47,000

Earnings Growth Potential: Medium

Total Jobs Held: 54,000

Job Outlook: Average increase

Annual Job Openings: 2,400

Related Jobs: Automotive body and related repairers; brickmasons, blockmasons, and stonemasons; carpenters; carpet, floor, and tile installers and finishers; cement masons, concrete finishers, segmental pavers, and terrazzo workers; painters and paperhangers; sheet metal workers

Personality Types: Realistic-Conventional

Did You Know?

You've probably seen stained glass windows in churches, where they have been used for about 1,000 years. They were actually controversial when they first were installed. Some priests liked them because pictorial windows could teach Bible lessons to illiterate churchgoers. Others complained that the bright colors distracted them from their religious devotions.

Hazardous Materials Removal Workers

At a Glance

These workers identify, remove, package, transport, and dispose of dangerous materials. They might deal with asbestos, lead, or radioactive materials. They also respond to emergencies where harmful substances are present. They use equipment ranging from brooms to personal protective suits, face shields, and respirators. Asbestos abatement workers and lead abatement workers remove asbestos, lead, and other materials from buildings scheduled to be renovated or demolished. Emergency and disaster response workers clean up hazardous materials after train derailments and trucking accidents. In facilities using radioactive materials, such as nuclear power plants, technicians and workers decontaminate areas and package radioactive materials for transportation or disposal.

Data Bank

Education and Training: Moderate-term on-the-job training

Average Earnings: $29,000–$49,000

Earnings Growth Potential: Low

Total Jobs Held: 42,000

Job Outlook: Above-average increase

Annual Job Openings: 1,800

Related Jobs: Fire fighters; insulation workers; painters and paperhangers; police and detectives; power plant operators, distributors, and dispatchers; sheet metal workers; water and liquid waste treatment plant and system operators

Personality Types: Realistic-Conventional

Did You Know?

We've probably all heard about the Chernobyl meltdown or massive oil spills. But much of the hazardous material that threatens our health daily can be found in our own homes, schools, and offices. Lead was a common ingredient in house paint until the 1970s, when researchers began proving that it is toxic to humans, especially children. Likewise, asbestos, which was commonly used for insulation and fireproofing, can be harmful when breathed in, causing lung disease. Workers involved in testing for and removing these substances should have excellent job opportunities.

Career in Focus: *Treatment, Storage, and Disposal Worker*

These workers transport and prepare materials for treatment or disposal. At incinerator facilities, they transport materials from the customer to the incinerator, where they are destroyed by fire. At landfills, they follow a strict procedure for processing and storing hazardous materials. They organize and track the location of items in the landfill and may help change the material from a liquid to a solid state in preparation for storage. These workers typically operate heavy machinery, such as forklifts, bulldozers, and large trucks.

Where and When

As the name implies, this is probably not the safest job around, but every precaution is taken to ensure worker health when dealing with hazardous materials. Some workers may wear fully enclosed protective suits, and safety measures and guidelines are strictly followed. The work can be physically demanding, as it involves considerable standing, stooping, and kneeling. Most hazardous materials removal workers work a standard 40-hour week, though overtime and shift work are common. Those who remove materials from schools and businesses often work nights and weekends.

For More Information

❋ LIUNA Training and Education Fund, 37 Deerfield Rd., Pomfret Center, CT 06259. Internet: www.liunatraining.org

Insulation Workers

At a Glance

These workers put insulation in buildings to keep the heat in during the winter and the heat out during the summer. Insulation workers cement, staple, wire, tape, or spray insulation between the inner and outer walls or under the roof of a building. They often use a hose or blowing machine to spray a liquid insulation that dries into place. These workers must wear protective suits, masks, and respirators. Insulation workers use a variety of hand tools—trowels, brushes, knives, scissors, pliers—and some power tools, such as saws and compressors. Many are self-employed.

Career in Focus: *Pipe Coverer and Insulator*

Though most insulation workers are generalists, some specialize in providing insulation for pipes, vats, tanks, boilers, and refrigeration units in commercial and industrial buildings. This insulation not only prevents the wasteful loss of heat, but prevents moisture condensation and dampens sound as well. Though they no longer use asbestos, these workers may use cork, plastic, and magnesia as insulating materials.

Where and When

Insulation workers work indoors in residential and industrial settings. The work involves lots of standing, bending, or kneeling, and they may also work from ladders or in tight spaces. Work around pipes with varying temperatures can cause burns, and particles from insulation materials can be irritating to the eyes, skin, and lungs. Workers follow strict safety guidelines to prevent injury or irritation. Most work 40 hours per week, though overtime is common.

For More Information

* National Insulation Association, 12100 Sunset Hills Rd., Suite 330, Reston, VA 20190-3295. Internet: www.insulation.org

* International Association of Heat and Frost Insulators and Allied Workers, 9602 Martin Luther King, Jr. Highway, Lanham, MD 20706-1839. Internet: www.insulators.org

* North American Insulation Manufacturers' Association, 44 Canal Center Plaza, Suite 310, Alexandria, VA 22314-1548. Internet: www.naima.org/pages/resources/training.html

Data Bank

Education and Training: Moderate-term on-the-job training

Average Earnings: $27,000–$47,000

Earnings Growth Potential: Medium

Total Jobs Held: 57,000

Job Outlook: Above-average increase

Annual Job Openings: 2,900

Related Jobs: Carpenters; carpet, floor, and tile installers and finishers; drywall and ceiling tile installers, tapers, plasterers, and stucco masons; roofers; sheet metal workers

Personality Types: Realistic-Conventional

Did You Know?

According to the U.S. Department of Energy, heating and air-conditioning account for 50 to 70 percent of the energy used in the average American home. And as any insulation installer will tell you, good insulation can cut energy costs dramatically. Growing concern about greenhouse gases also increases interest in energy efficiency and is good news for insulation workers.

Painters and Paperhangers

At a Glance

Painters and paperhangers make walls and other surfaces attractive by applying paint, varnish, stain, or wallpaper to them. Painters first apply a primer or sealer to prepare the surface before adding the finish coat. Painters then brush, roll, and spray the paints onto surfaces. Painters paint outside walls with special paints that protect them from weather damage. Paperhangers apply wallpapers and add decorative borders. When redecorating, they may first remove the old covering by soaking, steaming, or applying solvents. When necessary, they patch holes and take care of other imperfections before hanging the new wall covering. Nearly half of all paperhangers and painters are self-employed.

Data Bank

Education and Training: Moderate-term on-the-job training

Average Earnings: $28,000–$44,000

Earnings Growth Potential: Low

Total Jobs Held: 450,000

Job Outlook: Average increase

Annual Job Openings: 10,700

Related Jobs: Carpenters; carpet, floor, and tile installers and finishers; drywall and ceiling tile installers, tapers, plasterers, and stucco masons; painting and coating workers, except construction and maintenance

Personality Types: Realistic-Conventional

Did You Know?

Painting isn't always a matter of "slapping it on there" using a brush or roller. Today, painters use a wide range of techniques to jazz up walls. They might stencil, sponge, rag-roll, splatter, marbleize, or stipple paint onto a flat surface. They can also use appliqué or wallpaper borders. These days, many painters act as a kind of interior decorator, helping homeowners get the walls to look just right.

Career in Focus:
Maintenance Painter

While the majority of painters are either self-employed or work for contractors involved in new construction or remodeling work, some are hired as part of a general maintenance staff. These maintenance painters usually work for organizations that own or manage large buildings or complexes, such as apartments, schools, hospitals, factories, and government agencies. Their work is similar to that of other painters, except that the employment is much more steady and the work can be more routine.

Where and When

Most painters and paperhangers work 40 hours per week or less, and nearly a quarter work a variable schedule or only part time. The job can require considerable standing, climbing, and bending, and some of the work is done on scaffolding and ladders. Painters often work outdoors, but generally only when the weather allows. Those who must remove lead-based paint work in a self-contained suit to prevent contact or inhalation of hazardous materials.

For More Information

* Associated Builders and Contractors, Workforce Development Department, 4250 N. Fairfax Dr., 9th Floor, Arlington, VA 22203. Internet: www.trytools.org

* International Union of Painters and Allied Trades, 1750 New York Ave. NW, Washington, DC 20006. Internet: www.iupat.org

* National Center for Construction Education and Research, 3600 NW 43rd St., Bldg. G, Gainesville, FL 32606. Internet: www.nccer.org

* Painting and Decorating Contractors of America, 1801 Park 270 Dr., Suite 220, St. Louis, MO 63146. Internet: www.pdca.org

Plumbers, Pipelayers, Pipefitters, and Steamfitters

At a Glance

Plumbers, pipelayers, pipefitters, and steamfitters install, maintain, and repair many different types of pipe systems. Plumbers install and repair water, waste disposal, drainage, and gas pipe systems in homes and other buildings. They also install showers, sinks, toilets, and appliances. Pipelayers, pipefitters, and steamfitters install and repair pipe systems used in manufacturing, creating electricity, and heating and cooling buildings. They also install the controls that regulate these systems. Steamfitters specialize in installing pipe systems that move liquids or gases under pressure. Sprinklerfitters install automatic fire sprinkler systems in buildings.

Career in Focus: *Construction Plumber*

Construction plumbers are responsible for installing the new piping in a house or other building. They work from blueprints or drawings that show the planned location of pipes, plumbing fixtures, and appliances. To assemble a system, plumbers cut and bend lengths of pipe and connect them with fittings. After the piping is in place in the house, plumbers install the fixtures and appliances and connect the system to the outside water or sewer lines. Finally, using pressure gauges, they check the system to ensure that the plumbing works properly.

Where and When

Pipefitters and steamfitters generally work in industrial and power plants. Plumbers work in any commercial or residential setting where water and septic systems are required. Pipelayers work outdoors, sometime in remote areas. All of this work can be physically demanding, requiring extended periods of standing, lifting, crouching, and bending. Most work a standard 40-hour week, though those who provide maintenance services work evenings and weekends or are on call.

For More Information

* United Association of Journeymen and Apprentices of the Plumbing and Pipefitting Industry, Three Park Place, Annapolis, MD 21401-3687. Internet: www.ua.org

* Plumbing-Heating-Cooling Contractors—National Association, 180 S. Washington St., Falls Church, VA 22046-2935. Internet: www.phccweb.org

* American Fire Sprinkler Association, Inc., 12750 Merit Dr., Suite 350, Dallas, TX 75251-1273. Internet: www.firesprinkler.org

---

Data Bank

Education and Training: Short-term on-the-job training to long-term on-the-job training

Average Earnings: $34,000–$60,000

Earnings Growth Potential: Medium

Total Jobs Held: 556,000

Job Outlook: Above-average increase

Annual Job Openings: 19,800

Related Jobs: Boilermakers; construction and building inspectors; construction managers; electricians; elevator installers and repairers; heating, air-conditioning, and refrigeration mechanics and installers; industrial machinery mechanics and millwrights; sheet metal workers; stationary engineers and boiler operators

Personality Types: Realistic-Conventional

Did You Know?

We may think of indoor plumbing as a modern convenience, or maybe we just take it for granted. But did you know that cultures as far back as 2600 B.C. had flush toilets attached to a sewage system? The Indus Valley Civilization had one in nearly every house, predating Egyptian plumbing advances and the Roman aqueducts. Modern-day toilet paper, on the other hand, wasn't invented until 1857, by a man named Joseph Gayetty, who had his name printed on every sheet.

Roofers

At a Glance

Roofers install roofs made of tar or asphalt and gravel, rubber, metal, or shingles (themselves made of asphalt, slate, fiberglass, wood, or other material). They may install or repair the tiles on residential roofs, or repair old roofs on other buildings. Some may also waterproof concrete walls and floors. Roofers also install equipment that requires cutting through roofs, such as ventilation ducts and attic fans. Roofing has the highest accident rate of any of the construction trade occupations.

Data Bank

Education and Training: Moderate-term on-the-job training

Average Earnings: $27,000–$46,000

Earnings Growth Potential: Low

Total Jobs Held: 149,000

Job Outlook: Little change

Annual Job Openings: 3,000

Related Jobs: Carpenters; carpet, floor, and tile installers and finishers; cement masons, concrete finishers, segmental pavers, and terrazzo workers; drywall and ceiling tile installers, tapers, plasterers, and stucco masons; sheet metal workers

Personality Types: Realistic-Conventional

Did You Know?

Not surprisingly, roofing is one of the top ten most dangerous occupations, according to the Bureau of Labor Statistics. While the majority of accidents and injuries are caused by falls, some are caused by burns due to the heat of bitumen—the hot, tar-like material used as a sealant. Doctors have researched various means of treating such burns, particularly searching for ways to remove tar or bitumen from burned skin without causing further damage. The results of their findings? Use good old-fashioned butter.

Career in Focus: *Estimator*

In most trade construction jobs there is room for advancement within a company. Roofers, for example, can advance to the role of supervisor or estimator for a roofing contractor. Estimators need a variety of skills in order to do their job, including the ability to read blueprints and even a little sales experience. They travel to the site, discuss the needs of the client, and put in a bid to do the work. If the price is right, the company gets the job. Most self-employed roofers naturally do their own estimating.

Where and When

Roofing work involves climbing, bending, kneeling, and heavy lifting. It also involves work outside, sometimes in rainy conditions. Workers risk slips or falls, not to mention that roofs can become quite hot during the summer. Almost all salaried roofers work for contractors who determine their working schedule, though one in four is self-employed.

For More Information

* National Roofing Contractors Association, 10255 W. Higgins Rd., Suite 600, Rosemont, IL 60018-5607. Internet: www.nrca.net

* United Union of Roofers, Waterproofers, and Allied Workers, 1660 L St. NW, Suite 800, Washington, DC 20036. Internet: www.unionroofers.com

Sheet Metal Workers

At a Glance

Sheet metal workers use large sheets of metal to make ductwork for air-conditioning and heating systems. They also make roofs, rain gutters, skylights, outdoor signs, railroad cars, and other products. They may work with fiberglass and plastic. Sheet metal workers do both construction-related work and mass production of sheet metal products. Sheet metal workers study plans and specifications to determine the materials they will need. They then measure, cut, shape, and fasten pieces of sheet metal to make ductwork, countertops, and other custom products. They take the parts to the construction site, where they further assemble the pieces as they install them. Sheet metal workers in manufacturing plants make parts for products such as aircraft or industrial equipment.

Career in Focus: *HVAC Technician*

In addition to installation, some sheet metal workers specialize in testing, adjusting, and servicing existing air-conditioning and ventilation systems to make sure they work efficiently. Properly installed duct systems are a key component to heating, ventilation, and air-conditioning (HVAC) systems, which is why duct installers are sometimes called HVAC technicians. These sheet metal workers sometimes perform a complete mechanical inspection of a building's HVAC, water, and lighting systems.

Where and When

Sheet metal workers usually work in shops where they create heavy pieces or on site doing installation work. The job can involve considerable lifting, standing, climbing, and squatting. The work is done both indoors and out. Working with sharp metal, soldering and welding equipment, and scaffolds and ladders can be dangerous as well. Most sheet metal workers work a 40-hour week.

For More Information

* Fabricators and Manufacturers Association, International, 833 Featherstone Rd., Rockford, IL 61107-6301. Internet: www.fmanet.org

* International Training Institute for the Sheet Metal and Air-Conditioning Industry, 601 N. Fairfax St., Suite 240, Alexandria, VA 22314-2083. Internet: www.sheetmetal-iti.org

* Sheet Metal and Air Conditioning Contractors' National Association, 4201 Lafayette Center Dr., Chantilly, VA 20151-1209. Internet: www.smacna.org

* Sheet Metal Workers International Association, 1750 New York Ave. NW, 6th Floor, Washington, DC 20006-5301. Internet: www.smwia.org

Data Bank

Education and Training: Long-term on-the-job training

Average Earnings: $30,000–$57,000

Earnings Growth Potential: Medium

Total Jobs Held: 171,000

Job Outlook: Average increase

Annual Job Openings: 5,200

Related Jobs: Assemblers and fabricators; glaziers; heating, air-conditioning, and refrigeration mechanics and installers; machine setters, operators, and tenders—metal and plastic; machinists; tool and die makers

Personality Types: Realistic

Did You Know?

You may already know that many insulation workers in the 1970s were exposed to asbestos—an insulation material that causes cancer in humans. But did you know that sheet metal workers had high exposures, too? In a survey taken in the late 1980s, more than 31 percent of sheet metal workers in construction, shipyard, and refinery work showed signs of asbestos-related diseases. Nowadays, asbestos is rarely used in construction or manufacturing.

Structural and Reinforcing Iron and Metal Workers

At a Glance

These workers make the steel frames used to build bridges, high-rise buildings, and other structures. They also position and secure steel bars inside concrete in order to reinforce highways, buildings, bridges, and tunnels. In addition, they repair and renovate older buildings and structures. Even though the primary metal involved in this work is steel, these workers are still often known as ironworkers. These workers use a wide range of tools and heavy equipment to do their job.

Data Bank

Education and Training: Long-term on-the-job training

Average Earnings: $32,000–$61,000

Earnings Growth Potential: Medium

Total Jobs Held: 98,000

Job Outlook: Average increase

Annual Job Openings: 2,800

Related Jobs: Assemblers and fabricators; boilermakers; carpenters; cement masons, concrete finishers, segmental pavers, and terrazzo workers; construction equipment operators; construction laborers; construction managers; engineers; welding, soldering, and brazing workers

Personality Types: Realistic-Conventional-Investigative

Did You Know?

The suspension bridge with the longest central span, the Akashi Kaikyo Bridge, is located in Japan. It spans 1,991 meters (which makes it well over a mile long) and is supported by two 1,000-feet-high steel towers. It is more than 2,000 feet longer than the Golden Gate Bridge in San Francisco. How much steel does it take to make the world's longest bridge? A little more than 180,000 metric tons. That's about the same as the combined weight of 30,000 African elephants.

Career in Focus:
Ornamental Ironworker

Though most ironwork is not designed to be decorative (being sturdy and safe take priority), the work of ornamental ironworkers is different. They install stairs, handrails, curtain walls, and other miscellaneous metal items after the structure of the building has been completed. Ornamental ironworkers make sure that the pieces are properly fitted and aligned before bolting or welding them. They also dig postholes, mix concrete, and install ornamental fences.

Where and When

This work is usually done outside in all kinds of weather, though those working at great heights do not work during wet, icy, or extremely windy conditions. To prevent falls, ironworkers use safety harnesses, scaffolding, and nets for protection. Most structural and reinforcing iron and metal workers work in metropolitan areas, where most commercial and industrial construction takes place. Most work a standard week, though paid overtime is common.

For More Information

* International Association of Bridge, Structural, Ornamental, and Reinforcing Iron Workers, Apprenticeship Department, 1750 New York Ave. NW, Suite 400, Washington, DC 20006-5315. Internet: www.ironworkers.org/organization/Apprenticeship.aspx

* Associated Builders and Contractors, Workforce Development Department, 4250 N. Fairfax Dr., 9th Floor, Arlington, VA 22203-1607. Internet: www.trytools.org

* Associated General Contractors of America, Inc., 2300 Wilson Blvd., Suite 400, Arlington, VA 22201-5426. Internet: www.agc.org

Installation, Maintenance, and Repair Occupations

Computer, Automated Teller, and Office Machine Repairers

At a Glance

Computer repairers install and fix computers, printers, and other computer equipment. Some repairers work on both computers and office equipment. Automated teller repairers install and fix ATMs—the machines that allow customers to carry out bank transactions automatically—at banks and credit unions. Most repairers travel to customers' workplaces to make repairs. These workers, known as field technicians, often have assigned businesses to which they provide regular maintenance. Bench technicians, on the other hand, work in repair shops located in stores, factories, or service centers. To repair or adjust equipment, workers use hand tools, such as pliers, screwdrivers, soldering irons, and wrenches. They work in many industries, and some are on call 24 hours a day to make emergency repairs.

Did You Know?

You can find a personal computer in more than 80 percent of American homes, and millions more sit on desks in businesses and schools. As they break down or need upgrades, they provide work for computer repairers. The most common problems are malware (viruses, worms, spyware) and a buildup of plain old dust. Disk crashes also create headaches, especially for users who are careless about backing up important data.

Career in Focus: *Office Machine and Cash Register Servicer*

Anyone who has ever worked in an office environment has probably seen one of these workers. Office machine and cash register servicers work on photocopiers, cash registers, mail-processing equipment, and fax machines. Office machine repairers usually work on machinery at the customer's workplace. Common malfunctions are caused by worn or dirty parts or problems with lamps, lenses, or mirrors. Servicers clean, replace, or repair the necessary parts.

Where and When

Most of this work takes place in clean, well-lighted surroundings. Field repairers must travel frequently. Because machines such as computers and ATMs are critical for organizations to operate, repairers and technicians often work around the clock. Shifts are usually decided on the basis of seniority. Though the job isn't strenuous, repairers may be required to lift heavy equipment.

For More Information

* Electronics Technicians Association International, 5 Depot St., Greencastle, IN 46135. Internet: http://eta-i.org

* International Society of Certified Electronics Technicians, 3608 Pershing Ave., Fort Worth, TX 76107-4527. Internet: www.iscet.org

Electrical and Electronics Installers and Repairers

At a Glance

These workers install and repair electrical and electronics equipment. Many of them work for the Department of Defense, where they install radar, missile controls, and communication systems. Other electronic equipment repairers work for telephone companies, at hospitals, and in repair shops. They also may work in power plants and relay stations. Field technicians travel to factories or other locations to repair equipment. These workers often have assigned areas in which they perform preventive maintenance on a regular basis. Bench technicians work in repair shops located in factories and service centers, fixing components that cannot be repaired on the factory floor.

Career in Focus: *Motor Vehicle Electrical and Electronics Installer and Repairer*

These workers install, diagnose, and repair equipment in automobiles. Most installation work involves either new alarm or sound systems. Motor vehicle installers and repairers work with a growing range of electronic equipment, including DVD players, satellite navigation equipment, and passive and active car security systems.

Where and When

Some repairers work in comfortable repair shops while others may work on factory floors. Field technicians spend much of their time traveling to serve customers on site. Repairers may be required to carry heavy equipment and work in uncomfortable positions. Some risk of electric shock comes with the job, though precautions are taken against it.

For More Information

* ACES International, 5381 Chatham Lake Dr., Virginia Beach, VA 23464. Internet: www.acesinternational.org

* Electronics Technicians Association International, 5 Depot St., Greencastle, IN 46135. Internet: http://eta-i.org

* International Society of Certified Electronics Technicians, 3608 Pershing Ave., Fort Worth, TX 76107. Internet: www.iscet.org

Data Bank

Education and Training: Vocational/technical training

Average Earnings: $38,000–$57,000

Earnings Growth Potential: Low

Total Jobs Held: 161,000

Job Outlook: Little change

Annual Job Openings: 3,900

Related Jobs: Aircraft and avionics equipment mechanics and service technicians; broadcast and sound engineering technicians and radio operators; coin, vending, and amusement machine servicers and repairers; computer, automated teller, and office machine repairers; electricians; electronic home entertainment equipment installers and repairers; elevator installers and repairers; maintenance and repair workers, general; radio and telecommunications equipment installers and repairers

Personality Types: Realistic-Conventional-Investigative

Did You Know?

Just what makes a smart bomb smart? It is, in fact, its precision-guided control system (installed by electronics specialists). These bombs and missiles are guided by radio, laser, and even satellite systems to more accurately hit the intended target and reduce the number of surrounding casualties. Of course, a smart bomb is still only as smart as the person using it.

Electronic Home Entertainment Equipment Installers and Repairers

At a Glance

These workers install and repair radios, TV sets, stereos, video games, and other home electronic equipment. They also may install and repair home security systems, intercom equipment, and satellite systems. They run tests to find problems and adjust and replace parts. Small equipment is usually brought into repair shops to be handled by bench technicians. Field technicians, on the other hand, travel to customers' homes to do installations and repairs. Improvements in technology have miniaturized and digitized many audio and video recording devices, which has only made repair work harder. Improved technologies have also lowered the price of electronic home entertainment equipment to the point where customers often replace broken equipment instead of repairing it.

Data Bank

Education and Training: Vocational/technical training

Average Earnings: $25,000–$41,000

Earnings Growth Potential: Medium

Total Jobs Held: 51,000

Job Outlook: Average increase

Annual Job Openings: 1,400

Related Jobs: Coin, vending, and amusement machine servicers and repairers; computer, automated teller, and office machine repairers; electrical and electronics installers and repairers; electricians; home appliance repairers; maintenance and repair workers, general; radio and telecommunications equipment installers and repairers

Personality Types: Realistic-Conventional

Did You Know?

It can take decades for a new invention to catch on with the public. Push-button phones were first invented in 1896 and color television was first demonstrated in 1929, but neither product was in common use in America until the 1960s. Though it might take decades for a new invention to gain popularity, it sometimes doesn't take long for a new invention to be replaced or forgotten. Does anyone remember the laser disc?

Career in Focus: *Home Theater Installation Technician*

Big-screen televisions and surround-sound stereo systems have made it possible for people to create a theater-like experience in their own living room. This has created a need for home theater installation technicians, who specialize in installing home theater and satellite products. This job requires extensive travel to customers' homes, as well as complete knowledge of the equipment being installed and good people skills.

Where and When

Most repairers work in comfortable repair shops. Field technicians spend much of their time traveling to serve customers on site. Repairers may be required to carry heavy equipment and work in uncomfortable positions. They also must take precautions against electric shock. About one out of every three of these workers is self-employed.

For More Information

* Electronics Technicians Association International, 5 Depot St., Greencastle, IN 46135. Internet: www.eta-i.org

* International Society of Certified Electronics Technicians, 3608 Pershing Ave., Fort Worth, TX 76107. Internet: www.iscet.org

Radio and Telecommunications Equipment Installers and Repairers

At a Glance

These workers install, repair, and maintain complex telephone and radio equipment. Most work either in a phone company's central office or in the field at customers' homes or offices. Others work on equipment for cable TV companies, railroads, or airlines. Radio mechanics install and maintain radio transmitting and receiving equipment. Telecommunications equipment installers work on equipment that transmits voice signals, data, graphics, and video, for example, installing or repairing telephone wiring and equipment. When problems with telecommunications equipment arise, repairers diagnose the source of the problem by testing the equipment.

Career in Focus: *PBX Installer and Repairer*

These workers set up private branch exchange (PBX) switchboards, which relay incoming, outgoing, and inter-office calls within a single organization. They also install power systems, alarms, and telephone sets. The installer performs tests to verify that the equipment functions properly. Due to rapidly developing technologies, PBX installers must adapt and learn new technologies, including increasingly popular Voice over Internet Protocol (VoIP) systems.

Where and When

These installers and repairers generally work in clean, comfortable surroundings such as an office or a service center. Telephone installers and repairers may work on rooftops, ladders, and telephone poles, however. While outdoors, these workers are subject to various weather conditions. Most installers and repairers work regular business hours, though some companies require shift work to meet round-the-clock servicing hours.

For More Information

* International Brotherhood of Electrical Workers, Telecommunications Department, 900 7th St. NW, Washington, DC 20001.

* Communications Workers of America, 501 3rd St. NW, Washington, DC 20001. Internet: www.cwa-union.org/jobs

* National Coalition for Telecommunications Education and Learning, NACTEL, 6021 South Syracuse Way, Suite 213, Greenwood Village, CO 80111. Internet: www.nactel.org

* Society of Cable Telecommunications Engineers, Certification Department, 140 Philips Rd., Exton, PA 19341-1318. Internet: www.scte.org

Data Bank

Education and Training: Vocational/technical training

Average Earnings: $42,000–$64,000

Earnings Growth Potential: High

Total Jobs Held: 209,000

Job Outlook: Declining

Annual Job Openings: 3,700

Related Jobs: Broadcast and sound engineering technicians and radio operators; computer, automated teller, and office machine repairers; electrical and electronics installers and repairers; engineering technicians; line installers and repairers

Personality Types: Realistic-Investigative-Conventional

Did You Know?

We think of ourselves as living in the digital age, where everybody is "wired" into the information superhighway. But in fact only about 15 percent of the world's population has Internet access. Of course, it is different in the United States, where nearly 70 percent of the population uses the Internet regularly. And that number is growing, which could mean steady work for telecommunications installers.

Aircraft and Avionics Equipment Mechanics and Service Technicians

At a Glance

Aircraft and avionics mechanics and service technicians inspect airplanes for problems. They make repairs and test equipment to make sure it is working properly and to complete the inspections required by the Federal Aviation Administration (FAA). Some work on several different types of planes, whereas others specialize in just one. Some mechanics even specialize in one part of an aircraft, such as the engine or electrical system of a DC-10. Much of an aircraft mechanic's work is preventive maintenance (thankfully). Mechanics inspect aircraft engines, landing gears, instruments, brakes, and other parts of the aircraft, repairing and replacing them as necessary. They also keep maintenance records of the work they perform.

Data Bank

Education and Training: Vocational/technical training

Average Earnings: $43,000–$61,000

Earnings Growth Potential: Low

Total Jobs Held: 140,000

Job Outlook: Average increase

Annual Job Openings: 3,700

Related Jobs: Automotive service technicians and mechanics; electrical and electronics installers and repairers; electricians; elevator installers and repairers

Personality Types: Realistic-Conventional-Investigative

Did You Know?

How safe is air travel? Statistics show that a good percentage of Americans are afraid to fly, but those same people often don't think twice about driving on the interstate. Yet according to the U.S. National Safety Council, you are 20 times more likely to be killed in an auto accident than in an airplane accident. That's partly because aircraft and avionics mechanics follow strict procedures to keep the planes in tip-top condition, whereas many cars have defective brakes, bald tires, or other defects.

Career in Focus: *Avionics Technician*

Avionics systems are an integral part of aircraft design. Avionics technicians repair and maintain the components used for aircraft navigation and radio communications, weather radar systems, and other instruments and computers that control flight. Technicians also may be required to analyze and develop solutions to complex electronic problems. These duties may require additional training and education. But you want the person repairing your airplane's radar system to be well educated, don't you?

Where and When

Mechanics typically work in hangers or other indoor areas. They often work under pressure to maintain flight schedules and still ensure the safety of passengers. They often lift objects weighing more than 70 pounds, and mechanics must stand, lie, or kneel in awkward positions. Ear protection is usually worn when working on and testing engines. Most aircraft mechanics work 40 hours per week in shifts around the clock, though overtime is frequent.

For More Information

* Professional Aviation Maintenance Association, 400 N. Washington St., Suite 300, Alexandria, VA 22314. Internet: www.pama.org

Automotive Body and Related Repairers

At a Glance

Automotive body repairers fix automobiles damaged in accidents. Although some work on large trucks, buses, or tractor-trailers, most work on cars and small trucks. They straighten bent bodies, hammer out dents, and replace parts that can't be fixed. Their supervisors usually decide which parts to fix and replace and how long the job should take. Body repair work has variety and challenges: Each damaged vehicle presents a different problem. Using their broad knowledge of automotive construction and repair techniques, repairers must develop appropriate methods for each job.

Career in Focus: *Automotive Glass Installer*

Some body repairers specialize in installing and repairing glass in automobiles and other vehicles. They remove broken, cracked, or pitted windshields and window glass. They then apply a moisture-proofing compound along the edges of new glass, place the glass in the vehicle, and install rubber strips around the sides of the windshield or window to make it secure and weatherproof. These specialists tend to make less money on average than general automotive body repairers.

Where and When

Most of these repairers work a standard 40-hour week, though some overtime is possible. They work indoors in noisy and dirty body shops, often working in awkward positions. Cuts, burns, and injuries from power tools are possible, though serious accidents are usually avoided when safety guidelines are followed.

For More Information

* Automotive Careers Today, 8400 Westpark Dr., MS #2, McLean, VA 22102. Internet: www.autocareerstoday.org

* Automotive Service Association, P.O. Box 929, Bedford, TX 76095. Internet: www.asashop.org

* Inter-Industry Conference on Auto Collision Repair Education Foundation (I-CAR), 5125 Trillium Blvd., Hoffman Estates, IL 60192. Internet: www.collisioncareers.org

* Society of Collision Repair Specialists, P.O. Box 909, Prosser, WA 99350. Internet: www.scrs.com

* National Glass Association, 8200 Greensboro Dr., Suite 302, McLean, VA 22102. Internet: www.myglassclass.com

Data Bank

Education and Training: Long-term on-the-job training

Average Earnings: $29,000–$49,000

Earnings Growth Potential: Medium

Total Jobs Held: 186,000

Job Outlook: Little change

Annual Job Openings: 4,800

Related Jobs: Automotive service technicians and mechanics; diesel service technicians and mechanics; glaziers; heavy vehicle and mobile equipment service technicians and mechanics; painting and coating workers, except construction and maintenance

Personality Types: Realistic-Conventional

Did You Know?

A "crumple zone" is a feature of automobiles designed to prevent injury in an accident by absorbing the energy from impact. They are typically found in the front of automobiles and work by lengthening the time it takes for the vehicle to come to a complete stop. This, in turn, reduces the amount of force applied to the bodies of the driver and passengers. While their benefits in high-speed accidents are unquestionable, they do have one obvious disadvantage: They crumple, often totaling the front of the car. This results in higher repair costs and more complicated work for automotive body repairers.

Automotive Service Technicians and Mechanics

At a Glance

Automotive mechanics and service technicians repair and service cars, trucks, and vans that have gas engines. During routine service work, mechanics inspect, adjust, and replace vehicle parts. Mechanics must be quick and accurate when they are diagnosing mechanical problems. This job is becoming more technically demanding as automobiles become more complex. As a result, these workers are now usually called "technicians" rather than "mechanics." The increasing complexity requires workers who can use computerized shop equipment and work with electronic components, while maintaining their skills with traditional hand tools.

Data Bank

Education and Training: Vocational/technical training

Average Earnings: $26,000–$47,000

Earnings Growth Potential: High

Total Jobs Held: 764,000

Job Outlook: Little change

Annual Job Openings: 18,200

Related Jobs: Automotive body and related repairers; diesel service technicians and mechanics; heavy vehicle and mobile equipment service technicians and mechanics; small engine mechanics

Personality Types: Realistic-Investigative

Did You Know?

Voluntary certification by the National Institute for Automotive Service Excellence (ASE) has become the credential to have for automotive service technicians. Certification is available in eight different areas, from electrical systems to engine repair to heating and air-conditioning. Technicians generally must have two years of experience in each field to pass the exam and earn their certification. More than 2,000 high school and postsecondary training programs have been certified by the ASE.

Career in Focus: *Tune-up Technician*

Most vehicles require regular tune-ups in order to run efficiently. Tune-up technicians adjust the ignition timing and valves, and adjust or replace spark plugs and other parts to ensure the best engine performance. They often use electronic testing equipment to isolate and adjust malfunctions in fuel, ignition, and emissions control systems. Like most other mechanics, they must be familiar with computers as well.

Where and When

More than half of all service technicians work more than 40 hours per week, including evenings and weekends. They generally work indoors. They may be required to do heavy lifting. Minor cuts, burns, and bruises are common.

For More Information

* Automotive Careers Today, 8400 Westpark Dr., MS #2, McLean, VA 22102. Internet: www.autocareerstoday.org

* Career Voyages, U.S. Department of Labor, 200 Constitution Ave. NW, Washington, DC 20210. Internet: www.careervoyages.gov/automotive-main.cfm

* National Automotive Technicians Education Foundation, 101 Blue Seal Dr. SE, Suite 101, Leesburg, VA 20175. Internet: www.natef.org

* Accrediting Commission of Career Schools and Colleges, 2101 Wilson Blvd., Suite 302, Arlington, VA 22201. Internet: www.accsc.org

* Automotive Youth Educational Systems (AYES), 101 Blue Seal Dr. SE, Suite 101, Leesburg, VA, 20175. Internet: www.ayes.org

Diesel Service Technicians and Mechanics

At a Glance

Diesel mechanics and service technicians repair and maintain diesel engines in heavy trucks, buses, tractors, bulldozers, and cranes. They spend a lot of time doing preventive maintenance to make sure that the equipment operates safely and to reduce expensive breakdowns. It is common for technicians to handle all kinds of repairs, from working on a vehicle's electrical system one day to doing major engine repairs the next. This work is becoming increasingly complex, as more electronic components are used in diesel engines. Because of this new technology, technicians must regularly learn new skills.

Career in Focus: *School Bus Mechanic*

Each and every school day, buses transport millions of children to school through rain, sleet, and snow. Knowing the precious cargo they carry, school bus mechanics must be aware of the latest technologies in bus manufacturing. These mechanics often service every aspect of the vehicle, including the diesel engine. In small school districts, a single mechanic may be responsible for every aspect of the maintenance program. Because of the heavy responsibility they have, these mechanics are sometimes required to have a state certification in school bus inspection.

Where and When

Diesel technicians usually work indoors, though they sometimes make repairs to vehicles on the road. They are often required to do heavy lifting and stand or lie in awkward positions to make repairs. Like other automotive service technicians, they are prone to working more than 40 hours per week.

For More Information

* Association of Diesel Specialists, 400 Admiral Blvd., Kansas City, MO 64106. Internet: www.diesel.org

* National Institute for Automotive Service Excellence (ASE), 101 Blue Seal Dr. SE, Suite 101, Leesburg, VA 20175. Internet: www.asecert.org

* Accrediting Commission of Career Schools and Colleges, 2101 Wilson Blvd., Suite 302, Arlington, VA 22201. Internet: www.accsc.org

* National Automotive Technicians Education Foundation, 101 Blue Seal Dr. SE, Suite 101, Leesburg, VA 20175. Internet: www.natef.org

Data Bank

Education and Training: Vocational/technical training

Average Earnings: $33,000–$50,000

Earnings Growth Potential: Low

Total Jobs Held: 263,000

Job Outlook: Little change

Annual Job Openings: 7,500

Related Jobs: Aircraft and avionics equipment mechanics and service technicians; automotive body and related repairers; automotive service technicians and mechanics; heavy vehicle and mobile equipment service technicians and mechanics; small engine mechanics

Personality Types: Realistic-Conventional

Did You Know?

Diesel engines are heavier and last longer than gas engines. They're also more efficient because a diesel engine compresses its fuel—so it uses less to do more. Diesels get more power, get better fuel mileage, and are even better for the environment. Large trucks, buses, and trains have diesel engines, and nearly 40 percent of European cars run on diesel. So why isn't diesel more popular in the United States? In short, because it's harder to find, which makes it more expensive.

Heavy Vehicle and Mobile Equipment Service Technicians and Mechanics

At a Glance

These mechanics and technicians repair the machinery used in construction, logging, farming, and mining. They fix and maintain trenchers, backhoes, bulldozers, and cranes. They service and repair diesel engines and other machine parts. They may also repair the hydraulic lifts used to raise and lower scoops and shovels. Service technicians perform routine maintenance checks to ensure the equipment's performance and safety. In addition, service technicians adjust or replace defective parts and may also repair undercarriages and track assemblies. It is common for technicians in large shops to specialize in one or two types of repair. Technicians need training in electronics and the use of hand-held diagnostic computers to make engine adjustments and diagnose problems.

Data Bank

Education and Training: Long-term on-the-job training

Average Earnings: $34,000–$51,000

Earnings Growth Potential: Low

Total Jobs Held: 191,000

Job Outlook: Average increase

Annual Job Openings: 5,200

Related Jobs: Aircraft and avionics equipment mechanics and service technicians; automotive service technicians and mechanics; diesel service technicians and mechanics; industrial machinery mechanics and millwrights; small engine mechanics

Personality Types: Realistic-Conventional-Investigative

Did You Know?

Like many other industries, construction is highly sensitive to changes in the economy. When the economy experiences a downturn, investors are less likely to expand, new homes are less likely to be built, and bulldozers and cranes tend to sit idle. This in turn impacts those in the heavy vehicle and mobile equipment service trade. Still, most companies will try to retain experienced workers during slow periods, allowing for some job security.

Career in Focus: *Farm Equipment Mechanic*

What used to be a general repairer's job around the farm has evolved into a specialized technical career. These mechanics service, maintain, and repair farm equipment. They may also repair smaller lawn and garden tractors. Farmers have increasingly turned to farm equipment dealers to service and repair their equipment because the machinery is so complex. Farm equipment mechanics will generally work longer hours in the spring, summer, and fall, and much fewer hours in the winter.

Where and When

These service technicians usually work indoors, unless a repair is urgent or the machinery can't be moved from the worksite. Field service technicians work outdoors and spend most of their time away from the shop. Sometimes extensive travel is necessary. All technicians must be able to lift heavy parts and stand and lie in awkward positions while working. Minor cuts, burns, and bruises are part of the job. Most work a standard 40-hour week, though overtime is common.

For More Information

* Associated Equipment Distributors, 615 W. 22nd St., Oak Brook, IL 60523. Internet: www.aedcareers.com

* National Automotive Technician Education Foundation (NATEF), 101 Blue Seal Dr. SE, Suite 101, Leesburg, VA 20175. Internet: www.natef.org

* National Institute for Automotive Service Excellence (ASE), 101 Blue Seal Dr. SE, Suite 101, Leesburg, VA 20175. Internet: www.asecert.org

Small Engine Mechanics

At a Glance

The small engines that power motorcycles, motorboats, and outdoor power equipment share many characteristics with larger engines—including breakdowns. Small engine mechanics do routine engine checkups and repair everything from weed eaters to yachts. Motorcycle mechanics repair and overhaul motorcycles, motor scooters, mopeds, dirt bikes, and all-terrain vehicles. Other small engine mechanics service and repair lawnmowers, garden tractors, and chain saws. All engines require periodic service to minimize the chance of breakdowns and to keep them operating efficiently. Such routine maintenance is normally a major part of any mechanic's work. Many of these workers are self-employed.

Career in Focus: *Motorboat Mechanic*

Motorboat mechanics, or marine equipment mechanics, repair and adjust the equipment of boat engines. Most small boats have portable outboard engines that are removed and brought into the repair shop. Larger craft, such as cabin cruisers and commercial fishing boats, are powered by diesel or gasoline inboard or inboard-outboard engines, which are removed only for major overhauls. Most of these repairs are performed at the docks or marinas. Motorboat mechanics also may work on propellers, steering mechanisms, marine plumbing, and other boat equipment.

Where and When

Small engine mechanics usually work in well-lighted and ventilated repair shops, though motorboat mechanics commonly work outdoors at docks or marinas. Mechanics may work fewer than 40 hours a week during winter months, when motorcycles, motorboats, and lawnmowers are not in use (though we assume snow-blowers and snowmobiles need servicing, too).

For More Information

* Accrediting Commission of Career Schools and Colleges, 2101 Wilson Blvd., Suite 302, Arlington, VA 22201. Internet: www.accsc.org

Data Bank

Education and Training: Moderate-term on-the-job training to long-term on-the-job training

Average Earnings: $25,000–$40,000

Earnings Growth Potential: Low

Total Jobs Held: 70,000

Job Outlook: Average increase

Annual Job Openings: 1,900

Related Jobs: Automotive service technicians and mechanics; diesel service technicians and mechanics; heavy vehicle and mobile equipment service technicians and mechanics; home appliance repairers

Personality Types: Realistic-Conventional

Did You Know?

If you take a job in a restaurant, the restaurant usually supplies you with the pots and pans. Likewise, janitors aren't expected to bring their own mop and bucket. But mechanics often must provide their own hand tools for their work. Most beginning mechanics start out with the basics, such as wrenches, pliers, screwdrivers, and power drills. As they gain experience, they collect more tools. Experienced mechanics might have thousands of dollars invested in tools.

Heating, Air-Conditioning, and Refrigeration Mechanics and Installers

At a Glance

Heating and air-conditioning systems control the temperature, humidity, and air quality in most buildings. Refrigeration systems make it possible to store and transport food, medicine, and other perishable items. These mechanics install, maintain, and repair such systems. They may work for large companies or be self-employed. Technicians often specialize in either installation or maintenance and repair, although they are trained to do both. Because of the nature of the coolants used in air-conditioning and refrigeration, these workers must conform to strict guidelines to help protect the environment.

Data Bank

Education and Training: Vocational/technical training

Average Earnings: $32,000–$54,000

Earnings Growth Potential: Low

Total Jobs Held: 308,000

Job Outlook: Rapid increase

Annual Job Openings: 13,600

Related Jobs: Boilermakers; electricians; home appliance repairers; plumbers, pipelayers, pipefitters, and steamfitters; sheet metal workers

Personality Types: Realistic-Conventional

Did You Know?

People working in this job can have a strong impact on the environment. CFCs and HFCs are coolants used in air-conditioning and refrigeration systems. These chemicals are dangerous if they escape into the atmosphere, where they eat away at the ozone layer. Responsible technicians are careful to protect the environment from these chemicals. In fact, all technicians who work with them must be certified in their proper handling. Exams are administered by organizations approved by the U.S. Environmental Protection Agency.

Career in Focus:
Refrigeration Mechanic

Some mechanics may specialize only in refrigeration. Refrigeration mechanics install, service, and repair industrial and commercial refrigerating systems and a variety of refrigeration equipment. They follow blueprints to install motors, compressors, condensing units, evaporators, and other components. They connect this equipment to the ductwork, refrigerant lines, and electrical power source, and then charge the system with refrigerant and check it for proper operation.

Where and When

These mechanics and installers work in homes, stores, hospitals, office buildings, factories—just about anywhere. They may work outside in cold or hot weather or in buildings that are uncomfortable (the buildings usually don't have working heat or air-conditioning, after all). Hazards include electrical shock, burns, and muscle strain. The majority of mechanics and installers work at least 40 hours per week, though during peak seasons (the summer and winter) overtime is common.

For More Information

* Air-Conditioning Contractors of America, 2800 Shirlington Rd., Suite 300, Arlington, VA 22206-3607. Internet: www.acca.org

* Air-Conditioning, Heating, and Refrigeration Institute, 2111 Wilson Blvd., Suite 500, Arlington, VA 22201-3001. Internet: www.ahrinet.org

* Associated Builders and Contractors, Workforce Development Department, 4250 N. Fairfax Dr., 9th Floor, Arlington, VA 22203-1607. Internet: www.trytools.org

* Carbon Monoxide Safety Association, P.O. Box 669, Eastlake, CO 80614-0669. Internet: www.cosafety.org

* HVAC Excellence, P.O. Box 491, Mt. Prospect, IL 60056-0521. Internet: www.hvacexcellence.org

Home Appliance Repairers

At a Glance

Anyone whose washing machine has ever exploded in a bubbly, watery mess knows the importance of a dependable appliance repair person. Home appliance repairers—sometimes called service technicians—repair ovens, washers, dryers, refrigerators, and other home appliances. Some repairers work specifically on small appliances such as microwaves and vacuum cleaners; others specialize in major appliances such as refrigerators and dishwashers. After identifying problems, home appliance repairers replace or repair defective belts, motors, heating elements, switches, gears, or other items. When repairing refrigerators and window air-conditioners, repairers must take care to recover and recycle refrigerants. All of these repairers must keep good records, prepare bills, and collect payments.

Career in Focus: *Gas Appliance Repairer*

Many ovens use gas to produce heat rather than electricity. Repairers who specialize in gas appliances check the heating unit and replace tubing, thermocouples, thermostats, and valves. They may have to install pipes in a customer's home to connect the appliances to the gas line as well. They may have to saw holes in walls or floors and hang steel supports in order to hold gas pipes in place. They also answer emergency calls about gas leaks.

Where and When

Home appliance repairers either work in repair shops or make service calls to customers' homes. They may spend several hours a day driving to and from appointments. Repairers sometimes work in uncomfortable positions and tight spaces. Repairers must be conscious of the possibility of electrical shock and gas leaks. They usually work with little or no direct supervision. Most work a standard 40-hour week.

For More Information

* Professional Service Association, 71 Columbia St., Cohoes, NY 12047. Internet: www.psaworld.com

* International Society of Certified Electronics Technicians, 3608 Pershing Ave., Fort Worth, TX 76107. Internet: www.nastec.org

* United Servicers Association, 1 Presidential Way, Suite 106, Woburn, MA 01801. Internet: www.unitedservicers.com

Data Bank

Education and Training: Long-term on-the-job training

Average Earnings: $27,000–$43,000

Earnings Growth Potential: Medium

Total Jobs Held: 50,000

Job Outlook: Little change

Annual Job Openings: 900

Related Jobs: Coin, vending, and amusement machine servicers and repairers; electrical and electronics installers and repairers; electronic home entertainment equipment installers and repairers; heating, air-conditioning, and refrigeration mechanics and installers; small engine mechanics

Personality Types: Realistic-Conventional-Investigative

Did You Know?

The idea for the microwave oven started with a candy bar. Engineer Dr. Percy Spenser was working with radar equipment—more specifically a vacuum tube—when he noticed the candy bar in his pocket melting. Later experiments showed that the waves being emitted by the tube could pop popcorn and cause an egg to explode. Not long afterward, the first real microwave oven was built. It was nearly 6 feet tall and weighed more than 700 pounds. It probably would not have mounted easily under a kitchen cabinet.

Industrial Machinery Mechanics and Millwrights

At a Glance

A wide range of employees is required to keep sophisticated industrial machinery running smoothly—from highly skilled industrial machinery mechanics to lower skilled maintenance workers who perform routine tasks. Millwrights assemble and set up machines in factories or plants. They must understand how a machine functions to assemble and disassemble it properly; this may involve knowledge of electronics, pneumatics, and computer systems. Industrial machinery workers maintain and repair the machines to keep work on schedule. They maintain complete and up-to-date records to anticipate trouble and service equipment before factory production is interrupted. If an industrial machinery mechanic is unable to repair a machine and a major overhaul is needed, a millwright with expertise on the machine may be hired to make the repair.

Data Bank

Education and Training: Moderate-term on-the-job training to long-term on-the-job training

Average Earnings: $35,000–$55,000

Earnings Growth Potential: Low

Total Jobs Held: 408,000

Job Outlook: Little change

Annual Job Openings: 8,700

Related Jobs: Electrical and electronics installers and repairers; electricians; machinists; maintenance and repair workers, general; plumbers, pipelayers, pipefitters, and steamfitters; welding, soldering, and brazing workers

Personality Types: Realistic-Conventional-Investigative

Did You Know?

About 25 percent of these workers are union members. Labor unions represent workers' rights in negotiations with their employers and ensure fair pay and working conditions. Many workers in installation, maintenance, and repair occupations belong to unions. Those in industrial machinery repair may belong to one of several, including the United Steelworkers of America, the United Auto Workers, and the International Association of Machinists and Aerospace Workers.

Career in Focus: *Machinery Maintenance Worker*

These employees are responsible for cleaning machinery, performing basic diagnostic tests, checking performance, and determining whether major repairs are necessary. They must adhere to strict maintenance schedules. Maintenance workers may perform minor repairs, but major repairs are generally left to machinery mechanics. As such, maintenance workers tend to earn less than mechanics, but they also don't need the same qualifications. Short-term on-the-job-training and a high school diploma are usually all one needs to be a machinery maintenance worker.

Where and When

Factories and other facilities can't afford to have machinery out of service, so mechanics are often on call to make emergency repairs. Overtime is common: About 30 percent work more than 40 hours per week. These workers are subject to cuts, bruises, and muscle strain, and they often must work on top of ladders or in cramped conditions. To protect themselves, they wear hard hats, safety glasses, and hearing protection. Millwrights are typically employed on a contract basis and may spend only a few days or weeks at a single site. As a result, schedules of work can be unpredictable, and workers may experience downtime between jobs.

For More Information

✳ United Brotherhood of Carpenters/Millwrights, 6801 Placid St., Las Vegas, NV 89119. Internet: www.ubcmillwrights.org

Line Installers and Repairers

At a Glance

Line installers and repairers lay the wires and cables that bring electricity, phone service, and cable TV signals into our homes. They clear lines of tree limbs, check them for damage, and make emergency repairs when needed. They install new lines by constructing utility poles, towers, and underground trenches to carry the wires and cables. In addition to installation, these workers are responsible for the regular maintenance of electrical, telecommunications, and cable television lines. Bad weather or natural disasters can cause extensive damage to networks, so line installers and repairers must respond quickly to these emergencies to restore service.

Career in Focus: *Electrical Powerline Installer*

While the work performed by telecommunications and electrical powerline installers is quite similar, they are two distinct occupations. Working with powerlines requires specialized knowledge of transformers, electrical power distribution systems, and substations. Workers on electrical powerlines install and replace transformers, circuit breakers, switches, fuses, and other equipment to control and direct the electrical current. Naturally, they take safety precautions to prevent electric shocks.

Where and When

This job can be dangerous because installers and splicers work underground or high above ground with various chemicals and electricity. They lift equipment and work in a variety of uncomfortable positions. They may have to travel long distances, and they often work in a variety of weather conditions. Many work a 40-hour week, though emergencies may require overtime. For example, when severe weather damages communication and electrical lines, installers and repairers may work long, irregular hours to restore them.

For More Information

* American Public Power Association, 1875 Connecticut Ave. NW, Suite 1200, Washington, DC 20009-5715. Internet: www.appanet.org

* Center for Energy Workforce Development, 701 Pennsylvania Ave. NW, Washington, DC 20004-2696. Internet: www.cewd.org

* The Fiber Optic Association, 1119 S. Mission Rd. #355, Fallbrook, CA 92028. Internet: www.thefoa.org

* National Joint Apprenticeship and Training Committee (NJATC), 301 Prince Georges Blvd., Suite D, Upper Marlboro, MD 20774. Internet: www.njatc.org

Data Bank

Education and Training: Long-term on-the-job training

Average Earnings: $38,000–$65,000

Earnings Growth Potential: High

Total Jobs Held: 285,000

Job Outlook: Little change

Annual Job Openings: 7,300

Related Jobs: Electrical and electronics installers and repairers; electricians; power plant operators, distributors, and dispatchers; radio and telecommunications equipment installers and repairers

Personality Types: Realistic-Conventional-Investigative

Did You Know?

Fiber-optic cables are made of tiny strands of glass, generally no wider than human hair. These tiny strands carry light impulses that provide phone service, high-speed Internet communications, and TV reception to homes and businesses. One fiber-optic cable can carry the equivalent of more than 100,000 phone conversations at one time. Glass also is a cheaper material than copper, but splicing fiber-optic cable requires specialized equipment and training. Job prospects should be good for individuals with experience in working with such materials.

Maintenance and Repair Workers, General

At a Glance

General maintenance and repair workers have skills in many different crafts. They repair and maintain machines, mechanical equipment, and buildings. They also work on plumbing, electrical, and air-conditioning and heating systems. They build partitions; make plaster or drywall repairs; and fix or paint roofs, windows, doors, floors, and woodwork. They also maintain and repair specialized equipment and machinery found in cafeterias, hospitals, stores, offices, and factories. Typical duties include troubleshooting and fixing faulty electrical switches, repairing air-conditioning motors, and unclogging drains. General maintenance and repair workers inspect and diagnose problems and determine the best way to correct them, frequently checking blueprints, repair manuals, and parts catalogs. They also perform routine preventive maintenance and ensure that everything runs smoothly.

Data Bank

Education and Training: Moderate-term on-the-job training

Average Earnings: $27,000–$45,000

Earnings Growth Potential: Medium

Total Jobs Held: 1,361,000

Job Outlook: Average increase

Annual Job Openings: 35,800

Related Jobs: Boilermakers; carpenters; coin, vending, and amusement machine servicers and repairers; electrical and electronics installers and repairers; electricians; electronic home entertainment equipment installers and repairers; heating, air-conditioning, and refrigeration mechanics and installers; plumbers, pipelayers, pipefitters, and steamfitters; radio and telecommunications equipment installers and repairers

Personality Types: Realistic-Conventional-Investigative

Did You Know?

The general maintenance and repair worker is capable of fixing just about anything, so long as it doesn't require extensive knowledge or expertise. In that way he or she could be considered a "Jack of All Trades," a phrase meaning someone who is good at just about everything but does not excel at anything. The original figure of speech that this phrase comes from is "Jack of all trades, master of none, though ofttimes better than master of one."

Career in Focus: *Maintenance Supervisor*

General maintenance workers often use their work experience to become craftworkers, such as electricians or plumbers, later in their careers. Those in large organizations who don't specialize can still advance to become the maintenance supervisor. In addition to many of the responsibilities of the general worker, maintenance supervisors plan work schedules and coordinate the work of other maintenance staff. They are responsible for inspecting and evaluating the work of maintenance employees as well as being the first to respond in the case of a maintenance emergency.

Where and When

These workers may have to stand for long periods, lift heavy objects, and work in uncomfortable environments or on ladders. Cuts, shocks, burns, falls, and bruises are potential hazards. Most work a regular 40-hour week, though some work evening, night, or weekend shifts or are on call for emergency repairs. The level of direct supervision varies.

For More Information

* International Maintenance Institute, P.O. Box 751896, Houston, TX 77275-1896. Internet: www.imionline.org

* Society for Maintenance and Reliability Professionals, 8400 Westpark Dr., 2nd Floor, McLean, VA 22102-3570. Internet: www.smrp.org

Medical Equipment Repairers

At a Glance

Medical equipment repairers maintain, adjust, calibrate, and repair a wide variety of electronic, electromechanical, and hydraulic equipment used in hospitals and other medical environments, including health practitioners' offices. They may work on patient monitors, defibrillators, medical imaging equipment (X-rays, CAT scanners, and ultrasound equipment), voice-controlled operating tables, electric wheelchairs, as well as other sophisticated dental, optometric, and ophthalmic equipment. In some cases, medical equipment repairers perform routine scheduled maintenance to ensure that all equipment is in good working order. Less complicated equipment may need attention only when it breaks down.

Career in Focus:
Wheelchair Repairer

Wheelchair repairers usually also service motorized scooters, as well as wheelchair lifts and ramps. For a wheelchair tune-up, the repairer may clean and adjust the wheel bearings, test battery performance, check the air pressure of the tires, check that all bolts are tight, and note any signs of stress to the frame. Because a faulty wheelchair limits the user's mobility, repairers often have to make house calls for major repairs. Weekend work often is necessary.

Where and When

Medical equipment repairers usually work daytime hours but are often expected to be on call. Some work irregular hours and may be required to work overtime and under time pressure if an important piece of medical equipment malfunctions. Medical equipment repairers often must work in a patient environment, which has the potential to expose them to diseases and other health risks. Those who work as contractors often have to travel—sometimes long distances—to perform needed repairs.

For More Information

* Association for the Advancement of Medical Instrumentation (AAMI), 1110 N. Glebe Rd., Suite 220, Arlington, VA 22201-4795. Internet: www.aami.org

Data Bank

Education and Training: Associate degree

Average Earnings: $32,000–$55,000

Earnings Growth Potential: Medium

Total Jobs Held: 41,000

Job Outlook: Rapid increase

Annual Job Openings: 2,300

Related Jobs: Coin, vending, and amusement machine servicers and repairers; computer, automated teller, and office machine repairers; medical, dental, and ophthalmic laboratory technicians

Personality Types: Realistic-Investigative-Conventional

Did You Know?

Some amazing high-tech medical devices are in use now. For example, cryoguns shoot liquid nitrogen at warts, some skin cancers, and other skin defects to freeze them so they can be removed. Lasers are used to reshape the cornea of the eye for correct vision. Internal defibrillators provide electric stimulation to a heart that loses its correct rhythm. Ultrasonic liposuction equipment breaks up fat cells so the fat can be sucked out of the body. Each of these devices uses a different combination of technologies, and biomedical inventors put new devices to use each year. To stay employed, repairers need to update their skills regularly.

Production Occupations

Assemblers and Fabricators

At a Glance

Assemblers and fabricators put together complicated products such as computers, appliances, and electronic equipment. Their work is detailed and must be done accurately. They follow directions from engineers and use several tools and precise measuring instruments. Assemblers look for faulty parts and mistakes in the assembly process and then try to help fix problems before more defective products are produced. Some experienced assemblers work with designers and engineers to build prototypes or test products. Changes in technology have transformed the manufacturing and assembly process; automated manufacturing systems now use robots, computers, and programmable motion control devices. Assemblers must be comfortable using all of these new technologies.

Data Bank

Education and Training: Short-term on-the-job training to moderate-term on-the-job training

Average Earnings: $22,000–$36,000

Earnings Growth Potential: Low

Total Jobs Held: 1,951,000

Job Outlook: Declining

Annual Job Openings: 42,600

Related Jobs: Industrial machinery mechanics and millwrights; inspectors, testers, sorters, samplers, and weighers; machine setters, operators, and tenders—metal and plastic; welding, soldering, and brazing workers

Personality Types: Realistic-Conventional

Did You Know?

Manufacturing techniques are moving from traditional assembly line systems toward "lean" manufacturing systems. Lean manufacturing involves using teams of workers within "cells" to produce entire products. Team assemblers perform a group of tasks, rather than specializing in a single task as they would on an assembly line. The team also may decide how to assign the work and how to perform different tasks. This helps companies cover for absent workers, improve productivity, and respond more quickly to changes in demand.

Career in Focus: *Electrical and Electronic Equipment Assembler*

Electrical and electronic equipment assemblers build products such as electric motors, batteries, computers, and sensing equipment. Because dust might affect the operation of these products, electronic equipment assemblers tend to work in very clean, comfortable environments. There are about 200,000 workers directly employed in this field.

Where and When

Working conditions vary from plant to plant, but continue to improve. Most factories today are generally clean, well lit, and well ventilated. Some assemblers may come into contact with harmful chemicals or fumes, but safety precautions minimize any risk. Most full-time assemblers work 40 hours per week, though overtime and shift work is fairly common. The work can be repetitious and tedious.

For More Information

✳ IPC, 3000 Lakeside Dr., 309 S, Bannockburn, IL 60015
Internet: www.ipc.org

Food Processing Occupations

At a Glance

These workers are responsible for producing many of the foods found in your pantry and refrigerator. Food processing workers work in grocery stores and production plants. They may work in a small market, in a large refrigerated room, or on an assembly line. Meat, poultry, and fish cutters and trimmers cut meat into pieces that are suitable for sale. Many work in animal slaughtering and processing plants, while butchers usually are employed in grocery stores. Bakers produce cakes, breads, and other baked goods. In manufacturing, bakers produce goods in large quantities, using high-volume mixing machines, ovens, and other equipment. Deli workers make salads and side dishes at grocery stores.

Career in Focus: *Food Batchmaker*

Food batchmakers set up and operate equipment that mixes, blends, or cooks ingredients to produce food products according to formulas or recipes. They generally work in assembly-line production facilities where much of the process is automated, and they are sometimes involved in quality control. They spend most of the work day on their feet. Kind of like those elves that make the cookies, except batchmakers make lots of different products, and they don't live in trees.

Where and When

Working conditions vary considerably. Butchers and meat-cutters may work in slaughtering and processing plants or behind a meat counter. Those who work with meat and fish often work in cold, damp rooms to prevent the meat from spoiling. The cold, slippery conditions, sharp tools, and tiring, repetitive tasks make this one of the more dangerous jobs around. Bakers work in bakeries, hotels, restaurants, and supermarkets. They usually work in shifts, and morning, evening, weekend, and holiday work is common. Other food processing workers generally work in warm, noisy environments. Most work a regular 40-hour week, though that may include evenings and weekends.

For More Information

* Retail Bakers of America, 8400 Westpark Dr., 2nd Floor, McLean, VA 22102.

Data Bank

Education and Training: Short-term on-the-job training to long-term on-the-job training

Average Earnings: $20,000–$30,000

Earnings Growth Potential: Low

Total Jobs Held: 707,000

Job Outlook: Little change

Annual Job Openings: 23,400

Related Jobs: Chefs, head cooks, and food preparation and serving supervisors; cooks and food preparation workers

Personality Types: Realistic-Conventional

Did You Know?

The slaughtering and meatpacking industry is carefully regulated by the Food and Drug Administration (FDA), but it wasn't always. You may have heard of a book called *The Jungle*, by Upton Sinclair. Though the political novel is about the immigration experience, it is often remembered for its stomach-churning descriptions of the meatpacking industry at the turn of the 19th century. Its publication spurred the federal government to enforce stronger standards for both the safety of the workers and the general meat-eating public. In essence, the book helped create the FDA.

Computer Control Programmers and Operators

At a Glance

These workers use special computer numerically controlled (CNC) machines to cut and shape products such as car parts and compressors. These machines include lathes, milling machines, laser cutters, and water jet cutters. CNC programmers and operators follow blueprints from engineers to produce large quantities of a specific part. They use their knowledge of the working properties of metals and programming skills to design a set of instructions needed to make the product. These instructions are translated into a computer-aided manufacturing program containing a set of commands for the machine to follow. These commands describe where cuts should occur, what type of cut should be used, and the speed of the cut. In other words, these workers tell machines how to make stuff.

Data Bank

Education and Training: Moderate-term on-the-job training to work experience in a related occupation

Average Earnings: $29,000–$44,000

Earnings Growth Potential: Low

Total Jobs Held: 158,000

Job Outlook: Little change

Annual Job Openings: 4,000

Related Jobs: Computer software engineers and computer programmers; industrial machinery mechanics and millwrights; machine setters, operators, and tenders—metal and plastic; machinists; tool and die makers; welding, soldering, and brazing workers

Personality Types: Realistic-Conventional-Investigative

Did You Know?

While less-skilled CNC operators may need only a couple of weeks of on-the-job training, computer control programmers and skilled operators require more training and education. In fact, a growing number of them are receiving formal education from community or technical colleges. While these programs are still relatively new, they can provide the training needed to get a certification from the National Institute of Metalworking Skills, which in turn can expand career opportunities.

Career in Focus: *CNC Operator*

After the programming work is completed, CNC operators run the actual machines. They position the metal on the CNC machine and let the computer make the cuts. During a machining operation, the operator modifies the cutting program to account for any problems encountered. While many CNC operators are programmers as well, some manufacturers simply need CNC operators to be "button-pushers." They primarily start and stop machines, load cutting programs, and load and unload parts and tools. A single operator may monitor several machines simultaneously.

Where and When

Most computer control programmers and operators work a standard 40-hour week. They are increasingly working evening and weekend shifts, however, and overtime is common during peak production periods. Most machine shops are clean, well lit, and ventilated. Working around machine tools requires workers to wear protective equipment and exercise caution.

For More Information

✳ Fabricators and Manufacturers Association, 833 Featherstone Rd., Rockford, IL 61107 Internet: www.fmanet.org

Machine Setters, Operators, and Tenders—Metal and Plastic

At a Glance

Machine tool operators in the metalworking and plastics industries help produce most of the products we rely on daily. These workers fall into two groups: those who set up machines for operation and those who tend the machines while they work. They may work with drilling and boring machines, milling and planing machines, or lathe and turning machines. They work according to blueprints and other instructions to produce metal and plastic parts for everything from toasters to trucks. Because the setup process requires an understanding of the entire production process, setters usually have more training and are more highly skilled than those who simply operate or tend machinery.

Career in Focus: *Machine Setter, Operator, and Tender—Plastic*

Plastic parts are steadily replacing metal ones in all kinds of manufacturing. These workers are required to set up and tend machines that transform plastic compounds into a wide variety of goods such as toys, tubing, and auto parts. These products are manufactured by various methods. They may use injection molding to make a spatula, an extruding machine to make a window frame, or blow molding to create a two-liter soft-drink bottle.

Where and When

These workers tend to be on their feet most of the day in clean, well-lit, and well-ventilated labs and workshops. The machines they use can be dangerous, so strict safety rules are observed, including the use of safety glasses and earplugs. Most machine setters, operators, and tenders work 40 hours per week. Because many shops operate more than one shift each day, some operators work nights and weekends.

For More Information

* Fabricators and Manufacturers Association, 833 Featherstone Rd., Rockford, IL 61107 Internet: www.fmanet.org

Data Bank

Education and Training: Moderate-term on-the-job training to long-term on-the-job training

Average Earnings: $25,000–$38,000

Earnings Growth Potential: Low

Total Jobs Held: 1,028,000

Job Outlook: Declining

Annual Job Openings: 19,900

Related Jobs: Assemblers and fabricators; computer control programmers and operators; machinists; painting and coating workers, except construction and maintenance; tool and die makers; welding, soldering, and brazing workers

Personality Types: Realistic-Conventional

Did You Know?

They call it "labor-saving machinery" in part because it cuts down on the amount of physical work required. But that, in turn, cuts down on the number of workers. The new advances in computer-controlled machine tools and robots have had a dramatic impact on this industry, causing an overall decline in the number of new workers needed in this field. The result is that those with the most experience and education and who are willing to adapt to the ever-changing technology will have the best job prospects.

Machinists

At a Glance

Machinists make metal parts using lathes, drill presses, and milling machines. They often make specialized parts or one-of-a-kind items for companies that produce everything from cars to computers. Before they make a part, machinists must carefully plan and prepare the operation. After the layout work is completed, machinists position the workpiece on the machine tool, set the controls, and make the cuts. During the machining process, they must constantly monitor the rate and speed of the machine. Some machinists repair or make new parts for existing machinery. Because the technology in this field is changing rapidly, machinists must learn to operate a wide range of machines.

Data Bank

Education and Training: Long-term on-the-job training

Average Earnings: $30,000–$47,000

Earnings Growth Potential: Low

Total Jobs Held: 421,000

Job Outlook: Declining

Annual Job Openings: 5,600

Related Jobs: Computer control programmers and operators; industrial machinery mechanics and millwrights; machine setters, operators, and tenders—metal and plastic; tool and die makers

Personality Types: Realistic-Conventional-Investigative

Did You Know?

The vast majority of machinists work in manufacturing; however, a machinist's ability to create one-of-a-kind items makes the trade valuable in other fields as well. In fact, some machinists make copies of antique tools and machinery for museums and collectors. They use today's technologies to re-create yesterday's tools.

Career in Focus:
Production Machinist

Production machinists produce large quantities of one part, especially parts requiring great precision. Frequently, machinists work with computer control programmers to determine how the automated equipment will cut a part. The programmer may determine the path of the cut, while the machinist determines the type of cutting tool, the speed of the cutting tool, and the feed rate.

Where and When

Most machine shops are relatively clean, well lit, and ventilated, and exposure to noise and debris is limited. Machinists still must wear protective equipment like safety glasses. Machinists stand most of the day and may need to lift heavy workpieces. Many machinists work a 40-hour week, though evening and weekend shifts are becoming more common.

For More Information

✳ Fabricators and Manufacturers Association, 833 Featherstone Rd., Rockford, IL 61107 Internet: www.fmanet.org

Tool and Die Makers

At a Glance

Tool and die makers are among the most highly skilled workers in manufacturing. These workers produce tools, dies, and devices that enable machines to manufacture a variety of products—from clothing and furniture to heavy equipment and parts for aircraft. Tool makers create tools that cut, shape, and form metal and other materials. Die makers make the dies used to shape metal in stamping and forging machines. Some tool and die makers make prototypes of parts and then work with engineers to determine how best to manufacture the part. In addition to developing, designing, and producing new tools and dies, these workers also may repair worn or damaged tools, gauges, jigs, and fixtures. Tool and die makers must know about machining operations, mathematics, and blueprint reading.

Career in Focus: *Mold Maker*

A mold maker is not some scientist experimenting with bacteria and mildew in petri dishes. Rather, molds are used in a variety of manufacturing processes, most often to create plastic parts and goods. Mold makers specialize in creating the molds for the manufacturing industry. While some plastics companies may employ their own mold makers, the majority work out of specialty shops alongside other tool and die makers.

Where and When

Tool and die makers usually work in clean and cool tool-rooms. Workers follow safety rules and wear safety glasses, earplugs, gloves, and masks. They spend much of their time on their feet and may do moderately heavy lifting. Most work 40 hours per week, traditionally during normal business hours.

For More Information

＊ Fabricators and Manufacturers Association, 833 Featherstone Rd., Rockford, IL 61107 Internet: www.fmanet.org

Data Bank

Education and Training: Long-term on-the-job training

Average Earnings: $38,000–$59,000

Earnings Growth Potential: Low

Total Jobs Held: 84,000

Job Outlook: Declining

Annual Job Openings: 500

Related Jobs: Computer control programmers and operators; industrial machinery mechanics and millwrights; machine setters, operators, and tenders—metal and plastic; machinists; welding, soldering, and brazing workers

Personality Types: Realistic-Investigative-Conventional

Did You Know?

Many tool and die makers learn their skill through formal apprenticeship programs, which can take 4–5 years to complete. While requirements used to be limited to some on-the-job training and a certain number of courses, the National Institute of Metalworking Skills is developing new standards that would replace some of these requirements with competency tests. Don't say we didn't warn you.

Welding, Soldering, and Brazing Workers

At a Glance

These workers use the heat from a torch to melt and then permanently fuse metal parts together. Because of its strength, welding is used to build ships, cars, aircraft, and even space shuttles. Welding is also used to join beams when constructing buildings and bridges, and to join pipes in pipelines, power plants, and refineries. Welders may use a hand torch or a welding machine. There are about 100 different types of welding, though arc welding is the most common. Like welding, soldering and brazing use molten metal to join two pieces of metal. However, the metal added during the process has a melting point lower than that of the workpiece, so only the added metal is melted, not the workpiece itself. Highly skilled welders often are trained to work with a wide variety of materials in addition to steel, such as titanium, aluminum, or plastics.

Data Bank

Education and Training: Vocational/technical training

Average Earnings: $28,000–$42,000

Earnings Growth Potential: Low

Total Jobs Held: 466,000

Job Outlook: Declining

Annual Job Openings: 14,300

Related Jobs: Assemblers and fabricators; boilermakers; computer control programmers and operators; jewelers and precious stone and metal workers; machine setters, operators, and tenders—metal and plastic; machinists; plumbers, pipelayers, pipefitters, and steamfitters; sheet metal workers; tool and die makers

Personality Types: Realistic-Conventional

Did You Know?

Say the word *welder*, and many people picture a man in a hard hat and goggles. But many of today's welders are women, and they can trace their history to the shipyards of World War II. During the war, naval shipyards were so short of workers that they began hiring and training housewives and mothers to do the job. You may have heard of "Rosie the Riveter," who was the subject of a song, but you probably didn't know that pictures of "Wendy the Welder" also were published to boost wartime morale.

Career in Focus: *Cutter*

The work of cutters is closely related to that of welders. However, instead of *joining* metals, cutters use the heat from an electric arc, a stream of plasma, or burning gases to trim metal objects to specific dimensions. Cutters also dismantle large objects, such as ships, railroad cars, automobiles, buildings, or aircraft. Some operate and monitor cutting machines similar to those used by welding machine operators.

Where and When

These workers are exposed to a number of hazards, not the least of which are intense light, poisonous fumes, and very hot materials. They are like knights in armor, wearing safety shoes, goggles, hoods, and face shields. They may work both indoors and out, and may even work on scaffolding or platforms high off the ground. About half of these workers work a 40-hour week, though overtime is common, and some welders work up to 70 hours per week. In addition, some work in factories that operate around the clock, which requires evening and weekend shifts.

For More Information

* American Welding Society, 550 NW LeJeune Rd., Miami, FL 33126. Internet: www.aws.org

* Fabricators and Manufacturers Association, 833 Featherstone Rd., Rockford, IL 61107 Internet: www.fmanet.org

Bookbinders and Bindery Workers

At a Glance

Bookbinders and bindery workers use machines to bind the pages of books and magazines in a cover. These machines fold, cut, gather, glue, stitch, sew, trim, and wrap pages to form a book. Job duties depend on the kind of material being bound. In establishments that print new books, this work is done mechanically. In firms that do edition binding, workers bind books produced in large numbers or "runs." A small number of bookbinders work in hand binderies. These highly skilled workers design original or special bindings for limited editions, or restore and rebind rare books. Bookbinders and bindery workers in small shops may perform many binding tasks, while those in large shops usually are assigned only one or a few jobs.

Career in Focus: *Library Binder*

Library binders repair books and provide other specialized binding services to libraries. In libraries where repair work on rare books is needed, these bookbinders sew, stitch, or glue the printed sheets, shape the book bodies with presses and trimming machines, and reinforce them with glued fabric strips. Covers are created separately and then glued, pasted, or stitched onto the book bodies. If the book is especially old or rare, special precautions must be taken to preserve it.

Where and When

Binderies are noisy, and the job can be strenuous, requiring considerable lifting, standing, and carrying. Binders often work on an assembly line, and the task can be repetitive. Most work a 40-hour week.

For More Information

* Graphic Arts Education and Research Foundation, 1899 Preston White Dr., Reston, VA 20191. Internet: www.gaerf.org

* Printing Industries of America, 200 Deer Run Rd., Sewickley, PA 15143. Internet: www.printing.org

* NPES, The Association for Suppliers of Printing, Publishing, and Converting Technologies, 1899 Preston White Dr., Reston, VA 20191. Internet: www.npes.org/education/index.html

* National Association of Printing Leadership, 75 W. Century Rd., Suite 100, Paramus, NJ 07652. Internet: www.napl.org

Data Bank

Education and Training: Short-term on-the-job training to moderate-term on-the-job training

Average Earnings: $22,000–$37,000

Earnings Growth Potential: Low

Total Jobs Held: 67,000

Job Outlook: Declining

Annual Job Openings: 1,000

Related Jobs: Machine setters, operators, and tenders—metal and plastic; prepress technicians and workers; printing machine operators

Personality Types: Realistic-Conventional

Did You Know?

Long before the printing press was invented, people were experimenting with book binding. The craft began in Rome during the first century with the invention of the codex. A codex was simply a series of sheets of vellum or parchment folded in half and sewed together across the fold. This was a vast improvement over the scrolls that were most popular at the time. Codices were easier to carry, easier to search through, and allowed for writing on both sides. They were the precursors to our modern books.

Prepress Technicians and Workers

At a Glance

Prepress technicians and workers prepare materials for printing presses. They do typesetting, design page layouts, take photographs, and make printing plates. With personal computers, customers can now show printing companies how they want their printed material to look. It is increasingly common for prepress technicians to receive files from the customer electronically. These files need to be formatted to fit on the paper the customer wants to use. The technician then creates proofs of the pages to give to the customer for a final check. Technicians use laser "imagesetters" to expose digital images of the pages directly onto thin aluminum printing plates which are then used to make the final product.

Data Bank

Education and Training: Long-term on-the-job training to vocational/technical training

Average Earnings: $27,000–$45,000

Earnings Growth Potential: Medium

Total Jobs Held: 107,000

Job Outlook: Declining

Annual Job Openings: 900

Related Jobs: Artists and related workers; bookbinders and bindery workers; desktop publishers; graphic designers; printing machine operators

Personality Types: Realistic-Conventional

Did You Know?

Desktop publishing has changed the printing industry and the jobs of prepress workers. Today, they use high-tech computer programs to design and prepare materials for printing. These programs allow workers to separate color photos into the four basic colors that all printers use. The computer tells the printer precisely how much of each color of ink to apply so that the blend matches the original photos exactly. While this process is more efficient, it also means fewer jobs for prepress technicians.

Career in Focus: *Job Printer*

The printing process has three stages—prepress, press, and binding or postpress. Most of the time these three processes are handled by different workers who specialize in each stage. In small print shops, however, job printers are responsible for all three stages. They check proofs for errors and print clarity, correct mistakes, print the job, and attach each copy's pages together. They are the one-stop shopping of the printing world, though they are often not capable of handling large print runs.

Where and When

Prepress technicians and workers work in clean, comfortable environments with little noise. The extensive computer use can result in eyestrain and backaches. Platemakers who still work with chemicals run the risk of skin irritation. All of these workers are subject to the stress and pressure of tight deadlines. Most work an eight-hour day, though those employed by newspapers often work nights, weekends, and holidays.

For More Information

* Graphic Arts Education and Research Foundation, 1899 Preston White Dr., Reston, VA 20191. Internet: www.gaerf.org

* Printing Industries of America, 200 Deer Run Rd., Sewickley, PA 15143. Internet: www.printing.org

* NPES, The Association for Suppliers of Printing, Publishing, and Converting Technologies, 1899 Preston White Dr., Reston, VA 20191. Internet: www.npes.org/education/index.html

* NAPL, National Association of Printing Leadership, 75 W. Century Rd., Suite 100, Paramus, NJ 07652. Internet: www.napl.org

Printing Machine Operators

At a Glance

Printing machine operators prepare, run, and maintain the printing presses in a pressroom. They check the paper and ink, make sure paper feeders are stocked, and monitor the presses as they are running. To prepare presses for printing, machine operators generally install the printing plate, ink the presses, load paper, adjust the press to the paper size, and feed paper through the press cylinders. However, new technology skips these steps and sends the files directly to the press. Throughout the run, operators must regularly pull sheets to check for any printing imperfections, though much of this is now done by computers also. In most shops, press operators also perform preventive maintenance.

Career in Focus: *Screen Printing Machine Operator*

No doubt you have seen custom screen-printed t-shirts. Screen printing machines are capable of printing text and designs onto materials other than paper, including glass, plasticware, and cloth. Screen printing machine setters and operators determine all of the settings and adjustments necessary to create the design. They also monitor the printing process to ensure accuracy.

Where and When

This work can be physically and mentally demanding. Printing machine operators spend most of their time on their feet and are constantly under pressure to meet deadlines. Pressrooms are noisy, and working with the machinery can be hazardous, though new computerized controls make the job much safer. Many press operators work weekends, nights, and holidays, especially those who work for newspapers. Overtime is often needed to meet deadlines.

For More Information

* NPES, The Association for Suppliers of Printing, Publishing, and Converting Technologies, 1899 Preston White Dr., Reston, VA 20191. Internet: www.npes.org/education/index.html

* Printing Industries of America, 200 Deer Run Rd., Sewickley, PA 15143. Internet: www.printing.org

* Graphic Arts Education and Research Foundation, 1899 Preston White Dr., Reston, VA 20191. Internet: www.gaerf.org

* NAPL, National Association of Printing Leadership, 75 W. Century Rd., Suite 100, Paramus, NJ 07652. Internet: www.napl.org

Data Bank

Education and Training: Moderate-term on-the-job training

Average Earnings: $25,000–$43,000

Earnings Growth Potential: Medium

Total Jobs Held: 196,000

Job Outlook: Declining

Annual Job Openings: 4,100

Related Jobs: Bookbinders and bindery workers; machine setters, operators, and tenders—metal and plastic; prepress technicians and workers

Personality Types: Realistic-Conventional

Did You Know?

Before the Middle Ages, few people in Europe could read. Manuscripts had to be copied by hand, a task often performed by scribes who were employed by monasteries. Then, in 1456, Johannes Gutenberg made the first printing press using moveable type. His invention not only put a lot of scribes out of work, it also made books available to common people for the first time in history. Gutenberg's printing press is considered one of the most important inventions in human history. In fact, in 1999, the Arts & Entertainment network named Gutenberg the most influential person of the last millennium.

Textile, Apparel, and Furnishings Occupations

At a Glance

Textile workers operate the machines that make goods such as fibers, cloth, and upholstery. These goods are then used in all kinds of products from sweaters to sofas. Jobs may involve computers, large industrial machinery, or substantial handwork. Textile machine setters, operators, and tenders run machines that make textile products out of fibers. Textiles are the basis of towels, bed linens, and nearly all clothing, but they also are a key ingredient in products ranging from roofing to tires. Apparel workers make cloth, leather, and fur into clothing and other products. They may also repair torn or damaged items, or tailor them to fit a customer. Upholsterers are skilled craft workers who make new furniture or repair old furniture. Laundry and dry cleaning workers clean garments, linens, draperies, blankets, and other articles.

Data Bank

Education and Training: Short-term on-the-job training to long-term on-the-job training

Average Earnings: $19,000–$27,000

Earnings Growth Potential: Very low

Total Jobs Held: 787,000

Job Outlook: Declining

Annual Job Openings: 9,600

Related Jobs: Assemblers and fabricators; food processing occupations; jewelers and precious stone and metal workers; woodworkers

Personality Types: Realistic-Conventional

Did You Know?

Apparel workers are among the most rapidly declining work groups in the U.S. economy, in part because much of the work isn't being done in the U.S. anymore. Many U.S. companies are moving their production facilities abroad where labor is cheaper. Even tailors and dressmakers are feeling the sting, as it is now often cheaper to simply go out and buy new clothes rather than repair the old ones. Most of the patches you see on jeans today are there as a fashion statement, not to mend holes.

Career in Focus: *Shoe and Leather Worker*

Shoe and leather workers work in manufacturing or personal services. In shoe manufacturing, they operate machines that do the cutting, joining, and finishing needed to create footwear. In personal services, they repair and customize leather goods for the public. They construct, decorate, or repair shoes, belts, purses, saddles, luggage, and other leather products. Shoe and leather workers and repairers who own their own shops also must keep records and supervise other workers.

Where and When

Working conditions vary considerably, though most people in these occupations work a standard 40-hour week. Evening and weekend work is common, especially for those employed in laundry and dry cleaning or in retail stores. Many textile mills use rotating shifts, which can make for unusual schedules. Work in these occupations can be physically demanding and repetitive. Upholsterers, for example, stand most of the day and do a lot of bending and heavy lifting.

For More Information

* Drycleaning & Laundry Institute, 14700 Sweitzer Ln., Laurel, MD 20707. Internet: www.ifi.org

* American Apparel & Footwear Association, 1601 N. Kent St., 12th Floor, Arlington, VA 22209. Internet: www.apparelandfootwear.org

Woodworkers

At a Glance

Woodworkers use machines that cut, shape, assemble, and finish wood to make doors, cabinets, paneling, and furniture. In addition to these household goods, woodworkers also make sporting goods, such as baseball bats and oars, as well as musical instruments, toys, caskets, tool handles, and thousands of other wooden items. Precision woodworkers use hand tools to make rare or customized items. Production woodworkers use machines such as power saws, planers, sanders, and lathes. They may work in sawmills and plywood mills. Woodworkers have been greatly affected by the introduction of computer-controlled machinery, which has decreased the number of openings in this field.

Career in Focus: *Furniture Finisher*

Unlike those woodworkers who mass produce similar items, furniture finishers work on a job-by-job basis, often building one-of-a-kind pieces. These highly skilled precision woodworkers do all of the cutting, shaping, preparing, and assembling in order to make a finished product. For this reason, they normally need substantial training and an ability to work from detailed instructions and specifications.

Where and When

Working conditions vary by industry. Those in logging and sawmills have more physically demanding jobs and must adhere to rigid safety precautions. In furniture and cabinet manufacturing, employees still wear eye and ear protection and take precautions to guard against accidents. Prolonged standing, lifting, and fitting of heavy objects are common characteristics of the job.

For More Information

* Architectural Woodwork Institute, 46179 Westlake Dr., Suite 120, Potomac Falls, VA 20165. Internet: www.awinet.org

* WoodIndustryEd.org, c/o AWFS, 500 Citadel Dr., Suite 200, Commerce, CA 90040. Internet: www.woodindustryed.org

* WoodLINKS USA, P.O. Box 445, Tuscola, IL 61953. Internet: www.woodlinksusa.org

---

Data Bank

Education and Training: Moderate-term on-the-job training to long-term on-the-job training

Average Earnings: $22,000–$34,000

Earnings Growth Potential: Low

Total Jobs Held: 323,000

Job Outlook: Little change

Annual Job Openings: 8,900

Related Jobs: Carpenters; computer control programmers and operators; machinists; sheet metal workers; structural and reinforcing iron and metal workers

Personality Types: Realistic-Conventional

Did You Know?

Wood is one of the oldest materials to be shaped by man, whether it's making the shaft of a spear or carving out a canoe. Some of the stranger things to be created include a wooden car, wooden flowers, and wooden legs. However, through extensive testing, scientists have found that George Washington's false teeth were not, in fact, made of wood (as many of us were taught in elementary school). Rather his dentures were made of gold, ivory, lead, and human and animal teeth. So tongue splinters weren't a big problem, we guess.

Power Plant Operators, Distributors, and Dispatchers

At a Glance

Power plant operators control the turbines, generators, and boilers that generate electricity. Operators distribute power demands among generators, combine the current from several generators, and regulate the flow of electricity from the plant. When power requirements change, these workers start or stop generators and connect or disconnect them from circuits. Reactor operators are authorized to control the power output of the reactor in a nuclear power plant. The Nuclear Regulatory Commission (NRC) licenses operators of these plants.

Data Bank

Education and Training: Long-term on-the-job training

Average Earnings: $52,000–$74,000

Earnings Growth Potential: Low

Total Jobs Held: 50,000

Job Outlook: Little change

Annual Job Openings: 1,800

Related Jobs: Electrical and electronics installers and repairers; electricians; line installers and repairers; stationary engineers and boiler operators; water and liquid waste treatment plant and system operators

Personality Types: Realistic-Conventional

Did You Know?

Some parts of the world have grown accustomed to rolling blackouts—periods where they must go without electricity. But imagine being without power for more than two months. The longest peacetime blackout in history began on February 19, 1998, in Auckland, New Zealand. Four main power cables broke, causing electricity in the city center to be down for a total of 66 days.

Career in Focus: *Power Distributor and Dispatcher*

Also called load dispatchers or systems operators, these workers make sure that users receive enough electricity. They control the flow of electricity to industrial plants and substations, which supply everyone else's power needs. They monitor and operate current converters, voltage transformers, and circuit breakers. Dispatchers anticipate power needs, such as those caused by changes in the weather. They also handle emergencies, such as transformer or transmission line failures, by routing the electrical current around the affected areas.

Where and When

Because electricity is provided around the clock, this work is done in 8- or 12-hour shifts. Work on rotating shifts can be stressful and tiring because of disruptions in sleeping patterns. Those who work in control rooms generally sit or stand at a control station. The work requires constant attention. Those who work outside the control room may be exposed to danger from shocks, falls, and burns. Most workers at nuclear power plants are subject to random drug and alcohol tests.

For More Information

* American Public Power Association, 1875 Connecticut Ave. NW, Suite 1200, Washington, DC 20009-5715. Internet: www.appanet.org

* Center for Energy Workforce Development, 701 Pennsylvania Ave. NW, Washington, DC 20004-2696. Internet: www.cewd.org

* U.S. Nuclear Regulatory Commission, Washington, DC 20555-0001. Internet: www.nrc.gov

* North American Electric Reliability Corporation, 116-390 Village Blvd., Princeton, NJ 08540-5721. Internet: www.nerc.com

Stationary Engineers and Boiler Operators

At a Glance

Stationary engineers and boiler operators operate and maintain equipment that provides air-conditioning, heat, and ventilation to large buildings such as industrial plants. This equipment may include boilers, turbines, generators, pumps, and compressors, and may supply electricity, steam, or other types of power. These workers start up, regulate, repair, and shut down equipment. They ensure that the equipment operates safely and efficiently by monitoring meters and gauges. Stationary engineers typically use computers to operate the safety systems of new buildings and plants as well.

Career in Focus: *First-class Stationary Engineer*

There are several classes of stationary engineer licenses, each one specifying the type and size of equipment the engineer is allowed to use. A licensed first-class stationary engineer is qualified to run a large facility and operate equipment of all types and capacities. This person may be in charge of all mechanical systems in the building and may supervise the work of assistant stationary engineers, turbine operators, boiler tenders, and air-conditioning and refrigeration operators and mechanics. The license requires several years of on-the-job experience as well as passing a written examination.

Where and When

Stationary engineers and boiler operators generally work 40 hours per week all year round. Some facilities operate around the clock, creating the need for rotating shifts. These workers are often exposed to high temperatures, dust, dirt, and high noise levels. Workers spend much of their time on their feet. They may have to work in crouching and kneeling positions and crawl inside boilers to inspect, clean, or repair equipment.

For More Information

✳ International Union of Operating Engineers, 1125 17th St. NW, Washington, DC 20036. Internet: www.iuoe.org

✳ National Association of Power Engineers, Inc., 1 Springfield St., Chicopee, MA 01013. Internet: www.napenational.org

Data Bank

Education and Training: Long-term on-the-job training

Average Earnings: $41,000–$63,000

Earnings Growth Potential: Medium

Total Jobs Held: 42,000

Job Outlook: Little change

Annual Job Openings: 900

Related Jobs: Chemical plant and system operators; gas plant operators; industrial machinery mechanics and millwrights; maintenance and repair workers, general; petroleum pump system operators, refinery operators, and gaugers; power plant operators, distributors, and dispatchers; water and liquid waste treatment plant and system operators

Personality Types: Realistic-Investigative-Conventional

Did You Know?

Being a stationary engineer doesn't mean you can just sit in one place all day and monitor equipment (though the name may suggest otherwise). In fact, stationary engineers got their name to distinguish them from railroad and marine engineers. Although they don't chug down the rails or steam through the waves, they keep moving to handle many other maintenance responsibilities besides monitoring, cleaning, adjusting, inspecting, or repairing their usual equipment. They are often responsible for carpentry, plumbing, locksmithing, and electrical repairs. It would seem that stationary engineers are never in one place for very long.

Water and Liquid Waste Treatment Plant and System Operators

At a Glance

Water treatment plant operators make sure that the water we drink is safe. Water is pumped from wells, rivers, streams, and reservoirs to water treatment plants, where it is treated and distributed to customers. Wastewater travels through customers' sewer pipes to wastewater treatment plants. From there it is either treated and returned to streams, rivers, and oceans or reused for irrigation and landscaping. Operators in both types of plants control equipment that removes harmful materials, chemicals, and microorganisms from the water. They also control pumps, valves, and other equipment that moves the water or wastewater through the treatment process. They take water samples, perform analyses, and test and adjust chemicals in the water, such as chlorine. Occasionally, operators must work during emergencies, often caused by weather. Plant operators must also be familiar with federal and state regulations.

Data Bank

Education and Training: Long-term on-the-job training

Average Earnings: $31,000–$51,000

Earnings Growth Potential: Medium

Total Jobs Held: 113,000

Job Outlook: Rapid increase

Annual Job Openings: 4,700

Related Jobs: Chemical plant and system operators; gas plant operators; petroleum pump system operators, refinery operators, and gaugers; power plant operators, distributors, and dispatchers; stationary engineers and boiler operators

Personality Types: Realistic-Conventional

Did You Know?

In 1908, Jersey City became the first U.S. city to adopt permanent chlorination of its water supply. Cases of typhoid fever plummeted, and 1,000 other cities followed over the next decade. More recently, chlorine has been found to form harmful byproducts in drinking water, so researchers have been experimenting with using ozone and other chemicals and processes. Nevertheless, chlorinated water is thought to have saved more lives than any vaccine or antibiotic ever invented.

Career in Focus: *Water Treatment Plant Attendant*

Every ladder has a first rung. Trainees in water treatment plants usually begin as attendants where they learn the majority of their skills on the job. They do routine tasks such as record meter readings, take samples of wastewater and sludge, and perform simple work on pumps, motors, valves, and other plant equipment. This training is often combined with formal classroom experience.

Where and When

Water and wastewater treatment plant and system operators work both indoors and out. The work is physically demanding and is often performed in unsanitary locations. Because of this, operators pay close attention to safety procedures, especially around slippery walkways and dangerous gases. Because plants operate around the clock, operators work in rotating shifts, including weekends and holidays. They may be required to work overtime.

For More Information

* Association of Boards of Certification, 208 Fifth St., Suite 201, Ames, IA 50010-6259. Internet: www.abccert.org
* American Water Works Association, 6666 W. Quincy Ave., Denver, CO 80235. Internet: www.awwa.org
* National Rural Water Association, 2915 S. 13th St., Duncan, OK 73533. Internet: www.nrwa.org
* Water Environment Federation, 601 Wythe St., Alexandria, VA 22314-1994. Internet: www.wef.org

Inspectors, Testers, Sorters, Samplers, and Weighers

At a Glance

All products must meet certain quality standards before they can be sold to the public. These workers examine and sort products before releasing them to consumers. They may test by looking, listening, feeling, tasting, weighing, or smelling. Inspectors may reject a product, send it back to be fixed, or fix the problem themselves. Inspectors work in all kinds of industries producing all kinds of products, from food to clothing to glassware to cars. Some inspectors examine materials received from a supplier before sending them to the production line. Others inspect individual components or perform a final check on the finished product. Depending on their skill level, inspectors also may set up and test equipment, calibrate instruments, or simply record data.

Career in Focus: *Tester*

Testers repeatedly test existing products or prototypes under real-world conditions. For example, they may purposely abuse a machine by not changing its oil to see when it breaks down. They may devise automated machines to repeat a basic task thousands of times, such as opening and closing a car door. They subject products to extreme environments, such as scorching heat and freezing cold, to see how well they hold up. Through these tests, companies determine how long a product will last, what parts will break down first, and how to improve durability.

Where and When

Some inspectors may examine the same type of product for an entire shift, whereas others may inspect a variety. They are often on their feet all day and may be required to lift heavy objects. Plant conditions vary from noisy and dirty to clean and air-conditioned. Some inspectors do all of their analysis directly from electronic readouts on a computer. Evening, night, and weekend shifts are not uncommon, and overtime is sometimes required to meet production goals.

For More Information

* American Society for Quality, 600 N. Plankinton Ave., Milwaukee, WI 53203. Internet: www.asq.org

Data Bank

Education and Training: Moderate-term on-the-job training

Average Earnings: $25,000–$42,000

Earnings Growth Potential: Medium

Total Jobs Held: 465,000

Job Outlook: Declining

Annual Job Openings: 7,800

Related Jobs: Agricultural inspectors; construction and building inspectors; fire inspectors and investigators; occupational health and safety specialists; occupational health and safety technicians; transportation inspectors

Personality Types: Conventional-Realistic

Did You Know?

You have probably seen video footage of crash test dummies, but did you know that automobile safety testing actually started with human cadavers? Long before the invention of crash dummies, researchers used dead bodies to simulate the effects of car accidents. Then, in 1949, the first dummy was invented by Sierra Engineering Company. Named Sierra Sam, he was created for the United States Air Force in order to test aircraft ejection seats, finally answering the question "What kind of dummy would do such a thing?"

Jewelers and Precious Stone and Metal Workers

At a Glance

These workers use precious metals and stones such as gold and diamonds to design and manufacture jewelry. Some specialize in one area, such as buying, designing, cutting, repairing, selling, or appraising jewels. This work requires a high degree of skill and attention to detail. Jewelers use chemicals, sawing and drilling tools, and torches in their work. They may work for large jewelry manufacturing firms, for small retail jewelry shops, or as owners of their own businesses. Those who own or manage stores or shops also hire and train employees, order and sell merchandise, and perform other managerial duties. Gemologists and laboratory graders analyze, describe, and certify the quality and characteristics of gem stones. They often work as quality control experts for retailers, importers, or manufacturers.

Data Bank

Education and Training: Vocational/technical training

Average Earnings: $25,000–$45,000

Earnings Growth Potential: High

Total Jobs Held: 52,000

Job Outlook: Little change

Annual Job Openings: 1,400

Related Jobs: Artists and related workers; commercial and industrial designers; fashion designers; retail salespersons; sales representatives, wholesale and manufacturing; welding, soldering, and brazing workers; woodworkers

Personality Types: Realistic-Artistic

Did You Know?

One of the most famous jewels in the world is the Hope Diamond. This 451-carat blue diamond was found in the early 1600s and has passed from kings to commoners. It has been stolen and recovered, sold and resold, cut and recut. But its fame is due to the bad luck it seems to bring its owners. Through the years, some of its owners have been beheaded, been killed by wild dogs, or committed suicide. More than 20 deaths have been blamed on the gem. You can see it at the Smithsonian Natural History Museum in Washington, DC, though you probably shouldn't get too close.

Career in Focus: *Jewelry Appraiser*

Jewelry appraisers carefully examine jewelry to determine its value, after which they write appraisal documents. They determine the value of a piece by researching the jewelry market, using reference books, auction catalogs, price lists, and the Internet. They may work for jewelry stores, appraisal firms, auction houses, pawnbrokers, or insurance companies. Many gemologists also become appraisers.

Where and When

This work involves a great deal of concentration. The use of more comfortable jewelers' benches has eliminated most of the physical discomfort caused by spending long periods bent over in one position. Lasers, chemicals, sharp tools, and jewelers' torches all require proper safety precautions. In repair shops, jewelers usually work alone with little supervision. Those in retail stores may have extensive customer interaction. Because of the valuable nature of their products, jewelers must take involved safety precautions against theft.

For More Information

* Gemological Institute of America, 5345 Armada Dr., Carlsbad, CA 92008. Internet: www.gia.edu

* Jewelers of America, 52 Vanderbilt Ave., 19th Floor, New York, NY 10017. Internet: www.jewelers.org

* Manufacturing Jewelers and Suppliers of America, 57 John L. Dietsch Square, Attleboro Falls, MA 02763. Internet: www.mjsa.org

* Accrediting Commission of Career Schools and Colleges, 2101 Wilson Blvd., Suite 302, Arlington, VA 22201. Internet: www.accsc.org

Medical, Dental, and Ophthalmic Laboratory Technicians

At a Glance

These workers produce the devices that help patients see, speak, chew, or move better. Medical laboratory technicians construct artificial limbs, braces, and supports based on prescriptions from doctors. They are also referred to as orthotic and prosthetic technicians. Dental laboratory technicians make the products dentists use to replace decayed teeth. Using dentists' directions and molds of patients' mouths, they make dentures (false teeth), crowns, and bridges. In some laboratories, technicians perform all stages of the work, whereas in other labs, each technician does only a few specialized tasks.

Career in Focus: *Ophthalmic Laboratory Technician*

Ophthalmic laboratory technicians make prescription eyeglass or contact lenses. Some ophthalmic laboratory technicians manufacture lenses for other instruments, such as telescopes and binoculars. Ophthalmic laboratory technicians cut, grind, edge, and finish lenses according to specifications provided by opticians, optometrists, or ophthalmologists, and may insert lenses into frames to produce finished glasses. Although some lenses still are produced by hand, technicians are increasingly using automated equipment to make them.

Where and When

These technicians generally work in clean, comfortable laboratories where they have limited contact with the public. Most work a standard 40-hour week. At times they must wear goggles, gloves, and masks for safety. They may spend a great deal of time standing.

For More Information

* American Academy of Orthotists and Prosthetists, 1331 H St. NW, Suite 501, Washington, DC 20005. Internet: www.opcareers.org

* American Board for Certification in Orthotics, Prosthetics, and Pedorthics, 330 John Carlyle St., Suite 210, Alexandria, VA 22314. Internet: www.abcop.org

* Commission on Dental Accreditation, American Dental Association, 211 E. Chicago Ave., Chicago, IL 60611. Internet: www.ada.org/prof/ed/accred/commission/index.asp

* National Association of Dental Laboratories, 325 John Knox Rd., L103, Tallahassee, FL 32303. Internet: www.nadl.org

* Commission on Opticianry Accreditation, P.O. Box 142 Florence, IN 47020. Internet: www.coaccreditation.com

Data Bank

Education and Training: Moderate-term on-the-job training to long-term on-the-job training

Average Earnings: $25,000–$42,000

Earnings Growth Potential: Low

Total Jobs Held: 95,000

Job Outlook: Above-average increase

Annual Job Openings: 3,200

Related Jobs: Dentists; medical equipment repairers; opticians, dispensing; optometrists; orthotists and prosthetists; textile, apparel, and furnishings occupations

Personality Types: Realistic-Investigative-Conventional

Did You Know?

What did people do before they had porcelain dentures? When Queen Elizabeth I lost all of her front teeth, she put pieces of cloth under her lips to make her face appear fuller. Other members of the royal court had ornamental teeth made from silver or gold. Many early sets of dentures were made from bone or ivory, or from human teeth either donated by the dead (who didn't need them) or sold by the poor (who felt they needed the money more).

Painting and Coating Workers, Except Construction and Maintenance

At a Glance

Painting and coating machine operators cover everything from cars to candy with paints, plastics, varnishes, chocolates, or special solutions. Workers use various types of machines to coat a range of products, from giving paper its glossy finish to applying a mixture of silver, tin, and copper to glass to make mirrors. The most common methods of applying paints and coatings are spraying and dipping. Spray machine operators use spray guns to coat metal, wood, ceramic, fabric, paper, and food products with paint and other solutions. Other workers paint, coat, or decorate products such as furniture, glass, pottery, toys, cakes, and books. In response to concerns about air pollution and worker safety, manufacturers increasingly are using new types of paints and coatings on their products.

Data Bank

Education and Training: Short-term on-the-job training to moderate-term on-the-job training

Average Earnings: $25,000–$39,000

Earnings Growth Potential: Low

Total Jobs Held: 193,000

Job Outlook: Little change

Annual Job Openings: 5,800

Related Jobs: Automotive body and related repairers; machine setters, operators, and tenders—metal and plastic; painters and paper-hangers

Personality Types: Realistic-Conventional

Did You Know?

Some lucky coating workers get to operate enrobing machines. These gizmos coat bakery goods, candy bars, and other treats with melted chocolate, sugar, or cheese. So some of the same skills that might help you paint a car can also help you make a Milky Way. Smaller candy makers may use a hand-dipping method to get a chocolate coating, but this process is much more time intensive, not to mention all the chocolate lost by workers licking their fingers.

Career in Focus: *Automotive Painter*

Although the majority of painting and coating workers are employed in manufacturing, perhaps the best known group of workers refinishes old and damaged cars, trucks, and buses. Automotive painters use a spray gun to apply successive coats of paint until the finish of the repaired sections of the vehicle matches that of the original. To speed drying between coats, they may place the freshly painted vehicle under heat lamps or in a special infrared oven. These painters also may do special detailing work.

Where and When

Painting and coating workers typically work indoors and may be exposed to dangerous fumes, though the painting is done in ventilated booths and operators typically wear masks or respirators. Operators have to stand for long periods when using a spray gun, as well as bend, stoop, or crouch in uncomfortable positions. Most operators work a normal 40-hour week, but self-employed automotive painters often work more.

For More Information

✳ National Automotive Technician Education Foundation, 101 Blue Seal Dr., Suite 101, Leesburg, VA 20175. Internet: www.natef.org

Semiconductor Processors

At a Glance

Semiconductors, also known as microchips, are the tiny brains inside today's computers and high-tech equipment. Semiconductor processors are the workers who make these microchips. Semiconductors are produced in "cleanrooms"—production areas that must be kept free of any airborne matter, which can damage the chips. Processors must wear special coveralls called "bunny suits" to keep any dust away from the semiconductors. In creating these chips, operators use special equipment to imprint information on tiny silicon wafers. They spend a great deal of time at computer terminals, monitoring the operation of the equipment that makes the chips. They ensure that each of the tasks in the production of the chip is performed correctly.

Career in Focus: *Semiconductor Processing Technicians*

While technicians account for a smaller percentage of the workers in cleanrooms, they are crucial to the process. Technicians troubleshoot production problems and make equipment adjustments and repairs. They also take the lead in assuring quality control. To keep equipment repairs to a minimum, technicians perform diagnostic analyses to see whether an error is a flaw in one chip or in the process as a whole.

Where and When

Semiconductor processors work in rooms that must be kept free of dust and set at a comfortable 72 degrees. Workers wear suits that cover them entirely, minus the eyes which are protected by glasses. These workers may work with highly toxic chemicals, and they spend much of the day on their feet. The pace of the work is deliberately slow. Because these plants operate around the clock, night and weekend work is common.

For More Information

* Maricopa Advanced Technology Education Center, 4110 E. Wood St., Suite 1, Phoenix, AZ 85040. Internet: www.matec.org

* SEMI, 3081 Zanker Rd., San Jose, CA 95134. Internet: www.semi.org

* Semiconductor Industry Association, 181 Metro Dr., Suite 450, San Jose, CA 95110. Internet: www.sia-online.org

Data Bank

Education and Training: Vocational/technical training

Average Earnings: $26,000–$39,000

Earnings Growth Potential: Low

Total Jobs Held: 32,000

Job Outlook: Declining

Annual Job Openings: 600

Related Jobs: Assemblers and fabricators; engineering technicians; engineers; inspectors, testers, sorters, samplers, and weighers; science technicians; tool and die makers

Personality Types: Realistic-Conventional-Investigative

Did You Know?

Silicon Valley is the name given to the southern part of the San Francisco Bay area that became known for its creation of microchips. Over the past 20 years, the industry there has exploded. Now Silicon Valley has become synonymous with many high-tech products and inventions—and the people who got rich making them. In fact, the area has the highest number of millionaires per capita of anywhere in the United States.

Transportation and Material Moving Occupations

Air Traffic Controllers

At a Glance

Air traffic controllers are responsible for the safe movement of airport traffic both in the air and on the ground. With the help of radars, they direct landings, takeoffs, and ground movement of aircraft. They keep planes a safe distance apart during flights and inform pilots of current weather conditions. Their immediate concern is safety, but controllers also must direct planes efficiently to minimize delays. In emergencies they may search for missing aircraft. Airport tower controllers' main responsibility is to organize the flow of aircraft into and out of the airport. After each plane departs, airport tower controllers notify enroute controllers who take charge and ensure that the airplane safely arrives at its destination. There are 20 air route traffic control centers located around the country, each employing 300 to 700 controllers.

Data Bank

Education and Training: Long-term on-the-job training

Average Earnings: $70,000–$142,000

Earnings Growth Potential: Very high

Total Jobs Held: 26,000

Job Outlook: Average increase

Annual Job Openings: 1,200

Related Jobs: Airfield operations specialists

Personality Types: Enterprising-Conventional

Did You Know?

The process to become an air traffic controller is long and involved. A person must enroll in an FAA-approved education program and pass a pre-employment test. In addition, applicants must have three years of full-time work experience or have completed four years of college. After completing the FAA-approved program (and providing the applicant is under the age of 31), the applicant must pass a medical exam, undergo drug screening, and obtain a security clearance. If all of that goes well, the candidate then attends a 12-week training session at the FAA Academy in Oklahoma. After graduating from there, the trainee begins on-the-job training as a "developmental controller," which can last between two and four years. After all of this, he or she is finally certified to be a full-fledged air traffic controller.

Career in Focus: *Flight Service Specialist*

In addition to airport towers and centers, air traffic controllers also work in flight service stations operated at more than 100 locations. These flight service specialists provide pilots with information on the station's particular area, including terrain, weather information, suggested routes, and other information important to the safety of a flight. Flight service specialists help pilots in emergency situations and coordinate searches for missing or overdue aircraft. However, they are not involved in managing air traffic.

Where and When

Controllers work about 40 hours per week. Because most control towers and centers operate around the clock, controllers rotate night and weekend shifts. The job requires intense concentration, as controllers are expected to keep track of several planes at once. The mental stress can be exhausting.

For More Information

* Federal Aviation Administration, 800 Independence Ave. SW, Washington, DC 20591. Internet: www.faa.gov

* National Air Traffic Controllers Association, 1325 Massachusetts Ave. NW, Washington, DC 20005. Internet: www.natca.org

Aircraft Pilots and Flight Engineers

At a Glance

Aircraft pilots fly airplanes and helicopters, test aircraft, and sometimes fight forest fires. Pilots may work for large airlines, charter services, the government, or private businesses. They must plan flights, check the aircraft and weather conditions, and keep records of each flight. Flight engineers act as a third pilot on large aircraft, monitoring and operating many of the instruments and systems. Most pilots are airline pilots and copilots who transport passengers and cargo, but one out of five pilots is a commercial pilot involved in tasks such as dusting crops, spreading seed for reforestation, testing aircraft, directing firefighting efforts, tracking criminals, monitoring traffic, and rescuing and evacuating injured persons.

Career in Focus: *Flight Instructor*

Some pilots are flight instructors. They teach their students in ground-school classes, in simulators, and in dual-controlled planes and helicopters. They teach student pilots about flight procedures and techniques, prepare lesson plans, and evaluate and monitor student performance. A few specially trained pilots are examiners. They periodically fly with other pilots or pilot's license applicants to test their proficiency.

Where and When

While the "where" should be obvious (if they aren't in the cockpit, they probably should be), the "when" varies considerably. FAA regulations state that pilots flying large aircraft cannot fly more than 100 hours a month or 1,000 hours a year. Most pilots fly about 75 hours a month and spend another 75 hours performing nonflying duties. Flight assignments are based on seniority, and most pilots work an irregular schedule and spend a lot of time away from home (at the expense of the airline). Commercial pilots also have irregular schedules and work at odd hours.

For More Information

* Federal Aviation Administration, 800 Independence Ave. SW, Washington, DC 20591. Internet: www.faa.gov

* Air Line Pilots Association, International, 1625 Massachusetts Ave. NW, Washington, DC 20036. Internet: www.clearedtodream.org

* Helicopter Association International, 1635 Prince St., Alexandria, VA 22314. Internet: www.rotor.com

Data Bank

Education and Training: Vocational/technical training to bachelor's degree

Average Earnings: $71,000–$128,000

Earnings Growth Potential: High

Total Jobs Held: 116,000

Job Outlook: Average increase

Annual Job Openings: 5,300

Related Jobs: Air traffic controllers; airfield operations specialists

Personality Types: Realistic-Conventional-Investigative

Did You Know?

Not only are the earnings of airline pilots some of the highest in the nation, the job comes with its share of benefits as well. Airline pilots are usually eligible for life and health insurance, retirement benefits, and disability payments. They receive an expense allowance for every hour they are away from home and sometimes have an allowance for purchasing and cleaning their uniforms. In addition, pilots and their families usually are entitled to free flights. The drawback: The time away from home can be considerable, and the starting pay is often shockingly low.

Bus Drivers

At a Glance

Buses provide transportation for millions of people every year, from commuters to school children to vacationers. Bus drivers transport people from place to place following a time schedule and a specific route, sometimes collecting fares and keeping a log of their activity. Some transit bus drivers transport people long distances within a state or throughout the country. School bus drivers drive students to and from school. Drivers must operate vehicles safely and have a valid commercial driver's license. Bus drivers operate a range of vehicles, from 15-passenger buses to 60-foot buses that can carry more than 100 passengers.

Data Bank

Education and Training: Moderate-term on-the-job training

Average Earnings: $22,000–$37,000

Earnings Growth Potential: Medium

Total Jobs Held: 647,000

Job Outlook: Average increase

Annual Job Openings: 15,700

Related Jobs: Rail transportation occupations; taxi drivers and chauffeurs; truck drivers and driver/sales workers

Personality Types: Realistic-Conventional-Social

Did You Know?

More than 24 million students ride school buses every day in America. Some states now require that school buses be equipped with seat belts for all riders, and many other states are studying the idea. Proponents say seat belts will protect kids in a crash, but others say seat belts will slow down the time it takes to evacuate the bus in an emergency (not to mention give kids an additional means for torturing each other). It's a debate that has raged for decades.

Career in Focus: *Motor Coach Driver*

Some drivers operate motor coaches, which transport passengers on chartered trips and sightseeing tours. Drivers interact with customers and tour guides to make the trip as comfortable and informative as possible. They keep to strict schedules and follow the tour's itinerary. These drivers often act as customer service representative, tour guide, program director, and safety guide all in one. Trips frequently last more than a day.

Where and When

Most drivers work without any kind of direct supervision, but they also take full responsibility for their passengers. Intercity bus drivers may work nights, weekends, and holidays and spend much of their time away from home. Senior drivers may have regular weekly work schedules, but schedules of other drivers vary. School bus drivers work only when school is in session, many for 20 hours per week or less. Those who work on tour and charter buses may work on any day and all hours, including weekends and holidays. The Department of Transportation regulates how many hours bus drivers can drive in a given week.

For More Information

* Federal Motor Carrier Safety Administration, 1200 New Jersey Ave. SE, Washington, DC 20590. Internet: www.fmcsa.dot.gov

* National School Transportation Association, 113 S. West St., 4th Floor, Alexandria, VA 22314. Internet: www.yellowbuses.org

* American Public Transportation Association, 1666 K St. NW, Washington, DC 20006. Internet: www.apta.com

* United Motorcoach Association, 113 S. West St., 4th Floor, Alexandria, VA 22314. Internet: www.uma.org

Taxi Drivers and Chauffeurs

At a Glance

Taxi drivers and chauffeurs drive people in cars, limousines, and vans. Taxi drivers pick up passengers by "cruising" for fares, prearranging pickups, and picking up passengers from taxi stands. These professional drivers also help out-of-town business people and tourists get around in unfamiliar surroundings. Drivers should be familiar with streets in the areas they serve so that they can use the most efficient routes. They should know the locations of frequently requested destinations, such as airports, bus and railroad terminals, convention centers, hotels, and other points of interest. Chauffeur service differs from taxi service in that all trips are prearranged. Chauffeurs pamper their passengers by providing extras like newspapers, drinks, music, and television. All of these workers must lift heavy luggage and packages, drive in all kinds of weather and traffic, and sometimes put up with rude customers.

Career in Focus: *Paratransit Driver*

Many wheelchair-bound individuals may have difficulty getting into and out of a regular taxicab. Thankfully some taxi services have accommodations for such individuals. Some taxi drivers specialize in transporting individuals with special needs, such as those with disabilities and the elderly. These drivers, known as paratransit drivers, operate specially equipped vehicles. Some additional training on the equipment and passenger needs may be required.

Where and When

Driving for long periods can be tiring, stressful, and uncomfortable. Work hours of taxi drivers and chauffeurs vary greatly. Many work part time, and schedules can change from day to day. Drivers may be on call, and evening and weekend work is expected. The job is attractive to individuals seeking a flexible work schedule, however. Improvements in cars have made the job safer and more comfortable, including satellite tracking systems and automated dispatch systems. Many chauffeurs wear formal attire such as a uniform or tuxedo.

For More Information

* Taxicab, Limousine and Paratransit Association, 3200 Tower Oaks Blvd., Suite 220, Rockville, MD 20852. Internet: www.tlpa.org

* National Limousine Association, 49 S. Maple Ave., Marlton, NJ 08053. Internet: www.limo.org

Data Bank

Education and Training: Short-term on-the-job training

Average Earnings: $18,000–$28,000

Earnings Growth Potential: Low

Total Jobs Held: 232,000

Job Outlook: Above-average increase

Annual Job Openings: 7,700

Related Jobs: Bus drivers; truck drivers and driver/sales workers

Personality Types: Realistic-Enterprising

Did You Know?

Some jobs you might anticipate being dangerous and sometimes even deadly. Roofers, fishers, and logging workers, for example, constantly face hazards as part of their daily work. But did you know that taxi drivers rank in the top ten most dangerous jobs in the United States? Granted, much of the danger comes from automobile accidents, but taxi drivers—who often work alone, carry large amounts of cash, and work at all hours in all areas of a city—may also find themselves victims of robbery and homicide.

Truck Drivers and Driver/Sales Workers

At a Glance

Truck drivers move and deliver goods among factories, warehouses, stores, and homes. Even if some goods travel most of the way by ship, train, or airplane, almost everything is carried by trucks at some point in its journey. Drivers maintain their trucks, check for fuel and oil, make sure their brakes and lights work, and make minor repairs. They also load and unload the goods they transport. The duration of runs vary according to the types of cargo and the destinations. Local drivers may provide daily service for a specific route or region, while other drivers make intercity and interstate deliveries. Heavy truck and tractor-trailer drivers transport goods including cars, livestock, and other materials. Light or delivery services truck drivers operate vans and trucks weighing less than 26,000 pounds. They generally pick up or deliver merchandise and packages within a specific area.

Data Bank

Education and Training: Short-term on-the-job training

Average Earnings: $26,000–$43,000

Earnings Growth Potential: Low

Total Jobs Held: 3,189,000

Job Outlook: Average increase

Annual Job Openings: 86,200

Related Jobs: Bus drivers; Postal Service mail carriers; sales representatives, wholesale and manufacturing; taxi drivers and chauffeurs

Personality Types: Realistic-Conventional-Enterprising

Did You Know?

Long-distance trucking runs may last for several days or even weeks. Drivers stop only for gas, food, and loading and unloading. On such long runs, two drivers may work together. One driver sleeps in a berth built into the truck while the other drives. The berths often include refrigerators and televisions, though the quarters are still cramped.

Career in Focus: *Route Driver*

The primary responsibility of route drivers is to deliver and sell products over established routes. They sell goods or pick up and deliver items. They also respond to customer complaints and requests, take orders, and collect payments. Most have routes that deliver to businesses and stores rather than to homes. After completing their route, route drivers place orders for their next deliveries based on product sales and customer requests.

Where and When

Driving for many hours at a time and loading and unloading cargo can be tiring. Some long-distance truck drivers may spend most of the year away from home, while local truck drivers usually return home in the evening. The U.S. Department of Transportation regulates the working conditions for truck drivers. Long-distance drivers may drive for 11 hours or work for 14 after 10 hours off-duty. Drivers on long runs face boredom, loneliness, and fatigue, and they often work nights, holidays, and weekends.

For More Information

* American Trucking Associations, Inc., 950 N. Glebe Rd., Suite 210, Arlington, VA 22203. Internet: www.truckline.com

* American Trucking Associations, Inc., industry recruiting page: www.gettrucking.com

* Professional Truck Driver Institute, 555 E. Braddock Rd., Alexandria, VA 22314. Internet: www.ptdi.org

* The International Brotherhood of Teamsters, 25 Louisiana Ave. NW, Washington, DC 20001. Internet: www.teamster.org

Rail Transportation Occupations

At a Glance

Railroads deliver billions of tons of freight and millions of travelers per year to destinations throughout the country, while subways and light-rail systems transport millions of passengers around metropolitan areas. This job includes railroad workers as well as subway and streetcar operators. Railroad engineers operate locomotives that transport passengers and cargo. Conductors are responsible for the cargo and passengers on trains. Those assigned to passenger trains also ensure passenger safety and comfort as they go about collecting tickets and fares, making announcements, and coordinating activities of the crew. Brakemen remove cars and throw switches to allow trains to change tracks. Yardmasters coordinate the activities of workers engaged in railroad traffic operations.

Career in Focus: *Subway and Streetcar Operator*

Subway and streetcar operators generally work for public transit authorities instead of railroads. Subway operators control trains that transport passengers through cities and their suburbs. The trains run in underground tunnels, on the surface, or on elevated tracks. Operators must start, slow, or stop their train; make announcements to riders; open and close the doors of the train; and ensure that passengers get on and off the subway safely. Streetcar operators drive electric-powered streetcars, trolleys, or light-rail vehicles that transport passengers around metropolitan areas. They don't *all* work in San Francisco.

Where and When

Many rail transportation workers work nights, weekends, and holidays and may work more than a 40-hour week. The more desirable shifts are usually given based on seniority. Rail yard workers spend most of their time outdoors regardless of weather conditions. The work of conductors and engineers can be physically demanding as well. Those who work on trains operating between points hundreds of miles apart may spend a lot of time away from home.

For More Information

* Association of American Railroads, 425 3rd St. SW, Suite 1000, Washington, DC 20024. Internet: www.aar.org

* National Railroad Passenger Corporation, 60 Massachusetts Ave. NE, 4th Floor, Washington, DC 20002. Internet: www.amtrak.com

* United Transportation Union, 14600 Detroit Ave., Cleveland, OH 44107. Internet: www.utu.org

Data Bank

Education and Training: Moderate-term on-the-job training

Average Earnings: $39,000–$61,000

Earnings Growth Potential: Low

Total Jobs Held: 79,000

Job Outlook: Average increase

Annual Job Openings: 3,300

Related Jobs: Bus drivers; heavy vehicle and mobile equipment service technicians and mechanics; material moving occupations; truck drivers and driver/sales workers; water transportation occupations

Personality Types: Realistic-Conventional

Did You Know?

In the late 1800s, when the railroad was the fastest way to travel, wealthy people sometimes bought their own railroad cars. These cars were usually decorated with rich, expensive materials. Some even had luxury items such as sunken bathtubs, barber's chairs, and pipe organs. When they wanted to travel, these people simply had their cars hitched to a train. Most employed their own maids, chefs, and waiters to serve them on the trip as well. Some modern passenger trains still offer luxury travel accommodations, including fine linens and crystal stemware, impeccable service, and executive staterooms for sleeping. Pipe organs, however, are no longer available.

Water Transportation Occupations

At a Glance

Workers in water transportation operate all kinds of boats on oceans, lakes, rivers, canals, and other waterways. Captains or masters are in charge of a vessel and the crew. Deck officers or mates help the captain. Sailors and deck hands do maintenance, steer, and load and unload cargo. Pilots guide ships through harbors and narrow waterways. On larger coastal ships, the crew may include a captain, a mate or pilot, an engineer, and seven or eight seamen. Unlicensed positions on a large ship may include a full-time cook, an electrician, and mechanics.

Data Bank

Education and Training: Short-term on-the-job training to work experience in a related occupation

Average Earnings: $37,000–$69,000

Earnings Growth Potential: High

Total Jobs Held: 81,000

Job Outlook: Above-average increase

Annual Job Openings: 4,600

Related Jobs: Fishers and fishing vessel operators; heavy vehicle and mobile equipment service technicians and mechanics; job opportunities in the armed forces

Personality Types: Realistic-Enterprising-Conventional

Did You Know?

Merchant mariners working on ships on the Great Lakes typically work for 60 days straight and then have 30 days off. Most sailors are hired for one voyage at a time, and during the winter months when the lakes are frozen, there is no work at all. Compared to many deep-sea mariners, however, those working on the Great Lakes are often not very far from home.

Career in Focus: *Ship Engineer*

Ship engineers operate, maintain, and repair propulsion engines, boilers, generators, pumps, and other machinery. Merchant marine vessels usually have four engineering officers: a chief engineer and a first, second, and third assistant engineer. Assistant engineers stand periodic watches, overseeing the safe operation of engines and machinery. These individuals combine their technical skills with their knowledge of seafaring, and many of them have a college degree.

Where and When

The "where" is usually a boat of some kind, hopefully in a body of water of some kind. The "when" varies tremendously. Merchant mariners spend extended periods at sea, usually on voyages lasting several months. At sea, workers usually stand watch for 4 hours and then are off for 8 every day of the week. Workers on other ships may be on duty for 6 or 12 hours and then off for another 6 or 12. Extended periods of unemployment are common. People in water transportation work in all weather conditions, and the jobs come with their share of hazards. The work is physically demanding and the stress of being away from home for long periods can take its toll.

For More Information

* Maritime Administration, U.S. Department of Transportation, 1200 New Jersey Ave. SE, Washington, DC 20590. Internet: www.marad.dot.gov

* U.S. Coast Guard National Maritime Center, 2100 Second St. SW, Washington, DC 20593. Internet: www.uscg.mil/nmc

* The American Waterways Operators, 801 N. Quincy St., Suite 200, Arlington, VA 22203. Internet: www.americanwaterways.com

Material Moving Occupations

At a Glance

Material moving workers load and unload trucks and ships using cranes, bulldozers, shovels, and forklifts. They also move construction materials, logs, and coal around factories, warehouses, and construction sites. Material moving workers are categorized into two groups—operators and laborers. Operators use machinery to move construction materials such as earth, petroleum products, and other heavy materials. Some move materials onto or off of trucks and ships. They also may set up and inspect equipment, make adjustments, and perform minor repairs. Laborers manually handle freight, stock, or other materials; clean vehicles, machinery, and other equipment; and pack or package products and materials.

Career in Focus: *Hand Freight, Stock, and Material Mover*

These workers don't require cranes or bulldozers to do their work. Instead they manually move freight, stock, and other materials to and from storage and production areas, loading docks, delivery vehicles, ships, and containers. Their specific duties vary by industry. In factories, they may move materials or goods between loading docks, storage areas, and work areas. Specialized workers within this group include baggage and cargo handlers, who work in transportation industries, and truck loaders and unloaders.

Where and When

Material moving work is physically demanding and can be repetitive. Workers lift and carry heavy objects and stoop, kneel, crouch, or crawl in awkward positions. Some work at great heights, and many work outdoors in all kinds of weather. They often must wear gloves, hardhats, protective glasses, and other safety devices. Most material movers work eight-hour shifts, though overtime is common.

For More Information

* International Union of Operating Engineers, 1125 17th St. NW, Washington, DC 20036. Internet: www.iuoe.org

* National Commission for the Certification of Crane Operators, 2750 Prosperity Ave., Suite 505, Fairfax, VA 22031. Internet: www.nccco.org

* U.S. Department of Labor, Occupational Safety and Health Administration (OSHA), 200 Constitution Ave. NW, Washington, DC 20210. Internet: www.osha.gov

* Mine Safety and Health Administration, 1100 Wilson Blvd., Arlington, VA 22209-3939. Internet: www.msha.gov

Data Bank

Education and Training: Short-term on-the-job training to long-term on-the-job training

Average Earnings: $20,000–$31,000

Earnings Growth Potential: Low

Total Jobs Held: 4,584,000

Job Outlook: Declining

Annual Job Openings: 135,700

Related Jobs: Agricultural workers, other; building cleaning workers; construction equipment operators; construction laborers; grounds maintenance workers; logging workers

Personality Types: Realistic-Conventional

Did You Know?

This job category covers a wide range of titles, from excavating machine operators who use scoops to load trucks with gravel to ship loaders who use hoists to load and unload sea vessels. But perhaps the unsung heroes of the category are the refuse and recyclable material collectors—more commonly known as garbage collectors. These workers gather the refuse from homes and businesses all across the nation for transport to dumps, landfills, and recycling centers. It's a heavy job for a country where every person produces an average of four pounds of trash per day.

Job Opportunities in the Armed Forces

Job Opportunities in the Armed Forces

At a Glance

The U.S. Armed Forces is the country's largest single employer with more than 2 million people serving, of which 1.4 million are on active duty. Maintaining a strong defense requires many activities, such as running hospitals, repairing helicopters, programming computers, and operating nuclear reactors. Military jobs range from clerical work to professional positions to construction work. People in the military must serve for a specified time and can be moved from one base to another. Enlisted personnel, who make up about 85 percent of the Armed Forces, carry out the fundamental operations of the military in areas such as combat, administration, construction, engineering, health care, and human services. Officers, who make up the remaining 15 percent of the Armed Forces, are the leaders of the military, supervising and managing all activities.

Data Bank

Education and Training: Moderate-term on-the-job training to related work experience

Average Earnings: $18,800–$54,200 for enlisted personnel with 12–16 years of experience (officers can make considerably more)

Earnings Growth Potential: Cannot be determined

Total Jobs Held: 2,400,000

Job Outlook: Little change expected, but defense needs may change

Annual Job Openings: 184,000

Related Jobs: Almost all of them

Personality Types: All of them

Did You Know?

The military can provide you with the training to do almost any job once you've finished your commitment. The Armed Forces train welders, nurses, journalists, cooks, dental hygienists, metalworkers, surveyors, emergency management specialists, computer specialists, pilots, sailors, electronic equipment repairers, mechanics, and medical records technicians, to name just a few. Many employers like hiring former military personnel because they know about discipline, honor, and getting the job done. In addition, the Montgomery GI Bill helps veterans pay for continued education at many colleges, universities, and training schools.

Career in Focus: *Combat Specialty Occupations*

When most people think of the military, they think of those enlisted men and women in combat specialty operations. They are the soldiers, such as infantry, artillery, and special forces, who are most directly involved in combat. They conduct military maneuvers, offensive raids, intelligence, demolitions, and search and rescue missions using aircraft, helicopters, ships, tanks, subs, and all other kinds of equipment. Enlisted personnel in this category represent only 15 percent of the total manpower for the military, however.

Where and When

To say that working conditions vary in the military is an understatement. A mechanic onboard an aircraft carrier has a vastly different work environment than a military counselor working with soldiers returning from combat duty or a bomb recovery specialist looking for landmines in city streets. The "where" could be a naval base in Hawaii, a recruitment center in Iowa, or a cave in Afghanistan. The "when" for an officer on a submarine is completely different than for a public affairs officer in Washington, DC. It also goes without saying that the work can sometimes be hazardous, even during peacetime—though much of the military's workforce is never directly involved in combat.

For More Information

❋ U.S. Department of Defense. *Military Career Guide Online*. Internet: www.todaysmilitary.com

Appendix A: Job Titles by Personality Type

Saying someone has a good personality after a first date usually means the person wasn't much of a looker. But personality counts for a great deal, especially in the world of work. It can even be valuable as a means of focusing your career research.

Many career counselors believe that people are more satisfied in a job or career if it suits their personality; people will stay at a job longer and be more productive if they like what they do and whom they work with. The personality types used in the *EZ OOH* were developed in the 1950s by career development researcher John L. Holland, and his theory has since become the most widely used model for matching personality to career decisions. It is used in a wide variety of professional assessments and research materials, including the *Self-Directed Search* and the Department of Labor's Occupational Information Network.

This appendix offers an index of job titles found in the *EZ OOH* arranged by personality type. (The green jobs are not included here because personality type information is not yet available for them.) You can use this index to quickly locate the jobs that might best match your interests. Simply review the descriptions of the six personality types, find the one or two that best describe you and your work preferences, and then scan the jobs listed under those categories to find ones you want to read about.

Note that most occupations also are characterized by one or two secondary personality types. For example, Construction Managers has Enterprising as its primary personality type, but it also has Realistic and Conventional as secondary types. The occupations in this appendix are ordered first by their primary type and then by their secondary types. The ordering follows the pattern RIASEC, which consists of the first letter of each personality type: Realistic, Investigative, Artistic, Social, Enterprising, and Conventional.

If you want to find jobs that *combine* your primary personality type and a secondary personality type, look in the following table for RIASEC codes that match the two codes in either order. For example, if your primary personality type is Investigative and your secondary type is Realistic, you would look for jobs in the table coded IR. (You'd find seven, including Engineers.) You will also find jobs coded IR_, such as Computer Scientists (coded IRA) and Dentists (coded IRS). If you look further, you'll find still more jobs coded I_R, such as Optometrists (coded ISR). All of these jobs are worth considering. Finally, to cast an even wider net, you may want to consider reversing the codes you're looking for. In the current example, you might look for jobs coded RI or RI_, such as Engineering Technicians (coded RIC). But you need to keep in mind that these jobs may not be quite as satisfying because your primary personality type, though represented, does not dominate.

Descriptions of the Six Personality Types
Realistic

Realistic personalities like work activities that involve practical, hands-on problems and solutions. They enjoy dealing with plants; animals; and real-world materials such as wood, tools, and machinery. They also enjoy working outside, but often do not like paperwork or working closely with others.

Sample Work Activities: Build kitchen cabinets, install flooring in houses, drive a taxicab, maintain the grounds of a park, refinish furniture, put out forest fires, work on a fishing boat, assemble electronic parts.

Investigative

Investigative personalities like jobs that involve working with ideas and that require critical thinking and analysis. They like to search for facts and solve complex problems mentally rather than to persuade or lead people.

Sample Work Activities: Study rocks and minerals, do laboratory tests to identify diseases, conduct chemical experiments, investigate crimes, invent new foods, diagnose and treat sick animals, study the history of past civilizations.

Artistic

Artistic personalities like jobs that involve working with forms, designs, and patterns. They like self-expression and prefer to do their work without following a clear set of rules.

Sample Work Activities: Conduct an orchestra, write poems or novels, play a musical instrument, act in a movie, paint sets for a play, announce a radio show, sing in a band, design artwork for magazines, create dance routines for a show.

Social

Social personalities like work activities that assist others and promote learning and personal development. They like to teach, to give advice, to help, or to be of service to people in some way.

Sample Work Activities: Perform nursing duties in a hospital, teach children how to read, give career guidance to people, do volunteer work at a nonprofit organization, help families care for ill relatives, work with juveniles on probation, teach a high school class.

Enterprising

Enterprising personalities like work activities that involve starting up and carrying out projects. They like persuading and leading people, taking risks, and making important decisions. They prefer action rather than thought.

Sample Work Activities: Buy and sell stocks and bonds, manage a retail store, buy and sell land, market a new line of clothing, negotiate contracts for professional athletes, represent a client in a lawsuit, run a toy store.

Conventional

Conventional personalities like work activities that involve following set procedures and routines. They prefer working with data and details more than with ideas. They like working where there is a clear line of authority to follow.

Sample Work Activities: Proofread records or forms, use a computer to generate customer bills, organize and schedule office meetings, keep shipping and receiving records, develop an office filing system, handle bank transactions.

Index of Job Titles by Personality Type

Realistic

Agricultural Workers, Other   R

Cement Masons, Concrete Finishers, Segmental Pavers, and Terrazzo Workers   R

Fishers and Fishing Vessel Operators   R

Sheet Metal Workers   R

Automotive Service Technicians and Mechanics   RI

Veterinary Technologists and Technicians   RI

Conservation Scientists and Foresters   RIE

Camera and Photographic Equipment Repairers   RIC

Elevator Installers and Repairers   RIC

Engineering Technicians   RIC

Medical Equipment Repairers RIC

Medical, Dental, and Ophthalmic Laboratory Technicians   RIC

Radio and Telecommunications Equipment Installers and Repairers   RIC

Science Technicians   RIC

Stationary Engineers and Boiler Operators   RIC

Tool and Die Makers   RIC

Jewelers and Precious Stone and Metal Workers   RA

Musical Instrument Repairers and Tuners   RAC

Radiologic Technologists and Technicians   RS

Surgical Technologists   RSC

Taxi Drivers and Chauffeurs   RE

Correctional Officers   REC

Police and Detectives   REC

Water Transportation Occupations   REC

Athletes, Coaches, Umpires, and Related Workers   RES

Barbers, Cosmetologists, and Other Personal Appearance Workers   RES

Fire Fighters   RES

Animal Care and Service Workers   RC

Assemblers and Fabricators   RC

Automotive Body and Related Repairers   RC

Boilermakers   RC

Bookbinders and Bindery Workers   RC

Brickmasons, Blockmasons, and Stonemasons   RC

Broadcast and Sound Engineering Technicians and Radio Operators   RC

Carpet, Floor, and Tile Installers and Finishers   RC

Coin, Vending, and Amusement Machine Servicers and Repairers   RC

Construction Equipment Operators   RC

Construction Laborers   RC

Cooks and Food Preparation Workers   RC

Diesel Service Technicians and Mechanics   RC

Drywall and Ceiling Tile Installers, Tapers, Plasterers, and Stucco Masons   RC

Electronic Home Entertainment Equipment Installers and Repairers   RC

Food Processing Occupations   RC

Glaziers   RC

Graders and Sorters, Agricultural Products   RC

Hazardous Materials Removal Workers   RC

Heating, Air-Conditioning, and Refrigeration Mechanics and Installers   RC

Insulation Workers   RC

Logging Workers   RC

Machine Setters, Operators, and Tenders—Metal and Plastic   RC

Material Moving Occupations   RC

Painters and Paperhangers   RC

Painting and Coating Workers, except Construction and Maintenance   RC

Pest Control Workers   RC

Photographic Process Workers and Processing Machine Operators   RC

Plumbers, Pipelayers, Pipefitters, and Steamfitters   RC

Power Plant Operators, Distributors, and
  Dispatchers   RC

Prepress Technicians and Workers   RC

Printing Machine Operators   RC

Rail Transportation Occupations   RC

Roofers   RC

Small Engine Mechanics   RC

Textile, Apparel, and Furnishings Occupations   RC

Water and Liquid Waste Treatment Plant and System
  Operators   RC

Welding, Soldering, and Brazing Workers   RC

Woodworkers   RC

Agricultural Inspectors   RCI

Aircraft and Avionics Equipment Mechanics and
  Service Technicians   RCI

Aircraft Pilots and Flight Engineers   RCI

Carpenters   RCI

Computer Control Programmers and Operators   RCI

Computer Support Specialists   RCI

Computer, Automated Teller, and Office Machine
  Repairers   RCI

Construction and Building Inspectors   RCI

Drafters   RCI

Electrical and Electronics Installers and
  Repairers   RCI

Electricians   RCI

Fire Inspectors and Investigators   RCI

Forest and Conservation Workers   RCI

Heavy Vehicle and Mobile Equipment Service
  Technicians and Mechanics   RCI

Home Appliance Repairers   RCI

Industrial Machinery Mechanics and
  Millwrights   RCI

Line Installers and Repairers   RCI

Machinists   RCI

Maintenance and Repair Workers, General   RCI

Semiconductor Processors   RCI

Structural and Reinforcing Iron and Metal
  Workers   RCI

Watch Repairers   RCI

Bus Drivers   RCS

Building Cleaning Workers   RCE

Couriers and Messengers   RCE

Food and Beverage Serving and Related
  Workers   RCE

Grounds Maintenance Workers   RCE

Security Guards and Gaming Surveillance
  Officers   RCE

Truck Drivers and Driver/Sales Workers   RCE

Investigative

Agricultural and Food Scientists   IR

Atmospheric Scientists   IR

Biological Scientists   IR

Chemists and Materials Scientists   IR

Engineers   IR

Geoscientists and Hydrologists   IR

Veterinarians   IR

Computer Scientists   IRA

Medical Scientists   IRA

Physicists and Astronomers   IRA

Cardiovascular Technologists and Technicians   IRS

Dentists   IRS

Nuclear Medicine Technologists   IRS

Clinical Laboratory Technologists and
  Technicians   IRC

Environmental Scientists and Specialists   IRC

Social Scientists, Other   IA

Sociologists and Political Scientists   IAS

Audiologists   IS

Dietitians and Nutritionists   IS

Epidemiologists   IS

Diagnostic Medical Sonographers   ISR

Optometrists   ISR

Physicians and Surgeons   ISR

Podiatrists   ISR

Psychologists   ISA

Urban and Regional Planners   IEA

Management Analysts   IEC

Market and Survey Researchers   IEC

Computer Systems Analysts   IC

Occupational Health and Safety Specialists   IC

Computer Network, Systems, and Database
Administrators   ICR

Computer Software Engineers and Computer
Programmers   ICR

Mathematicians   ICA

Pharmacists   ICS

Economists   ICE

Operations Research Analysts   ICE

Artistic

Makeup Artists, Theatrical and Performance   AR

Photographers   AR

Television, Video, and Motion Picture Camera
Operators and Editors   AR

Artists and Related Workers   ARE

Architects, except Landscape and Naval   AI

Landscape Architects   AIR

Gaming Services Occupations   AIC

Technical Writers   AIC

Interpreters and Translators   AS

Dancers and Choreographers   ASR

Authors, Writers, and Editors   AE

Interior Designers   AE

Musicians, Singers, and Related Workers   AE

Commercial and Industrial Designers   AER

Fashion Designers   AER

Floral Designers   AER

Graphic Designers   AER

Models   AER

News Analysts, Reporters, and Correspondents   AEI

Social

Home Health Aides and Personal and Home Care
Aides   SR

Licensed Practical and Licensed Vocational
Nurses   SR

Massage Therapists   SR

Occupational Therapist Assistants and Aides   SR

Physical Therapist Assistants and Aides   SR

Athletic Trainers   SRI

Fitness Workers   SRE

Dental Hygienists   SRC

Nursing and Psychiatric Aides   SRC

Radiation Therapists   SRC

Occupational Therapists   SI

Registered Nurses   SI

Social Workers   SI

Teachers—Postsecondary   SI

Chiropractors   SIR

Emergency Medical Technicians and
Paramedics   SIR

Physical Therapists   SIR

Physician Assistants   SIR

Respiratory Therapists   SIR

Respiratory Therapy Technicians   SIR

Counselors   SIA

Instructional Coordinators   SIA

Speech-Language Pathologists   SIA

Child Care Workers   SA

Recreational Therapists   SA

Teachers—Kindergarten, Elementary, Middle, and
Secondary   SA

Teachers—Preschool, Except Special Education   SA

Teachers—Special Education   SA

Teachers—Vocational   SA

Teachers—Adult Literacy and Remedial
Education   SAE

Teachers—Self-Enrichment Education   SAE

Health Educators   SE

Recreation Workers   SEA

Customer Service Representatives   SEC

Probation Officers and Correctional Treatment
Specialists   SEC

Teacher Assistants   SC

Eligibility Interviewers, Government Programs   SCE

Enterprising

Sales Engineers   ERI

Chefs, Head Cooks, and Food Preparation and Serving
Supervisors   ERC

Construction Managers   ERC

Farmers, Ranchers, and Agricultural Managers   ERC

Engineering and Natural Sciences Managers   EI

Lawyers   EI

Actors, Producers, and Directors   EA

Public Relations Specialists   EAS

Judges, Magistrates, and Other Judicial Workers   ES

Announcers   ESA

Education Administrators   ESC

Flight Attendants   ESC

Funeral Directors   ESC

Human Resources Assistants, except Payroll and
Timekeeping   ESC

Human Resources, Training, and Labor Relations
Managers and Specialists   ESC

Medical and Health Services Managers   ESC

Administrative Services Managers   EC

Air Traffic Controllers   EC

Financial Managers   EC

Industrial Production Managers   EC

Private Detectives and Investigators   EC

Property, Real Estate, and Community Association
Managers   EC

Purchasing Managers, Buyers, and Purchasing
Agents   EC

Real Estate Brokers and Sales Agents   EC

Retail Salespersons   EC

Sales Representatives, Wholesale and
Manufacturing   EC

Securities, Commodities, and Financial Services Sales
Agents   EC

Travel Agents   EC

Demonstrators and Product Promoters   ECR

Food Service Managers   ECR

Computer and Information Systems Managers   ECI

Advertising Sales Agents   ECA

Advertising, Marketing, Promotions, Public Relations,
and Sales Managers   ECA

Insurance Sales Agents   ECS

Lodging Managers   ECS

Meeting and Convention Planners   ECS

Office and Administrative Support Supervisors and
Managers   ECS

Opticians, Dispensing   ECS

Personal Financial Advisors   ECS

Sales Worker Supervisors   ECS

Top Executives   ECS

Computer Operators   CR

Inspectors, Testers, Sorters, Samplers, and Weighers   CR

Medical Transcriptionists   CR

Meter Readers, Utilities   CR

Occupational Health and Safety Technicians   CR

Pharmacy Technicians and Aides   CR

Postal Service Clerks   CR

Postal Service Mail Carriers   CR

Postal Service Mail Sorters, Processors, and Processing Machine Operators   CR

Weighers, Measurers, Checkers, and Samplers, Recordkeeping   CR

Surveyors, Cartographers, Photogrammetrists, and Surveying and Mapping Technicians   CRI

Dental Assistants   CRS

File Clerks   CRE

Police, Fire, and Ambulance Dispatchers   CRE

Shipping, Receiving, and Traffic Clerks   CRE

Stock Clerks and Order Fillers   CRE

Statisticians   CI

Archivists, Curators, and Museum Technicians   CIR

Actuaries   CIE

Financial Analysts   CIE

Paralegals and Legal Assistants   CIE

Library Technicians and Library Assistants   CSR

Medical Assistants   CSR

Librarians   CSE

Social and Human Service Assistants   CSE

Appraisers and Assessors of Real Estate   CE

Bill and Account Collectors   CE

Billing and Posting Clerks and Machine Operators   CE

Bookkeeping, Accounting, and Auditing Clerks   CE

Brokerage Clerks   CE

Cargo and Freight Agents   CE

Cashiers   CE

Claims Adjusters, Appraisers, Examiners, and Investigators   CE

Cost Estimators   CE

Counter and Rental Clerks   CE

Court Reporters   CE

Credit Authorizers, Checkers, and Clerks   CE

Data Entry and Information Processing Workers   CE

Desktop Publishers   CE

Loan Interviewers and Clerks   CE

Medical Records and Health Information Technicians   CE

Payroll and Timekeeping Clerks   CE

Procurement Clerks   CE

Production, Planning, and Expediting Clerks   CE

Secretaries and Administrative Assistants   CE

Tax Examiners, Collectors, and Revenue Agents   CE

Tellers   CE

Dispatchers, except Police, Fire, and Ambulance   CER

Gaming Cage Workers   CER

Office Clerks, General   CER

Accountants and Auditors   CEI

Budget Analysts   CEI

Insurance Underwriters   CEI

Communications Equipment Operators   CES

Hotel, Motel, and Resort Desk Clerks   CES

Interviewers, except Eligibility and Loan   CES

Loan Officers   CES

Order Clerks   CES

Receptionists and Information Clerks   CES

Reservation and Transportation Ticket Agents and Travel Clerks   CES

Appendix B: Job Titles by Education and Training Requirements

According to the U.S. Department of Labor, an associate, bachelor's, or higher degree is the minimal requirement for 12 of the 20 fastest-growing occupations in the country, from dental hygienists to financial examiners. While it is no guarantee to getting a particular job, your education and training history is a primary qualification for even being *considered* for most jobs. The good news is there are millions of careers out there for all education levels (provided you have at least a high school diploma and are willing to learn on the job).

Because the number of jobs you have to choose from is dependent in part on your education or at least the education you are willing to get, we've broken the *EZ OOH* job titles down by their *minimal* education and training requirements. (Some of the job titles appear for multiple levels of education or training because specializations within the large occupation have differing minimal requirements, and the green jobs aren't included because education information is not yet available for them.) We recommend that you look for jobs that match your current level of education, but also ask yourself how far you are willing to go to get the job of your dreams. Consider the education and training level you would be willing to get, and look for jobs that match those criteria as well. Granted, postsecondary education isn't cheap, but there are resources out there that can help you fund your educational goals. In fact, you can find many of them referenced in the next appendix.

Jobs Requiring Work Experience in a Related Job

Agricultural Workers, Other

Building Cleaning Workers

Chefs, Head Cooks, and Food Preparation and Serving Supervisors

Computer Control Programmers and Operators

Construction and Building Inspectors

Correctional Officers

Dancers and Choreographers

Fire Fighters

Food Service Managers

Grounds Maintenance Workers

Industrial Production Managers

Lodging Managers

Police and Detectives

Private Detectives and Investigators

Real Estate Brokers and Sales Agents

Sales Representatives, Wholesale and Manufacturing

Sales Worker Supervisors

Secretaries and Administrative Assistants

Teachers—Postsecondary

Teachers—Self-Enrichment Education

Water Transportation Occupations

Jobs Requiring Short-Term On-the-Job Training

Animal Care and Service Workers

Assemblers and Fabricators

Barbers, Cosmetologists, and Other Personal Appearance Workers

Bill and Account Collectors

Bookbinders and Bindery Workers

Building Cleaning Workers

Cashiers

Child Care Workers

Cooks and Food Preparation Workers

Couriers and Messengers

Desktop Publishers

Floral Designers

Food and Beverage Serving and Related Workers

Food Processing Occupations

Gaming Cage Workers

Grounds Maintenance Workers

Home Health Aides and Personal and Home Care Aides

Library Technicians and Library Assistants

Material Moving Occupations

Nursing and Psychiatric Aides

Occupational Therapist Assistants and Aides

Office Clerks, General

Painting and Coating Workers, except Construction and Maintenance

Pharmacy Technicians and Aides

Physical Therapist Assistants and Aides

Plumbers, Pipelayers, Pipefitters, and Steamfitters

Postal Service Mail Carriers

Receptionists and Information Clerks

Recreation Workers

Retail Salespersons

Security Guards and Gaming Surveillance Officers

Shipping, Receiving, and Traffic Clerks

Taxi Drivers and Chauffeurs

Teacher Assistants

Textile, Apparel, and Furnishings Occupations

Truck Drivers and Driver/Sales Workers

Water Transportation Occupations

Jobs Requiring Moderate-Term On-the-Job Training

Advertising Sales Agents

Animal Care and Service Workers

Announcers

Assemblers and Fabricators

Bookbinders and Bindery Workers

Bookkeeping, Accounting, and Auditing Clerks

Broadcast and Sound Engineering Technicians and Radio Operators

Bus Drivers

Cargo and Freight Agents

Carpet, Floor, and Tile Installers and Finishers

Cement Masons, Concrete Finishers, Segmental Pavers, and Terrazzo Workers

Computer Control Programmers and Operators

Construction Equipment Operators

Construction Laborers

Cooks and Food Preparation Workers

Correctional Officers

Customer Service Representatives

Demonstrators and Product Promoters

Dental Assistants

Drywall and Ceiling Tile Installers, Tapers, Plasterers, and Stucco Masons

Fishers and Fishing Vessel Operators

Food Processing Occupations

Forest and Conservation Workers

Grounds Maintenance Workers

Hazardous Materials Removal Workers

Industrial Machinery Mechanics and Millwrights

Inspectors, Testers, Sorters, Samplers, and Weighers

Insulation Workers

Loan Officers

Logging Workers

Machine Setters, Operators, and Tenders—Metal and Plastic

Maintenance and Repair Workers, General

Material Moving Occupations

Medical Assistants

Medical, Dental, and Ophthalmic Laboratory Technicians

Models

Painters and Paperhangers

Painting and Coating Workers, except Construction and Maintenance

Pest Control Workers

Pharmacy Technicians and Aides

Printing Machine Operators

Rail Transportation Occupations

Roofers

Secretaries and Administrative Assistants

Security Guards and Gaming Surveillance Officers

Small Engine Mechanics

Social and Human Service Assistants

Surveyors, Cartographers, Photogrammetrists, and Surveying and Mapping Technicians

Textile, Apparel, and Furnishings Occupations

Water Transportation Occupations

Woodworkers

Jobs Requiring Long-Term On-the-Job Training

Actors, Producers, and Directors

Air Traffic Controllers

Announcers

Artists and Related Workers

Athletes, Coaches, Umpires, and Related Workers

Automotive Body and Related Repairers

Boilermakers

Brickmasons, Blockmasons, and Stonemasons

Carpenters

Carpet, Floor, and Tile Installers and Finishers

Cement Masons, Concrete Finishers, Segmental Pavers, and Terrazzo Workers

Claims Adjusters, Appraisers, Examiners, and Investigators

Cooks and Food Preparation Workers

Dancers and Choreographers

Drywall and Ceiling Tile Installers, Tapers, Plasterers, and Stucco Masons

Electricians

Elevator Installers and Repairers

Farmers, Ranchers, and Agricultural Managers

Fire Fighters

Flight Attendants

Food Processing Occupations

Glaziers

Heavy Vehicle and Mobile Equipment Service Technicians and Mechanics

Home Appliance Repairers

Industrial Machinery Mechanics and Millwrights

Interpreters and Translators

Line Installers and Repairers

Machine Setters, Operators, and Tenders—Metal and Plastic

Machinists

Material Moving Occupations

Medical, Dental, and Ophthalmic Laboratory
Technicians

Musicians, Singers, and Related Workers

Opticians, Dispensing

Photographers

Plumbers, Pipelayers, Pipefitters, and Steamfitters

Police and Detectives

Power Plant Operators, Distributors, and Dispatchers

Prepress Technicians and Workers

Purchasing Managers, Buyers, and Purchasing Agents

Sheet Metal Workers

Small Engine Mechanics

Stationary Engineers and Boiler Operators

Structural and Reinforcing Iron and Metal Workers

Textile, Apparel, and Furnishings Occupations

Tool and Die Makers

Water and Liquid Waste Treatment Plant and System
Operators

Woodworkers

Jobs Requiring Vocational/Technical Training

Aircraft and Avionics Equipment Mechanics and
Service Technicians

Aircraft Pilots and Flight Engineers

Automotive Service Technicians and Mechanics

Barbers, Cosmetologists, and Other Personal
Appearance Workers

Broadcast and Sound Engineering Technicians and
Radio Operators

Claims Adjusters, Appraisers, Examiners, and
Investigators

Computer, Automated Teller, and Office Machine
Repairers

Court Reporters

Diesel Service Technicians and Mechanics

Drafters

Electrical and Electronics Installers and Repairers

Electronic Home Entertainment Equipment Installers
and Repairers

Emergency Medical Technicians and Paramedics

Fitness Workers

Gaming Services Occupations

Heating, Air-Conditioning, and Refrigeration
Mechanics and Installers

Insurance Sales Agents

Jewelers and Precious Stone and Metal Workers

Library Technicians and Library Assistants

Licensed Practical and Licensed Vocational Nurses

Massage Therapists

Medical Transcriptionists

Nursing and Psychiatric Aides

Prepress Technicians and Workers

Radio and Telecommunications Equipment Installers
and Repairers

Real Estate Brokers and Sales Agents

Semiconductor Processors

Surgical Technologists

Teachers—Preschool, Except Special Education

Travel Agents

Welding, Soldering, and Brazing Workers

Jobs Requiring an Associate Degree

Appraisers and Assessors of Real Estate

Broadcast and Sound Engineering Technicians and
Radio Operators

Cardiovascular Technologists and Technicians

Clinical Laboratory Technologists and Technicians

Computer Network, Systems, and Database Administrators

Computer Support Specialists

Dental Hygienists

Diagnostic Medical Sonographers

Engineering Technicians

Fashion Designers

Funeral Directors

Interior Designers

Medical Equipment Repairers

Medical Records and Health Information Technicians

Nuclear Medicine Technologists

Occupational Health and Safety Technicians

Occupational Therapist Assistants and Aides

Paralegals and Legal Assistants

Physical Therapist Assistants and Aides

Police and Detectives

Radiation Therapists

Radiologic Technologists and Technicians

Registered Nurses

Respiratory Therapists

Science Technicians

Secretaries and Administrative Assistants

Veterinary Technologists and Technicians

Jobs Requiring a Bachelor's Degree

Accountants and Auditors

Agricultural and Food Scientists

Aircraft Pilots and Flight Engineers

Architects, Except Landscape and Naval

Archivists, Curators, and Museum Technicians

Artists and Related Workers

Athletic Trainers

Atmospheric Scientists

Authors, Writers, and Editors

Biological Scientists

Budget Analysts

Chemists and Materials Scientists

Clinical Laboratory Technologists and Technicians

Commercial and Industrial Designers

Computer Network, Systems, and Database Administrators

Computer Software Engineers and Computer Programmers

Computer Systems Analysts

Conservation Scientists and Foresters

Construction Managers

Cost Estimators

Counselors

Dietitians and Nutritionists

Engineers

Financial Analysts

Graphic Designers

Health Educators

Human Resources, Training, and Labor Relations Managers and Specialists

Insurance Underwriters

Landscape Architects

Market and Survey Researchers

Meeting and Convention Planners

News Analysts, Reporters, and Correspondents

Occupational Health and Safety Specialists

Personal Financial Advisors

Probation Officers and Correctional Treatment Specialists

Property, Real Estate, and Community Association Managers

Public Relations Specialists

Recreational Therapists

Sales Engineers

Science Technicians

Securities, Commodities, and Financial Services Sales Agents

Social Workers

Surveyors, Cartographers, Photogrammetrists, and Surveying and Mapping Technicians

Tax Examiners, Collectors, and Revenue Agents

Teachers—Adult Literacy and Remedial Education

Teachers—Kindergarten, Elementary, Middle, and Secondary

Teachers—Special Education

Technical Writers

Television, Video, and Motion Picture Camera Operators and Editors

Jobs Requiring a Bachelor's or Higher Degree Plus Work Experience

Actors, Producers, and Directors

Actuaries

Administrative Services Managers

Advertising, Marketing, Promotions, Public Relations, and Sales Managers

Artists and Related Workers

Computer and Information Systems Managers

Education Administrators

Engineering and Natural Sciences Managers

Farmers, Ranchers, and Agricultural Managers

Financial Managers

Human Resources, Training, and Labor Relations Managers and Specialists

Judges, Magistrates, and Other Judicial Workers

Management Analysts

Medical and Health Services Managers

Musicians, Singers, and Related Workers

Purchasing Managers, Buyers, and Purchasing Agents

Teachers—Vocational

Top Executives

Jobs Requiring a Master's Degree

Archivists, Curators, and Museum Technicians

Counselors

Economists

Environmental Scientists and Specialists

Geoscientists and Hydrologists

Instructional Coordinators

Librarians

Occupational Therapists

Operations Research Analysts

Physical Therapists

Physician Assistants

Psychologists

Social Scientists, Other

Social Workers

Sociologists and Political Scientists

Speech-Language Pathologists

Statisticians

Urban and Regional Planners

Jobs Requiring a Doctoral Degree

Agricultural and Food Scientists

Biological Scientists

Computer Scientists

Mathematicians

Medical Scientists

Physicists and Astronomers

Psychologists

Teachers—Postsecondary

Jobs Requiring a Professional Degree

Audiologists

Chiropractors

Dentists

Lawyers

Optometrists

Pharmacists

Physicians and Surgeons

Podiatrists

Veterinarians

Appendix C: Additional Sources of Career Information

Career Resources

While each entry in the *EZ OOH* recommends resources to further explore that particular job, there are many general resources that weren't listed. This appendix explains some of the more common career and education print resources and Web sites that you can use to further your research. Gathering as much information as possible will help you make a more informed decision and find a satisfying and rewarding career.

Personal contacts. Don't underestimate the power of the people you already know such as friends, colleagues, and family. Not only can they answer questions about a particular job, they can also put you in contact with people who can help you further. Such networking can help you make a decision about your career path and may also help you get a job once you've decided.

Local libraries. Libraries contain a tremendous amount of information on jobs and how to get them. They can also provide access to e-mail and the Internet for those individuals who don't have access at home. In addition to valuable reference books (such as those listed later in this appendix), libraries may have information on job openings, colleges and financial aid, vocational training options, specific businesses, and trade magazines that can provide occupational information for specific industries. Librarians can help you find the information you need; after all, that's what they get paid for (see page 96 if you don't believe us).

Professional societies, trade groups, and labor unions. These groups are associated with workers in specific occupations. They are great resources for information on training requirements, earnings, and listings of local employers. Many offer apprenticeships for specific careers or can put you in contact with other organizations that can provide the training you need. Many of the sources listed at the end of each job description are professional societies, trade groups, and labor unions. In addition, the *Encyclopedia of Associations* (available at your local library) can give you the contact information you need for a particular organization.

Employers. Though contacting them requires some courage, employers are the main source of information on specific jobs. They can give you information on openings, application requirements, earnings and benefits, and advancement opportunities. Even if employers have no job openings, they can still provide the information you need to decide whether the job is right for you to begin with.

Informational interviews. People already working in a particular field often are willing to speak with people interested in joining their field. An informational interview will allow you to get good information from experts in a specific career without the pressure of a job interview. These interviews allow you to determine how a certain career may appeal to you while helping you build a network of personal contacts.

Postsecondary institutions. Colleges, universities, and other postsecondary institutions frequently have career centers and libraries with information on different careers, job listings, and alumni contacts in various professions. They may have career counselors to help students and alumni as well. Anyone enrolled in a postsecondary school or thinking about enrolling should be sure to take advantage of these resources.

Guidance and career counselors. Counselors can help you decide which careers might suit you best by determining your strengths and interests. They can help you evaluate your options and search for a job in your field or select a new field altogether. They can also help you further your education. Some counselors offer interview coaching, resume writing, and help with filling out applications. Counselors are most commonly found in high school guidance offices, college and vocational and technical school career planning and placement offices, community organizations, vocational rehabilitation agencies, and state employment service offices.

Internet resources. Many online career resources include job listings, resume posting services, and information on job fairs, training, and local wages. Most of the resources listed at the end of each job description have Internet addresses as well. In addition, individual companies may include job listings on their Web sites with information about required credentials, wages and benefits, and contact information. When using Internet resources, be sure that the organization is a credible, established source of information.

Online Sources from the Department of Labor and the Federal Government

* **Career OneStop.** Provides a wide range of workforce assistance and resources. Internet: www.careeronestop.org

* **O*NET Online.** This resource can provide even more information on specific occupations. Internet: www.onetcenter.org

* **Bureau of Labor Statistics.** The Department of Labor's Bureau of Labor Statistics publishes a wide range of labor market information. Internet: www.bls.gov

* **Career Guide to Industries.** This publication discusses careers from an industry perspective. The *Career Guide* is also available at your local career center and library. Internet: www.bls.gov/oco/cg/home.htm

* **Wage Data.** For information on occupational wages. Internet: www.bls.gov/bls/blswage.htm

* **Education and Training Administration.** For information on training, workers' rights, and job listings. Internet: www.doleta.gov/jobseekers

* **USA Jobs.** Information on obtaining civilian positions within the federal government. Internet: www.usajobs.opm.gov

* **Today's Military.** For information on careers in the military, the Montgomery G.I. Bill, and military service. Internet: www.todaysmilitary.com

* **Equal Employment Opportunity Commission.** Information on how to file a charge of discrimination based on race, color, religion, sex, national origin, age, or handicap. Internet: www.eeoc.gov

Organizations for Specific Groups

Disabled workers:

* **State Vocational Rehabilitation Agency.** State counseling, training, and placement services for those with disabilities. Internet: http://www.workworld.org/wwwebhelp/state_vocational_rehabilitation_vr_agencies.htm

* **National Organization on Disability.** Information on employment opportunities, transportation, and other considerations for people with all types of disabilities. Internet: www.nod.org

* **Job Accommodation Network (JAN).** Information on making accommodations in the work place for people with disabilities. Internet: www.jan.wvu.edu

* **Disability Information.** A comprehensive federal Web site of disability-related resources. Internet: www.disabilityinfo.gov

Blind workers:

* **National Federation of the Blind, Job Opportunities for the Blind (JOB).** Information on the free national reference and referral service for the blind. Internet: www.nfb.org

Older workers:

* **National Council on the Aging.** Internet: www.ncoa.org
* **National Caucus and Center on Black Aged, Inc.** Internet: www.ncba-aged.org

Veterans:

* **Credentialing Opportunities Online (COOL).** Explains how Army soldiers can meet civilian certification and license requirements related to their Military Occupational Specialty (MOS). Internet: www.cool.army.mil/index.htm

Women:

* **Department of Labor, Women's Bureau.** Resources for women in the workforce. Internet: www.dol.gov/wb

Education and Training Resources

Each entry in the *EZ OOH* provides the minimal education requirements for that job. This section explains the major sources of education and training required for most occupations in more detail. It also provides resources to help you get the education and training you need. Readers interested in researching jobs by the education and training level required should see Appendix B.

Four-year colleges and universities. Colleges and universities provide the knowledge and background necessary to be successful in many fields. They also can help place students in internships or co-ops to learn a job hands on. For more information on colleges and universities, go to your local library, consult a counselor, or contact individual colleges. Also check with your state's higher education agency.

A list of these agencies is available on the Internet: http://wdcrobcolp01.ed.gov/Programs/EROD/org_list.cfm?category_cd=SHE

Junior and community colleges. Junior and community colleges offer programs that lead to associate degrees and training certificates. Community colleges tend to be less expensive than four-year colleges and universities, generally have more adult and part-time students, and are more tailored to the needs of local employers. Many offer weekend and night classes. For students who may not be able to enroll in a college or university because of their academic record, limited finances, or distance, junior or community colleges are a place to earn credits that can be applied toward a degree at a four-year college. For more information on junior and community colleges, go to your local library, consult a counselor, or contact individual schools. Also check with your state's higher education agency.

A list of these agencies is available on the Internet: http://wdcrobcolp01.ed.gov/Programs/EROD/org_list.cfm?category_cd=SHE

Vocational and trade schools. These schools offer courses designed to provide hands-on experience. They tend to concentrate on trades, services, and other types of skilled work. Graduates of vocational and trade schools generally have an advantage over informally trained or self-trained job seekers. These schools also help students acquire any license or other credentials needed to enter the job market. For more information on vocational and trade schools, go to your local library, consult a counselor, or contact individual schools. Also check with your state's director of vocational-technical education.

A list of state directors of vocational-technical education is available on the Internet: http://wdcrobcolp01.ed.gov/Programs/EROD/org_list.cfm?category_cd=VTE

Apprenticeships. An apprenticeship provides work experience as well as education and training for those entering certain occupations. Apprenticeships are offered by sponsors, who employ and train the apprentice. Apprenticeships generally last between one and four years. Some apprenticeships allow the apprentice to earn an associate degree. A state agency approved completion certificate is granted to those completing programs.

Information on apprenticeships is available from the Office of Apprenticeship on the Internet: www.doleta.gov/oa/.

Employers. Many employers provide on-the-job training. On-the-job training can range from spending a few minutes watching another employee demonstrate a task to participating in formal training programs that may last for several months. In some jobs, employees may continually undergo training to stay up to date with new developments and technologies or to add new skills.

Military. The United States Armed Forces trains and employs people in more than 4,100 different occupations. For more information, see "Job Opportunities in the Armed Forces" in this book.

Financial Aid Resources

Many people fund their education or training through financial aid or tuition assistance programs. Federal student aid is available as grants, work-study programs, and loans. All federal student aid applicants must first fill out a Free Application for Federal Student Aid (FAFSA), which provides a Student Aid Report (SAR) and eligibility rating. Forms must be submitted to the school, which then determines the amount of aid you will receive. The following resources can help you get the aid you need:

✳ For information on applying for federal financial aid, visit the FAFSA Internet site: www.fafsa.ed.gov.

✳ A U.S. Department of Education publication describing federal financial aid programs, called *The Student Guide*, is available at www.studentaid.ed.gov/students/publications/student_guide/index.html.

✳ Information on federal programs is available from www.studentaid.ed.gov and www.students.gov.

✳ Information on state programs is available from your state's higher education agency. A list of these agencies is available on the Internet: http://wdcrobcolp01.ed.gov/Programs/EROD/org_list.cfm?category_cd=SHE.

Grants. A grant is money that is given to pay for education or training and any associated expenses. Grants are considered gifts and are not paid back. They are typically given on the basis of financial need. Federal grants are almost exclusively for undergraduate students.

Additional information on grants is available on the Internet: www.studentaid.ed.gov.

Federal Work-Study program. The Federal Work-Study program is offered at most institutions and consists of federal sponsorship of a student who works part time at the institution he or she is attending. The money a student earns through this program goes directly toward the cost of attending the institution. There are no set minimum or maximum amounts for this type of aid, although, on average, a student can expect to earn about $2,000 per school year.

General information on the Federal Work-Study program is available at http://studentaid.ed.gov/PORTALSWebApp/students/english/campusaid.jsp.

Scholarships. A scholarship is money donated to a student to help pay for his or her education or training. Scholarships are based on financial need, academic merit, athletic ability, or a wide variety of other criteria set by the organizations that provide the scholarships. Frequently, students must meet minimal academic requirements to be considered for a scholarship. Other qualifying requirements—such as intended major field of study, heritage, or group membership—may be added by the organization providing the scholarship. Information on scholarships is typically available from high school guidance counselors and local libraries.

The College Board has information on available scholarships at www.collegeboard.com/pay.

Student loans. Many institutions, both public and private, provide low-interest loans to students and their parents or guardians. The federal government also provides several types of student loans based on the applicant's financial need.

The College Board has information on available loans at www.collegeboard.com/pay.

Employer tuition support programs. Some employers offer tuition assistance programs as part of their employee benefits package. The terms of these programs depend on the firm. Consult your human resources department for information on tuition support programs offered by your employer.

Military tuition support programs. The United States Armed Forces offer various tuition assistance and loan repayment programs for military personnel. For more information go to www.todaysmilitary.com.

State and Local Resources

Most states have career information delivery systems (CIDS), which may be found in secondary and postsecondary institutions, as well as libraries, job training sites, vocational-technical schools, and employment offices. A wide range of information is provided, from employment opportunities to unemployment insurance claims.

Alabama

Labor Market Information Division, Alabama Department of Industrial Relations, 649 Monroe St., Room 422, Montgomery, AL 36131. Telephone: (334) 242-8859. Internet: http://dir.alabama.gov

Alaska

Research and Analysis Section, Department of Labor and Workforce Development, P.O. Box 25501, Juneau, AK 99802-5501. Telephone: (907) 465-4500. Internet: http://almis.labor.state.ak.us

Arizona

Arizona Department of Economic Security, P.O. Box 6123 SC 733A, Phoenix, AZ 85005-6123. Telephone: (602) 542-5984. Internet: https://www.azdes.gov

Arkansas

Labor Market Information, Department of Workforce Services, #2 Capital Mall, Little Rock, AR 72201. Telephone: (501) 682-3198. Internet: www.discoverarkansas.net

California

State of California Employment Development Department, Labor Market Information Division, P.O. Box 826880, Sacramento, CA 94280-0001. Telephone: (916) 262-2162. Internet:www.labormarketinfo.edd.ca.gov

Colorado

Labor Market Information, Colorado Department of Labor and Employment, 633 17th St., Suite 600, Denver, CO 80202-3660. Telephone: (303) 318-8850. Internet: http://lmigateway.coworkforce.com

Connecticut

Office of Research, Connecticut Department of Labor, 200 Folly Brook Blvd., Wethersfield, CT 06109-1114. Telephone: (860) 263-6275. Internet: www.ctdol.state.ct.us/lmi

Delaware

Office of Occupational and Labor Market Information, Department of Labor, 19 West Lea Blvd., Wilmington, DE 19802. Telephone: (302) 761-8069. Internet: www.delawareworks.com/oolmi/

District of Columbia

D.C. Department of Employment Services, 64 New York Ave. NE, Suite 3000, Washington, DC 20002. Telephone: (202) 724-7000. Internet: www.does.dc.gov/does

Florida

Labor Market Statistics, Agency for Workforce Innovation, 107 E. Madison St., MSC 110—Caldwell Building, Tallahassee, FL 32399-4111. Telephone: (850) 245-7105. Internet: www.labormarketinfo.com

Georgia

Workforce Information and Analysis, Room 300, Department of Labor, 223 Courtland St., CWC Building, Atlanta, GA 30303. Telephone: (404) 232-3875. Internet: www.dol.state.ga.us/em/ get_labor_market_information.htm

Guam

Guam Department of Labor, 504 D St., Tiyan, Guam 96910. Telephone: (671) 475-0101. Internet: http://guamdol.net

Hawaii

Research and Statistics Office, Department of Labor and Industrial Relations, 830 Punchbowl St., Room 304, Honolulu, HI 96813.
Telephone: (808) 586-9013.
Internet: www.hiwi.org

Idaho

Research and Analysis Bureau, Department of Commerce and Labor, 317 West Main St., Boise, ID 83735-0670.
Telephone: (208) 332-3570.
Internet: http://lmi.idaho.gov

Illinois

Illinois Department of Employment Security, Economic Information and Analysis Division, 33 S. State St., 9th Floor, Chicago, IL 60603.
Telephone: (312) 793-6521.
Internet: http://lmi.ides.state.il.us

Indiana

Research and Analysis—Indiana Workforce Development, Indiana Government Center South, 10 N. Senate Ave., Indianapolis, IN 46204.
Toll-free: (800) 891-6499.
Internet: www.in.gov/dwd

Iowa

Policy and Information Division, Iowa Workforce Development, 1000 E. Grand Ave., Des Moines, IA 50319-0209.
Telephone: (515) 281-5387.
Internet: www.iowaworkforce.org/lmi

Kansas

Kansas Department of Labor, Labor Market Information Services, 401 SW Topeka Blvd., Topeka, KS 66603-3182.
Telephone: (785) 296-5000.
Internet: http://laborstats.dol.ks.gov

Kentucky

Research and Statistics Branch, Office of Employment and Training, 275 E. Main St., Frankfort, KY 40621.
Telephone: (502) 564-7976.
Internet: www.workforcekentucky.ky.gov

Louisiana

Research and Statistics Division, Department of Labor, 1001 N. 23rd St., Baton Rouge, LA 70802-3338.
Telephone: (225) 342-3111.
Internet: www.laworks.net

Maine

Labor Market Information Services Division, Maine Department of Labor, 45 Commerce Dr., State House Station 118, Augusta, ME 04330.
Telephone: (207) 623-7900.
Internet: http://maine.gov/labor/lmis

Maryland

Maryland Department of Labor Licensing and Regulation, Office of Labor Market Analysis and Information, 1100 N. Eutaw, Baltimore, MD 21201.
Telephone: (410) 767-2250.
Internet: www.dllr.state.md.us/lmi/index.shtml

Massachusetts

Executive Office of Labor and Workforce Development, Division of Career Services, 19 Staniford St., Boston, MA 02114.
Telephone: (617) 626-5300.
Internet: www.detma.org/LMIdataprog.htm

Michigan

Bureau of Labor Market Information and Strategic Initiatives, Department of Labor and Economic Growth, 3032 W. Grand Blvd., Suite 9-100, Detroit, MI 48202.
Telephone: (313) 456-3100.
Internet: www.milmi.org

Minnesota

Department of Employment and Economic Development, Labor Market Information Office, 1st National Bank Building, 332 Minnesota St., Suite E200, St. Paul, MN 55101-1351.
Toll-free: (888) 234-1114.
Internet: www.deed.state.mn.us/lmi

Mississippi

Labor Market Information Division, Mississippi Department of Employment Security, 1235 Echelon Pkwy., P.O. Box 1699, Jackson, MS 39215.
Telephone: (601) 321-6000.
Internet: http://mdes.ms.gov

Missouri

Missouri Economic Research and Information Center, P.O. Box 3150, Jefferson City, MO 65102-3150.
Toll-free: (866) 225-8113.
Internet: www.missourieconomy.org

Montana

Research and Analysis Bureau, P.O. Box 1728, Helena, MT 59624.
Toll-free: (800) 541-3904.
Internet: www.ourfactsyourfuture.org

Nebraska

Nebraska Workforce Development—Labor Market Information, Nebraska Department of Labor, 550 S. 16th St., P.O. Box 94600, Lincoln, NE 68509.
Telephone: (402) 471-2600.
Internet: www.dol.nebraska.gov/nwd/
center.cfm?PRICAT=3&SUBCAT=4Z0

Nevada

Research and Analysis, Department of Employment Training and Rehabilitation, 500 E. Third St., Carson City, NV 89713.
Telephone: (775) 684-0450.
Internet: www.nevadaworkforce.com

New Hampshire

Economic and Labor Market Information Bureau, New Hampshire Employment Security, 32 S. Main St., Concord, NH 03301-4857.
Telephone: (603) 228-4124.
Internet: www.nh.gov/nhes/elmi

New Jersey

Division of Labor Market and Demographic Research, Department of Labor and Workforce Development, P.O. Box 388, Trenton, NJ 08625-0388.
Telephone: (609) 984-2593.
Internet: www.wnjpin.net

New Mexico

New Mexico Department of Labor, Economic Research and Analysis, 401 Broadway NE, Albuquerque, NM 87102.
Telephone: (505) 222-4683.
Internet: www.dws.state.nm.us/dws-lmi.html

New York

Research and Statistics, New York State Department of Labor, W. Averell Harriman State Office Campus, Building 12, Albany, NY 12240.
Telephone: (518) 457-9000.
Internet: www.labor.state.ny.us

North Carolina

Labor Market Information Division, Employment Security Commission, 700 Wade Ave., Raleigh, NC 27605.
Telephone: (919) 733-2936.
Internet: www.ncesc.com

North Dakota

Labor Market Information Manager, Job Service North Dakota, 1000 E. Divide Ave., Bismarck, ND 58506.
Toll-free: (800) 732-9787.
Internet: www.ndworkforceintelligence.com

Ohio

Bureau of Labor Market Information, Ohio Department of Job and Family Services, 420 E. 5th Ave., Columbus, OH 43219.
Telephone: (614) 752-9494.
Internet: http://ohiolmi.com

Oklahoma

Labor Market Information, Oklahoma Employment Security Commission, P.O. Box 52003, Oklahoma City, OK 73152.
Telephone: (405) 557-7172.
Internet: www.ok.gov/oesc_web/Services/
Find_Labor_Market_Statistics/index.html

Oregon

Oregon Employment Department, Research Division, 875 Union St. NE, Salem, OR 97311.
Telephone: (503) 947-1200.
Internet: www.qualityinfo.org/olmisj/OlmisZine

Pennsylvania

Center for Workforce Information & Analysis, Pennsylvania Department of Labor and Industry, 220 Labor and Industry Building, Seventh and Forster Sts., Harrisburg, PA 17121.
Toll-free: (877) 493-3282.
Internet: www.paworkstats.state.pa.us

Puerto Rico

Department of Work and Human Resources, Ave. Muñoz Rivera 505, Hato Rey, PR 00918.
Telephone: (787) 754-5353.
Internet: www.dtrh.gobierno.pr

Rhode Island

Labor Market Information, Rhode Island Department of Labor and Training, 1511 Pontiac Ave., Cranston, RI 02920.
Telephone: (401) 462-8740.
Internet: www.dlt.ri.gov/lmi

South Carolina

Labor Market Information Department, South Carolina Employment Security Commission, 631 Hampton St., Columbia, SC 29202.
Telephone: (803) 737-2660.
Internet: www.sces.org/lmi/index.asp

South Dakota

Labor Market Information Center, Department of Labor, P.O. Box 4730, Aberdeen, SD 57402-4730.
Telephone: (605) 626-2314.
Internet: http://dol.sd.gov/lmic

Tennessee

Research and Statistics Division, Department of Labor and Workforce Development, 220 French Landing Dr., Nashville, TN 37245.
Telephone: (615) 741-1729.
Internet: www.state.tn.us/labor-wfd/lmi.htm

Texas

Labor Market Information, Texas Workforce Commission, 9001 N. IH-35, Suite 103A, Austin, TX 75753.
Toll-free: (866) 938-4444.
Internet: www.tracer2.com

Utah

Director of Workforce Information, Utah Department of Workforce Services, P.O. Box 45249, Salt Lake City, UT 84145-0249.
Telephone: (801) 526-9675.
Internet: http://jobs.utah.gov/opencms/wi

Vermont

Economic and Labor Market Information, Vermont Department of Labor, P.O. Box 488, Montpelier, VT 05601-0488.
Telephone: (802) 828-4000.
Internet: www.vtlmi.info

Virgin Islands

Bureau of Labor Statistics, Department of Labor, 53A & 54AB Kronprindsens Gade, St. Thomas, VI 00803-2608.
Telephone: (340) 776-3700.
Internet: www.vidol.gov

Virginia

Virginia Employment Commission, P.O. Box 1358, Richmond, VA 23218-1358.
Toll-free: (800) 828-1140.
Internet: www.vec.virginia.gov/vecportal/index.cfm

Washington

Labor Market and Economic Analysis, Washington Employment Security Department, P.O. Box 9046, Olympia, WA 98507-9046.
Telephone: (360) 438-4833.
Internet: www.workforceexplorer.com

West Virginia

Workforce West Virginia, Research, Information and Analysis Division, 112 California Ave., Charleston, WV 25303-0112.
Telephone: (304) 558-2660.
Internet: http://workforcewv.org/lmi

Wisconsin

Bureau of Workforce Information, Department of Workforce Development, P.O. Box 7944, Madison, WI 53707-7944.
Telephone: (608) 266-7034.
Internet: http://worknet.wisconsin.gov/worknet

Wyoming

Research and Planning, Wyoming Department of Employment, 246 S. Center St., Casper, WY 82602.
Telephone: (307) 473-3807.
Internet: http://doe.state.wy.us/lmi

Other Career Reference Materials

The *EZ OOH* is an ideal resource to get you started on your career search, but finding, getting, and keeping the right job requires more than just one book. The following resources, available from JIST, can help you further your career exploration and get the job you want.

Enhanced Occupational Outlook Handbook: Featuring more than 8,000 job descriptions, this reference book contains the full descriptions for each job in the *Occupational Outlook Handbook* plus related jobs from the U.S. government's Occupational Information Network (O*NET) database and *Dictionary of Occupational Titles*. Ideal for in-depth research.

O*NET Dictionary of Occupational Titles: This is the only print edition of the Department of Labor's O*NET database and includes information for more than 900 occupations.

The *Best Jobs* Series: This series of books provides job descriptions of the best-paying and fastest-growing jobs based on any number of factors. Find the best jobs for your personality or your education level, the best jobs for introverts or those who don't want to work behind a desk, the best jobs to get through apprenticeships, or the best jobs for the 21st century.

The *Help in a Hurry* Series: Once you've used the *EZ OOH* and other career resources to discover the job of your dreams, let these quick and insightful books help you get it. Includes books to help you with career choices, resumes, interviews, and cover letters.

For more information about these and other career reference and exploration resources, please visit www.jist.com.

Editors' note: This section was adapted from the "Sources of Career Information" section of the *Occupational Outlook Handbook*. Specific non-government institutions, addresses, and Web sites are provided for your own research and do not constitute a specific endorsement by the Department of Labor or JIST Publishing.

Index of Job Titles